Breaking Silence

ADVANCING HUMAN RIGHTS

Sumner B. Twiss, John Kelsay, and Terry Coonan, Editors

Breaking Silence: The Case That Changed the Face of Human Rights
  Richard Alan White

For All Peoples and All Nations: The Ecumenical Church and Human Rights
  John S. Nurser

Breaking Silence

The Case That Changed the Face of Human Rights

RICHARD ALAN WHITE

GEORGETOWN UNIVERSITY PRESS / Washington, D.C.

Georgetown University Press, Washington, D.C.
© 2004 by Georgetown University Press. All rights reserved.
Printed in the United States of America

10   9   8   7   6   5   4   3   2   1   2004

Library of Congress Cataloging-in-Publication Data

White, Richard Alan, 1944–
   Breaking silence : the case that changed the face of human rights / Richard Alan
White.
      p.   cm.—(Advancing human rights series)
   ISBN 1-58901-032-9 (cloth: alk. paper)
   1. Human rights—Paraguay.   2. Political persecution—Paraguay.   3. Filártiga,
Joelito, 1959–1976.   4. Torture—Paraguay.   5. Paraguay—Politics and
government.—1954–1989.   6. Filártiga, Joel.   I. Title.   II. Series.
JC599.P3W48   2004
323′.044′09892—dc22   2004004292

Joelito was only one who died of torture that day. One among hundreds every day, all around the world. But they go unnoticed, forgotten, without any testimony. It is as if their suffering and deaths never happened.

—DR. JOEL FILÁRTIGA

Breaking Silence is dedicated to those whose deaths did happen—and continue to happen.

CONTENTS

FOREWORD

THIS REMARKABLE BOOK gives readers a unique look into the most celebrated legal case in the international human rights field. Ironically, in 2004, at the very time this book is being published, the Justice Department of President George W. Bush is challenging that decision.

The story, which resulted in the *Filártiga v. Peña* case, involved the death of a young man, Joelito Filártiga, who was tortured and killed by an agent of Paraguayan dictator Alfredo Stroessner in 1976. Joelito's sister, Dolly, came to the United States and was advised that she could sue the murderer of her brother under an ancient but newly rejuvenated statute that might give her damages in a civil lawsuit against the alleged murderer, Mr. Américo Peña-Irala, who had moved to the United States. The statute, called the Alien Tort Claims Act (ATCA), was issued by the very first Congress in 1789.

Federal judge Eugene Nickerson, to whom Dolly and her father, Dr. Joel Filártiga— who joined the suit filed by the Center for Constitutional Rights (CCR)—presented the case, declined to extend jurisdiction in the civil suit. In his view, the long-neglected ATCA statute did not confer jurisdiction on a foreign national for a tort committed in Paraguay. In the legal community, that result was not unexpected.

But the CCR lawyers' appeal to the Second Circuit Court was sensationally successful. The Appellate Court reversed the trial judge and remanded the Filártigas' case to the District Court for a hearing. The trial resulted in a decree that ordered the defendant to pay $10.375 million to the Filártigas in compensatory and punitive damages.

In short, the Appellate Court judges who wrote the 1980 reversal found that Joelito had been tortured and killed by a public official, and that such conduct clearly violated the customary norms of international law. In part, they relied upon Article 5 of the Universal Declaration of Human Rights, which proclaims that "no one shall be subjected to torture or to cruel, inhuman or degrading treatment or punishment."

The Filártiga family's success has inspired some seventy progeny cases. Throughout the 1980s, these cases expanded the scope of the *Filártiga* interpretation of ATCA to include not only torture but also "disappearances," extrajudicial executions, crimes against humanity, and genocide. Initially, these decisions were brought against government officials in countries such as Argentina, Chile, El Salvador, the Philippines, and the former Yugoslavia.

Beginning in the mid-1990s, a second wave of *Filártiga* progeny cases moved beyond individual human rights violators to class-action suits against corporations.

Today, there are dozens of pending class-action suits against corporate defendants ranging from oil conglomerates destroying the Amazon rain forest to designer clothing companies exploiting workers' rights in their developing-world sweat shops.

In response to complaints by some U.S. corporations, the U.S. Justice Department under President George W. Bush is attempting to reverse the *Filártiga* precedent. It argues that ATCA is a statute that furnishes only jurisdiction and not a cause of action. In effect, it claims that whereas the law does allow the courts to accept ATCA cases, it would require a separate act by Congress expressly to give people the right to actually file the suit. This new position reverses the position of the Justice Department under the Jimmy Carter administration. At that time, the Department of Justice intervened on behalf of the Filártigas, contending strongly that the human rights standards invoked by the victims' position reflected the view of President Carter. He said that the supremacy of human rights was the soul of his foreign policy.

Even after the Supreme Court pronounces on this issue, the legal question will not be resolved. In anticipation that limitations may be placed on ATCA, in 1992 Congress passed the Torture Victim Protection Act (TVPA), which, on the basis of the *Filártiga v. Peña* decision, allows U.S. citizens as well as aliens to sue for torture and summary executions committed in a foreign country. If the Supreme Court restricts the remedy of ATCA, it is not clear whether this would also apply to TVPA. Moreover, should it become necessary, defenders of ATCA intend to sponsor congressional legislation that will accord ATCA the necessary cause-of-action provision.

According to some diplomats, the holding in *Filártiga*—that aliens in the United States can reach the assets of individuals in other nations—is an infringement by the courts upon the constitutional right of the executive branch to conduct foreign relations. Some commentators also affirm that various U.S. corporations are being unjustly charged with violations of international law in Burma, Colombia, Nigeria, and elsewhere.

A few leaders and jurists in foreign countries are protesting the reach of a statute that was passed by the very first Congress of a new nation devoted to the pursuit of justice, arguing that it is surely anomalous that lawyers seldom used ATCA for some 190 years. But that statute made the United States a defender of international law, and it established that ours is a country that guarantees indemnification of aliens for wrongs done to them, when those wrongs are not remedied where they took place and when those wrongs are violations of the international law that is applicable to every human being on the planet.

Regardless of the ultimate decision of the courts on ATCA, the *Filártiga* case will still be a monument to a new interpretation of international law with profound significance for the jurisprudence of federal courts in America.

———— *llll* ————

This inspiring narrative by historian Richard Alan White provides a wealth of new information about the *Filártiga* case and the inner workings of the human rights community—as well as the U.S. government. The author knew the murdered Joelito and continues his close personal friendship with the Filártiga family. He put himself at great risk by remaining in Paraguay and working with the Filártigas as they decided to break the silence of a painfully oppressive society.

White's meticulous research is combined with a journalistic sensibility. He offers a stunning account of the horrific murder scene in Paraguay, then the longest reigning dictatorship in Latin America, and he describes in detail how the human rights community—from members of the Carter administration to professional advocates—rallied to seek justice for the Filártigas.

As a member of Congress, I voted in 1976 for the passage of the Foreign Sovereign Immunities Act. I thought then that it was a measured and carefully crafted law by the U.S. State Department that spelled out the limitations on the powers of all sovereign nations. I am not certain that I would vote for it now, however. The world has changed. Some claim that the concept of national sovereignty needs to be reexamined, and that the United States should be a leader in developing laws that will punish violations of international law even when they are committed against a noncitizen of the United States. ATCA and TVPA are designed to accomplish that objective.

It is fair to say that the *Filártiga* case changed history. We owe Richard Alan White an enormous debt of gratitude for his courage, his research, his perseverance, and his willingness to tell this story—a story that shows, unflinchingly, that human rights matter.

ROBERT F. DRINAN, S.J.

ACKNOWLEDGMENTS

IN RECOGNITION OF my appreciation for the people and institutions that have contributed moral, academic, technical, and financial support during the twenty-eight years it took for this work to come to completion, I owe special gratitude to Sharon O'Day, Laurie Solak, and Mitchell Alan White for research assistance; to Natalie Ann White for editorial work; to Richard Brown, Sandra Coliver, Mary Ellsberg, Joyce Kornblatt, Bert Lockwood Jr., Celeste Meza, Steven Schneebaum, Charles Pinkney Reed, Peter Weiss, and Michelle Zarella for manuscript suggestions; to Michelle Burgess, Tashy Calway, Arline Chase, Harvey Cheezem, Al D'Amato, Rose DiRenzo, and Eva Jane Simmons for technical assistance; to Celeste Aguilera Caló, Cristina Aldereti, Oscar Dario Croce, Gladys Crosky, Nancy de Guillen, Raymond Mendez P. Hines, Marina Mendez Paiva, and Victor Ortiz Montaner for transcriptions and translations; to Walter Gaffney and Jeannette Rodgers of La Esperanza Fund, Stephen Marks of the Ford Foundation, Don McNeill of the McNeill Family Foundation, and Raymond Simmons for financial assistance; to E. Bradford Burns, Marketta Freund, Charles Goldberg, Barbara Kelly, Gerald and Bobby Nehman, Mario Pastore, Alvin Rosenbloom, and Herman Ziering for their support of the Filártigas' cause; to Drs. Robert Burr, William Hurwitz, Herman Kabat, and Richard Lords for helping me through times of physical difficulties; and especially to Richard Pierre Claude and Henri J. M. Nouwen for their friendship and unqualified support through these years. The art that appear before each chapter are the drawings of Dr. Joel Filártiga, with the exception of the drawing before chapter five, which was done by Dr. Filártiga's daugher, Analy.

I would also like to take this opportunity to thank the people whose contributions are described in *Breaking Silence*, as well as all the others who helped in many ways but are too numerous to mention here, and those who cannot be named because, even at this time, they could still be harmed should their participation become known.

Regardless of these enormous contributions, I accept full responsibility for all translations and any conceptual or factual errors.

PROLOGUE

Dr. Joel Filártiga and I met through our mutual friend Roberto Thompson, then the editor of *ABC Color*, Paraguay's largest newspaper. Roberto had agreed to publish an article of mine about the Jesuit Missions of Paraguay, in four consecutive Sunday Supplements. After reading the first installment, Filártiga stopped by the office in Asunción to check out the rest of the essay. And, in a burst of generosity and creativity, on the spot he drew pen-and-ink drawings for the remaining three episodes.

But it was not until two years later that I first met Filártiga, when in 1975 I returned to Paraguay to continue my dissertation research on Dr. José Gaspar Rodriguez de Francia, the controversial George Washington figure of Paraguayan independence. Through our long discussions of world events and Paraguayan politics and history, Joel and I discovered a shared philosophy of life and grew to become close friends. He drew illustrations for each chapter of my book, graphically capturing their central themes. At his rural clinic in Ybycuí, I came to admire his philanthropic work with the peasants. There I grew to love the whole Filártiga family, and I developed an independent friendship with Joelito, Joel's sixteen-year-old son.

During this time, we set into motion plans for Filártiga to come to UCLA to display his art and draw attention to conditions in Paraguay. Joel's January 1976 trip was a great success, his speeches and exhibitions expanding to other institutions throughout southern California.

Just six weeks after Filártiga's return to Paraguay, Joelito was tortured to death by the police of General Alfredo Stroessner. By then, I had received my Ph.D. in Latin American history from UCLA and was preparing to return to Paraguay as an Organization of American States postdoctoral fellow to conduct further historical research.

At the behest of my friends, I arrived in Paraguay to live in the Filártigas' home. For the next seven months, I shared their terror, agonies, and degradation. As a trained historian, I happened to be on the scene before, during, and after what turned out to be a historical event. As Dr. Filártiga years later ironically observed: "It was almost as if you won the lottery—backwards." It is only because of these improbable circumstances that it has been possible to write *Breaking Silence* from the vantage point of a participant-observer.

Following Joelito's murder, the Filártigas did not buckle under to the fear and misdirected shame that is characteristic of human rights victims, not unlike those of child sexual abuse and domestic violence. Contrary to the reasonable expectations of the dictatorship, they refused to go along with the official cover-up and discreetly bury Joelito. Instead, breaking the silence of human rights victims, the Filártigas did everything in their power to reveal the truth.

Upon arriving in Paraguay in 1976, I joined the Filártigas in their cause, tapping into the network of media, political, and other influential people I had built as a graduate student researching my doctoral dissertation in Paraguay. My semiofficial status at the U.S. Embassy as a Fulbright-Hays scholar had accorded me wide-ranging access, both within the American community as well as among Paraguayan intellectuals and politicians.

Also, my historical work on Dr. Francia attracted quite a bit of attention. The Instituto de Investigaciones Históricas Dr. José Gaspar Rodriguez de Francia gave me the honor of becoming its only non-Paraguayan member. Even before I had completed the final version of *Paraguay's Autonomous Revolution: 1810–1840*, it had been translated and published in three lengthy installments in *Estudios Paraguayos*, the academic journal of the Catholic University. Its first Spanish edition came out a few months later.

Because of this, I was regularly invited to give newspaper interviews and lectures on Paraguayan history. The public exposure created the opportunity to form personal relationships with a number of influential people, some of whom later greatly contributed to the Filártigas' struggle; from Congressman Domingo Laino, the leader of Paraguay's principal opposition political party, to Colonel Robert LaSala, the disillusioned Green Beret Vietnam veteran serving as a U.S. military adviser to the Paraguayan Army.

As I helped investigate the murky circumstances of Joelito's death, I began collecting primary and secondary source materials on the *Caso Filártiga*, an undertaking I continued after returning to the United States, throughout the following years of organizing, and again later during the late 1980s and 1990s as I conducted the research for *Breaking Silence*.

Over these years, I maintained contact with the Filártigas, and worked with human rights activists and nongovernmental organizations supporting the family's pursuit of justice in Paraguay and the United States. Along the way, I conducted scores of interviews and follow-ups with the principals, amounting to well over 100 hours of taped recordings. All were transcribed, and when necessary translated into English. This material was then catalogued according to subject matter and transferred onto computerized note cards. Finally, the information was printed onto thousands of cross-referenced note cards.

Other kinds of primary source information that were integrated into this database include private correspondence, diaries, journals, and contemporary chronicles of events, both written and tape recorded; documentation from various human rights, legal advocacy, and Latin American support organizations; internal documents from the files of the Anti-Smuggling Unit of the U.S. Immigration and Naturalization Service (INS); previously classified U.S. Department of State cables, obtained under the Freedom of Information Act; letters of support and inquiry from members of the U.S. Congress to the government of Paraguay, the INS, the Department of State, and the U.S. Embassy and consulate in Paraguay; as well as official court documents and trial transcripts from the legal proceedings in both Paraguay and the United States. The *Breaking Silence* research archive amounts to some 12,000 pages of documentation, from which 87 Thematic Chronologies were compiled and, in turn, distilled into a 178-page Master Chronology. This archive will become publicly accessible in a university law library or other appropriate institution, as well as in the Paraguayan Archivos de Horror, as the formerly secret records of General Stroessner's police state have come to be known.

In citations from secondary sources—such as newspaper and magazine articles—I have used exact quotations for all references. In writing the dialogue, I have employed primary sources, relying upon the recorded interviews or contemporary records of at least one of the participants, and as often as possible using their exact words. As a further check for accuracy, in the great majority of cases, it has been possible for the people involved to review the dialogues in which they appear. Because a tape recorder was not running at all times, the dialogues are necessarily neither literal nor precise verbatim exchanges but rather substantively reliable reconstructions.

In a few cases, I have disguised the identities of people who—even today—could be harmed should their participation become known, by changing names and other identifying facts; to this end, in one instance I melded two people into a composite character.

By the methodological standard of the professional historian, *Breaking Silence* is an unusual documentary presentation. I feel secure characterizing it as a work of dramatic nonfiction.

The personal, moral, political, and legal significance of *Breaking Silence* should be gauged from the point of view of the Filártiga family's tragedy, as it grew from yet another routine torture-murder by a tinhorn dictator in the middle of South America to acquire the status of a landmark U.S. legal precedent with increasing international significance, and from which hundreds of torture survivors have benefited. The overall historical integrity of this saga should be judged from the perspective of a painstakingly documented account of that family's defiance of oppression, resulting in what Dr. Filártiga calls "a touch of justice."

present

DR. JOEL FILÁRTIGA

Renowned Paraguayan Artist

in a public lecture

"Art as Social Criticism
in Latin America"

Illustration © J. Filártiga

Dr. Filártiga reflects in both the style and content of his art the human anguish and suffering he has observed as a medical doctor who has been treating peasants in the interior of Paraguay for over twenty years. Since the early 1950's, his works have been displayed in Europe and throughout Latin America and continue to appear in Paraguay's major art galleries and private collections.

A follower of Mexican muralists Orozco and Siquieros, Filártiga has mastered a dynamic technique that combines expressionism and surrealism. The Ascunción periodical "La Tribuna" comments that the painting of Filártiga is " . . . above all, the pure and unmasked encounter with psychic pain . . . psychic because it has neither blood nor skin . . . no human anatomy; but it is Truth because ultimately Truth is Pain, just as it brings forth Glory, Love, Happiness."

Dr. Filártiga will be in residence at UCLA January 26-30 for his lecture, discussions and the exhibition of his work, which will be on display in the second floor Kerckhoff Hall exhibition area.

Wednesday, January 28, 1976   **3 P.M.**   **Bunche Hall 9383**
No Admission Charge   Public Cordially Invited

CPL 1/14 - 1/29/76

Publicity leaflet from Dr. Filártiga's 1976 Southern California tour.

ONE

FTER THE FUNERAL, Dr. Joel Filártiga came home to a dead telephone. All night Joel had tried getting through to me, dialing my number in California and hearing a ring—and then the operator would break in, announce that all international lines were busy, and disconnect the call.

Now there could be no doubt. The dictator's secret police had isolated him, cutting him off from reaching help abroad.

Filártiga looked around the living room at his family. Beyond exhaustion from their vigil, his wife and three daughters stared helplessly back at him. For the first time since the murder, Joel felt raw fear.

That afternoon, Dr. Filártiga had a long talk with a friend at the Embassy of Peru. The next day, the diplomatic mail pouch carried his letter out of Paraguay.

Asunción—March 31, 1976

Dear friend Richard,

They have struck me a devastating blow. The lords of darkness and death have robbed me of my son Joel. They brutally tortured him and then they killed him. Today I buried him.

I am strong, but I would ask that some friend from the university, or from the "Paraguay Project," come here to be with me during this painful trance, yet another trial for this battered body that has never been able to inure itself to more and more pain.

I do not know why they killed him. But I am sure your help, and that of the other people there, will help me unravel this wrenching tragedy.

We have given a martyr to the cause of man's freedom against the shadowy and sinister forces of death.

I wait for you.

Letters no longer arrive. I do not know why, and I wait for them so.

Joel, senior
3-31-76

I wait for you. SOS
I will send photographs.

Asunción, Marzo 31, 1976

Querido amigo Richard,

Me han dado un golpe artero. Los dueños de la muerte y de la noche me han robado a mi hijo Joel. Lo martirizaron brutalmente y lo mataron. Hoy lo enterré.

Tengo fortaleza pero pediría la presencia de algún amigo de la universidad, o del "Paraguay Project", para que me acompañe en este doloroso trance, una prueba más para este curtido cuerpo nunca acostumbrado a más y más dolores.

Yo no entiendo por qué fue, pero vuestra ayuda y la de las gentes de allí, me ayudarán a desmadejar esta desgarrante tragédia.

Dimos un mártir a favor de la libertad del hombre contra las fuerzas obscuras y cibernéticas de la muerte.

Os espero.

No me llegan más cartas. No se por qué y tanto las espero.

Joel el grande

31 - III - 76

Os espero. S.O.S.

Mandaré fotografías.

1

It took nearly two weeks for Dr. Filártiga's letter to reach me in Los Angeles.

Those first few months of 1976 had been an exceptionally fulfilling time for me. With all but a few remaining formalities to complete my Ph.D. in Latin American history at UCLA, I had received a postdoctoral fellowship to return to South America. And on top of everything else, the Filártiga family had invited me to stay with them at their home in Asunción, the capital of Paraguay.

On April 13, it all blew apart. Again and again, I called the Filártigas' number in Asunción, only to get busy signals. Finally, asking the local operator to try, I was told that the telephone was "out of order."

I tried getting through to Dr. Filártiga's rural clinic, but the operator at the telephone kiosk there said the family had left the village. Nobody knew when, or even if, they would be back.

At last, I called a mutual friend of ours, Roberto Thompson. In the four years since meeting Roberto, we had come to know each other well. Still, because the Paraguayan secret police routinely monitored international calls, especially those of former political prisoners like Roberto, our conversation would have to be guarded.

"Hola Roberto. Como has estado? Habla—"

Recognizing my voice, he broke in before I could identify myself. "Fine, just fine. And yourself?" he said casually in English.

Taking his cue, I switched to English as well. "Actually, I'm a little confused. Yesterday I received a letter from a friend, and I can't seem to get through to him by phone. Do you know what I'm talking about? I mean—"

"Yes, of course," he interrupted again, in the same nonchalant voice.

"So tell me," I asked, "is there any possibility of an accident of some kind?"

Roberto answered in precisely chosen words: "No. There's no question of that. Something very bad happened. It definitely wasn't an accident."

"Ah well, my information is several weeks old. I was just wondering how things are now?"

A brief pause. "Better. At first it was very difficult. But people are feeling stronger now."

It was my turn to hesitate. "Listen, Roberto," I said carefully, "if it isn't inconvenient, could you do me a favor and let him know that everyone up here has been informed of what happened. And if he still feels it's necessary, I could come right away. But there are some important things that should be taken care of first. So he must call, or send a telegram or something, to let me know."

"Yes. I see," Roberto replied, now clearly uneasy.

"If I don't hear from him, I'll assume things aren't so bad now, and will keep to my plans. Anyway, I'll be getting a letter to him. Do you think you could pass that message along?"

"But of course."

2

I had met Roberto when I first visited Paraguay in 1972, to conduct research on a Fulbright-Hays doctoral dissertation fellowship. Because the U.S. Congress funds the national scholarship program, Fulbright scholars travel abroad under government auspices. In practice, this semiofficial status means automatic acceptance by the American community, endless invitations to diplomatic parties to meet the host county's dignitaries, and introductions to local notables who can help you out.

Roberto, then the editor-in-chief of Paraguay's principal newspaper, was one of the first contacts set up by the U.S. Embassy. We hit it off right away and he extended me every courtesy: from the use of a desk in the city room to having an after-work beer with other Paraguayan professionals. In fact, it was thanks to Roberto that I came to know Dr. Filártiga.

Unlike in the United States, in Latin American countries history plays an overtly political role. Indeed, the tradition of publishing historical essays in newspapers often is used by these governments to create a "usable past"—to foster nationalism and buttress their legitimacy with the real, or invented, glories of their country's history.

In any event, in 1973 Roberto published a lengthy article of mine on the Jesuit Missions of Paraguay, in four consecutive *ABC Color* Sunday Supplements. After reading the first installment, Joel stopped by the newspaper to check out the rest of the essay.

Dr. Filártiga, who is also an accomplished artist, evidently liked the remaining three installments. On the spot, he appropriated Roberto's desk, and he made pen-and-ink drawings, graphically capturing the articles' central themes.

After seeing Filártiga's drawings, I was delighted and wanted to meet him. However, not until two years later, when I next returned to Paraguay, did we get together.

By then, mid-1975, Roberto's political fortunes had taken a turn for the worse. Sacked from his job at *ABC Color* for exposing a particularly sensitive case of government corruption, he had been arrested, imprisoned, and tortured by Investigaciones, the Paraguayan political police. As further punishment, General Alfredo Stroessner had also banned him from practicing his profession.

Even though the dictator prohibited Roberto from working as a journalist, the owner of the newspaper continued to pay his regular salary for a year. So we worked out a deal in which Roberto would translate my dissertation into Spanish and *ABC Color* would serialize the entire work in its Sunday Supplements.

One afternoon shortly after we began working together, Roberto showed up at my place with two strangers. One, a well-dressed, handsome teenager, hung back, appraising me with friendly, if somewhat reserved, curiosity.

The other, a middle-aged man exuding a confident good humor, openly sized me up. His goatee and girth contributed to a Hemingway-like presence, and his glistening coffee irises comfortably locked onto my eyes.

"Richard," Roberto began, "I'd like to introduce Dr. Filártiga and his son Joelito. They've—"

"So this is the Yanqui," the vibrant stranger broke in with a smile, "who dares to write the history of our country?"

"And you can only be," I quipped back, "that audacious artist who had the gall to doctor it when I wasn't looking."

And for the rest of the day, there went my disciplined writing schedule.

3

We settled under the enormous mango tree that shaded the front yard of my house. I told Joel about the materials I had found in the National Archives, which gave the lie to the traditional history books that berated Paraguay's founding father as the archetypical Latin American tyrant. I went on about how Dr. Francia—the George Washington of Paraguay—was really a populist who championed the common people at the expense of the privileged classes, those same elites who had gone on to write their embittered version of history.

Joel told me about the rural clinic he ran, the only private medical facility in the village of Ybycuí, eighty miles outside the capital. He explained how, after graduating from medical school eighteen years before, his decision to become a country doctor had scandalized Asunción society, all but branding him a traitor to his class. Why, people openly questioned, would this son of such an old and distinguished family, this brilliant young physician, shun a lucrative medical career in the capital, electing instead to tend to peasants in the impoverished countryside?

As our friendship grew, I asked Filártiga to read the manuscript of *Paraguay's Autonomous Revolution* and to compose pen-and-ink drawings for each chapter. He invited me to visit his clinic.

As much as my work benefited from Joel's artistic contributions, my visits to Ybycuí proved to be of far greater value. There I found a world that otherwise I would never have known. And it was there that I grew to know the Filártiga family.

Nidia, at thirty-eight, was five years younger than her husband. Possessing inexhaustible energy, she seemed to be in constant motion. As the clinic's administrator and head nurse, Nidia tackled the endless problems of keeping a developing-world rural medical facility on track. No task was too menial—she spent hours everyday cooking and washing—or overly daunting—assisting Dr. Filártiga from the most routine procedure to major surgery.

Generally unaware of the admiration of the staff and patients, Nidia did recognize the necessity of deliberately downplaying her physical beauty. Otherwise, authentic human contact with the peasants they served, people who already held the Filártigas in awe, became all but impossible.

Only on those rare occasions when we would go to a restaurant would Nidia put aside her drab work clothes. Bringing out her fetching appearance, she let out her blond hair, highlighted her bottle-green eyes with a touch of makeup, and displayed her trim figure in a dress left over from her upper-class youth.

Nidia quickly, and completely, won me over.

Dolly, a strong-willed young woman, and at nineteen the eldest of the Filártiga children, worked alongside her parents in all aspects of clinic life. Some months before we met, however, partly in search of greater independence from her father—who indeed was capable of being a stern taskmaster—Dolly had decided to spend the weekdays at the family house in Asunción, where she could take advantage of the better educational opportunities.

At fourteen, Analy, the quietest of the children, also did her share of the work. And another helper, Katia, at eleven the baby of the family, brightened a room simply with her sparkling presence.

4

The clinic itself can only be described as a marvel of necessity. Nothing was wasted. For bandages, threadbare sheets were cut up and disinfected in boiling water, over and over, until they literally fell apart. Even gauze and disposable syringes, after being sterilized, were reused.

Dr. Filártiga's workload consisted of twenty to thirty consultations a day, as well as averaging several major procedures or operations a week. And while he kept rudimentary patient records on card files, not even an informal bookkeeping system existed. In any event, there was no real need for one. Joel personally knew each of his patients, almost without exception peasant farmers eking out a subsistence living. For those few who had any spare cash, he adjusted his fees according to an informal sliding scale based upon their ability to pay.

Basically, though, the clinic operated on an exchange-of-services basis. Almost everyone contributed in kind: bringing a chicken or some vegetables, chopping wood, digging a new well, helping out with the cooking and laundry, making repairs, or adding on a new room. "In my whole life here," Joel told me, "I have never had to buy anything to eat. And the clinic, under my direction, has been built by the peasants with their work."

Over the years, the clinic had grown from two small rooms to a modest compound. By 1975, it consisted of the Filártigas' living quarters, a combination consultation and examination room, an operating room, a workshop, an institutional-sized kitchen, and three hospital-type rooms, accommodating several patients each. As is customary throughout Latin America, even in most respectable hospitals, relatives of the patients attend to their nonmedical needs, such as serving their meals, washing them, and helping them to the toilet.

Patients began arriving before dawn. Many came from the distant reaches of the Ybycuí Valley, often spending five or six hours traveling in rickety, old, ox-drawn carts to reach the clinic.

Occasionally, there were others who came quietly in the middle of the night. For the security of all concerned, these people did not mix with the regular patients. They received medical treatment and, if necessary, convalesced in the semiprivacy of the Filártigas' living quarters. They departed as discretely as they arrived.

Ordinarily, though, barring life-or-death emergencies, the people gathered in the front yard, softly talking among themselves in Guaraní, stoically waiting for Dr. Filártiga to open up at 6:00 A.M.

Paraguay is the only officially bilingual country in Latin America. Spanish is the language of government and commerce; Guaraní is the native Indian tongue, spoken by the vast majority of the population, especially in the *campo* where most people have, at best, a cursory knowledge of Spanish. An insight into Paraguay's bilingual culture can be seen in the saying: "One makes business in Spanish—and love in Guaraní."

It is also true that one gets sick in Guaraní. Many times I would hear Dr. Filártiga speaking Spanish with a patient, only to shift to Guaraní as soon as they began the medical consultation.

Watching people arrive at the clinic, I noticed that a few, like the mayor of Ybycuí, dressed in middle-class garb. But these were the exception. Peasants, clothed in sweat-stained hand-me-downs, made up the vast majority of Filártiga's patients.

One morning, as I helped lift a man curled up in pain from the back of an ox cart, my eyes fixed upon the inch-thick, deeply gouged soles of his bare feet. The realization struck me that he had never worn shoes; that a lifetime of working in the fields had so deformed his feet that, should he somehow find the money to buy a pair of footwear, his gnarled feet could never fit in them.

5

That afternoon I saw Joel explode in frustration. In his cluttered office after lunch, he was telling me about the chronic medical problems he treated. Filártiga blamed the dictatorship's indifference for many of his patients' ailments. He explained how not only the myriad of maladies stemming from undernourishment and contaminated water—such as gastric enteritis and parasites—but also tuberculosis and leprosy, easily could be prevented through basic public health programs.

Rather naively, I questioned what was being done.

"What do you think?" he replied wearily. "So long as General Stroessner and his mafia run Paraguay only for their own personal benefit, without a care about the misery and death their greed causes, what can be done?"

"Well," I said, "have you tried contacting any of the international health organizations?"

"Richard, you do not understand." Joel sighed and sat back behind his desk. "I will give you one small example of the way things work here. A few years ago, the big cotton growers began using Folodol M60. It is a very powerful insecticide to protect their crops. And it works very well. There are no more cotton blights. And they are making more profit than ever.

"But it is also a very potent toxin. And the people who must work those fields day after day, week after week, year after year, end up poisoned. Many get sick. Some die!

"Here—I will show you." Leaping to his feet, Filártiga began rummaging through the drawers of a cabinet. "Never mind, I will tell you," he said in growing frustration, apparently unable to find the patient records he sought.

"Now, I have all these cases of appendicitis and spontaneous abortions. And almost all of them are workers from the cotton fields!" He slammed his fist down on the desk. "This never was the case before they started using Folodol M60. And last year alone, three people died!"

"So what's being done about it?"

"What is being done?" he exclaimed, his frustration bursting to the surface. "Nothing, absolutely nothing. That is what is being done. Stroessner's on the side of the greedy growers. The government does absolutely nothing to control them."

Flushed with emotion, Joel paused for a deep breath, and then went on. "I wrote a letter to the minister of health. Nothing happened. I wrote letters to the newspapers. None of them dared publish them. I have talked with other doctors. They say they have the same problems. I tell everyone I talk to, and nothing changes. The big cotton growers just go on using more and more agritoxins. And more and more poisoned workers arrive at the clinic. And some of them die!"

Anchored behind his desk, gripping its oaken bulk, he finally calmed down. Then, with a touch of resignation in his voice, he chided, "Well, so now you know what is not being done. And even worse, what cannot be done."

6

The people's esteem for Dr. Filártiga far surpassed the respect usually accorded small-town physicians. They not only depended upon Joel for their medical needs but regarded him as their political champion as well. For more than two decades, since Stroessner seized power in the 1954 military coup, so many people had been tortured and murdered for attempting to better their lot that they had long since abandoned any illusion as to their fate should they openly oppose the dictatorship.

Even Dr. Filártiga, whose upper-class background afforded him a good deal of protection, was not immune. Three times he had been arrested and tortured. The last time, in 1966, accused of giving medical aid to members of an armed resistance movement cost him weeks of beatings and electric shocks. And, of course, the inevitable dips in the *pileta*.

Pileta is Spanish for swimming pool. In the lexicon of Paraguayan torture, however, it is a bathtub filled with vomit, urine, feces, blood, and other bodily fluids in which victims—usually under the supervision of a police physician—are immersed, until they lose consciousness. Only to be revived, and torment to begin all over again.

Fortunately, at the time Filártiga's mother, Lidia, held the influential post of president of the Women's Auxiliary of Stroessner's Colorado Party. To her horror, she learned that the ominous green X, which marked those slated for execution, appeared next to her son's name on the prisoner list.

Lidia begged, bribed, and cajoled her powerful contacts in the regime until she got Joel's death status rescinded, and his sentence reduced to internal exile. For nine months Filártiga languished in the remote hamlet of Mbuyapey, where each morning he was required to report to the police station. During his banishment, the people of Ybycuí held weekly Masses to pray for the safe return of their maverick physician-artist-philanthropist-champion.

7

The people's love of their doctor's son equaled that for his father. In some ways, it was even more intimate because Joelito did not carry the baggage of his father's awesome status. Joelito had grown up with these people. And, in the lapses caused by the activist lifestyle of his parents, the people of Ybycuí became something akin to a second, extended family that raised him. He knew and fully accepted them; they knew and fully accepted him: embracing him as one of their own, teaching him their culture and wisdom.

Joelito enthusiastically pitched in with all tasks around the clinic. Because of his mechanical aptitude, he spent a good deal of time repairing equipment and serving as the clinic's driver—delivering medicines and checking on the progress of patients, bringing to the clinic people too ill to make it on their own, especially those from the outlying regions of the Ybycuí Valley.

Early one morning as I accompanied Joelito on his rounds, we came across a pickup soccer game. Joelito pulled over and, jumping out, said, "Come on. Let's go kick the ball around a while."

I tried to beg off. "I've never played soccer in my life. I don't even know the rules."

"You don't know how to play soccer?" He looked at me in amazement. "Everybody plays soccer. Come on. Let's go."

"No. Look, I'm serious," I persisted, "I'd just spoil the game. When I was growing up we played another kind of football, American football. And that was a long time ago."

"How old are you anyway?" he asked.

"Thirty."

"See. You're not so old." Joelito broke into that easy, open laugh of youth. "Come on. It doesn't matter. Don't be afraid."

And then, as if it resolved everything, he added, "They're all my friends. It doesn't matter. They won't mind. You're my friend, too. Come on. It'll be fun. Let's go!"

It was fun.

8

When we got back to the clinic, Dr. Filártiga had just finished a grueling three-hour cesarean section on Señora Mariana Brizuela. Even as Mariana still lay unconscious, recovering from the anesthesia, Joelito began cleaning up the operating room.

I followed Joel into to the living room where, with an exhausted sigh, he flopped on the sofa. "A delicate operation," he said. "The baby was—"

"Papi, Papi, come quick!" Joelito shouted, bursting into the room, "Señora Brizuela's dead!"

With the surprising agility some heavyset men possess, Dr. Filártiga sprang from the sofa and ran to the operating room. I noted Mariana's lack of breathing, her chalky death pallor, and silently agreed with Joelito—obviously she was dead.

Seeing the alarm on Dr. Filártiga's face was confirmation. But, not visible to me, his medical sixth sense was kicking in.

While furiously spinning the hand crank that tilted the old operating table to lower Mariana's head, Filártiga began snapping out orders. "Nidia, bring five milligrams of Levofed. Now! Prepare another five of adrenaline. And the same of Doca! Hurry!"

By the time the table was fully repositioned, Nidia had two of the hypodermic needles ready. "But," she explained, "there's no Doca."

What followed appeared more like a choreographed show than a life-and-death medical emergency.

In one continuous motion, Filártiga swooped the first syringe from Nidia's outstretched hand and plunged it through the plastic IV bottle of saline solution already inserted in Mariana's vein. And, as Nidia injected the adrenaline in her other arm, he instructed her, "We'll use Effortil instead of Doca. It's almost the same generic composition."

A moment later, as Filártiga checked Mariana's pulse with one hand, Nidia placed the Effortil syringe in his other. Without breaking stride, he jabbed it deep into Mariana's buttock. Then, with Joelito holding her steady, he balled both hands into fists and began external cardiac massage, a procedure he continued for the next half hour while Nidia and Joelito took turns wiping away the sweat running down his face.

At last, Mariana began breathing, her blood pressure rose, she opened her eyes. "Doctor, how is my baby?"

"He is perfect. A fine, healthy boy." Flexing his hands to restore circulation, Filártiga continued checking her blood pressure and pulse. "And how do you feel, Mariana?"

"Tired. A little sore," she answered groggily. Small wonder. Mariana was still strapped to the tilted operating table and, in fact, would have to remain in that position for the next four hours.

"Can I go to my room now? I want to see my baby and my husband," she pleaded.

"Not just now, my daughter," Dr. Filártiga said. "You have had a hard time. Your blood pressure is still low. I am going to keep you here for a little while longer. Somebody will be with you all the time. Now go back to sleep and rest."

Returning to the living room, I asked Joel, "What happened to Mariana? When I first saw her, she sure looked dead to me."

"Almost. Another few minutes and I do not think that the Levofed and Effortil could have raised her blood pressure in time. She came very close."

Once again collapsing on the sofa, he lit his pipe and explained in detail. "Mariana suffers chronic low blood pressure. With the excessive loss of liquids when she gave birth, she went into acute circulatory shock. It is a very severe condition. The body temperature and blood pressure drop drastically. And this cuts off the circulation of blood to the brain. The patient then enters into a coma, and the heart stops. It was very close.

"To be truthful," he finished, "at first I did not think she would live. It was a miracle."

Yes, I thought, a miracle. A miracle that you left the city and set up your clinic in this remote village. A miracle that you immediately diagnosed Mariana's condition and knew what to do. A miracle that, because of the years practicing medicine with chronic shortages of medicines, you have developed an encyclopedic knowledge of their generic compositions and substituted Effortil when there was no Doca. A miracle that Nidia, without any formal training, has become a most incredibly competent operating room nurse. And a miracle that young Joelito, while scrubbing the operating room instruments, kept a conscientious eye on Señora Brizuela and told you as soon as she went into shock.

Yes, I thought, a miracle.

9

At first, Joelito would stop by my place to deliver one of his father's drawings, or to drop off a bottle of molasses or a chunk of cheese that Nidia sent from Ybycuí. Then he began just coming over without any special reason.

Much like at the clinic, Joelito naturally slipped into helping out around my rented house in Asunción—stacking firewood, repairing a leaky faucet, and generally doing what ever needed to be done. It did not take long to develop an independent friendship of our own.

Everyone knows a Joelito—an easygoing, secure young man with the aura of a natural leader. In Joelito I saw one of those special people who, as he made his way through life, was sure to fulfill his promise.

Despite the difference in age, Joelito's openness pretty much precluded taboo subjects between us. I asked him what his father thought of the Playboy Bunny sticker he had plastered on the rear window of the family car.

"Oh, he complains that it's embarrassing. You know how serious Papi is. But when he tells me to take it off, I just laugh, and ask him that if it's so bad then why doesn't he take it off himself? Then he laughs, too. And we both end up laughing about it."

"Do you have any idea," I said, "how lucky you are to be able to laugh like that with your father?"

"What do you mean?" he asked, genuinely perplexed.

"Look, most fathers just boss their kids around. It's a lot easier than putting up with all the hassle of treating you with respect, like a real person. I never laughed like that with my father."

"You mean you and your father weren't friends?" he asked incredulously.

"Friends? No, you couldn't say we were friends," I told him and changed the subject. "Anyway, what do you plan to do with the last 700 months of your life?"

"Seven hundred months?"

"Sure. You're sixteen now," I said. "If you live to the average age of seventy or so, that's about fifty-five years, about 700 months."

Joelito took a moment to absorb the new concept. "That's an awful long time. Too long to worry about," he laughed.

"I know a lot about how bad things are here and I'm going to help change them. But I want to be successful and happy, too. Not like Papi. He's always angry about something.

"He says that you can't be successful and good at the same time here in Paraguay. He says to become wealthy you have to prostitute yourself and work with the dictatorship. To be good you have to suffer and fight."

"So how about you?" I pressed. "What are you going to do?"

"I'm going to be a doctor like Papi. And an architect, too," Joelito said. "And I want to be an artist like Papi, because you can make changes with art, too.

"You've seen my drawings. What do you think?" he asked without a trace of self-consciousness.

"They're really good," I told him truthfully. Joelito's talent was already pressing the limits of his father's instruction, his drawing taking on a distinctive style of his own.

"And what about you?" Joelito asked. "What are you going to do with your last 500 months?"

Somewhat taken aback by his agile math, a few beats passed before I answered. "Well, in a couple of weeks I'll be going back to UCLA to finish up my dissertation, the book that Roberto translated and your father made the drawings for.

"Then, I hope to come back here to work on another book. After that, I don't know. Probably teach at some university."

"You're just like Papi. Always working. Always so serious. Will you be happy being a professor?"

Again I stalled, half toying with the idea of weaseling out from giving an honest answer to Joelito.

"You know," I said, "I don't even think about being happy anymore. Somehow that has just slipped away."

"See. You and Papi need more happiness."

10

Throughout that exceptionally raw Paraguayan winter of 1975, Filártiga and I spent many evenings relaxing near the warmth of my fireplace. Our discussions ranged from art and history to philosophy, from United States foreign policy to world politics, from the practice of medicine in Paraguay to the inner workings of Stroessner's dictatorship.

"Richard," Joel explained, "I will tell you a good way to begin understanding how Stroessner and his cronies function. Imagine that your mafia gained control of an entire country—that they became the government.

"That is why Paraguay, with a population of less than three million, is the world's largest importer of American cigarettes. Of course very few remain here, because they are smuggled into countries all around South America."

Filártiga paused long enough to light his pipe. "It is said that smuggling is Paraguay's biggest business. It makes perfect sense when you add in the whisky, narcotics, electronics, perfumes, and all the other luxury goods.

"There even is a traffic in rare animals—flamingos from Argentina, panthers from the jungles of Brazil, other endangered species protected by international treaties. Rich people in Paris and New York pay exorbitant prices to impress their friends with such exotic pets."

"Government-sponsored organized crime," I agreed, throwing a piece of wood on the fire. "It really is like a mafia setup."

"Yes. But worse. Because they have the power of a sovereign nation-state. So who is to stop them? They can get away with anything."

"Anything?"

"Anything," Filártiga insisted. "Even selling Paraguayan citizenship to Nazi war criminals. It is no secret. I have seen the naturalization papers of Dr. Josef Mengele"— the Angel of Death from Auschwitz concentration camp.

11

Of course, it took more than corruption to hold together Stroessner's gangster regime. I asked Joel about the secret police.

"Investigaciones are entirely separate from the Army," he explained. "Not that one is less vicious than the other. Stroessner plays them off against each other, promoting a rivalry. In fact, the political police are so powerful that they serve as a check against the possibility of a military coup.

"The *campo* is mostly left to the Army, the urban centers to Investigaciones. Like the old Nazi Gestapo, their primary purpose is to repress political dissent. But both rely on a vast network of *pyragués.*"

"*Pyragués?*"

"Informers. The human pestilence that permeates the fabric of Paraguayan society," he said. "According to an old Guaraní legend, the *pyragué* is a mythical being. His feet are encased in thick mats of hair, so he can silently sneak up to your house at night and listen in on your secrets.

"*Pyragués* are everywhere. They can be waiters in restaurants, household servants, taxi drivers, shoeshine boys. Whatever they hear or see, they report to Investigaciones. They get paid even for passing on rumors. You do not have to be a 'subversive' to be arrested. Just suspicion can be enough."

"What do you have to do to become a suspect?" I asked.

"There is no clear line," Filártiga said. "Sometimes just speaking out against the regime is enough. When workers try to form a union, or peasants join together in an agricultural cooperative, that certainly is enough. But lots of times nothing is enough."

"Nothing? Nothing is enough?"

"You never know," Joel said. "Let me tell you about my old friend Alberto Carlés."

Filártiga drew closer to the fire. "Alberto is an economist. We grew up together. We went to school together. I am the godfather of his first son. But we do not see much of each other anymore. We do not even celebrate the holidays together—not because we do not want to, but because it could cause suspicion.

"If I must see him, I always park my car a few blocks away from his house. He does the same. Otherwise, the *pyragués* would eventually notice a pattern."

In a calm, matter-of-fact tone, he went on. "You know I do not belong to any political party. But I am known as a dissident. Maybe someday I will be arrested again. And then Alberto could be arrested too. For nothing. Because we are friends and spend time together. That could be enough.

"It is a way to terrorize the people. And it works. That is why we say that here in Paraguay, people 'walk with fear.'"

12

Stoking the fire, I contemplated life in Paraguay's police state. Misconstruing my concern for apprehension, Joel tried to allay my anxiety.

"Oh, you have got nothing to worry about. You are a Yanqui. They do not treat Yanquis like they do Paraguayans. Your embassy would cause too much trouble. And Stroessner needs United States support to stay in power.

"The only way that they would take you is if they caught you red-handed, working with an armed resistance group. Now that would be a triumph. They would have a foreigner to prove their international communist conspiracy. Then, for sure, you would be a guest of Investigaciones."

"No. That's not what I'm thinking," I said, perhaps laughing a bit too loudly. "Actually, I was thinking about something we might arrange when I get back to UCLA."

Joel did not say anything, but his body language perked up.

"What do you think?" I suggested. "Maybe we could get you invited to the university as a guest lecturer, give an art exhibition, talk about your work at the clinic?"

13

Four months later, in January 1976, Joel arrived in Los Angeles. Allyn Sinderbrand, who, while visiting me in Paraguay, had come to admire Filártiga had taken charge of the preparations. She had enlisted volunteer students and faculty, putting together a team whose advance work would have done a presidential candidate proud. Leaving the airport, she showed Joel one of the publicity leaflets.

14

Joel's visit to California exploded into a whirlwind of activity. The *Los Angeles Times* and both major Spanish newspapers—*Los Angeles Express* and *La Opinión*—ran feature articles. The local NBC television station aired a lengthy news special, "The Albert Schweitzer of Latin America." And an independent filmmaker, Jim Richardson, took it upon himself to produce a short documentary that portrayed Dr. Filártiga and his work.

Momentum snowballed. Joel received more invitations to speak and exhibit his art at private homes, churches, and other universities. Meeting with colleagues at UCLA, the University of Southern California, and the City of Hope's medical complex, he collected donations of medical supplies. And, in a flash of inspiration, he renamed his clinic in Paraguay the SANATORIO LA ESPERANZA—CLINIC OF HOPE.

The attention even enveloped Filártiga personally. A dentist friend sat him down for a marathon six-hour overhaul of his mouth, and a professor of medicine at one of the area's medical centers ran him through an exhaustive physical examination.

To provide Filártiga and his work with continuing support, the informal network of people coalesced into the "Paraguay Project." We arranged a series of successful fundraisers; like the art exhibition held at the home of Leonard Nimoy—Mr. Spock of *Star Trek* fame—who graciously refrained from even raising an eyebrow as we took his Picassos off the walls to hang up the Filártigas.

Along with the impressive amount of medical supplies, we raised $5,000 to purchase a new Packard Bell cardioscope and defibrillator for the clinic, the first such sophisticated medical technology in Paraguay outside the capital of Asunción.

On his return trip, Filártiga stopped in Mexico City and Buenos Aires—where other friends organized yet more lectures and art exhibitions. He finally arrived home in late February to a hero's welcome. While we were delighted to learn of the television and newspaper coverage extolling his triumphant international tour, the *ABC Color* feature article—which led off with a reproduction of the UCLA leaflet announcing Filártiga's lecture, "Art as Social Criticism in Latin America"—caused a pang of apprehension.

The final results of Joel's medical examination had been mailed to his house after the test and, to no one's great surprise, had arrived opened. Overall, finding Filártiga's health satisfactory, the report sternly warned that "the combination of your overweight condition and your incipient coronary artery disease makes you a candidate for serious and possibly fatal heart disease."

The medical report went on to say that Filártiga should lose twenty to thirty pounds as soon as possible and, most emphatically, "avoid all stress, both physical and emotional."

In a backhanded way, Filártiga felt that the news of his heart disease could prove beneficial. For, together with his rising international prominence, it might serve as a restraint against the police arresting and torturing him again.

It was a sound assumption. The torturer's job is not to kill the victim. The purpose of torture is to break the prisoner's will, perhaps to extract information, certainly to so debase the victims that they abandon their "subversive" activities and cower before the power of the police state. In fact, the inadvertent death of a "client" is the torturer's worst possible blunder, a professional disgrace.

To make sure that everyone knew the score, Filártiga all but advertised his heart condition. In keeping with his absentminded reputation, as he hustled through his hectic schedule of interviews and appearances, he would often leave behind copies of his California medical report.

15

In early March, the Paraguay Project people in LA and I began receiving disturbing press clippings and letters from Filártiga and other Paraguayan friends. The dictatorship, announcing the emergence of an armed resistance group, had launched another of its periodic waves of repression. Because of the anti-Stroessner implications of my book, *ABC Color* had backed out of the arrangement to serialize it. But then the Catholic University agreed to publish the entire work in its academic journal. And, though I might find a less than heartfelt welcome when I returned to Paraguay in a few months, it was Filártiga's immediate safety that most concerned everyone.

As a precaution, I wrote the London Secretariat of Amnesty International. I sent Amnesty biographical information on Filártiga and myself, as well as the names, addresses, and phone numbers of several Paraguayan opposition leaders to contact in the event of our arrest or disappearance.

In early April I received a reply from Amnesty's Campaign for the Abolition of Torture. Dick Oosting, the joint campaign organizer, said, "It goes without saying that if we were to receive word of you or your colleagues/friends having landed into trouble in Paraguay, we will try to do what we can, and as quickly as possible. I hope you realize, though, that one cannot expect wonders from Amnesty interventions, whatever the level or quantity."

Oosting's candor was a bit sobering, though hardly unexpected. What came next, however, was something of a surprise. "I have passed copies of your letters and enclosures to Edy Kaufman, the researcher responsible for Paraguay, and he will write to you separately," Oosting told me. "I hope all will go well, and hope that it will be possible for you to assist us in our work on Paraguay, as much as your other commitments allow you to do so. I am sure Edy will have a few questions in this respect!"

I had not expected to be recruited by Amnesty, but that was just fine with me—in fact, more than fine. Anticipating Kaufman's letter, I wrote him with a few questions of my own and offered to do what I could to help out. Shortly before I departed for Paraguay, his reply arrived.

"Many thanks for your letter of 7 April and the very kind offer of assistance during your stay in Paraguay. This will undoubtedly be invaluable to us," Kaufman wrote. "The innocuous address to which you can write to us is: 77 Dorchester Place, London

NW1," he told me, before offering his "Many best wishes for your forthcoming trip (and safe return)."

Of course, by the time Kaufman's letter reached me in Los Angeles, I had received Dr. Filártiga's letter. Yet, because the circumstances surrounding Joelito's murder remained so vague, there was little chance of getting Amnesty involved at this early stage. In any event, we had already mobilized the many friends and admirers Dr. Filártiga had made on his visit to California just two months before. Spontaneously, people took up a collection, and they gave me the proceeds to deliver to Joel upon my arrival in Paraguay.

Far more important, scores of condolence letters went out to the Filártigas from the Paraguay Project people. We organized a telegram and letter-writing campaign to members of Congress, as well as officials in the Ford administration; and we made certain that General Stroessner received copies of all the correspondence. To provide a measure of protection, it was essential to impress upon the dictator that now, more than ever, Filártiga could be counted on for unconditional support.

I still did not understand what had happened to Joelito, and I was equally in the dark about the Filártigas' situation. On May 13, after spending a few days with friends and family in New England, I boarded the first leg of Braniff's infamous fifteen-hour milk run down the spine of South America to Paraguay.

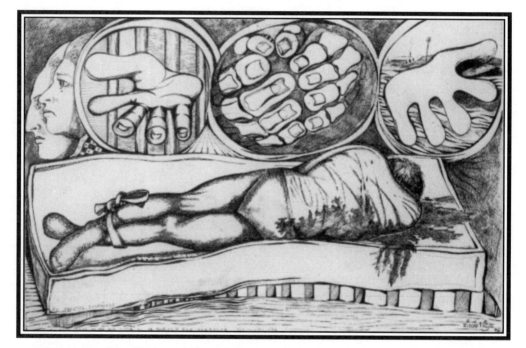

The night of Joelito's murder, the police forced Dolly to carry her brother's
tortured corpse to their house on a bloodstained mattress.

TWO

THE FILÁRTIGAS MET ME at Asunción's Aeropuerto Presidente Stroessner. The vibrant Nidia of my memory appeared drawn and shaky in her ankle-length black dress. Joel was disheveled and hyper. His mischievous brown eyes, which had so captivated his admirers in California only a few months before, now seemed more like open wounds.

We had barely exchanged *abrazos* in the terminal when Dr. Filártiga began blurting out an all but incoherent explanation of what had happened.

"They say it was a crime of passion! That is what the government and the press are calling the *Caso Filártiga*. A crime of passion! That Duarte came home and caught his wife Charo in bed with Joelito and killed him in a fight. But it is all a lie!

"Duarte is in jail, but they let Charo go without even making her give a deposition. And now she has disappeared. Now she will never get to tell the truth.

"We filed our own lawsuit against Police Inspector Peña and the others who murdered Joelito. Our lawyers said Nidia should file because I was not clean. Because I am a known dissident, they said it would be better that way.

"Then the police arrested Nidia and Dolly. But all that is a lie, too. It was just a way to try and make us abandon the case against them."

Confused by this startling news, I turned to Nidia. "You and Dolly were arrested? What for? When did this happen?"

"You do not know, Richard?" she said, a questioning expression overlaying the fatigue on her face. "Dolly wrote you a letter when we were in the prison. She told you everything."

"I didn't receive it. It never arrived," I replied. "The only letter I got was the one Joel sent through the diplomatic pouch saying Joelito had been killed."

A flash of disappointment crossed Nidia's face, and a film of resignation dulled her green eyes as she accepted that the news of their imprisonment had not made it to the world outside Paraguay.

"Well," Nidia explained, "it was about a month after Joelito's death, after we filed the suit against Inspector Peña and the others. They said that Dolly and I broke into Peña's house and attacked them, that we tried to beat them up. They accused us of trespassing and assault, and the court ordered us arrested.

"But we hid out with friends and Papi took out a public notice in *ABC* denouncing why we were going to be arrested. It was so ridiculous. Nobody believed it.

"Finally, our lawyer took us to the court and we surrendered." Nidia stopped talking and seemed to drift away for a few moments.

"It was April 28. I remember because it was Analy's fifteenth birthday. Poor Analy. You know how special it is to every girl, because that is when she becomes a woman. But we could not celebrate her fifteenth birthday because Dolly and I were in the Buen Pastor prison."

As we stood in the dingy reception area outside the custom's exit, friends and families meeting other arriving passengers swarmed around us. A number of people recognized Dr. Filártiga and Nidia, whose pictures had been regularly appearing in the press. Oblivious to their stares, Joel paid them no attention.

"Arresting Nidia and Dolly was too much! Everybody knew it was just another machination to persecute us.

"They murdered Joelito," he insisted. "And then because we seek justice in the courts, they arrest his mother and sister! Because we wouldn't stay silent, like we were supposed to. Because we want the truth known, they throw Nidia and Dolly in prison like common criminals.

"Even here in Paraguay that's too much," Joel railed, his voice growing louder. "Public opinion became outraged. For the first time people started to talk openly against the police. Some came to me and said that they would arrange to kill Peña. But I told them no. Because it's not just Peña. It's the whole system that is to blame for Joelito's death.

"The *Caso Filártiga* is a great public scandal. There's never been anything like it. The police saw that arresting Nidia and Dolly was only making things worse for them, so they had to let them go.

"But Nidia and Dolly are still not free of the charges. Our lawyers say that probably nothing more will come of it, that it'll just be forgotten. But their case is still technically alive in the court. And in this country nothing is certain. If Nidia and Dolly are ever convicted, that would put our case against Peña in jeopardy. So as a guarantee I joined the suit against them too."

By now, the agitated scene in the bustling airport had attracted a small crowd. A couple of soldiers carrying machine pistols wandered over in our direction. In his excitement, Filártiga did not notice. But Nidia took him by the arm and shuffled us out of the building.

1

In the car Filártiga began unloading again. "The first thing I did was take photographs to prove Joelito was tortured. I have been tortured. And I have treated many people after they have been tortured by the police. I know when someone's been tortured. And I know Joelito was tortured! By professionals. I have proof. You'll see. I'll show you.

"Judge Martínez signed the death certificate that the coroner made when Joelito was killed. But it's a lie. I had three colleagues of mine do an autopsy that same afternoon. It shows that the coroner's report is a lie. But they lied, too."

"Your colleagues lied, too?" I asked. "You said that their autopsy proved that the official death certificate was falsified."

"That's right," Joel answered, "but they really did not tell the truth either.

"The death certificate mentions only a few abrasions and one puncture above the heart. And that wound did not even exist! The coroner only said that to support the official crime-of-passion cover-up story, which is that the husband Duarte stabbed Joelito to death in a fight.

"In their autopsy report my colleagues described many, many more wounds. Far too many to be caused in a fight. But they were afraid to write down all of the wounds because they knew that only torture could have caused them."

Joel paused, took several deep breaths. It seemed to help organize his thoughts but did nothing to improve his driving, leaving me white-knuckling the handhold as he ripped through the streets of Asunción.

"Two weeks later," he picked up, "a good friend did a third autopsy. Dr. Hernán Godoy. His report is the most honest. But even he did not tell the whole truth.

"I showed him where Joelito had been burned by electric shocks. He said he had doubts, so I asked the assistant to make an incision. Then it was easy to see how deep the burns were. Old Dr. Godoy is a very good forensic surgeon. But he was afraid to put 'electric burns' in his report. He just wrote the word 'burns' in brackets with a question mark.

"I asked him, 'Doctor, why don't you put down they are electric burns?' He said, 'You learn with the years there are many things that cannot be told as they are. Forgive me, my son.' Those were his words to me."

After Joel finished telling me how even his colleagues feared to report their forensic findings honestly, he fell quiet. Nidia sat silently in the front seat, staring out the windshield. I pondered how the dictatorship's repression had permeated all aspects of Paraguayan society, even to the ethical degradation of the medical profession.

2

Without warning, Filártiga's angry voice shattered our pensive mood. "All the judges are corrupt and do what they are told. The courts are controlled by Stroessner. Diógenes Martínez is the judge who came out at three in the morning to Inspector Peña's house, to put his seal on the false death certificate. And the same Diógenes Martínez now has been put in charge of our case against Peña and the others who killed Joelito!

"But nobody believes the police," Joel went on. "Hundreds of people came to the wake. With their own eyes they saw the torture wounds all over Joelito's body. And I took photographs as proof. The camera does not lie. And the newspaper *Aquí* published them. Now, everyone knows the truth."

I knew Stroessner kept the press on a short leash, and knew how Roberto Thompson had been arrested and tortured for disclosing government corruption. And had not Joel just told me that the press was going along with the crime-of-passion whitewash? So how was it that *Aquí* would expose the official cover-up of police torture and murder?

And what was the sense in bringing legal action against a police inspector in a police state anyway?

Jet lagged and overwhelmed by the Filártigas' rambling explanation, all the unfamiliar names left me confused. About the only thing that came through in my muddled mind was that I still understood next to nothing about what was happening.

To change the subject, I asked about the piles of rotting garbage that spilled onto the streets of Asunción. Joel slammed on the brakes, stopped the car in the middle of the narrow street, and launched into a tirade. "The capital has been stinking for weeks. All because one of Stroessner's cronies ate the whole month's sanitary budget. So there's no money to run the garbage trucks or pay the workers."

Thrusting his arm out the window, Filártiga pointed at a cat-sized rat ambling among the trash heaps alongside several children playing in the refuse. He raged, "Many children have contracted acute dysentery because of this hygienic disgrace. Already three have died of rabies from rat bites.

"And nobody is ever punished. That's the way the system always works." By now Joel was yelling. "They steal money to build their big houses and take vacations in Miami. And the pleasures of these criminals is paid for by sickness and death!"

Trembling with fear, with both her hands Nidia grabbed Joel's outstretched arm, which was shaking with fury. "Papi, Papi," she pleaded. "Stop! For the love of God, shut up. The police will come. It does no good. You'll only bring more trouble. Please, Papi. Stop yelling!"

"No! I'll never shut up!" Filártiga exploded as he wrenched his arm free. "They'll never shut me up! This is the same system that killed Joelito. Nothing can ever make me shut up!"

3

Even before I could get settled into my room, Joel called me into the parlor. Nidia and Dolly joined us. On the coffee table were the color pictures of Joelito's body.

"Look here," Filártiga said, pointing to the welts that striped Joelito's back. "See how they all run in an almost perfect lateral pattern? That means he was held down, so he could not move when the torturers whipped him.

"And these," he explained dryly, pointing his pen at three round blistering scabs, "are the electric burns. They measured to a depth of five centimeters. I have treated people with burns like these before. I have had burns like this."

Dr. Filártiga's eyes remained fixed on the photographs as he continued speaking in the didactic tone of a lecturer. "Such burns are made by the *picana eléctrica*. It is a high-voltage rheostat with dials to adjust the electricity. Attached at the end of the cables are metal rods.

"When the voltage is increased, the shock is intensified and the electricity burns through the skin into the flesh. The *picana* causes extreme pain. Unbearable pain. It is a favored form of torture used by the police."

"What about these gashes?" I asked, indicating several wide cuts on the upper left side of Joelito's back. "Is that how they killed Joelito?"

"No," Filártiga answered. "I believe he died of cardiac seizure induced by excessive shocks.

"Those are puncture wounds made by a knife after he was already dead. A very big knife. Like a bayonet. It is the work of an expert—almost surgical in their precision. The major arteries were severed, but there was no bleeding there. That means the heart had already stopped."

"Why would they do that," I wondered. "If Joelito was already dead, what's the sense of stabbing him?"

"Part of their cover-up. To disguise that he died under torture—give credibility to their crime-of-passion story that the husband, Hugo Duarte, killed Joelito in a fight.

"Also, by severing the arteries," Filártiga concluded, "it was not possible to fully embalm the cadaver. In the heat at this time of year, that ensured we had to inter him right away. To hide the evidence of their crime in the grave."

4

No big political or ideological considerations led me to join the Filártigas' fight. Certainly I wanted to know the truth behind Joelito's death. But, in any normal sense, I never made a conscious decision. It was no more complicated than a gut-level rejection of the vicious part of our human nature responsible for the torture-murder of Joelito, and the devastation it had wrought upon these good people.

Living with the Filártiga family meant reliving their torment. We went over and over, and delved deeper and deeper into the tragedy that had shattered their lives.

With an obsession born of desperation, Nidia squirreled away anything to do with the case—legal documents, newspaper articles, photographs, letters, anonymous notes, and even the bloodstained mattress that had been used the night of the murder to carry Joelito's body home.

To a good degree, we all shared Nidia's mania. Our pursuit often took us down dangerous, sometimes reckless, avenues. We searched for information among friends and neighbors and lawyers and reporters, from priests and confidential informants to U.S. Embassy contacts and members of the opposition political parties, even from sympathetic Paraguayan government officials and the armed resistance group fighting against the dictatorship.

Along with gathering material on Paraguayan human rights violations for Amnesty International, I began my historical research at the National Archives. Most of my time, however, was spent trying to make sense of Joelito's murder.

The skills I had developed as a historian were not unlike those needed to investigate the death of Joelito: gathering and analyzing enormous amounts of raw data, culling out the relevant facts from the confusing and often contradictory mass of material, and then digging further into the most promising leads. With luck, logic, and the information provided by the Filártigas, bits and pieces of the puzzle started falling into place.

Even so, it took months before a coherent picture began to appear. As is so often the case in Latin America, or for that matter anywhere in the world, the murky events surrounding human rights murders were shrouded in a complex interplay of personal animosities and political ambitions.

5

In the early 1970s, Dr. Filártiga realized that the family needed a place in Asunción, so they purchased a lot in the barrio of Sajonia. On a cobblestone street just off Avenida Carlos Antonio López, a lovely four-lane boulevard divided by a tree-lined grassy mall, they began to build a house.

Inevitably, during his weekend visits to the capital, people came to Filártiga for medical treatment. Though some were residents of the upper-middle-class neighborhood, most of his patients by far arrived from the poorer sections of the town. Just as at his clinic in Ybycuí, those unable to pay in cash put in a couple of hours work cleaning up, laying bricks, or otherwise helping out.

The Filártigas' place soon became an informal meeting spot for artists, poets, writers, and students. As with Dr. Filártiga's patients, no appointment was necessary. People were welcome to just drop by.

Rather than relying on the mass media, Joel and his friends kept abreast of what was really going on in a more reliable way—they talked with each other.

Filártiga's informal salon centered on poetry and literary readings, artistic displays, and heated debates about current events and Paraguayan history, or simply on passing time with the eccentric and outspoken local celebrity.

In 1974, at the age of eighteen, Dolly moved from the family's home in Ybycuí to the house in Asunción. To provide a measure of security, Filártiga hired a live-in handyman, Bernardino Ortiz. And, then too, Grandma Lidia made daily visits, to keep a stern eye on things.

Dolly lobbied for her younger siblings to join her in Sajonia, where they also could get a better education. To their delight, Joel and Nidia finally acquiesced. Joelito—who Filártiga rationalized had matured beyond his sixteen years and would be a moderating influence on his rebellious sister—and Analy, then fourteen, joined Dolly in Asunción. Little Katia, still only eleven, remained at the clinic with her parents in Ybycuí.

The Filártiga children quickly made friends with the other young people in the barrio. The house became a beehive of activity, with all kinds of people wandering in and out, especially during the weekends when Joel and Nidia were in town. The neighborhood youngsters found Dr. Filártiga and his friends fascinating. They would gather around, watching and listening to their irreverent expositions on Paraguay and the world at large.

Nidia became a confidant to the young women. In the nonjudgmental manner that came from her years at the clinic, she was always available to offer advice and a sympathetic ear. Nidia became a person, for many the only person, with whom women could freely confide their most intimate problems.

The Filártigas became beloved and respected in the Sajonia barrio.

6

At the other end of the neighborhood's spectrum were Police Inspector Américo Peña-Irala and his common-law wife, Juana Villalba.

Even by the liberal sexual mores of Paraguayan culture, for years the other barrio residents had held Juana in less than high esteem. Perhaps influenced by their growing animosity, Juana left Sajonia in the 1960s. In 1973 she returned with her four children—daughter Charo, and sons Nery, Jorge, and Felipe—by then all teenagers, and a fifth child, ten-year-old Candido. Juana had accumulated quite a bit of money, enabling her to buy a comfortable residence just three houses from the Filártigas. Shortly after, Américo Peña moved in with her.

Dolly's account, compared with the vehemence of others with whom I spoke, is quite restrained. "They were the rich ones in the neighborhood. Then Juana chose to live with Peña and they used everything up. They bought a nice car and would go to Argentina and Brazil to take their vacations, or for a weekend to the Foz de Iguazu cataracts just to have fun. They went out to eat in restaurants a lot. Juana always wore expensive cloths. They were big shots.

"They would drink a lot in the house. Finally, they became almost like hermits. Nobody liked them. They didn't have any friends in the barrio. Sometimes they would have parties, but only with other police."

By early 1976, three more people had joined the household. To help out with the cooking and housework, Juana took in her thirteen-year-old niece Blanca Fernandez. The other new occupants were Charo's husband Hugo Duarte Arredondo and their newborn son.

The son of a prominent attorney, at twenty-two Hugo Duarte was a medical school dropout, who worked the night shift as a clerk at the downtown Hotel Guaraní. Because of the Villalba family's reputation, Duarte's parents had fiercely opposed his marriage to Charo. And so the hapless Duarte, mocked as a spoiled blowhard by the other young people, and ridiculed by even his wife, found himself living under the barrio's most infamous roof.

If people scorned Juana for her lifestyle, they feared Peña. A burly man with jet black hair and accusing green eyes, the inspector cut an imposing figure in his sharply pressed khaki police uniform. Indeed, the intimidating image Peña projected was on the mark.

Even without condescending to speak with his civilian neighbors, the cop was the source of aggravation in Sajonia. Arriving home after a night shift, Peña would pull up to the wrought iron fence and lean on the horn until someone would come running out of the house to swing open the gates for him.

Everyone walked on eggs when Peña was around. Slouched in his favorite recliner, he would watch the soccer games on television, ordering whoever was closest at hand to bring him a snack or a beer. Then, too, Peña was a mean drunk. The Villalba kids complained that all too often he would vent his drunken rage by beating the hell out of the women and children.

People could not help but hear such violence—especially during Paraguay's sweltering summers, when everyone's windows were open. Then, the clamor thundering from Peña's house tore apart the barrio's tranquillity, sending the neighborhood's guard dogs into a barking frenzy.

Such was the general loathing of Peña that, as the neighbors watched the police inspector drive off to work, they took to saying, "There he goes again. Off to torture someone."

7

By Latin American standards, General Alfredo Stroessner's police state ranked in the moderately repressive category. Normally, the selective persecution of the "communist subversives" and their sympathizers proved sufficient for the routine maintenance of the dictatorship.

However, when Stroessner suspected that serious opposition might be brewing, he unleashed his thugs. During periodic waves of repression, the police and army rampaged through their inventory of terror: mass arrests and routine torture, arbitrary "disappearances" and extrajudicial executions.

Filártiga had told me about the Investigaciones secret police. I learned about the army from another impeccable source, U.S. Army lieutenant colonel Robert LaSala.

I met Bob in 1975 at the embassy's Fourth of July party. Only months after the humiliating finale of the Vietnam war, political passions still burned at flash-point levels. I had learned the wisdom of avoiding military types at embassy functions.

It seems that I possessed a remarkable ability to infuriate almost anyone in uniform—even when hardly trying. But at the reception, my friend Father John Vesey, a Catholic missionary, laughed aside my protests and introduced Colonel LaSala. A full ten minutes passed without the "V" word being spoken.

Then the colonel tapped my drink with his, and in a quiet toast said, "Thank God it's finally over. We had no business being there in the first place." A bit later, Bob mentioned his master's thesis, and I offered a casual invitation to show him around the National Archives. The next morning, he showed up to begin work.

Over the following weeks, I found Bob to be an authentically moral person—and more than a bit disillusioned with Stroessner's regime. More quickly than I could have imagined, a mutual respect developed between us, until the last barriers of suspicion disappeared.

To get around the Paraguayan authorities, Bob offered me the use of the Army Post Office service to get letters into and out of the country. I gratefully accepted, and a few days later I went to his office at the U.S. Military Mission. Bob appeared to be edgy, so I asked what was wrong.

"Nothing special, really," he replied. "I guess this job is getting to me."

I knew that during his three years in the country, his disdain for the Paraguayan Army had grown to outright contempt.

"What's the matter, Bob?" I chided good-naturedly, "have your brother officers defending this mecca of freedom been behaving less than gentlemanly?"

His head snapped up and he shot me a glare. I gave him my most disarming smile and was rewarded with a short, bitter laugh.

"Yeah, the same old crap," he said. "This morning at the county team meeting I ran it all by the guys again. Nobody gives a shit."

"What did you tell them?"

"The same thing I've been saying all along: Cut off military assistance. The Paraguayan officer corps is the most corrupt I've ever come across. They're only interested in enriching themselves. The conscripts under their command receive little or no military training. Basically, they're used as slave labor on the officers' ranches. Or they're put to work on the houses that they're building for themselves, with materials diverted from the construction of military installations—materials subsidized by U.S. foreign aid.

"You can't really call them an army," he went on. "They're not professional soldiers. They function as an internal police force. They're nothing more than peasant beaters."

8

In December 1975, the simmering conflict with several of the peasants' self-help organizations, burst into the open. The Paraguayan Army began destroying the "subversive" peasant cooperatives sponsored by the Catholic Agrarian Leagues and the Protestant Friendship Mission.

By early 1976, the situation had escalated to where the country was bracing for more than just another of its periodic waves of repression. For the first time in a decade, Stroessner's peasant beaters faced the possibility that someone might actually shoot back at them.

On March 15, in neighboring Argentina, the armed forces overthrew President Isabel Perón and launched their "dirty war" against that country's insurgents. The Argentine counterinsurgency campaign presented a serious threat to the newly formed Paraguayan armed resistance group, the Political-Military Organization (Oganización Político Militar, OPM). A few months before, the OPM guerrillas had set up their headquarters in Argentina, just across the Paraguay River in the relative safety of the border town of Corrientes. But now they faced the threat of getting swept up in the Argentine military's rampage.

Despite the OPM's enterprising name, these guerrillas were not truly a military force. Lacking arms and experience, they avoided the trademark tactics of guerrilla warfare. Not only did they refuse to engage in political assassination, they never even pulled a bank robbery or carried out a kidnapping to finance their operations. Instead, they concentrated on educating the Paraguayan peasants about their basic legal rights and on organizing them into self-defense groups.

With their security jeopardized in Argentina, the OPM prepared to move its base of operations to Paraguay. Unknown to the guerrillas, Stroessner's secret police had planted several *pyragués* high among their ranks. Tightening surveillance at the principal border crossing points, Investigaciones geared up their informer networks to gather more precise intelligence and identify suspected OPM sympathizers.

Dr. Filártiga's notoriety as a former political prisoner and outspoken critic of the regime brought him under suspicion. Indeed, the circumstantial evidence stacked up against him was impressive. On top of speaking out for the peasant's rights, his Clinic of Hope freely provided medical care to the 40,000 peasants of the Ybycuí Valley. Then, too, he recently had made an international tour through California, Mexico City, and Buenos Aires, where his lectures and art had exposed the regime's corruption and human rights violations.

And finally, the Filártiga family's frequent trips to visit Nidia's mother in Posadas, Argentina—one of the places from which the OPM guerrillas were expected to cross into Paraguay—all combined to make Joel a prime suspect.

9

Police Inspector Américo Peña saw a golden opportunity to advance his career and at the same time vent his vengeance against the Filártigas.

By the end of March 1976, the political tension brewing in Paraguay was rapidly reaching a boiling point. On Friday, March 26, a worried Dr. Filártiga, Nidia, and Katia left the clinic in Ybycuí and rushed to Asunción. When they arrived in Sajonia, Joel called the family together in the master bedroom. He closed all the windows and curtains, locking in the summer's sultry heat.

"We must all be extra careful during these days," Joel told the children who were arrayed around their parents, sitting on the brown tile floor. "Things are very dangerous right now.

"This afternoon the army set up a roadblock in Paraguarí, where the dirt road from Ybycuí meets the main highway from Posadas," he went on. "Everyone was stopped. Every car, truck, bus, motorcycle, ox cart. Everyone. Nobody was passed through. They made us all get out while an officer verified our identification documents.

"One of the officers pronounced my name in a loud, deliberate voice. That struck me as odd. And you know there never used to be a control there. So I asked him what was going on. He said, 'It's because of the coup in Argentina, many guerrillas are escaping from there and coming back to Paraguay.'

"I said to him, 'I think you know me well. How long have I lived in this area? I am not a guerrilla. Why so much control? Why are you searching my car?'

"He looked down at our documents. And he said again, 'Doctor Joel Holden Filártiga.'"

"Of course, he knew who Papi was," Nidia said, wiping sweat from her forehead with a handkerchief. "But before he let us go, he wrote down our names and identification card numbers on a list.

"And just in the ten minutes we were there," she went on, "the soldiers took two young campesinos who were riding in a bus. I don't know why they were arrested or what happened to them afterward. But you can guess."

They all knew Dr. Filártiga's policy, "to give medical care to any person who asks for it, at any time, at any hour, at any distance." However, for the sake of their children's safety, neither Joel nor Nidia mentioned that at that moment two OPM members were convalescing at the clinic, one for the treatment of a gastric ulcer, the other for an acute case of hemorrhoids.

In the oppressive heat and humidity of the closed bedroom, Joel looked hard at his four children, one at a time, to make sure he held their full attention. "You have all known the waves of repression that come every three or four years. And you know they are the most difficult times.

"Those are the times when they have persecuted us the most—the times when they have ransacked the clinic, the times when they have arrested me, the times when they have tortured me. Those have been very hard times for the family. Yet, one way or the other, we have always survived.

"But this time," Joel warned, sweat now running down his face, "is going to be the worst of all."

10

Throughout their young lives, all the Filártiga children had helped people hunted by Stroessner's peasant beaters to receive refuge and medical care at the clinic. Hiding and helping people on the run was part of growing up a Filártiga. So, even though the OPM patients had not been mentioned, by this point in the family crisis meeting, both Joelito and Dolly realized that their father had had contact with the guerrillas. They exchanged knowing glances, a silent agreement that they must tell him everything.

Before either could speak, however, Joel went on. "The repression this time will be far, far worse—much worse than anything you have ever known. They are after the OPM. The last time there was a guerrilla movement was in the 1960s. I saw how they annihilated them. If in ten people one was suspected, they took everyone. That is how I was arrested and tortured. I remember—"

"Papi," Joelito broke in impulsively, "there's something going on with Peña I have to tell you. There are a lot of things, but the most—"

"That's right," Dolly interrupted, "You don't know how much Peña and Juana hate us. It began months ago when the Villalba kids used to tell them, 'Oh, Dr. Filártiga's family is so wonderful, why can't you be like them.' That's when they really started hating us and Peña ordered them to stay away.

"But that's impossible because Charo and Joelito and Analy go to school together every day. And, you know how the Villalba kids always come weekends to see you and Mamá, like everyone else. Anyway, they still come to the house all the time. Sometimes, they even sneak out at night and come over to listen to music and talk. They tell us everything."

Dolly stopped and looked at her brother. But Joelito, sitting on the floor anxiously biting his fingernails, let the chance to speak pass.

Dolly went on. "Like when Peña caught little Blanca—she's Juana's niece and lives with them. Well, he saw Blanca talking with this guy, he's kind of her boyfriend. Peña doesn't like him because he's just a helper at the Shell station, and he ordered Blanca not to see him anymore. Then he caught them together again. And do you know what Peña did? He cut off her hair, like a military cadet!

"And that's not all," Dolly said, turning to Nidia. "Mamá, you remember about a month ago when Charo came over with her baby? She told us about the fight she had with Peña, when he tried to tell everybody what to do—to impose his order in the house. Charo yelled at him that he didn't have the right to be the boss because he was taking her mother's money, more than he was giving."

"Yes, that is what Charo said," Nidia confirmed. "And she was crying, because there is something very wrong there. Not that Peña's always trying to make love to her. That is nothing new."

"She was crying," Dolly explained, "because her mother is not the same, because Juana just lays in bed all day. Charo told me her mother was depressed because they've spent all of her money."

"So that is why," Joel reflected, "Charo said Peña wants me to give him a $1,500 loan. They must think I brought back lots of dollars from the United States. They have squandered Juana's money and are probably in debt, too."

"Papi, I'm scared," Analy said, "Charo told us Peña is bragging that he's going to make everything all right. That he is going to catch a big fish and get a promotion and they'll be rich again.

"Papi." Analy's voice quivered. "Charo says that Peña is hunting you."

11

Joel got up from the bed and ambled to a chair next to the small mahogany table that held his pipe rack. With apparent indifference, he selected a favorite briar and painstakingly filled the bowl. Using the time to think, he took long, slow draws until the pipe was burning smoothly.

"I wish you would all stop worrying about Peña's ambitions," he announced in a reassuring tone that masked his true concern. "As long as we are all careful, he presents no danger to me."

Katia left her spot on the floor and took Joel's place next to Nidia on the bed. Holding her mother's hand, she asked the question that was first on all their minds.

"Papi, how come you are not afraid of Peña, like everyone else?"

"I will explain it, my little angel," Joel answered, forcing a smile for his youngest daughter.

"You have lived all your life here, and Paraguay seems like the most important place in the world. But in reality we are a poor, little country. The newspapers in the big, rich countries hardly ever write stories about us in Paraguay. And that is the way Stroessner wants it.

"Because when they do," he explained, "they almost always denounce the government's crimes. Like the way Stroessner gave protection to the heroin smuggler Joseph Ricord and his whole Latin Connection. Or how the Aché Indians are hunted for sport, like animals."

"But Papi," she persisted, "why aren't you scared of Peña?"

Filártiga, concentrating on Katia, missed the anxious looks flashing between Joelito and Dolly.

"My dear, if you would kindly permit me to finish," Joel replied indulgently. "Above all things, Stroessner wants to present a good face to the world. It is very important for him to hide the truth."

"How come?"

"Because bad publicity hurts the dictatorship in many different ways. For example, Stroessner gets lots of money from the rich countries. And a dirty face means that he would not get as much."

Joel derived so much satisfaction from teaching his children these political lessons, he momentarily forgot about the danger. But Dolly and Joelito worried that they must tell their father what was going on.

"Do you understand what I have explained so far?" Joel asked Katia.

"Yes, Papi," she said, "except why Peña doesn't scare you."

"Be patient," Joel replied and drew on his pipe. "I have friends in some of the rich countries. Sometimes I meet them here, and when they go back home they invite me to visit them. They arrange exhibitions of my art, and I talk about the clinic and tell everyone about Stroessner. This way, I make lots of other friends. They buy my art and give money and medicines and equipment for the clinic. They arrange for television and radio interviews. And they write articles in newspapers and magazines."

"Doesn't that make the president mad at you?" Katia wanted to know.

Joel laughed with delight at the perceptiveness of his youngest daughter. Nidia wrapped an arm around Katia and said, "Yes, he is very angry with Papi. But he must be careful. If they do something bad to Papi only because of what he says, Stroessner knows that there would be a worldwide scandal. Because Papi's friends would write lots and lots against Stroessner. And he is afraid of that."

"So," Katia beamed, "the president is scared of Papi?"

In the tension-filled atmosphere, Katia's naiveté hit everyone as hilarious. Joel was still laughing when Nidia answered. "No, my love, it is not that easy. What worries Stroessner are the big problems that a scandal would cause."

"Anyway," Joel assured Katia with more conviction than he felt, "that is why I am not afraid of Peña. You see, it does not matter how ambitious he is—or how much he hates me. Without proof of something subversive, Stroessner will not allow Peña to do anything."

Perhaps it was his father's apparent complacency, or maybe Joelito just could not hold it in any longer, but that is when he finally opened up.

"Papi, please! That's what I have to tell you," Joelito blurted. "Nery Villalba took *The Open Veins of Latin America*. And Charo says that Peña has it."

Ashen-faced, Nidia turned to Joel. He lowered his head and began massaging his temples.

12

Several months earlier, during their Christmas visit to Nidia's mother in Posadas, Filártiga had bought a copy of *The Open Veins of Latin America* and smuggled it back to Ybycuí. The book, written by the veteran journalist Eduardo Galeano, had become an instant classic. In his muckraking style, the Uruguayan newsman drew together the historical inequities and present-day injustices that bleed the life out of Latin America. In fact, *The Open Veins* offers such provocative insights that it was required reading at UCLA. Its scathing exposé of the Stroessner regime, however, placed it at the top of Paraguay's banned-books list.

Now, Filártiga's mind raced to reconstruct the events leading up to Joelito bringing the subversive book to Asunción. During his regular work visits to the clinic in January 1976, Joelito began reading *The Open Veins*. At the time Dr. Filártiga was preparing to leave Ybycuí for his big trip to the United States, Mexico, and Argentina. Joelito badgered him to let him take the book to Sajonia, to finish it during his father's absence. Filártiga finally acquiesced and gave his son the book, along with strict instructions to read it only in private and to always keep it well concealed.

In the hectic activity since Dr. Filártiga's return to Paraguay, the entire matter of *The Open Veins* had been swept from his mind.

13

Joelito sat statue-still, cross-legged on the floor, staring down at the large brown tiles. Dolly seemed about to say something, but Filártiga held up his hand to still her.

"Joelito, tell me, how could this happen?" he asked in weary resignation.

"Papi, I'm sorry," Joelito said shakily. "I'll never make a mistake like that again. I promise."

"That's not important right now," Filártiga said. "Tell me everything."

Joelito, rising to his feet, regained some composure. "After you left, I started reading *The Open Veins* again. It's not like any of the books we have at school. It tells the truth about how things really work. Papi, it's just like everything you're always saying.

"It explains how the elites in Latin American countries get rich by teaming up with the international corporations, and all the ways that their system steals our wealth. Now I really understand. I got super excited and wanted to tell some of my friends."

"Is that what you and your friends talked about?" Filártiga asked.

"Yes. But only the truth," Joelito moaned. "Like that animals are more valuable than people. If one of their horses falls sick, they send for a veterinarian. But, when a campesino worker gets sick, the landowners never get a doctor for them."

"Joelito," he asked gravely, "are you or any of your friends involved with Father Sanmartí?"

During the past months, the Jesuit Cristo Rey High School had come under suspicion as a center of OPM activities. The police, tipped off by their *pyragüés*, put a number of student activists and professor Miguel Sanmartí, along with several other Spanish-born priests, under surveillance. Even though Joelito attended the Comuneros High School, inevitably there existed an overlap in the rise of student political awareness throughout Asunción.

"Oh, no. I swear to God, Papi. We haven't had anything to do with Father Sanmartí or any of that," Joelito swore. "I didn't even show the book to anyone. All we ever did was talk. Well, sometimes we would end up in little arguments. Like when you and your friends talk about politics."

"Then how did Nery Villalba get hold of *The Open Veins*?"

14

Joelito sat down on the bed. Subconsciously mimicking his father, his head dropped into his hands and he massaged his temples.

"It was a couple of weeks ago," he said without looking up. "Nery and I were in my room talking about how the system needs repression to work—how people are sometimes killed just so that big, respectable companies like Coca-Cola can do business in Latin America. He never knew any of these things before. And he became really excited, too, and wanted to know more.

"I had *The Open Veins* under my pillow. And he just leaned back and found it. I grabbed it right away. He kept begging me to borrow it. So, I told him it wasn't mine. That it's your book and he'd have to ask your permission. I knew he'd never do that.

"Afterward I couldn't find it and figured he took it anyway. When I asked him, he said he had it and promised to return it the next day. But, the next day he said he had lent it to his brother Jorge. Every time I told him to give it back, he had another excuse and promised to return it the next day.

"I knew how mad you'd be," Joelito said, finally looking up. "I tried everything to get it back before you found out. Last week, I told Nery I was going to beat him up if he didn't bring it back right away. He said he'd go get it. But he didn't come back. And I can't find him anywhere. Then the day before yesterday, Charo said Nery doesn't have the book any more. Peña took it away from him.

"Papi, I know I failed you," Joelito cried. "Just tell me what to do. I'll do anything you say."

In the hellish heat of the closed room, Filártiga sat in deep concentration, sifting and sorting through the information. Apart from the buzzing mosquitoes, the only sound was the tapping of the pipe stem against his teeth. At last, he broke the spell.

"No, Joelito," Filártiga said, raising his eyes to the ceiling. "I'll not lie to you. There's nothing that you, or any of us, can do about it now. It was a stupid mistake to let Nery steal *The Open Veins* from you. I thought you were smarter than that.

"But I doubt that just because Peña has a book of mine it presents such a serious threat as you fear."

With everyone braced for an outburst of anger, relief surged through the stifling room.

"Papi, I don't understand," Joelito said, his voice a mix of apprehension and hope. "Peña swears he's going to get you."

"I do not know what he plans to do. But, I think he will need more than one of my books—even if it is *The Open Veins*."

"But how can you be sure?" Joelito pressed.

"I can't be sure!" Filártiga snapped in exasperation. "Nobody can be sure of anything anymore."

15

"Stroessner is ruthless," Filártiga explained, after getting a grip on his fear, "but he is also intelligent and shrewd. He understands that as far as the outside world is concerned, what I read is little different than what I say. It may cast suspicion, but it is insufficient to move against me.

"And there is something else," Joel mused. "You remember when I was in California and they found I have heart disease? The medical report is very explicit. If I suffer any kind of severe shock, it could cause a heart attack and kill me. Investigaciones know this. I have told everyone, and let people read the report. Sometimes I pretend to forget and leave copies behind.

"If I die in the hands of the police, there would be an international scandal like never before. And Stroessner knows how much that would cost him."

16

"It is true, we can't know what Peña might do," Joel told his family. "But what concerns me most is this fierce new repression." Turning to Dolly, Joelito, and Analy, he said, "You have grown up protecting people from the police and attending to their victims. You have seen tortured people with your own eyes. But none of you have suffered it on your own bodies. And you do not really believe anything will ever happen to you.

"But you could not be more wrong. And that's why I am scared half to death!"

Filártiga sprang to his feet, throwing his unlit pipe and handkerchief on the chair. His saturated clothes clung to his body, sweat rolled down his face, soaking his beard and splattering on the tile floor, marking his path.

"Between the three of you," he challenged, "is there one who can tell me what is the greatest danger we face?"

From their positions on the floor, Joelito, Dolly, and Analy stared mutely up at their father.

"All right then," Joel said, "first I will tell you what it is not. It's not letting Nery steal *The Open Veins*. It's not that Peña now has the book. It's not even how Peña may be able to use it against me—although all that is bad enough.

"It is Joelito's indiscretion of indiscriminately talking about such things. That in his enthusiasm, he tried to educate his friends, without even seeing the tremendous risks involved.

"And not just Joelito. Just because your classmates stupidly do the same thing is no excuse. You all know there are *pyragués* in your schools. Yet you still joined in these political discussions, as if nothing has changed. And you know better."

Again Filártiga paused, his breathing great heaves, as he took a long look at each of his children.

"So how did you make such a horrible mistake of judgment this time? Because this time, except for Bernardino, you are alone here during the week and think you're grown up. Because this time, your adolescent confidence concealed the jeopardy that you have placed yourselves in. That you placed our family in. That you placed your friends in.

"Joelito," Filártiga asked rhetorically, "do you think you have some special immunity because your name is Filártiga? Apart from Peña, can you tell me how much more attention you have attracted from the police?

"I don't say these things out of anger," Filártiga said, with the anger of parents throughout the world, filled with the primal fear for their children. "I say them because I'm terrified. And I don't know how to make you understand that the old rules don't count anymore."

17

Three days later, the snap of boots on Sajonia's cobblestone pavement echoed in the unnatural stillness of the night. Covering the short distance, they arrived at the stained oak door of the Filártiga house. A series of hard raps rattled the massive portal.

Dolly woke with a start. It was nearly 4 A.M., Tuesday, March 30. Since the family crisis conference, she had not slept well. Dolly wanted to believe it was one of her father's drunken friends making such a racket at this late hour. But opening the door, she came face-to-face with Major Inspector Domingo Galeano, the commander of the Sajonia police barracks.

"You are Señorita Dolly Filártiga?" he asked politely.

"Yes, Señor," she acknowledged nervously, noticing the uniformed officers flanking him. "Why are you here? Is there some trouble?"

"There is a small problem with your brother at Inspector Peña's house," he replied. "If you would please come with us, all will be explained."

Dolly protested that she first had to change out of her nightgown. Inspector Galeano assured her that was unnecessary. It would just take a moment. He beckoned her to follow him outside into the hot night.

The street was ghostly still. No flashing lights or squawking radio noises came from the two squad cars. Even the other policemen appeared subdued. Those who spoke did so in hushed tones.

At Peña's house, a column of police were stationed along the length of the driveway. The light from the street lamps glistened off their lacquered helmets and polished black boots; they stood grim-faced at parade rest, clutching their rifles. To reach the entrance of Peña's house, Dolly realized, she had to pass directly along the police phalanx.

"Señor," she asked Galeano, "where is my brother?"

"He is inside," the inspector assured her. "Come. I will take you to him."

The eerie atmosphere from the street permeated the house. Even though there were several more uniformed officers and a couple of official-looking men in suits, those who conversed did so in whispers. Oddly, none of the people who lived there were present. Inspector Galeano steered Dolly through the hallway to Charo and Duarte's bedroom. From the open doorway, Dolly saw Joelito.

Her brother lay face down on a mattress with his back to her, partially covered by a bloody sheet. Denying what her senses told her, she ran to his side.

"Joelito! Joelito, get up!" Dolly begged. She grabbed his shoulder and frantically shook him. "Joelito, wake up!" she implored. "Please, Joelito, please get up!"

Because of her years at the clinic, Dolly was no stranger to death. Yet, her mind refused to accept what Joelito's cold skin and the rigidity of his body told her. Irrationally, Dolly continued to shake him, pleading. "Joelito, please. Come on. Get up and let's go home."

At last her defense mechanisms crumbled and she had to accept the truth. She collapsed on top of Joelito, clutching his body with all her might, weeping uncontrollably.

Dolly ignored the voices ordering her to stand up. She just wanted to stay there, wailing over her brother's body. She felt her hands and arms being pried apart, and she was ripped away from Joelito. Half in panic, Dolly burst through the surrounding people, blindly bolting down the hallway.

Suddenly, a powerful pair of arms seized her around the waist. Her mind cleared enough to see Peña blocking her way. For some reason, the first thing Dolly noticed was Peña's lack of clothes. Instead of a uniform like the other police, he wore only boxer shorts.

"Señor Peña," Dolly yelled, "what have you done to my brother?"

"Stop screaming!" Peña hissed. "Your brother got what he's been looking for for some time now."

With the enormous strength born of desperation, Dolly shoved the burly cop aside and raced down the hallway and through the door. Just as she reached the driveway, though, Inspector Galeano stopped her.

"Señorita, where are you going?" he demanded. "You must take your brother's body out of here immediately."

"I'm going home," Dolly cried. "Let me think. I don't know what to do. I have to think."

"Don't worry about anything," the inspector assured her. "We have taken care of everything. This is the coroner, Doctor Molinas. He has prepared the death certificate. And Judge Martínez, over there, has already put his official stamp on it. So, you see, Señorita, all is in order for you to take your brother home."

"I don't care!" Dolly yelled. "Leave me alone. I have to think."

At that moment, Peña caught up with them.

"Shut up!" he snarled. "Stop shouting. You'll wake up the neighbors. Don't talk. Don't cry. Don't do anything. Nobody has to know."

"Don't worry about the neighbors," Dolly shouted, and in a frantic display of bravado she told Peña, "Tonight you have the power over me. But soon the whole world is going to know. You don't know who you've touched. I am a Filártiga!"

Breaking away from them, Dolly ran home and locked the door. While trying to control her sobbing, she managed to tell Analy that Joelito was dead. Desperately they hugged each other and cried, and cried, and cried.

Shortly, the banging at the door began again. They refused to answer. The sisters embraced each other all the harder. The insistent blows grew sharper, as if delivered by a rifle butt.

Bernardino Ortiz, the caretaker who lived there and looked after the house during the week, offered to speak with the police. But Dolly approached the door and yelled, "We're not coming out until Papi gets here."

"Yes, you are," Inspector Galeano shot back. "If you don't come right now and take your brother's body away, we're going to throw it out in the street."

It was too horrible to contemplate. Dolly imagined Joelito laying in the gutter, buzzing insects swarming on his bloody body.

Dolly and Bernardino returned to Peña's house. They tried to carry Joelito home on the mattress. But he was too heavy. And the rigor mortis tended to make his body slip to the sides of the flimsy, single mattress. Finally, a neighbor came out to lend a hand. When at last they reached the Filártiga house, he asked where they should put the body.

Dolly looked around. Impulsively, she swept everything off the dining room table. On its polished surface, they placed Joelito's whipped, slashed, and electrically burned corpse.

**No Paraguayan newspaper dared publish this drawing of
General Stroessner's hand in the *Caso Filártiga.***

THREE

I T BEGAN AS A DAY like any other at the clinic. I awoke at five o'clock and drank some *yerba mate* tea. We made a list of the patients waiting outside. There were twenty-one. We gave them their numbers and started to work.

"But at 10:05 in the morning, a messenger from the Antelco telephone kiosk in town arrived to tell me that my son Joelito had suffered a tragedy. He gave no further information."

None other was necessary.

Throughout the world, the word "tragedy" carries an ominous connotation—a fatal auto crash, a fire that destroys one's home, cutting life short. In Stroessner's Paraguay, however, all too often it conveyed a far more sinister meaning.

"When I heard that Joelito had suffered a tragedy, I knew," Joel told me. "Not the details. So I held on to some hope. I prayed it was not true. But in my heart I knew. I felt like a robot."

Filártiga sent a nurse to fetch Katia from school and told the remaining patients why he could not attend to them. The family was leaving immediately for the capital. The news gripped the people of Ybycuí, who had known and loved Joelito all his life. They needed no further explanation either.

When eleven-year-old Katia arrived home, she found her mother in a state of near hysteria. "Mamá," she asked, "what happened? Carmen said Joelito had an accident."

"Yes," Nidia said, embracing her daughter, "there has been an accident."

Within minutes they were on the road, speeding to Asunción. As they passed Paraguarí, Joel noticed that the military checkpoint had been dismantled. He mentioned it to Nidia, but she was past the point of caring.

The rest of the trip is burned into Katia's memory. "With no warning, Mamá suddenly threw open the door of the pickup and tried to throw herself out. But Papi grabbed her. And we stopped for a little while.

"I kept asking what happened to Joelito, but they'd only say there was an accident. All the way they didn't speak to each other. Mamá just kept crying."

Screeching around the corner from Avenida Carlos Antonio López onto the small side street in Sajonia where they lived, Filártiga hit the brakes just in time to avoid smashing into the crowd.

From sidewalk to sidewalk, police, soldiers, journalists, neighbors, and many other people filled the block. Still before noon, fewer than eight hours since Dolly had called

Grandma Lidia and her uncle Neneco, the news of Joelito's death already had sped through Asunción's word-of-mouth grapevine.

Recognizing Dr. Filártiga, the police cleared a path to his house. They even opened the garage doors so that he could drive straight in, avoiding the milling mass of people.

Inside was nearly as crowded as the street. After greeting his mother, Joel turned to his brother. Neneco lowered his eyes and murmured, "They killed your son."

These four simple words vanquished any slim hope that Joel and Nidia had prayed for. An icy clarity overtook Dr. Filártiga as the reality of Joelito's death settled into his being. Katia sought comfort in her grandmother's bosom. A piercing scream burst from Nidia's throat as she crumpled to the floor. Wailing hysterically, she tore at her clothes.

Dr. Filártiga picked up his wife and carried her to their bedroom. After administering a sedative, he left her with friends and made his way to the dining room, where Joelito lay on the table.

With clinical detachment, he spent the next hours conducting a thorough examination of his son's body. There could be no mistake. Joelito had been professionally tortured.

"I know what happened," Joel agonized. "But how can I make the world know what happened?"

1

During all that day and night and the next day, relatives, friends, acquaintances, patients, colleagues, and students converged on the Filártigas' house. There were hundreds of people, perhaps even a thousand or more.

Childhood friends and relatives who for years had avoided being seen publicly with the Filártigas, in spite of the affection they shared, cast aside the risks to themselves. Even cousin César Filártiga, the secretary of Stroessner's prestigious Advisory Council, and his sons came. And while all knew that Joelito had "suffered a tragedy," few were prepared for what awaited them.

A defense mechanism exists in Latin American dictatorships when it comes to the grieving for human rights victims. The author Gabriel García Márquez captured this denial of a terrorized people in his novel *One Hundred Years of Solitude*. As the soldiers are loading the bodies of the striking workers they had massacred onto railroad cars to be taken away, García Márquez portrays the townsfolk going about their daily routines, as if nothing out of the ordinary had occurred.

It is within this context that Peña and his accomplices anticipated how the Filártigas would react; to pretend to accept the fiction that Charo's husband, Hugo Duarte, had killed Joelito, conceal the truth, and discreetly bury him for fear of reprisals against other members of the family. Indeed, the hastily contrived scheme to pass off the torture-murder as a crime of passion rested upon the perfectly sensible assumption that the Filártigas would go along with the official cover-up. That is why, when Peña ordered Dolly to shut up and quietly take away Joelito's body, he insisted that, "Nobody has to know."

But Dr. Filártiga did not buckle under to the fear and self-directed shame—not unlike that of child sexual abuse or domestic violence victims—as the conspirators expected. Instead, breaking the silence of human rights victims, he did everything in his power to reveal the truth.

As the waves of mourners passed through his home, Filártiga told everyone that the crime-of-passion story was a lie. To spare Nidia further trauma, when she made an appearance at the wake, he made sure that Joelito was covered. Otherwise, Filártiga would rip away the sheet from his son's brutalized body, forcing all to see the gruesome torture wounds that took the boy's life.

At the first sight of Joelito's mutilated corpse, people were shocked by the obscenity before their eyes. Their second reactions ranged from indignation to rage, from stupefaction to terror. More than one group of students, filled with the fury of youthful righteousness, vowed, "Don't worry, Dr. Filártiga, we the young people will punish those responsible for doing this to Joelito."

Drama and irony marked the arrival of Augustina Miranda, the personal secretary of Stroessner and a close friend of Lidia, Filártiga's mother. Augustina took one look at the savaged body of the boy she had known, her hands shot up to cover her eyes, and she cried, "Oh my God, this can't be. It just can't be. Doctor, please don't show me this thing." Fleeing to her car, Augustina ordered her chauffeur, "Get me away from here at once."

2

That afternoon, Filártiga sent for Horacio Galeano Perrone, one of Paraguay's most prominent criminal lawyers, with a reputation for taking on controversial cases. Horacio's conservative suits, meticulously trimmed dark hair, and air of casual confidence gave him a central-casting image of the well-connected politico of Stroessner's ruling Colorado Party that he was.

Horacio described to me what happened when he arrived at the Filártigas' house. "After we were introduced, Dr. Filártiga immediately took me to his son's body. It was laying on the table, on a bloodstained mattress, covered with a sheet. He took it off and showed me the wounds, the burns, the whip marks, and the stabs.

"At the time, I'd been a lawyer for eight years but I'd never seen anything like this. Dr. Filártiga explained in detail the torture methods that caused each of the injuries. It was horrifying.

"He was a very calm man. The mother, yes, she was crying in the next room— crying uncontrollably. But he kept his serenity very well.

"We lawyers must maintain a certain professional detachment. If we become nervous and say, 'My God, what a disaster'—well, you see.

"To serve our clients, we must retain our composure in these things. And I believe I did.

"But, inside," Horacio said, "I felt a great indignation, right? Because I'd never seen a tortured man. Really, I'd never seen one before. Then it came to mind what comes to everyone's mind. How this young man must have suffered. He had been a good-looking boy.

"Yes, inside one feels indignation and fear," the thirty-year-old father of three ended, "because you know that men who act that way, to do what they did, are dangerous. If they're capable of this, they're capable of other things."

3

To refute the official coroner's statement, Galeano Perrone and Filártiga decided upon an independent medical report. After calling around, Dr. Filártiga finally found three colleagues who agreed to come right over.

When they had finished their work, Joel asked for help with one last task. Disappearing into the bedroom, he returned in a few minutes with a thirty-five-millimeter camera and three rolls of film.

Maintaining his mask, he directed them how to position, and reposition, Joelito's corpse. For the next half hour, Dr. Filártiga systematically photographed every mark defiling his son's remains.

4

The following day, Wednesday, March 31, the funeral procession slowly wound its way through the streets of Asunción to the family crypt at the Cementerio del Sur. The morning newspapers all carried front-page articles, though timidly limiting their coverage to the official crime-of-passion story. But the grapevine had already spread the truth throughout the capital.

People responded with a spontaneous show of sympathy. While mild by world standards of dissent, in Paraguay's police state, their public demonstration of support for the Filártigas was a courageous act of solidarity. A member of the funeral party described it to me.

"Here in Paraguay," he explained, "it is common to go out and watch when a funeral passes by. But this was something special. It was an impressive caravan. A great number of cars, over 100 cars. Everyone knew it was *that case*. In big white surgical tape, they put the name FILARTIGA on the hearse.

"When they saw the caravan coming, thousands and thousands of people came out of their homes and shops, and lined up along the sidewalks. They were very quiet. Almost no one spoke. They just stood there in silence in the hot sun. Many of the men took their hats off.

"It made the police very nervous. Nothing like that had ever happened."

When they got back to Sajonia, the Filártigas found dozens of police stationed along their street. A good-sized cluster was posted by Peña's house, apparently to ensure the inspector's privacy. Another, smaller knot loitered in front of the Filártiga house, to discourage visitors and intimidate the family.

Once inside, the sharp, metallic snap of the police racking their rifle bolts reverberated through the house, rankling everyone's already frayed nerves.

Yet, Filártiga found it more irritating than frightening. The noise made it difficult to concentrate on what he had to do next. At last, his stressed-out mind focused. He had spent the night trying to get the news of Joelito's murder to his friends in California. We could put international pressure on Stroessner. For the family to have at least a measure of protection, he knew, the police had to be restrained.

In his addled condition, it took a half hour of frustrated searching to find his address book. At last he was ready to call. The phone was dead.

"Dolly!" Joel bellowed, "the phone is cut off. They're isolating us, so I can't tell the world what has happened. I'm going to the Peruvian Embassy to see Juan Andrés Cardozo. I have to send a letter to Richard."

As he hurried out, Filártiga shouted over his shoulder, "Where are Katia and Analy?"

"Katia's with grand Mamá," Dolly snapped back. "And Analy went straight to her room as soon as we got home. She locked the door and won't come out."

For four days Analy stayed in her room. Other than to accept an occasional plate of food, which she hardly touched, she refused to see or speak to anyone. Analy was under assault by the terrifying images of the wrenching, incomprehensible death of her brother.

Like Joelito, Analy had inherited their father's artistic talent. She would spend hours working on a drawing, capturing her demons in powerful pen-and-ink expressions of her anguish. After finishing a piece, in a violent catharsis Analy would tear it up, but Nidia managed to salvage a few. Perhaps the most captivating, later dubbed "the Devil Drawing" by the press, became a highlight in the newspaper campaign waged by the Filártigas.

5

Across the dining room table the day after Joelito's funeral, Dr. Filártiga stared at the young reporter from the tabloid *Aquí*.

Stroessner's regime viewed *Aquí* as an unwitting ally. Even though it boasted an enormous circulation, it was allowed far greater freedom than the establishment press. The scandal sheet's weekly ration of sensationalist stories provided an entertaining distraction for the masses. Its staple blood-and-guts photo essays, often hinting at government involvement, graphically reinforced Paraguay's culture of terror.

From the dictatorship's point of view, *Aquí* was a useful tool. Its shoddy apolitical reputation precluded any possibility of influencing international opinion. Even within Paraguay, no one Stroessner deemed to be "significant"—professionals, intellectuals, diplomats, church officials, or the political opposition—took it seriously.

Filártiga knew all this. He also was aware of the enormous influence that William Randolph Hearst's progeny exercised upon the common people. And he did not consider them insignificant.

Joel understood that public opinion was among their very few weapons to get the truth out. With Stroessner's repressive apparatus already stretched by its hunt for the OPM insurgents, raiding peasant cooperatives in the countryside and keeping a lid on the student unrest in the cities, the last thing the general wanted was to further rile up the people. Which, of course, was precisely what Filártiga set out to do.

Even so, on that Thursday afternoon of Holy Week, Joel was not prepared for the news brought by the young *Aquí* journalist.

Aquí came out on Fridays. And the next day was Good Friday, the day of Christ's crucifixion.

In Latin America, the world's largest bastion of Roman Catholicism, Holy Week marks the end of the forty self-sacrificing days of Lent. Far more important than the popular Christmas holidays, for the church, Semana Santa is the most revered time of the year. Special celebrations observe the sanctity of each day, culminating on Easter Sunday, the commemoration of Christ's resurrection.

In expressions of devotion, many priests lead pilgrimages of the faithful to local shrines. Also, during Holy Week, in the desperate hope of relieving their plight, it is customary among the impoverished, diseased, and undereducated masses to make special acts of supplication to a favored saint. Officially the church frowns upon such unorthodox practices. Even so, wisely it turns a blind eye to these widespread acts of popular religiosity.

"Dr. Filártiga," said the eager *Aquí* reporter, sitting across the table where Joelito's body had lain, "maybe you don't know everything that's going on, but lots of people already believe that your son is a saint—common people, like your patients and the people you're known to stick up for.

"On the way here, I stopped at the cemetery. And do you know what I found? I saw thirty or forty people praying to Joelito in front of his pantheon. And there are candles, countless votive candles, burning everywhere, by the door, on the windowsills, even on the ground."

"Yes, someone said something about this after the memorial Mass this morning," Joel wearily replied. His grief and the pressures of the past sixty sleepless hours had pushed him beyond exhaustion. "But nobody mentioned anything about Joelito being a saint."

"Well, I don't exactly mean a saint," the journalist equivocated. "More like a *beato*. You know, a blessed soul, a holy soul who sits close to God and has His ear and can put in a good word so that people's prayers are answered.

"Already there's talk about the poor widow who was being thrown out of her little house because she couldn't pay the rent. But after she petitioned Joelito for help, on her way home she found a fat wallet on the sidewalk, with thousands of *guaraníes*. And her problems were solved."

"How in God's name did all this start?" Filártiga wondered aloud.

"Well, you know how superstitious people can be," the reporter replied. "The way they see it, both Jesus and Joelito were innocent victims, killed by a tyrant during Semana Santa, even though they hadn't committed any crime. And they weren't just killed. Both were first tortured and then stabbed before their bodies were returned to their families. Because of Joelito's suffering, just like Jesus, people believe he's a martyr, too. They figure that he must be given a special place in heaven, next to God, because he died just like His own Son."

The fantastic tale astonished Joel. Slowly he slipped back into the chair and stared at a point somewhere beyond the dining room wall without seeing it. Or, perhaps, he was the only one who did see it.

Although never encouraged by the church, during the coming years the legend of Beato Joelito flourished. Miracles attributed to him drew such multitudes to the cemetery, it became next to impossible for relatives to peacefully visit the Filártiga pantheon. Owners of other burial vaults complained. Caretakers demanded extra pay to clean up the daily mess left behind by the crowds.

Abruptly, Filártiga sprang straight up in the chair. With a glare that pinioned the unsuspecting reporter to his seat, he growled, "So this is what *Aquí* wants! Advertise my son as a *beato* to sell your newspaper! Commercialize Beato Joelito to make money!"

"No, no!" the startled journalist protested. "We can't even mention that. We can get away with a lot, but there are limits. If we promoted Joelito as a *beato* murdered by the police, they would shut down the paper. To say nothing of what Investigaciones would do to us personally."

"What you do plan to do?" Filártiga demanded, regaining a modicum of control, if not civility.

"Look. You've seen the cowardly articles the newspapers put out yesterday and today," the young man scoffed. "You know how they are. And you can only expect more of the same from them. Everybody knows the police killed your son, but they'll never risk their necks and publish the truth."

"And *Aquí* will tell the whole truth?"

"Please, doctor. You know that's not possible," he conceded, "but we will tell more of the truth than any other paper in Paraguay."

"Perhaps you can do even better than you think," Filártiga said.

"What do you mean?"

"I mean what you cannot *tell*, you can *show*. Let people *see* the truth."

"I'm not sure that I understand you," the reporter said, unable to hide his anticipation.

From his briefcase, Joel pulled two photographs of Joelito's tortured body and slid them across the polished table.

6

I spent the morning of May 14, the day after moving in with the Filártigas, at that same dining room table, reviewing my notes and working through boxes of newspaper clippings and other documents. The family had left early to attend the daily memorial Masses that were held for Joelito.

Instead of the slow healing process of adjusting to Joelito's death and getting on with their lives, the Filártigas committed their all to exposing the truth. Nothing else mattered. Nothing. Since his son's murder, Dr. Filártiga had not even returned to his Clinic of Hope in Ybycuí.

With the exception of Joel's clinical description of how Joelito had been tortured, the family's attempts to explain what happened ended up like stream-of-consciousness ramblings. Beaten down to intellectual disorientation and emotional volatility, at several points the Filártigas hardly knew I was there. Furiously scribbling notes, my attempts to slow down their gushing paroxysms amounted to a perfect exercise in futility.

That first day, Joel, Nidia, and Dolly had unloaded with a cacophony of incomplete, irrelevant, and contradictory details, indiscriminately mixed with rumors, speculations, and a few solid facts. Inevitably, certainly understandably, our discussion was far less an explanation for me than a catharsis for them.

For them, their trusted friend had finally had arrived. For them, unrealistically exaggerating my ability to help, I was a well-known North American historian with United States Embassy connections come to join their struggle for justice. For them, I represented hope.

So it was that next morning I came across the April 2, Good Friday, edition of *Aquí*. Its banner headline screamed, "Sorrowful Passionate Drama: The Crime of Sajonia." A blown-up photo of Joelito's body filled the rest of the front page.

Scanning the piece, I came across another picture of Joelito, along with the scanty information released by the police supporting their crime-of-passion whitewash. With disgust, I recalled Dr. Filártiga telling me how he had given the photographs to the *Aquí* reporter, and his promise that they would get out more of the truth than any other paper in Paraguay.

I was about to toss the tabloid aside, when the boldface subtitles of two inside articles caught my attention:

Horrible Cruelty

The killing of Filártiga was carried out with refined cruelty, according to information obtained from the victim's family. The motive has already been established: the relationship he was carrying on with the wife of the murderer, as was proven last Monday night. . . .

Filártiga perished after horrible suffering and torture, caused by the criminal actions of a demented person. It appears that he was first beaten, which made it possible to then tie his feet and hands together (as is seen in one of the photographs) and later tortured: his body is covered with innumerable burn marks—similar to those made by a cigarette—and extremely painful slashes.

Finally, Filártiga was stabbed up to five times. . . .

How could *Aquí* get away saying Joelito had been tortured, even with all their equivocations? What followed was even more baffling.

A Question

The victim's family asks, without having received any answers, how is it possible that one man, physically smaller than Filártiga and alone in a small room, could inflict such savagery. This is the basis for thinking that the killer did not act alone, although it is only conjecture. What is certain is that before dying Filártiga suffered horrifying agony, after which he was treacherously stabbed.

The police authorities—as is explained in another paragraph of this article—are maintaining a hermetic silence concerning the investigative procedure, since it seems that they have not yet completed all aspects of the investigation, and the case could lead to the incrimination of more than one person. . . .

In striking contrast, the establishment newspaper articles were gleaned exclusively from the phony police report. All avoided the awkward questions raised by the facts of Joelito's murder. And since none had bothered to interview the Filártigas, there were no statements from the family.

7

The *Caso Filártiga* presented a conundrum for the establishment press. It was just the kind of spectacular story that journalists drool over: A tantalizing tangle of sex and murder in the upper class. The cuckold husband arrested and charged. The victim, the son of the country's internationally renowned philanthropist-physician-artist. And the public clamoring for every juicy detail.

In Stroessner's Paraguay, there was no need for official censorship—self-censorship did the job. Of course, everyone knew the police had a hand in killing Joelito. If it was a government-sponsored operation, the press could not touch it. Yet, if it was the work of an independent police squad, then the story just might be fair game. Still, with the official cover-up tale and the confusion surrounding the "Crime of Passion in Sajonia," the press kept their heads down.

Even *Aquí* took painstaking measures to cover itself. Avoiding editorial comment, it based its coverage of the *Caso Filártiga* exclusively on verifiable sources: quotes and attributions from the Filártiga family, authentic photos of Joelito, citations from official documents.

Even so, going through the back copies, I found that *Aquí* grew bolder in presenting the Filártigas' accusations, and pointing out the inconsistencies in the crime-of-passion farce.

For example, *Aquí*'s April 9 cover story could almost have been prepared by a Madison Avenue public relations firm hired by the Filártigas. In its six-page feature, the caption accompanying one of the gruesome shots of Joelito's body read, " 'Those who killed my son are nothing less then beasts,' said Dr. Filártiga, the father of the victim. The statement is not exaggerated, if one looks at this photograph taken the morning he first saw the dead seventeen-year-old youth. There are more signs of torture than fatal wounds."

But the article's pièce de résistance was the grisly two-page centerfold of Joelito's corpse. After making a point of the terrible pain inflicted by the lashes and burns, the caption concluded, "The relatives of the victim are convinced that the young man was killed in another place and later his body was brought to Américo Peña's house."

8

The *Caso Filártiga* was not the only hot story during this time of fast-breaking news. Five days after Joelito's murder, Saturday, April 3, the police captured an OPM leader attempting to enter Paraguay from the Argentine border town of Posadas. According to the official report, he "quickly confessed"—the code phrase that everyone knew meant police torture. In this case, the word passed along the grapevine held that the forces of law and order had been greatly assisted in obtaining the quick confession by their tested technique of ramming a crowbar into the victim's anus.

Before dawn the following day, Easter Sunday, Investigaciones' rapid-strike brigade had surrounded two houses in Asunción. As reported by the domesticated media, the OPM extremists answered police pleas to peacefully surrender with intense gunfire, forcing the authorities to respond in kind.

In all of the shoot-outs between the police and the OPM, not one of Stroessner's men was killed, and only two were wounded. In contrast, dozens of the poorly armed OPM rebels lost their lives. Those unlucky enough to be taken alive all quickly confessed before dying in police custody.

Indeed, the press could not have been more helpful to the dictatorship's campaign. They published full-page pictorial features of the ten most "dangerous extremists," designed to be torn out and carried around for handy reference. With Paraguay's per capita income of less than $500 a year, the wanted poster's $5,000 reward provided a powerful incentive for informers.

One of the first targets was the prestigious Cristo Rey Catholic High School in Asunción. Among the Jesuit teachers the police arrested was Father Miguel Sanmartí, whom they charged with being the "intellectual author" of the OPM movement.

Ironically, the successful raid by Stroessner's forces presented the dictator with a dilemma. The Paraguayan Constitution guarantees the archbishop of Asunción a place on Stroessner's Advisory Council. Over the years, the country's highest-ranking Catholic prelates had willingly accepted the perks of this institutional collaboration. However, upon assuming office in 1971 as archbishop, Ismael Rolón surprised the nation. In a public act of protest, he declared that as long as the regime continued to violate his flock's basic human rights, the church's seat on the council would remain vacant. In the five years since, with Stroessner's peasant beaters stepping up their persecution of the Christian Peasant Leagues and other self-help programs, church–state relations had plummeted to historic lows.

Whatever else could be said of Stroessner, even his enemies acknowledged the general's political acumen. He knew that "quick confessions" from the Jesuit priests, or for that matter any brutality inflicted upon the clerics, would make them martyrs in the eyes of the nation's overwhelmingly Catholic population.

The last thing Stroessner wanted was to get the people so riled up that their outrage would override his cultivated culture of fear. Yet simply releasing the troublesome priests would be seen as giving in to the church, a sign of weakness undermining his authority.

Investigaciones found the solution. None of the Jesuits were Paraguayan citizens. They all had been born abroad, most in Spain. So, in an expedient move, the government simply deported them. Their secular Paraguayan staff, however, did not fare as well.

9

If the regime regarded the church as an obstacle around which to tread softly, the Filártigas found it not only a source of spiritual comfort but also one of the few available avenues to pursue their struggle for justice.

In the Catholic tradition, memorial Masses are celebrated to pray for the souls of the deceased. To let people know the time and place of the ceremony, their loved ones place paid announcements in the newspapers.

As I scanned the press clippings, I saw that at least one memorial service each day was held for Joelito at churches spread out through the different barrios of Asunción. Also, services were held in many of the rural towns where Dr. Filártiga attended to the poor, especially in Ybycuí. The nuns from the convent there, who regularly sent people to the clinic for free treatment, organized many memorial Masses for Joelito. In the capital, the Filártiga family arranged for most of the services. Surprisingly, though, others took it upon themselves to sponsor other Masses—from relatives to Joelito's friends, from informal groups of artists to the professional association of physicians.

In Stroessner's Paraguay, these seemingly innocuous religious acts amounted to demonstrations of solidarity with the Filártigas. Even in the midst of the massive repression, and knowing full well that Investigaciones sent plainclothes police to the Masses, day after day people packed the churches. Often, after filling all the seats and standing room inside, the overflow gathered at the doorways and open windows.

After the formal service, many people lingered to talk with the family. Mostly these were ordinary folks who admired the Filártigas for standing up to the police. Nidia, Dolly, and Joel seized the opportunity to turn these occasions into public forums.

The Filártigas passionately told their story and answered questions. Accusing the police of murdering Joelito, they denounced the court's complicity in the cover-up. People were always impressed, even awed, by their fearless, straightforward talk. But it was the color photographs of Joelito's savaged corpse that had the greatest impact.

Filártiga had to make extra copies of the photos—especially the one that showed Joelito lying on his back, his youthful body obscenely defiled by torture. In the months and years ahead, while the *Caso Filártiga* slogged along its uphill battle, that photo became one of our most powerful weapons. It broke down people's psychological defenses, overcoming their apathy, fear, and cynicism.

"Most people react with outrage. Some cannot take it and turn away in anger," Joel told me. "At first, when we would talk to people after the Masses, we handed them out just so they could see. But then we found that none of the pictures were ever given back. Now dozens of color photos of Joelito's tortured body are all over the capital, all over Paraguay. I even sent some to friends in the United States and other countries.

"When I took them, it was only as proof that Joelito had been tortured by professionals. Until they were developed, I did not know that one of the rolls was color. And even then I did not imagine what it was. Only after seeing how it moved people's emotions did I realize it was a godsend."

10

Surprisingly, the corrupt Paraguayan courts provided another way for the Filártigas to pursue their fight. Just as they never missed a memorial Mass, they attended every legal proceeding dealing with Joelito's case, no matter how insignificant.

By the time the family came home on my second day with them, I had nearly finished working my way through the piles of documents. Only a hint of their mania cast its shadow over the papers strewn about the dining room.

It was almost as if my old friends had returned. Almost.

The toll wrought by their fear and fatigue was obvious. Nor could they disguise the pain and emptiness left by Joelito's loss. Even so, there was no mistaking the love and trust that formed the foundation of our friendship.

Anxious to get on with it, Joel waved a hand at the litter of papers and said, "So?"

"So?" I echoed in exasperation, casting my own hand over the clutter. "So, I've spent all day digging through this can of worms, and the only thing I'm sure of is that my back hurts more than my head aches. So, I'm astonished at what you've accomplished. Though I still can't say I really understand what's going on. So, I think we need to have a very *serious* talk. Not like yesterday."

"So," Filártiga mimicked, with another sweeping motion that managed to take in the heap of papers while at the same time dismissing my complaint, "where do we begin?"

Impressed by Joel's equanimity, I apologized for taking my irritation out on them. Nidia and Dolly assured me that they understood, they did the same thing all the time.

"The legal procedures have me the most confused," I said. "The press coverage is the least confounding part. And from what I picked up from you yesterday, I can see how at the Masses you're able to get out information to the people that even *Aquí* can't publish. I realize everything is intermingled, but let's start with the trial."

Over the years I had learned the basics of Paraguay's legal system. Even so, going through the court documents and newspaper accounts, the actions of the courts made no sense at all.

"It has been like a roller coaster," Joel acknowledged.

"The judges, especially at first, seemed to behave normally," I began. "That is, with the arrogance of Torquemada presiding at the Spanish Inquisition. They made no effort to conceal their collaboration with the police. But then, at other times it appears they back off—like the day before yesterday, when Judge Martínez ruled in your favor against Duarte's motion to dismiss.

"And what about the change in the attitude of your lawyers? At first they acted like frightened llamas, and now they've become panthers with one foot still in the jungle. Even insulting the court in their briefs, and Judge Martínez says nothing. What's going on?"

"The truth is, we do not really comprehend it all either," Joel admitted. "There is much about which we can only speculate."

"OK, let's fill in some of the blanks. I'll conduct a formal, tape recorded interview. We'll start at the beginning and work our way up to the present."

<h1 style="text-align:center">11</h1>

A couple of days after Joelito's death, the court accepted the police crime-of-passion report and charged Charo's husband, Hugo Duarte, with the murder. The first sign that the cover-up threatened to run off track came several days after that, when Nidia filed her lawsuit. To avoid accusations that Joel might use the trial for political purposes, he remained in the background, not joining the suit.

Under Napoleonic Law, the victim has the right to act as an adjunct to the state attorney prosecuting the case. The legal counsel of the victim, or in this case the victim's family, effectively becomes part of the prosecuting team.

On April 7, Nidia's lawyers, together with the state attorney prosecutor, filed an amplification petition. This petition requested that the court amplify the scope of the trial to include not only Duarte but also "the organizers, accomplices, and anyone else involved in covering up the murder."

"We were all so scared," Nidia recalled. "Our lawyers, Francisco Villate and José López Viera, warned us not to speak in the courtroom—because the police could arrest us right there. They explained how dangerous what we were doing was. We did not say any names in our amplification petition, but everybody knew an expanded investigation would lead straight to Peña and the police."

"Wait a minute," I said, "I thought your lawyer was Horacio Galeano Perrone, the man who was so upset when he saw Joelito at the wake."

"Well, yes, he is now. With the others. But at first Judge Martínez. . . . He is the same judge who they sent to Peña's house the night they killed Joelito. At first he only gave permission for Villate and López Viera to join the state attorney's prosecution team. Not until later did Martínez grant Galeano Perrone's request to become part, too."

"It is all part of the legal harassment against us," Dolly put in, "to protect the police and wear us down."

"Anyway," Nidia went on, "we filed the amplification motion to include the others because we wanted Charo to come and tell what really happened."

From my readings, I knew that Hugo Duarte's wife, Charo, had been detained as a material witness and ordered to give a deposition. Charo's firsthand account was critical to the official court case, and perhaps even more important in the court of public opinion.

I had also learned the Paraguayan Penal Code stipulates the following: "A husband, who in the act of unexpectedly surprising his woman in flagrante delicto of adultery, kills, injures or abuses her or her accomplice . . . is exempt from criminal responsibility." And what about a wife who catches her husband with his lover, I wondered?

Even though the courts never invoke this antiquated law anymore, Nidia's attorneys thought it was entirely possible, even probable, that Duarte intended to use it as his defense. Their reasoning rested on Duarte's otherwise inexplicable behavior in the trial.

Hugo Duarte, following the advice of his high-powered lawyer father, Pedro Duarte, refused to answer any questions about what happened that night. For that matter, he would not say anything at all, leaving the question of his guilt unchallenged. Ordinarily it would be an open-and-shut case.

But it would not be if Charo backed up the crime-of-passion police report. Then Judge Martínez could dismiss all charges on the grounds of justifiable homicide. And Duarte would walk.

If, however, Charo told the court what she honestly knew about what occurred the night of Joelito's murder, the police cover-up would be placed in peril—and so would she.

"On the day Charo was to testify," Dolly picked up the story, "we waited in the courtroom, crammed in with all the reporters, lawyers, police, and spectators. We could hear people whispering about how the police must have threatened Charo during the nine days they'd had her in jail.

"We remained silent, like the lawyers told us. But because Charo hated Peña and always confided in us, and especially because of her friendship with Joelito, we held out hope that she would tell the truth.

"At last, they brought her in." Dolly concluded, "Everybody stopped talking. Charo kept her head down. The guards took her to a chair next to her lawyer, Rafael Dujak, who is a partner in the law firm of Hugo Duarte's father. Everybody waited to see what she would do."

But, evidently, Charo had given in to neither the threats of the police nor the demands of her conscience.

Breaking with court procedure, before requiring her to give her deposition, the judge allowed her lawyer to introduce a motion. Decrying that his client had been illegally deprived of her liberty, he pleaded that Charo's deposition be postponed, and asked for her immediate release. In that way, he reasoned, she later could testify without the pressure of being a prisoner. It was such an obvious gambit that gasps filled the courtroom.

Judge Martínez did not question the dubious logic of the plea. Neither did he opt for the simple solution to depose Charo, sitting there in court, after which she would be free to leave. Rather, taking the matter under consideration, he remanded her back to the women's Buen Pastor prison.

Forty-eight hours later, after scheduling her deposition ten days hence, Martínez ordered Charo's release. And then, when she failed to show up on April 19, he simply rescheduled her deposition for two weeks later.

Again Charo missed her deposition hearing. Her mother, Juana Villalba, sent the court a note saying that she had disappeared. The very next day, May 4, Judge Martínez sprang into action and issued an arrest warrant for Charo.

12

Many other petitions and counterpetitions filled the courts during the initial phases of the trial. Two days after Charo's release, on April 12, Duarte's defense team filed a creative appeal to have the case dismissed.

"What's this Special Appeal?" I asked, shaking my head. "From what I can make out, it's almost like Duarte's lawyers have started another trial against Nidia."

"The court's actions are not determined by the rule of law," Joel sighed. "It is politics that count. It is complicated."

"That much is apparent," I said. "But until I understand what has gone on, I can't understand what is happening now."

Filártiga lit his pipe and reviewed Duarte's Special Appeal. "They claim we cannot expand the case to include anyone else, that our amplification petition is invalid."

"How so?"

"I can only tell you what Horacio Galeano Perrone told us," Joel replied. "The argument of their Special Appeal is that according to the police report Joelito and Duarte got in a fight and inflicted injuries upon each other. In such cases of mutual combat, the law requires that both people be arrested. And neither party has the right to make accusations against the other. In the legal proceeding, only the court can file charges.

"So, since Nidia represents Joelito," Filártiga said wearily, "their Special Appeal contends that the law prohibits her from bringing charges against Duarte—or even amplify the original charges to include anyone else."

"Unbelievable!" I exclaimed.

"That's what Horacio said," Dolly broke in. "He saw its stupidity right away. It's just another way to protect the police."

The blatant unfairness of the Special Appeal ploy fueled the people's support for the Filártigas. And it squeezed the weak-willed Judge Martínez into a bind—in fact, in a double bind.

To grant the Special Appeal could very well backfire. Certainly it would throw up a legal shield for the police, which surely would further inflame public opinion. And that, coming at the height of the tremendous repression sweeping the nation, Stroessner wanted to avoid.

To deny the Special Appeal, however, raised other dangers: Peña and his accomplices could turn on Judge Martínez—and his family.

The judge found himself treading through a minefield, the risk of a fatal misstep too great. Opting for the time-honored bureaucratic solution, Martínez stalled, and he took the Special Appeal under consideration, where it was still awaiting his ruling.

13

Meanwhile, the homicide trial was moving right along. The next day, April 13, the court granted the Filártigas' request for a third examination of Joelito's body. That afternoon Judge Martínez, Dr. Filártiga, Nidia, and Dolly met at the cemetery with Paraguay's top forensic pathologist.

In comparison with the other two medical reports, Dr. Hernán Godoy's findings were the most honest. Yet, while he did record the full extent of Joelito's injuries, even he equivocated. As Godoy later confided to Filártiga, he could not truthfully identify the three electric shock torture burn wounds, listing them instead simply as "burns."

A week later, on April 20, Dolly and Peña gave their depositions. Dolly recounted the horrors of that night, which had already appeared in *Aquí*, but now were prominently picked up in the establishment press. Peña stuck to his bare-bones story: Awakened by the sounds of a fight, he rushed to the bedroom, only to find Joelito's lifeless body and, like any solid citizen, he called the police.

At the same moment that Peña was recounting his fable in Judge Martínez' Sixth Criminal Court, down the hall in the First Criminal Court, the police launched their attack against Nidia and Dolly.

14

Accused of bursting into Peña's house and attacking Jorge Villalba, the two women were charged with "forcibly entering a domicile and assault." On the spot, the judge issued an arrest warrant for the culprits.

Clearly, it was another machination to derail Nidia's amplification motion. Paraguayan law prohibits a defendant in a criminal suit from being a plaintiff in any other criminal case. Even so, it is hard to conceive of a more witless move.

In the excitement and confusion of our marathon session the previous day, several times the Filártigas had tried to explain the bizarre story of Nidia and Dolly's arrest. And I still did not have it straight. After a light dinner on the patio, we returned to the dining room and went over it again.

"Well," Nidia began, "someone who works at the courthouse learned about the arrest warrant. She knew we were being falsely accused and warned us. At first I was very indignant—the idea of being arrested in our own house like criminals!

"And then, the more we thought about it, the more frightened we became. Once the police took us away in the car, it would be the same as being kidnapped. They could do anything they wanted. What guarantee did we have that we would ever get to the courthouse? They could just disappear us. Who knows?"

"Those were the worst days of terror," Dolly said. "A while after Joelito's funeral, the telephone started working again. All night long it would ring. We had to answer, because it might be a medical emergency for Papi. That's when the death threats started."

"Tell me about the death threats," I prompted. "What did they say?"

"Things like, 'Do you want another dead child? Ha, ha, ha.' Or 'Doctor, you are wrinkled. We are going to iron you out.' You know, things like that."

"And sometimes they didn't say anything," Nidia said, "but you could hear them breathing. Or they'd play music into the phone—classical music. It was a kind of a constant torture every day.

"Anyway," she went on, "because of the danger of being taken away by the police, we decided to run away so they couldn't get us. Lots of people offered to hide us. We stayed in hiding with friends for about a week. Until after Papi took out a big *solicitada* in the newspaper denouncing the charges against us, to guarantee our safety."

It took a moment to locate the *ABC Color* clipping in the stack I had assembled dealing with Nidia's and Dolly's arrest. After reviewing the facts of Joelito's murder and the farce of the trial, Filártiga's lengthy public announcement detailed this new persecution, decrying that "Because of this absurdly false accusation, the judge has ordered the imprisonment of my wife and daughter. Now, three weeks since the crime, this new travesty is added."

15

Joel's *solicitada* not only assured Nidia's and Dolly's safety; it was also a public relations coup. In Latin America, the reverence for motherhood approaches that for sainthood. The idea of throwing Nidia in jail for seeking the truth about the murder of her son ignited a furious outcry. The blasphemy of persecuting the grief-stricken mother, along with Joelito's sister, as Filártiga said, was "too much."

Infuriated by the arrest warrant for Nidia and Dolly, people spoke out against the injustice. The revulsion even included many high-ranking government officials. Some impassioned believers of Beato Joelito compared Nidia to the Virgin Mary and vowed vengeance.

On the morning of April 28, after hiding out for a few more days while the public's anger reached its peak, their lawyer, Horacio Galeano Perrone, drove Nidia and Dolly to the courthouse so they could turn themselves in. In a spectacularly asinine move, the judge ordered their immediate imprisonment. His arrogance served the Filártigas' cause well, inflaming public ire all the more.

"Everyone was very sympathetic to us," Nidia recalled. "Even the two policemen in the courtroom were so embarrassed that they apologized when they took us away. In the afternoon, Papi came to be with us for a while.

"The nuns in charge of the Buen Pastor prison were especially kind. They brought tea and stayed with us talking a long time, saying that everything was going to be all right."

"Richard, it was so absurd," Dolly laughed. "When we got there, the nuns didn't want us. So we said please take us. The judge ordered it and we have to be in here so that we can get out!

"But the nuns said you didn't do anything wrong, you shouldn't be here. We had to beg them to let us into jail!"

Galeano Perrone immediately filed a petition for their "conditional freedom." Later that day, when the news spread that the women were actually spending the night behind bars, if possible, people became even more incensed.

At this point, most likely word came down from on high. The first thing in the morning, the judge granted their release, and Nidia and Dolly were home in time for lunch.

To keep up the harassment, however, the charges remained pending. And the court confiscated their passports, presumably to thwart the accused commandos from escaping Stroessner's justice, although any Paraguayan can travel to neighboring Brazil and Argentina using only their national identification cards.

16

I flipped through the stacks of condolence letters. Neatly bound with black cloth ribbons, they stood out among the disorganized contents of the boxes.

Most came from California, but there were a good number from all over the United States, as well as from Latin America and Europe. There were scores from prestigious California universities and medical centers, but also quite a few from places like the Mayo Clinic, Yale, and Harvard. A dozen or so came from journalists who had covered Dr. Filártiga's U.S. tour. But the vast majority, well over 100, were written on letterhead stationery from doctors, dentists, public health officials, clergy, and artists.

Picking up a handful of letters, Nidia quietly asked, "You did this?"

"It was all of Joel's friends in California," I replied. "Joelito's murder hit people hard. They wanted to do something to help, anything. At least to write you to express their sorrow.

"It seemed best to organize a letter-writing campaign—sort of the way Amnesty International does. We thought that the international pressure on Stroessner would give you some protection. That's why many people typed them on official stationery, instead of properly handwriting them."

"Papi showed them in many places," Nidia said, "and so did Dolly and I—at the churches, in the market, even in the court. Everywhere. People were very impressed."

I glanced over to catch Joel's attention. Tuned out for the moment, he was engrossed in sketching a drawing. I asked Nidia, "I see that many of those in English have Spanish translations."

"Papi could read most of what they said," she explained, "but friends and students also helped. Many arrived open, and we think that others did not get to us at all. Still, there are so many!

"After dinner with friends we would stay up all night drinking coffee, making translations so Dolly and I could understand them, too. One would say, 'I know some of it.' And another would say, 'I can translate some parts. I am studying English at school.' Each one would add something.

"The mail comes in the morning. And as soon as I got it, I would tell Papi 'there are more letters.' He felt so relieved. He would lay down in bed and read them. Over and over again. Then cry a little. And he would say, 'This gives me strength.'"

17

"It is true," Joel murmured, joining in. "The letters helped me a lot because I felt very isolated and persecuted here. It was good to know I had support from friends in foreign countries.

"And the feeling of being supported helped me keep my emotional stability and diminished my anger. I had a lot of anger and desire to kill." He paused a beat. "I carried a weapon with me at all times, ready to commit suicide at any moment."

The expressions on Nidia and Dolly's faces confirmed my suspicion that in revealing his homicidal and suicidal impulses, Joel had not been entirely truthful. An accurate answer would have included the present as well as the past.

"Maybe we exaggerated a little bit too," Nidia told me, with the hint of a sad smile. "When we showed them to cousin César and other people from the government, we'd say, 'Look at this! Papi's friends all over the world are making a great international scandal.' And that the Organization of American States was sending you to investigate.

"You know that you're very well known here," she went on. "Because of all the articles in the newspapers and the university journals and your book. But they think you're more than just a historian. Your friendship with Congressman Domingo Laino, the leader of the biggest party of opposition in Paraguay. The way you worked with him when he was in so much trouble last year. Even taking over his classes at the university. And how you opened the doors of the embassy for him, so that now he is even invited to the receptions. And lots of other things too, like arranging for Papi's trip to the United States."

By the internal logic of Paraguay, because of the history of intervention by the "Colossus of the North" in the affairs of Latin American nations, Nidia's explanation was reasonable. She was wrong, but understandably so. Indeed, a lot of people in Stroessner's paranoid police state had made the same assumption, thinking I was somebody with real clout. Of course it was nonsense. In a moment, Nidia continued.

"Well, every day more letters arrived, and we kept showing them around. Papi said that if the lawyers believed we counted with powerful international support, it would give them courage to be strong. And he was right."

"When did the letters begin arriving?" I asked Nidia.

"Whole bunches started coming while Dolly and I were still in hiding, before Galeano Perrone took us to surrender."

The timing fits, I thought. "That explains a lot," I said aloud. "Your lawyers taking the offensive, even becoming offensive. And Judge Martínez putting up with it."

18

Before long, another piece of the puzzle fell into place. Since Nidia and Dolly technically could no longer be plaintiffs in any criminal suit, Horacio Galeano Perrone and Filártiga prepared a second, even stronger amplification motion. Counting on the public furor and the Filártigas' apparently enormous international support, after bringing Nidia and Dolly to the court to surrender on April 28, Galeano Perrone dropped the bombshell on the unsuspecting Judge Martínez.

The new amplification motion was similar to Nidia's petition, except that Dr. Filártiga was now the plaintiff. It requested that the homicide charge against Hugo Duarte be expanded to include any other accomplices or persons involved in covering up Joelito's death.

However, Joel's amplification motion went a lot further, asking the court to indict as codefendants five people who lived in Peña's house, and had been there at one time or another during the night of the murder—specifically, Américo Peña and Juana Villalba, and her children Jorge, Nery, and Charo.

Audaciously, Filártiga's new amplification petition claimed that on the night of Joelito's murder, "The extent of judicial negligence was not limited to the judge's ignorance, but was compounded by the scientifically inept report presented by the forensic physician present, along with the lack of diligence and perseverance of the chief of the police district who also was present."

And further, that during the initial police investigation, "all these functionaries made no attempt to determine the real nature of the crime. Instead, by their ignorance and actions, conceived of in bad faith, they have thrown a cloak of darkness over it to protect the true perpetrators of the death of my son."

19

Strange how one's mind will latch on to some little thing. Joel's amplification petition went on to list a score of facts contradicting the police cover-up. But it was the last point, tagged on almost as an afterthought, that most caught my attention.

On the night they killed Joelito, no one heard a peep from the neighborhood's guard dogs of Sajonia. Usually, any disturbance touched off a barking frenzy, shattering the barrio's tranquillity, especially during the summer when everyone slept with their windows open.

In *Silver Blaze*, Sherlock Holmes exposes the villain as the owner of "the dog that didn't bark." For the sleuth deduced that if a stranger had committed the theft, the animal would have sounded off. Likewise, the silence of the barrio's guard dogs gave the lie to the police crime-of-passion story. For, if Joelito had died in a violent fight with an enraged husband in Peña's house, the dogs would have broken into a fit of howling, waking up the whole neighborhood.

20

I read *Aquí's* April 30 edition with some amusement. The cover story consisted of lengthy excerpts from Joel's new amplification motion's juiciest sections. By then, even the straight press was reporting fresh developments in the *Caso Filártiga*. Of course, Joel had leaked the dynamite document.

And on top of everything else, his amplification motion produced another unexpected bonus. It smoked out the heretofore unknown Special Appeal. Up to this point, Judge Martínez had kept it a secret. According to Paraguayan legal window dressing, however, now he had to formally notify the Filártigas.

One week later, on May 5, Nidia's lawyers filed a brief contesting the Special Appeal ploy to prohibit amplifying the case—or even bring charges against Hugo Duarte—because of the alleged mutual combat. Clearly, Duarte had taken a beating the night of the murder. However, the cabby who drove Duarte home from his hotel job gave a deposition saying that he "neither saw nor heard 'a fight or scuffle' coming from the place, during the half hour he spent in front of Duarte Arredondo's house while waiting to be paid his taxi fare."

These were the same attorneys who only weeks before had warned Nidia and Dolly not to say a word in the courtroom because they could be killed. Now, at the Special Appeal hearing, they pointed out to Judge Martínez that the medical examination of the three independent physicians, as well as Dr. Godoy's report, contradicted the coroner's "superficial findings" made the night of Joelito's death. Consequently, they pronounced to the court, "we intend to file the corresponding criminal action against Dr. Molinas as an accomplice to this shameful crime."

Suddenly, as Nidia's attorneys were wrapping up their assault against the mutual combat Special Appeal ruse, Dr. Filártiga went ballistic. His belligerent accusations resounded throughout the courtroom, denouncing the corrupt proceedings, Judge Martínez' obstruction of justice, and anything else he could think of.

To all it was obvious that Filártiga had passed the point of caring what happened to him. Normally, the bailiffs would have made short work of any such disruption. Perhaps it was compassion for a crazy man, but something checked their hand, and they managed to peacefully drag Joel outside.

Clearly, Judge Martínez had lost control of the trial. Here was a routine, if sloppily contrived, crime-of-passion homicide case cooked up by the police. With the collaboration of the coroner, the judge, and even the allegedly cuckolded husband, everyone had expected the Filártigas to act rationally and go along with the whitewash. Instead, the *Caso Filártiga* had turned into the most controversial case in living memory.

None of the conspirators had imagined the Filártigas' tenacity to get at the truth, their reckless disregard of the consequences. None had figured on the family's campaign for justice to touch the hearts of so many, to rally public opinion. None had expected the *Caso Filártiga* to attract such international attention.

And now the conspirators saw that their cover-up plan was falling apart.

21

Even so, our knowledge of the events surrounding the killing of Joelito was still far from complete. Filártiga settled back among the clutter of the dining room, gathering his thoughts.

"Most likely," he said, "Peña and his gang abducted Joelito on their own initiative. To torture him for information. To connect me with the Christian Peasant Leagues and the OPM. To make a name for themselves. It seems unlikely they had clearance from higher up.

"The police already knew the OPM was moving their base of operations here to Paraguay. But the rebels had not started coming in yet. Peña's police squad killed Joelito five days before the first of them fell prisoner.

"They would have taken me," Filártiga said. "Except for the fear that I could die under the torture because of my heart condition. But with a confession from Joelito implicating me, they could openly arrest me."

Joel paused to rub his eyes, took a look at Nidia sitting across the table, and went on.

"We suspect Jorge or Nery Villalba came over and lured Joelito out of the house. They could have told him Charo needed to see him, to come get *The Open Veins*, or something. Maybe they thought Dolly and Analy knew where he went. We do not know.

"Anyway, without official sanction, they took Joelito someplace else and interrogated him—probably at the police headquarters here in Sajonia. Then, unexpectedly, under the torture he died. And in their panic they brought his body to Peña's house and mounted the crime-of-passion cover-up.

"They sent a police van to bring Dr. Molinas and Judge Martínez. Likely they were chosen because both are young and inexperienced, in their twenties and new to their jobs. They would have thought it was an official operation, and been ordered to cooperate. Then they called Duarte at work at the Hotel Guaraní. When he got home, they forced him to go along with the plan."

The rest of the story became even more sketchy, far more conjecture than facts. The dictatorship's concerns over the *Caso Filártiga* only partially coincided with those of Peña and the other conspirators: Their big worry was to extricate themselves; the regime wanted to avoid a scandal that could attract international attention and inflame the populace.

The Paraguayan courts can be a paragon of simplicity. Routinely, the give and take of everyday corruption prevails. But with political cases, or other matters that catch the dictator's interest, someone from the inner circle lets the presiding judge know His Excellency's wishes. And that's that.

About this time, Judge Martínez must have received one of these visits. For, a week after Nidia's lawyers filed their scathing May 12 brief, he denied Duarte's Special Appeal motion. In the light of Martínez' collaboration with the police, his ruling against the Special Appeal—which was meant to prevent the Filártigas from expanding the case to include the others—seemed a major legal victory.

"So what if it is Stroessner's intention to calm things down that accounts for Martínez's ruling?" I asked. "At least it opens up the court's investigation into the participation of the police."

"That is what we thought, too," Joel said. "Until Galeano Perrone explained that legally it amounts to nothing—that it is a political machination."

"Back up a bit. A political machination?"

"Yes. A classic Stroessner manipulation. By denying the ridiculous mutual combat Special Appeal, the public is deceived into thinking that the wheels of justice turn.

"Martínez' decision against the Special Appeal," Joel said, "recognizes only the right to submit our amplification motion, for us to petition the court to expand the charges against anyone else. But without actually granting our amplification motion, there can be no investigation into the part Peña and the others played in killing Joelito."

And, of course, Judge Martínez had judiciously avoided any such ruling.

22

As I marveled at the ways of the dictatorship, Nidia picked up a wrinkled sheet of paper. She smoothed it out on the table, her hands unconsciously playing with the page torn from a cheap student's notebook. I looked at the scribbled note:

> *Doña Nidia*
>
> *I want you to call me between 2:15 and 2:30. I want to speak with you.*
>
> *Charo*
>
> *If I do not answer, do not speak. Hang up.*

"It was in a box of papers," I said. "Is it important?"

"Yes. I mean no," Nidia replied. "No, not anymore. The next-door neighbor of Peña found it in his garden, the day after Charo got out of jail. He brought it to us right away. She must have thrown it over the wall, because it was wrapped around a stone and tied with string. Actually, he found three of them. One said that if she did not answer the phone, that meant *he* was there, and to call back at eight o'clock. Did you find them too?"

"No, just this one."

"Well, it was so soon after Joelito died," she went, "not even two weeks. And with the death threats and the motion to amplify the case and everything else. . . . That one time Dolly and I saw Charo in court, we hardly spoke to her at all. As soon as we looked at each other, the three of us started to cry. And before we knew it, the police took her away.

"Anyway, when we received the notes, I wasn't thinking very clearly. I made a terrible mistake. When I called, Juana answered. Instead of hanging up, I asked to speak with Charo. And then Juana hung up.

"Now Charo's disappeared." Nidia's voice trembled. "She didn't go back to school, and nobody in the neighborhood has seen her. We fear the worst. Now we'll never know for sure what really happened the night they killed Joelito. It's my fault."

With the end of the story, an almost tangible force settled upon us. It held us in its seductive embrace—measureless, slow-motion time.

Nidia looked down at her lap. Dolly listlessly shuffled papers about the table. Joel absently sketched on a pad. I stared at my notes.

Something weird was going on. And I did not like it at all. I had been sucked into the mire of the Filártigas' despair. I took a long, hard look at my friends. The torpor completely absorbed them.

Blowing the chance to talk with Charo only partially accounted for the Filártigas' desolation. Its treacherous vine was much stronger. It wrapped their souls in endless, futile speculation. What they should have done. What they could have done—or not done. Anything at all that might have changed the course of life's flow, no matter how insignificantly, just enough so that it would have missed killing Joelito.

The insidiousness with which the trap pulled me in triggered a flash of rage.

"Nidia's slip-up isn't the only mistake that's been made. It's easy to look back and find things to blame ourselves for. I *know* I can!"

To Dolly I said, "When Peña told you to shut up and not wake the neighbors, you yelled back that everybody was going to know." Turning to Nidia, "And you, in pain and shock from the most devastating loss a mother can suffer, you began the legal battle." Grabbing Joel's arm, "And your first thought, right after you saw that Joelito had been tortured, was to tell the whole world."

The downdraft from the two Casablanca ceiling fans chilled the goose bumps on my scalp.

"It's time for a reality check," I went on. "Look at all you've accomplished. I'm impressed. I'm more than impressed. I'm amazed. It's beyond incredible.

"In this war with the police, you've fought off their assaults. You forced Stroessner to back down and order the court to reject their Special Appeal. All over Paraguay, you *have* gotten the truth out. Everybody knows the police tortured and murdered Joelito."

Dr. Filártiga recovered first. "To do nothing was intolerable. But I fear," he said, in a voice that showed he truly was afraid, "it has only begun. Like a wounded bear, they are more dangerous than ever. For now, political restraints hold Peña and his police gang in check. For now. But Stroessner will not easily abandon them. And, as you've seen, there's no telling what they'll do next.

"From the beginning," Joel said, "I knew that to survive, the case had to be known internationally—beyond the control of Stroessner. I had a mountain in front of me and I did not know how to deal with it. That's why I wrote to you the same day we buried Joelito.

"When Colonel LaSala brought me your letter, it gave me great hope. I could only think that our survival depended on international support. What I needed was efficiency and clarity. Then I felt sure to have an efficient friend by my side."

Before I could say anything, Dolly shook me even further. "All through those terrible days, Papi kept saying that if they killed him, it wouldn't be the end. Because you'd be here to take over. You know, we should never give up. We must carry on the fight for Joelito under your orders."

The full implications hit me. They imagined me as some kind of high-powered operator, someone who could actually organize the international support the family and their struggle needed.

I wanted to scream that they had blown out of all proportion anything that I was even remotely capable of doing, that their expectations bore absolutely no relationship to reality—and, most of all, that I resented the hell out of them forcing their desperation on me.

23

Instead, attempting to put things in perspective, I told them, "Right now I am looking at that mountain in front of me. I can only promise that no matter what happens, we won't give up.

"But to think that I'm some kind of super gringo that can wave a magic wand and straighten everything out is pure fantasy. I simply don't have that kind of influence or contacts."

"You work for Amnesty International, don't you?" Dolly retorted. "You arranged for all the letters, didn't you?"

"Organizing a letter-writing campaign of Joel's friends is one thing," I replied. "It had nothing to do with Amnesty. In fact, it was I who sent Amnesty background materials on us and asked them to help if we got in trouble. They said they would do what they could, and then they asked me to help out with their human rights work while I'm here in Paraguay.

"So, yes," I told Dolly, "you can say I work for Amnesty. But right now, I still don't even know what that means. Anyway, setting up a permanent shield of international support is something else. That would take an organization."

"Like Amnesty International?"

"Yes. Like Amnesty."

"Then why won't you get them to do it?" Dolly demanded.

"It's not that I won't. It's that I can't. I don't even think that it's possible right now," I explained. "We know the police murdered Joelito. But with this crime-of-passion trial, and Duarte not contesting the charges, everything is too confused for Amnesty to get involved at this point.

"First, we have to show them that the *Caso Filártiga* is a legitimate human rights case. That Joelito was the victim of political torture and murder. I'm not saying that it can't be done. But it's going to take a lot of time and work before we can count on Amnesty's support."

Again a silence fell over the room, the family wrestling with their shattered expectations. At last, seeing my own despondency, Nidia said, "Please don't worry, Richard. We understand. Just your being here gives me more will to live. I had lost the will to live. I didn't want to eat or anything. I only wanted to look at the young men who looked like Joelito. Now that you are here, I have more strength. It seems as if we're safer."

Dolly, however, still could not let it go. "Well, how about your friends at the embassy?"

"I do know a few people at the embassy," I said. "But truthfully, they are mostly acquaintances, not really friends. In any event, I haven't had a chance to talk with anyone yet."

I had no idea if there was anyone who would be willing to stick their necks out. And even if I did find someone, I did not know just what they could do to help anyway.

"First thing tomorrow morning," I promised, "I'll start contacting people."

An OPM poster, with the guerillas' "Victory or Death" motto.

FOUR

WHEN WE TURNED OFF the paved highway onto the dirt road to Ybycuí, the going got rough. Bob Garrison backed off, putting more distance between us and the roiling plume of red dust thrown up by Filártiga's speeding pickup.

"I'm glad it's Saturday afternoon siesta time," Bob quipped. "The way Joel drives the clinic would be filled with new patients before we even got there."

"Strange," I said, "such a gifted physician is also one of the world's worst drivers."

"I'll bet they're pretty nervous right now," Bob said. "This is the first time they've been back since Joelito's death?"

"Right. Today's May 22. They killed him on March 30. Seven weeks."

"Must be hard."

"Uh-huh," I mused, putting off for the moment Bob's comment. There was something I wanted to clear up before we reached town.

"By the way," I said, "last night Filártiga told me you have the honor of being the first U.S. diplomat ever to visit the clinic, or for that matter, Ybycuí."

"We're going to cause quite a stir among the local big boys," I predicted. "That'll help the myth of Dr. Filártiga's heavy international support. Within the hour they'll be on the phone, letting the *jefes* in Asunción know how the Filártigas arrived home escorted by two U.S. diplomats."

"Two?" Bob said.

"Sure. Seeing us ride into town in this big American car, with its *cuerpo diplomático* license plates, and they'll assume we're both from the embassy. And a first-rate impress-the-shit-out-of-you-act calls for at least two envoys from the world's most powerful nation, don't you think?"

Bob's answer was a satisfied chuckle.

Settled in the bucket seat, I marveled at how much had been accomplished in the ten days since arriving in Paraguay. Everything had gone smoothly at the Organization of American States office when I checked in to officially activate my research grant. The staff at the National Archives greeted me like a long lost relative. And I managed to track down some old acquaintances from the embassy. In fact, it was at the home of Jerry Nehman, an agricultural economist who I had become friendly with the year before, that I met Bob and Maria Garrison.

Naturally, the after dinner talk turned to the *Caso Filártiga*. Garrison, the director of the Paraguayan–American Cultural Center, was the best informed. Everyone who frequented the center knew Filártiga, if not personally then through his art, and sympathized with his struggle.

The talk went on for hours. The more they learned about what the Filártiga family was going through, the greater became their admiration—and indignation.

Out of the blue, Bob casually mentioned that he would like to meet Dr. Filártiga, and perhaps pay a visit to the Clinic of Hope.

The young black diplomat's nonchalant manner did not fool anyone. We all knew of Stroessner's hypersensitivity to international pressure. Everyone recognized the enormous gift to the Filártigas' cause that Bob's act of solidarity was. Delighted, we arranged to have lunch with the family the next afternoon.

Filártiga and Garrison hit it off, and Joel invited him to visit the clinic. Yet, when Bob suggested we go to Ybycuí that same weekend, Joel became ambivalent. Pleading that the struggle sapped the family's time and energy, he suggested we hold off for a while.

The way Joel put it seemed reasonable. The Filártigas were at it every day, morning to night. Even so, I was not buying it. And I was afraid that if we did not move right away, the opportunity could very well be lost. What if Bob changed his mind or became too busy? What if the ambassador saw Garrison's involvement in the *Caso Filártiga* as interference in the internal affairs of the host country—a high diplomatic taboo—and forbade him from making the trip?

After lunch, I pulled Joel aside. He saw it coming. Even before I really got started, with a deep sigh that fell somewhere between resignation and relief, Joel raised both hands in mock surrender.

1

Now, as we entered Ybycuí, Filártiga's green pickup, with the red crosses Joelito had painted on the doors, slowed to crawl. After fifteen minutes creeping along the nearly deserted streets, Bob asked, "What's he doing? I thought they were eager to get to the clinic?"

"Not so much eager," I replied, "as anxious. There's more going on than I thought at first."

"How's that?"

"To start with, when Dr. Filártiga didn't return after Joelito's murder, Stroessner's flunkies out here started a rumor campaign. They said that the clinic was closed for good—that Filártiga had a nervous breakdown and the Board of Medicine was revoking his license."

"Damn. I didn't know that," Bob said. "But I mean right now. Why is he meandering back and forth on the streets at a snail's pace?"

"Well, right now, I'd say he's putting on a show to wake up the people. Letting them know he's not slinking back into town, a broken man.

"These people have been beaten down for so long that suspicion has become a part of the culture. It'll take a bit of effort for the Filártigas to reestablish the old confidence."

"If the situation here is so critical," Bob asked, "why has he waited so long to come back?"

"Good question. Joel and I talked about it, playing into the rumor campaign, jeopardizing their life's work. How they had to get the clinic up and running again, even if only on a part-time basis at first. Not only to squelch the rumors but also to tend to his patients and maintain their trust. But. . . ." I let it fade, collecting my thoughts.

Filártiga began a second swing through town. People were now coming out, waving from their doorways.

"But?" Bob prompted.

"But. . . ." Again I hesitated. No sense getting into the guilt driven family shouting matches. Or Filártiga's erratic suicidal, and homicidal, episodes.

Only days before, Joel had spotted Inspector Peña ahead in the traffic on Avenida Carlos Antonio López. Something snapped. He ordered Medina, his handyman who was driving, to catch up. At the red light, they managed to pull up alongside the cop on the outside lane. Filártiga, in the passenger seat, was three feet from the man responsible for the death of his son. The distance was reduced to a foot when his trembling hand stretched out the window, pointing a pistol at Peña's head.

According to a shaken Medina, who told us the story as soon as they got back, Joel yelled, "Face me, *cabrón*, so I can look you in the eyes and kill you right."

Peña ducked down, hit the gas and jumped the light. In his powerful car, the cop easily lost Filártiga's old pickup. Strangely, there was no police follow-up. The confrontation between Filártiga and Peña was being played out on another level.

Within the family we talked openly about Joel's "lapses," but there was no reason to lay it on Bob.

"So why haven't they returned?" he prompted me again.

"Look. Joel would keep saying how they had to get back here," I said. "But then he'd always find some excuse to beg off. You saw how he tried to squirm out of it the other day at lunch. After you left I pressed him for an explanation. It's rather complicated."

"No problem. Evidently, we have the time," Bob replied, glancing ahead at the Filártigas poking along.

"Last year," I began, "Joelito and Analy moved to Asunción to live with Dolly. Mostly to get a better education. Joelito didn't lose touch with people here, though, or drift away from the family, as you might expect. During vacations, whenever he could finagle it, Joelito would take one or both of his sisters and drive out, if only for the day.

"At the core, the Filártigas were an extremely close-knit family. But during Joel and Nidia's hectic weekend trips to Asunción, it was impossible to find good time together. They were constantly on the go, running around trying to attend to everyone and get everything done.

"So, you see, the house in Sajonia is only that—a house. The clinic here has always been the Filártigas' home. It's here that Joel and Nidia have spent their lives together, where the kids grew up."

Bob took it all in. "We haven't passed the clinic yet, have we?"

"No. And now everyone in town knows they're back," I said, pointing to the people greeting them. "And he's still avoiding the clinic. I imagine they're working themselves up to it."

"Working themselves up to it?" Bob asked.

"Yeah, I'm afraid so. In Asunción things have slowed down to where they can be dealt with in one or two days a week. Yet the Filártigas stay on. They drive themselves into a perpetual state of numbed exhaustion—to blunt the loss left by Joelito.

"Ybycuí is entirely different than Asunción for the Filártigas," I said. "Here, in the slower rhythm of the countryside, they can't sustain the obsessive pace that blunts their grief.

"Out here the family's going to have to relive Joelito's death all over. Out here, there're going to be a lot of very lonely, painful nights. Out here, there's no escaping it.

"What it comes down to is that the Filártigas have avoided coming home—a home that always has been filled with Joelito."

"God," Bob said, almost in veneration.

2

Four days later, the Filártigas were back in Asunción. Duarte's attorneys had appealed Judge Martínez' ruling denying the mutual combat Special Appeal ruse. To Horacio Galeano Perrone's consternation, Joel headed straight to the lawyer's office to help prepare the opposing brief.

Most afternoons, Galeano Perrone found the Filártigas ensconced in his office. They insisted on getting into every aspect of the case. Horacio acknowledged that they did come up with some good ideas and invaluable information. But these nuggets were buried in wild speculation and irrelevant anecdotes. And further aggravating Horacio and his staff, Filártiga critiqued every detail of their work while cajoling anyone he could buttonhole to take ever bolder action.

With Joel's return to the clinic, Horacio dared hope things would calm down. Yet, in less than a week, the Filártigas were back at it, reducing his offices to pandemonium.

Horacio groused about how Filártiga ignored his broad hints, blunt suggestions, and finally unabashed pleas to stop his constant meddling. He begged me to do whatever I could.

By then I was also pretty well exasperated. We did find some solace in sharing our frustration. I promised Horacio to have a heart-to-heart with Joel. But we both knew what that would be worth and resigned ourselves to the immutable.

3

The Filártigas did not rush back only to keep the lawyers on their toes. After Bob and I returned to Asunción late that Saturday night, and the stream of visitors flowing through the clinic dried up, the floodgates of grief burst.

Now, as we all gathered around the dining room table in Sajonia, Nidia told me what happened. "We were getting ready to go to bed when Dolly and I started crying," she said. "It was very hard being alone at the clinic that first night. Well, anyway, after everybody left, we started crying. And then Papi started crying, too.

"He just kept on crying. Harder and harder. Papi's whole body shook tremendously. One fierce convulsion after another, almost like a seizure. He was curled up on the bed, and kept crying harder and harder. He couldn't stop."

Nidia slowly clasped and unclasped her hands. "Dolly and I became frightened. We laid down beside Papi and hugged him for a long time. Like a baby, we kept rocking him back and forth until at last he fell asleep. The next day wasn't so bad. Lots of people kept coming. But Sunday night, again Papi began to cry uncontrollably. We comforted him like before. And then again last night."

All the while Nidia related these intimate details, Joel sat quietly with us, nodding his head in affirmation.

"This morning, when we received word of the appeal," Nidia finished, a sheepish grin playing across her lips, "Papi said that Galeano Perrone needed our help. So, right away we loaded up everything and came straight back."

While Nidia recounted the story, I had noticed a pile of burlap sacks stacked in the kitchen. As much out of curiosity as something to say, I asked what they were.

Dolly explained how everyone who came to the clinic—from the nuns at the convent to townsfolk and peasants—had brought something to eat. The Filártigas could not possibly use the mountain of meats, cheeses, honey, and produce. So, as always when they found themselves with an abundance of foodstuffs, they brought it to Asunción to distribute among the people.

Over Dolly's shoulder, I noticed Joel give Nidia a furtive look. To me, he said, "We must now go see a patient. If it is not inconvenient, we would appreciate it if you would come with us."

Obviously, he did not want to say any more in front of their daughter. Getting ready in my bedroom, I pondered the invitation. I had pocketed some cash and my passport when Joel came in. Uncharacteristically, he shut the door behind him and handed me an old U.S. Army Colt .45 pistol.

4

I looked into Filártiga's weary eyes. In the steadiest tone I could manage, I asked, "What's this for?"

"That's entirely up to you," Joel replied, dropping into the chair next to my bed. He opened his doctor's satchel and took out a small black leather pouch. Inside was his own handgun.

"If you are uncomfortable, leave it here." He said simply, "I only offer you the choice."

"Choice?" I replied. "You haven't even told me what's going on."

Actually, I had a good idea. Still, I wanted Joel to spell it out. "Do you honestly think it's fair to ask this of me? I haven't forgotten what you told me last year, how Investigaciones would love to catch a foreigner with the 'subversives' as evidence of their international communist conspiracy.

"That's what it comes down to, doesn't it? Or am I wrong?"

"No," Joel said, his voice now edged with tension. "But there is more involved. The patient is a woman in her mid-twenties. Soledad is in the seventh month of a difficult pregnancy. She has already experienced serious complications. Without medical attention, there is a strong possibility that Soledad's life, and the fetus, could be lost."

"I still don't see what it has to do with me."

Dr. Filártiga drew a deep breath, arched his head toward the ceiling, and in his clinical voice explained. "When I became a physician, I swore the Hippocratic oath. For more than twenty years, I have been faithful to that obligation. Soledad's husband, Juan Carlos da Costa, was among the first of the OPM to fall prisoner. He was not just another militant. He was the *comandante* of the OPM. The information Juan Carlos gave up in his quick confession has been devastating.

"Juan Carlos counted heavily on Soledad. She has a doctorate in jurisprudence and is very capable. Effectively she already was *co-comandante*. With her husband's death, she has become the *comandante* of the OPM. Soledad and the two other highest leaders are hiding here in Asunción."

Filártiga grew still. At length, he lowered his gaze from the ceiling and spoke to me directly. "They are the most hunted people in Paraguay. You have seen their pictures in the newspapers?"

"In the boxes of documents, I found a tear-out sheet. A 'Wanted Poster,' with the photos of ten people."

"That is right. But since that was published, seven have been killed. The police took some alive. We must assume that they too were tortured into quick confessions." Joel spoke quietly. "If you are taken with us, it will make no difference to Investigaciones if you are armed or not."

My protest activities in the States were poor preparation for this. Sure, once at a demonstration I had taken a police beating, but this was in another league altogether.

Intellectually, I had accepted the risks of joining the Filártigas' cause. Emotionally, however, I had not dealt with what it really meant. "I still don't understand what this is all about. You and Nidia can take care of your patient. There's no need for me to go."

"Soledad's medical condition has nothing to do with why they have asked to meet you," Joel said. "When we were waiting for you to arrive, I gave them your book on Paraguay's independence revolution. And told them about you."

"Told them what about me?"

"You know. Your embassy connections. Your international clout. You know."

"And you know that's wishful fantasy that has nothing to do with reality."

"Yes. *Now* I know!" Filártiga shot back. "But then, it is what I believed. They had killed Joelito. They had killed almost all of the OPM leaders. They were killing more and more people every day. We did not know what to think, we did not know what to do."

So, I thought, you endowed me with these imaginary powers. You created a super-ally, to keep your hopes alive, someone who offered a chance of survival.

"The last time we saw Soledad and the others," Joel went on, "just before you got here, they asked if it would be possible to talk with you."

"Why would they want to meet with me?"

Filártiga looked me straight on and, without a trace of apology, said, "Because they need your help. They are marked for execution. *And worse.*"

Filártiga still had not regained perspective, refusing to let go of the myth that I could never live up to. To say I felt resentful and put upon would be a monumental understatement. Holding myself in check, I fell back on the bed. The realization dawned that it also might be I, and not just the Filártigas, who lacked perspective.

Even after Joelito's murder and everything else that was happening to them, they continued to give medical care to Soledad, the most hunted person in Paraguay. The deeper I looked, the clearer it became that if I turned my back on the rebels, I would be abandoning the Filártigas. Then the full implications of what Joel said struck home, when he said that if they were captured they faced death, *and worse.*

At any time the OPM guerrillas could be taken prisoners, and the police would get their quick confession. Joel and Nidia would be arrested because they were helping them. And that would be it for the *Caso Filártiga* struggle.

I picked up the heavy weapon. Hefting it from hand to hand, I weighed Filártiga's choice.

"An aphorism of Alberto Schweitzer's may be relevant to your decision," Joel told me as he rose from his chair. "'Pain,' he said, 'is a crueler master than death itself.'"

Yeah, we all have to die. But we don't all have to be tortured to death.

5

I had imagined the OPM fugitives cowering in an attic, like Anne Frank and her family hiding from the Nazis. So it was something of a letdown to find the rebels living quite normally with a family in a middle-class barrio, not far from the center of Asunción.

Mario and Clotilde Ríos, both longtime OPM activists, rounded up their brood of kids for bed and excused themselves. The handsome living room, with its white stucco walls and red tiled floors, was filled with dark wood furniture upholstered in brown leather. The guerrillas, whose not entirely successful attempts at disguise made them look like young professionals, fit right in.

Over her naturally black hair, Soledad wore a light wig. And like the other *compañeros*, she had darkened her complexion with one of those instant tanning stains. Angry red blotches marred their faces, leaving the impression of a mild skin disease. Salvador and Francisco had sacrificed their mustaches and changed their hair styles from the Wanted Poster. When they went out, all sported clear horn-rimmed glasses that matched the new photos on their false identification cards.

Early each morning, the two men dressed in jackets and ties, and they left the house with Mario Ríos as if going off to the office. But they spent their days coordinating the work with the scattered remnants of the OPM. To further avoid arousing suspicion among the neighbors, Soledad played the role of Salvador's pregnant wife.

With the highest price on her head, Soledad rarely risked going about Asunción during the daytime. At night, however, she often moved about the city, carrying out her duties of holding together the decimated OPM structure.

With quiet authority, *Comandante* Soledad explained their predicament. "The Argentine coup forced us to return to Paraguay prematurely. Of course we knew about the *pyragüés*. What we didn't realize was how deeply the informers had penetrated our organization. The police knew the precise time and place that some of our people would be crossing the frontier.

"The Investigaciones Special Brigade tortured confessions from many. Sometimes, even before we knew that our people had fallen and could warn the others, it was too late. The police had already mounted their attacks."

Soledad paused. "That's what happened to my husband, Juan Carlos. Six weeks ago, April 9. Investigaciones assaulted the house where he and three others were hiding. They took him before he could take his own life."

Soledad sipped her coffee. "In the following two weeks, what took us years to build was destroyed. Anyone suspected in the least was taken, tortured. The police—"

At that moment the front door burst open, its cast-iron handle smashing into the stucco wall. Distorted by the massive adrenaline rush, it all happened in slow motion. Without conscious thought, the barrel of my pistol was lining up on the backlit figure in the doorway.

Many times I have thought about that moment. Probably, it was the scrawniness of the silhouette dashing through the doorway that prevented me from pulling the trigger and blowing a hole through eleven-year-old Mariolito Ríos.

It was over before anyone fully realized what had happened. I managed to get the gun back into my belt before my hands began shaking. Everyone started talking at once.

The commotion brought Mario rushing into the living room. Instantly sizing things up, he snatched up his son and angrily bawled out little Mariolito. As he carried the terrified youngster back to the bedrooms, Mario apologized to us for his boy's actions.

Of course, Mariolito was not to blame. Late getting home, he acted like any boy his age. Making a mad dash, he misjudged the force when he slammed into the door. And almost died for it.

I looked around. Everyone was on their feet, yet no one else had drawn a weapon. It was my turn to apologize, the amateur who had overreacted. They all assured me that I had done nothing wrong.

"The only thing I did right," I said in disgust, "was not kill the boy."

"No!" Soledad countered. "We have become accustomed to this life, and to children running in and out of the house all day. For you, it is new."

For fifteen minutes, we rehashed every detail of the tragedy that almost was. And, as far as concerned the OPM fugitives—and Joel and Nidia too, for that matter—that was the end of it. It took me a lot longer to quell the dread.

6

Soledad picked up her story. "In truth, maybe one out of five that have fallen prisoner, has anything to do with the OPM. The repression is often used to settle old scores—against anyone, not just politically, but personally too. And of business rivals bribing the police to arrest others. Like an auction where the loser ends up in an Investigaciones dungeon."

"What about charges?" I asked.

"All constitutional guarantees are suspended under Stroessner's State of Siege. Not that he really needs a pretext. But it provides a veneer of legality for the international community."

"No. No, I mean with the businesspeople. What happens to the ones who lose the bidding?"

"Oh. They negotiate with some other faction in Investigaciones to get out. They inform on the one who denounced them, and they may have him arrested because of some other shady business dealings they know about. Actually," she explained with dry humor, "they are not our greatest concern."

Getting back on track, she went on, "So many people have been arrested that the jails can no longer contain them, so the government opened a concentration camp. Emboscada is located in the campo, about eighty miles from Asunción, over very rough roads and with no accommodations to spend the night. This is to isolate the prisoners from their families and lawyers and the press.

"Already Emboscada holds hundreds of people," she elaborated. "And construction cannot keep up with the new prisoners that they bring in. You're a Latin American scholar. You know concentration camps have never been part of our history, our culture. Emboscada has added a new dimension of terror. We are guilty of more than our share of atrocities. But concentration camps are an imported evil."

Impressed by Soledad's sincerity and humility, I asked what they were going to do.

"The only thing we can—try to keep as many people alive for as long as possible."

"Why don't you get out of Paraguay?" I wanted to know.

"How? Where can we go?" she responded. "At first some of our people gained political asylum in the democratic embassies here in Asunción. It will take a while before they'll be allowed to leave, to be escorted to the airport and sent into exile. The diplomatic compounds of Peru and Venezuela are overflowing. Refugees are camped out on the lawns, in the gardens, everywhere.

"But Stroessner has now completely surrounded the friendly embassies with soldiers. And Investigaciones police are permanently stationed at the gates. They photograph everyone who enters, friends and relatives bringing food and things. Sometimes, even these people are arrested for being OPM messengers."

"There wasn't anything unusual at the U.S. Embassy, the couple of times I've been out there." I knew the answer to this provocative question, but I wanted to see how she would handle it.

"Yes. Well, I'm sure you know." Soledad looked me straight in the eye but did not quite succeed in concealing her embarrassment from me. "The policy of the United States is to never grant political asylum, to anyone."

7

Returning to why the rebels did not just get out of the country, I asked, "Why don't you go back to Argentina, blend into the million Paraguayans already living there for economic reasons?"

"That's all changed, too," Soledad said ruefully. "Paraguay's become a prison. The military has set up checkpoints, some of them roving roadblocks, even on back-country dirt roads. And the control at the frontier is almost complete. Investigaciones takes anyone the *pyragués* finger."

"Cross the rivers at night, in small boats," I suggested.

"Some have tried. But in Argentina and Brazil the military dictatorships now hunt our people—and return them to Paraguay. And Stroessner sends back anyone caught in Paraguay.

"All the countries here in the Southern Cone are now military dictatorships, bound together by their fascist ideology. Not only Brazil and Argentina, but Bolivia and Chile too. Even Uruguay, the Switzerland of South America, has fallen to military rule. And they function as a network, coordinating their repression across international borders, under what they call the Doctrine of National Security."

When *Comandante* Soledad finished her political exposition, she smiled and said abruptly, "Right now, we must see how my baby is doing." And she followed Joel and Nidia to a rear room for her prenatal checkup.

I sat with Salvador and Francisco, making getting-to-know-you small talk. Did I play chess? No. I found it addictive, and too consuming. So I was saving it until I was in jail and had plenty of time on my hands. Were they soccer fans? Fanatical. That was one of the things they missed most living underground, no longer being able to attend the games at the stadium. Both had graduated from the university. Salvador took a degree in political science. Francisco was a mechanical engineer.

When Filártiga returned, he indicated that it was time to leave. "Hold on a minute," I objected, and turning to Soledad said, "Before we go, there's something we need to clear up."

"Of course," she said. "Nidia said they meant to bring the children some honey from Ybycuí. When they do, maybe you could also come? There're some things we'd like to discuss with you."

"That's what we have to get straight," I blurted out. "I'm afraid Joel has given you the wrong impression. The truth is, I don't have the slightest idea of how to raise international pressure on Stroessner to make him loosen up."

Soledad actually laughed. "Don't worry. You can't think that we expect you to have a magic stick to wave and make all our troubles go away?"

8

"The only purpose military aid can possibly serve is to strengthen the hold of dictatorships on their people."

It was neither Soledad nor Dr. Filártiga who leveled this condemnation of U.S. assistance. Coincidentally, though, it was made on the same day the Filártigas rushed back from the Clinic of Hope and I first met the OPM insurgents.

On May 25, 1976, Ed Koch, the brash member of Congress and future mayor of New York City, delivered the rebuke on the floor of the U.S. House of Representatives, in his "Why Are We Assisting Paraguay?" speech.

A few weeks later, Colonel Bob LaSala gave me a copy of the *Congressional Record* containing Koch's rebuke of Stroessner and his peasant beaters. With a grin, Bob noted, "It looks like Jimmy Carter isn't the only one talking about human rights these days."

That evening, we made photocopies of the English original and Joel arranged for several trusted anti-Stroessner secretaries to type up fifty Spanish translations. Stapled to the English *Congressional Record* reproductions, they made an impressive packet.

We spread them around Asunción, mailing copies to embassies and newspapers, to international organizations, and even to Paraguayan government offices. From diplomatic receptions to private conversations, the idea that human rights in Paraguay had found a spot on the U.S. political agenda, as part of the presidential election campaign, caused more than a little interest. By our next visit with the OPM, Koch's speech had become *the* hot topic in town.

"We've been hearing about this," Soledad exclaimed. Nidia, Joel, and I sat back and watched our friends consume the Spanish translation.

"Look," Soledad announced, "he says that even though the Department of Defense report 'states flatly that there is no active insurgency threat to the Government of Paraguay, Stroessner uses his powers to conduct widespread random arrests to intimidate the general population and to hold a number of his political opponents in prison without trial for years, and the United States continues to provide training and equipment to Paraguay's military.'

"This is very important," Soledad said, "to have a high government official expose the truth like this."

"It could be," I equivocated, not wanting to burst their bubble. I told them about Senator Frank Church's hard-hitting investigation of some of the most powerful institutions, especially the CIA.

"What I'm getting at," I explained, "is the Church Committee hearings' revelations dominate the political landscape these days. Koch's denunciation is not of the highest priority up there."

"But not for us in Paraguay," Soledad noted astutely.

"No, not for us," I agreed. "It's the telescope phenomenon."

They looked at me for an explanation.

"In Paraguay, things can't be sugarcoated. The wealth simply does not exist. Injustices and exploitation are right up front, not like in the States. Even the middle class lives with the constant threat of poverty always looming over them, just waiting to snatch away everything they have."

"You see in black and white," Dr. Filártiga put in, "when you watch your children die of malnutrition. Or of a common childhood disease that a ten-centavo immunization would prevent."

"Right," I agreed. "So from our perspective here, a condemnation like Koch's carries the force of obvious truth. Compared with its effect in the States, it hits us with a powerful impact, as if magnified through a telescope."

"So you mean," Soledad said, "that the Congressman's speech will help us because people here perceive that Stroessner has lost the confidence of his *patrón*. Or because they think that the United States government finally realizes that he has gone too far and now is going to take serious measures. Even though that may not be so?"

"Something like that," I said. "It's too soon to tell. But Koch's speech is promising."

"More than that," Soledad retorted. "Already what he has accomplished is formidable."

I clamped my mouth shut. I did not think Koch had done anything especially courageous by jumping on Jimmy Carter's human rights bandwagon in an election year. Still, his speech had given the OPM fugitives a morale boost. And after three terrible months of suffering one devastating blow after the next, that was no small thing.

9

Soledad finished Koch's speech. "Listen to this, the way he comes right out and tells how the regime functions: 'Further, Stroessner has violated both international treaties and universally recognized human rights in the conduct of Paraguay's internal affairs, in which the military plays a vital role, not only as the power behind the government but also as an integral part of police operations.'

"And look," she said, pointing to another section, "here he denounces the dictatorship for persecuting even *suspected* enemies with 'torture, disappearances and other gross violations of human rights.' And he backs it all up with specific examples."

I, too, had been struck by the remarkable similarity among people from such radically diverse political worlds. The Paraguayan dissidents, a military adviser from the embassy, and a member of the U.S. Congress all so closely shared the same view of Stroessner that they used nearly the same words in their condemnations. And the common link went even further. The case studies that Koch used to support his accusations were drawn from a half-dozen international organizations.

"I didn't know that the UN or the OAS was involved in human rights," Soledad went on. "And except for Amnesty International, I haven't even heard of the others. What is it that they do?"

"I'm afraid that I don't know all that much about them either," I admitted.

My declaration of ignorance came as something of a shock. "But you must know something about them!" Salvador protested.

"I have picked up some general information," I replied. "To be honest, though, it's only been since Joelito was killed that I've really become involved in human rights. I'm no expert."

"Still, you do know more than any of us," Soledad said in her comandante voice. "International human rights is such a vague concept. It's so nebulous. I don't even comprehend how these organizations function on an everyday basis, in real life. And to us, this knowledge is of enormous importance."

Rationally, I knew she was right. I was the best source of information they had. Even so, I felt like a fraud. Shrugging in acceptance, I began arranging my thoughts.

Soledad asked me to hold on, and the guerrillas dashed back to their rooms. When they returned with student notebooks and ball-point pens, a sobering comparison with my seminars at UCLA hit me. This was no academic exercise.

"OK," I began, "international organizations involved in human rights can be divided into two major types: those funded by governments, like the UN or the OAS, and those independently organized, like Amnesty or the International League for Human Rights, that Koch mentions. They're called nongovernmental organizations, NGOs for short."

"What's the difference?" Soledad asked.

"As a general rule, the NGOs are made up of activists. Human rights is what they do, their raison d'être," I explained. "Whereas, in the governmental organizations, human rights work is more or less a poor cousin, low on the institutional totem pole, almost a concession to their formal mandates. And they're staffed by underworked and overpaid career bureaucrats, who're all too often concerned with promotions and pensions rather than enforcing human rights. Even if they could."

No sooner had these words left my mouth than I regretted them. "That's a bit unfair," I relented. "There are many good people in the governmental organizations who are disgusted with the institutional hypocrisy and do what they can from within the system."

"What did you mean when you said, 'Even if they could?'" Salvador asked.

"What it comes down to," I explained, "is that most of the governments that make up the UN and the OAS really don't care about human rights. In fact, most of them are openly hostile. They say that how they treat their citizens is their own business, strictly an internal matter—that the entire concept of international human rights is a violation of their national sovereignty. And they stick together to undermine effective human rights enforcement.

"Let me give you a fact, to put it in perspective," I went on. "In all these years since World War II, despite the treaties these governments have all signed, daily they continue to violate international human rights. Yet not a single one of them has been brought to task. At the very best, in a handful of cases, the human rights activities of the governmental organizations have resulted in a public embarrassment for the violator nation."

I stood, walked around, stretching to relieve my chronic back pain. I could have used another few minutes before continuing, but Soledad cut short my respite.

"So," she wanted to know, "how do the nongovernmental offices, the international human rights NGOs, function?"

"It's not much of an exaggeration," I replied, "to say that the NGOs are just about the opposite of governmental organizations. Their people are better known for burning out than for pursuing the good life. They're shamefully overworked and underpaid. And forget about prestige. They're looked down upon by the career-track human rights bureaucrats."

"So how do the NGOs get people to work for them?" Soledad asked.

"Human rights activists work out of commitment. Because they believe in the cause."

Soledad seemed less than convinced.

"Where's the mystery?" I asked her. "Why have you worked for years to build the OPM? And international human rights activists don't have to risk their lives—*and worse.*"

10

Dusk had snuck up on us. Yet nobody turned on a light. Going right to the bottom line, Soledad asked, "Where do the NGOs get their money? They can't operate without finances."

"True enough," I agreed. "But there's no secret there either. Some are funded by church groups and labor unions, and grants from foundations. And they all raise money just like any other not-for-profit organization: membership dues, direct mail campaigns, fundraising events. Some have angels, patrons who support their work financially."

"And the people who work at the NGOs? Are they like you, former Vietnam war protesters?"

"No way," I objected. "I'm something of an anomaly. Joel and Nidia are my friends. Joelito was my friend. To me human rights are very personal. They're another breed entirely."

Comandante Soledad's sharp mind circled back around. "And how are the strategy and tactics of the NGOs different?"

It took a couple of beats to frame my answer. "For one thing, we used civil disobedience and all sorts of outrageous actions to shake things up. The NGOs make every effort to be accepted. They work out of proper offices. Women usually wear skirts. Jackets and ties for men."

"I know how tedious that can be," Salvador sympathized, alluding to his cover of going to the office each morning.

"Oh, no. It's not a disguise at all," I said. "It's who they are. It reflects their self-image as respectable professionals."

The OPM guerrillas exchanged perplexed expressions. Salvador asked, "Are you saying that the NGOs can't be trusted?"

"Not in the least," I assured them. "I'm not even being critical. Just factual. All I'm saying is that's who they are. In fact, a good number of them come from the upper social classes."

"Isn't that a contradiction?" Soledad said.

"Why?" I asked her. "What's your class background, Doctora?"

Comandante Soledad snapped me a sharp look. Then her eyes crinkled, and she chuckled.

"Do you receive money from Amnesty International?" Soledad asked.

"No." Looking at Joel and Nidia, I said, "In Sajonia, I don't have any living expenses. And anyway, although they don't know it, the OAS research grant is subsidizing my human rights work."

"So, in effect, many of you work for nothing? Some even spend their own money," Soledad concluded.

"You could look at it that way," I conceded. "Then again, how much is your salary as comandante of the OPM?"

By then my back was really hurting. And the dysentery that was plaguing me did nothing to improve my disposition. I really wanted to get back to my bed and bathroom.

11

Comandante Soledad, however, had other ideas. "All right, what about Amnesty?" she asked. "We've talked about them before, but I still don't have a concrete idea of how international human rights works. When Investigaciones takes someone, for example, and everyone knows that they have him. Tell us what happens? Step by step."

Even though darkness had fully fallen, still no one bothered with the lights, the glow from the street lamps being sufficient for note taking.

"Sure," I said, resolving to keep it short. "Remember, Amnesty has no enforcement power. Their big stick is exposure—that they can cost Stroessner millions in foreign aid, hold up loans from the global financial institutions, discourage businesses from investing in Paraguay.

"But to your hypothetical case," I said. "First of all, Amnesty must have the basic facts. That's why when you tell me about a political prisoner, I'm always asking for more specific details."

"OK," Soledad said, "Then what happens?"

"The staff at the Secretariat in London gathers evidence until they're convinced they have a legitimate human rights case. Then, AI's Campaign Against Torture division launches an Urgent Action. With telegrams and letters, they let the government know that Amnesty knows about so-and-so's circumstances, and asks them for an accounting of the case."

"I imagine that Stroessner simply ignores them," she said.

"Of course. But it puts Stroessner on notice. The victim is no longer simply another unknown prisoner, forgotten in a Paraguayan dungeon. There are people in the outside world who know, who are paying attention, who care."

"Fine," Soledad said, "then what happens when nothing happens?"

"The Secretariat sends the case to an 'adoption group,' a half-dozen or so Amnesty volunteers in another country, never the same one where the victim is. And they keep up the pressure, sometimes for years, asking about their adopted political prisoner—organizing petitions from churches, universities, and professional organizations, enlisting influential people to join the campaign. And as new material comes in about their adopted prisoner, they forward that to the authorities, to let them know they have their own sources of information.

"The fact is that Urgent Action campaigns and adoption groups really do help the prisoners. Compared with other Investigaciones prisoners, they receive a lot better treatment. Sometimes, the government just quietly releases them."

Soledad nodded tentative acceptance.

"In part, it's the telescope phenomenon at work again. The idea is to never let Stroessner forget that he may have the *power* to imprison, torture, and kill. But nothing gives him the *authority* to do so. And it's going to cost him."

12

All during this discourse, I stole glances at Joel and Nidia. In Sajonia, I had my own upstairs set of rooms, with a semiprivate entrance. Even so, we did all live in the same house. The Filártigas could not help noticing the people who, sometimes late at night, climbed the outside stairway to my place. On faith, they accepted my explanation that these visits had to do with my human rights work.

What I neglected to tell the OPM was that I was organizing four other information networks. And, like them, I was instructing these people on how to sift through the blizzard of rumors and pin down the solid facts about human rights violations that Amnesty needed.

There was a group from the church, and another based at the two major universities in Asunción; a third came from the American community; and the last was made up of members of the opposition political party led by my friend Congressman Domingo Laino. Everyone worked on a volunteer basis, often without the knowledge of their bosses, and in some cases, in direct violation of the policies of the group or institution to which they belonged.

I juggled the days and times of our meetings so that no group learned about the others. And I told no one how I got around Investigaciones' scrutiny of mail coming into and leaving Paraguay.

Also, I stayed clear of the Paraguayan human rights NGOs, knowing that they were infiltrated by *pyragués* and that Amnesty would receive their information in any event.

Colonel Bob LaSala sent my reports out of the country by slipping them into the regular Army Post Office mail run. Since the APO goes only to and from the States—there is no service from one foreign country to another—they ended up taking a round-about route to England.

After being sorted out in Miami, the reports went on to Tashy Calway in Massachusetts, an old and dear friend going back to high school days. She made photocopies to save for me. The same was true of other sensitive documents, and my taped interviews. Of course, I could not chance keeping any of these materials in Stroessner's police state.

Tashy forwarded the originals to the drop address in London. Each day, someone from Amnesty picked up the material from abroad, and at the Secretariat the staff would get to work.

Just as I withheld information from my people in Paraguay, London did the same with me. So I had no idea they were pushing to meet the July publication deadline for a special booklet exposing Stroessner's latest wave of human rights violations.

Soledad's voice brought me back to the present. "What is this International League for Human Rights that Congressman Koch refers to?"

"I don't know," I confessed, "and no one here I've talked with does either."

We soon would. The ILHR was planning a high-profile on-site investigation of human rights conditions in Paraguay. Coincidentally, their mission was set for early July, the same month Amnesty would drop its bombshell.

Our ignorance of the ILHR's mission, which was openly being discussed in the United States, had nothing to do with security. The reason was far more mundane. As often as not, information that was public knowledge in the centers of world power simply never found its way to the relative backwater that was Paraguay.

Not that it would have mattered much, even if we had known of the ILHR's upcoming mission. The crisis that exploded in the Filártiga family consumed our every moment. One day—and I do not exaggerate—I could not find the five minutes to go to the bathroom.

13

The day the madness began, the Filártigas got a very late start leaving the clinic in Ybycuí. About three in the morning, as they reached the outskirts of Asunción, Nidia had an anxiety attack, loudly lamenting Joelito's death and all the fearful things that now confronted them.

In the twenty-minute drive through the city to Sajonia, Joel succumbed to his own demons. By the time they turned onto the cobblestone street where we lived, he had also gone over the edge.

"I'll show you there's nothing to fear," he shouted, jerking the pickup to a halt. Leaving its clattering diesel engine running, he grabbed a bar of soap from his medical bag and scrambled over the ornamental wrought-iron fence in front of Peña's house. In bold script, he wrote VIVA JOELITO across the windshield of the police inspector's car.

From the Filártigas' driveway, Joel's ranting penetrated my bedroom. But the angry argument did not wake me. For, like the rest of the family, I no longer slept.

Among the first things I noticed after arriving in Paraguay was that the trauma of Joelito's death and the hyperintensity of the struggle had so profoundly afflicted the Filártigas that they were no longer able to sleep—a condition that my own psyche soon adopted.

For the rest of my stay in Paraguay, sleep, in any conventional sense, became impossible. Most nights I would lie down for a few hours, more to relieve my aching back pain than from fatigue. At best, I reached a light alpha state of relaxation. But I never lost consciousness. Always, I was aware of every mosquito in the room. And there was no groggy waking up. Any sound, no matter how slight, made me instantly and fully alert.

By the time the noisy argument moved inside, Dolly and I were waiting in the living room. Frantically, Nidia tried to tell us what had happened. Joel, still nowhere close to rational, attempted an absurd justification.

"Peña's not the Almighty," he raged. "He's a coward. I heard him moving around inside the house. But he didn't dare come out and face me like a man!

"I did it only to show Nidia that Peña's a coward. To help her overcome her fear!" he insisted.

"You're the crazy one," Nidia shot back. "And you're going to get somebody else killed. Just like you did Joelito!"

Oh shit, I thought, the toothpaste is out of the tube and there is no way we are ever going to get it back in. The unspeakable had been spoken. The enormity of it stunned us. Nidia, Dolly, and I looked at each other in horror.

Joel grasped his chest, gasped for breath, and crumpled to the floor. I carried him to the couch. When he could finally speak, he asked Nidia to get a nitroglycerin tablet from his satchel.

I took in the scene. Filártiga refused to go to the hospital. Nidia and Dolly comforted him, wiping the beads of sweat from his face with a damp cloth. They bemoaned that the shock of Nidia's cutting accusation had triggered a heart attack, just as the California medical report had warned.

But I knew better: The extensive examination Filártiga underwent had detected no heart disease; it was in the hope of giving Joel some protection against being arrested and tortured again that I had persuaded my physician friend to falsify the test results.

It never occurred to any of us how horrendously our plan would backfire.

We had no inkling of Peña's ambitions, his rogue operation. Nor did we know, of course, the tragic irony that Joelito's heart, as is not uncommon among young athletes, was incapable of withstanding the extremes of electric shock torture.

The false medical report was my idea. This was the "mistake" I had alluded to when Nidia was beating herself up for blowing the telephone call with Charo. Sure, Filártiga had enthusiastically agreed to the phony medical report that promised him protection. Yet there was no getting around that it was I who initiated this link in the chain of events that ended up killing Joelito. Logically, I knew we had done nothing intentionally to merit blame. But reason held little sway as I dealt with my guilt.

Already the well-meaning deception gone wrong had cost Joelito's life and resulted in Nidia and Dolly being thrown in jail. Yet the dictatorship had left Dr. Filártiga alone, despite his outrageous provocations. But if they ever found out that he really did not suffer from heart disease. . . .

To pursue the truth, we had to keep up the lie.

14

Watching Joel's wife and daughter minister to him, I felt more the hypocrite than ever. Still, I had doubts. Filártiga might be putting on an act, or his chest pains could be psychosomatic. And, then again, he actually could be having a heart attack.

The tremendous strain of the past months certainly could have done it. Knowing Joel's character, it was inconceivable that he would consciously pull such a cruel hoax. The more I thought about it, the more I became convinced that it really did not matter if it was clinical pathology or a psychologically induced symptom. Real or imagined, Joel was suffering the pains of a coronary seizure.

And now that the evil genie was out of the bottle, there was no going back. By accusing Joel of responsibility for Joelito's murder, from now on it would be fair game, the ultimate weapon to bludgeon him in the emotional maelstrom that was the family's torment.

Already Joel's "lapses of sanity" scared the hell out of me. No doubt the vitriolic accusations to come would drastically inflame his guilt and feed his self-destructiveness. That he would become yet a greater menace to himself, and everyone else around him, seemed inevitable.

I knew that logic stood little chance. Even so, a try seemed better than doing nothing. Once we had all calmed down, I gave it a shot.

"We're not going to help anything by falling into this snake pit and biting each other. This kind of blame game within the family is one that only Peña and his criminal buddies can win.

"Nidia," I said, turning to her, crumpled on the couch next to her prostrate husband. "We all know how outspoken Joel is, but in your heart you know he does not bear culpability for what happened. We all know what it is that gives rise to psychopaths like Peña. That's where the blame rests. It's Stroessner's vicious dictatorship that's responsible for Joelito's death."

Insofar as my plea was factual, it was absolutely correct. But I had skirted the truth: If Dr. Filártiga had not been an active political opponent of the dictatorship, Joelito *would* still be alive.

15

Thankfully, the Filártigas were too befuddled to catch the flaw in logic. Or perhaps they were just too worn out to argue. We went on talking past dawn and well into the morning. I told them of my fears that in the fury of their fights, the accusation for Joelito's death again would be hurled at Filártiga. That I worried he would become ever more erratic, how that could get not only him, but all of us, killed—*and worse.*

Contritely, everyone agreed that it was unconscionable to lay the blame on Joel. Filártiga slowly recovered. The family came together. Nidia could not have been more sincere in her apologies and, with Dolly, vowed never to say such a thing again. And, of course, during the very next family blowout, they both stabbed and twisted that blade of guilt.

16

A few days later, Joel and Nidia were driving past the presidential palace. As they approached the permanent checkpoint, the soldiers of the Batalón Escolta waved them over. That morning an automobile mechanic had told Filártiga how ranking government officials avoided the tedious ID verification conducted by Stroessner's Praetorian guard at the checkpoint.

Without warning Nidia, when they reached the guard post, rather than pulling over as the soldiers directed, Joel ignored them and slowly maneuvered around the barricades. He continued on for another twenty feet to a brightly painted yellow telephone pole, came to a complete stop, and then drove on. Nidia was seized with terror.

When they got back, Nidia managed to tell us about Joel's latest self-destructive flirtation.

"What the hell were you doing?" I exploded, "pulling a suicidal stunt like that?"

"It was an act of defiance. To demonstrate to myself that I'm not afraid," he answered with a shrug, as if that settled it.

"With Nidia right there next to you?" I raged. "What if the mechanic was wrong? What if they arrested you both and got your quick confessions? What about the rest of us?"

Joel sat mutely at the dining room table, refusing to consider, or even acknowledge, that he had done anything amiss. I became even more irate.

"Like a self-centered weakling, you gave in to your pain and guilt. Gambling everything for self-pity. As if you are the only one who matters."

Filártiga's sphinxlike demeanor began to crack. Furious, I pulled out all the stops.

"You'd have destroyed your family. You'd have betrayed me, and the OPM. You'd have lost any chance of gaining support from Amnesty or anyone else. You'd have lost the battle against Peña and Joelito's other murderers. They'd be laughing over our graves."

More doubt showed in Filártiga as he squirmed in the chair. By then I did not give a damn.

"I came to Paraguay to help a friend, a man I admired and respected," I told him. "But after what you did today, I don't see that man anymore. I came here to join your struggle, not to be tortured to death because of your self-indulgence.

"I've learned not to make critical decisions when I'm this furious. So, before leaving your madhouse, I'm going to cool off for a while. But I can't imagine what could change my mind."

I turned to Nidia and Dolly. "If you want to go with me, be ready in an hour."

Our friendship all but over, Joel absorbed what was happening. Drawing upon the inner strength that he found right after Joelito's death, he made an astonishing turnabout.

"There is no time to waste," he said abruptly. His voice held the same authority that so impressed me the day I arrived, when he clinically described the details of Joelito's torture wounds. "We must warn Soledad and the others of the threat I pose!"

17

That evening, Joel, Nidia, and I sat with our OPM friends at the safe house. Step by step, leaving nothing out, we related the series of events leading to the crisis.

"With the pressure the Filártigas have endured," Soledad said to me, "we feared something like this would happen. Actually, it's what I've been wanting to talk to you about.

"We're in a very difficult situation. Joel's the only doctor, and Nidia the only nurse, who will deliver my baby." Soledad exchanged a warm look with them.

International law provides for medical neutrality during times of civil strife. But in Stroessner's Paraguay, that meant nothing.

"Our safety in this house is compromised," Soledad said, no accusation in her voice. "As soon as possible, we must move—to another place unknown to Joel and Nidia."

Speaking directly to Filártiga, she matter-of-factly asked, "Don't you agree?"

"Absolutely," Joel replied. "Sometimes these impulsive emotions overwhelm me. I am a danger to us all. It must be corrected."

No one offered a note of dissent.

"I refuse," he went on, "to continue under these circumstances. Not only should I be disinformed, I demand to be disinformed. Richard will stay in contact. It's the only way."

Before I could protest Filártiga's presumption, Soledad spoke up.

"It's not so simple," she said in a tone that focused everyone's attention. "We have been trying to arrange for a backup house, in the event of such an emergency. But everyone is too scared to accept us. The fact is, we have no place to go."

Soledad's revelation was a blow. We had not realized the gravity of their situation and, by extension, our own. Joel recovered first.

"Then we will find a house to rent for you," he stated.

"Again, I only wish the answer was so easy," Soledad told him. "We can't go out like normal people looking for a house. And you can't do it. The reason we're moving is to disinform you."

I sat on the edge of the chair, forearms resting on my thighs. With my head lowered, I absently studied the random swirls in the floor tiles. All conversation stopped. I became aware of the silence. I looked up. Everyone in the room was staring at me.

This enigmatic Devil Drawing, by Joelito's fifteen-year-old sister Analy, captivated the public.

FIVE

SOME WEEKS LATER, the crisis had passed. The place the OPM settled into—the big house of a former hacienda surrounded by an eight-foot wall—lay so far out in Asunción's urban sprawl that banana trees still crowded along its dirt streets.

My five human rights reporting groups started showing results, their information increasingly more accurate and thorough. And, at the Archives, the historical research was going so well that the OAS extended my grant.

Best of all, though, Joel and Nidia picked up their lives in Ybycuí. At the Clinic of Hope, they instituted "Free Thursdays," an innovation that to this day keeps the memory of Joelito alive.

"It seems redundant," I flippantly commented, when Filártiga told me about it. "You never charge anyone anyway."

"You are missing the point." Feigning exasperation at my density, and unable to conceal a touch of pride, he explained. "Thursdays have become our busiest day. People come not just to honor Joelito. They come to show solidarity. It is a repudiation of the regime.

"Once a week people use their diseased bodies to make a political demonstration at the clinic. And it does not go unnoticed."

Respectfully, I appraised my friend. Filártiga's seemingly innocuous Free Thursdays provided much more than dignified free medical care. It gave his patients the opportunity to express their love for the special young man who had spent his short life with them, whom they considered one of their own. By demonstrating their support for the Filártigas, it offered a relatively safe way of spitting in the dictatorship's eye. And, because Joel and Nidia engineered and participated in the conspiracy, it helped reestablish their bond with the people.

Life almost took on an air of normality. Then, late one afternoon while I was organizing my research note cards on the back patio, the Filártigas came busting in. Excitedly, they told me the fantastic news: A totally unexpected development had brought the struggle back to the fast lane, the one with no speed limit.

1

"After lunch we stopped by my mother's house," Joel began. "An Investigaciones officer sent me a message through an influential friend of hers. He has proof that Peña killed Joelito."

The story unfolded with Nidia's description of how they raced to the downtown office building where the cop moonlighted as a security guard. Joel was so hyped that when he swung into the no-parking zone outside, one tire ended up on the curb. Leaving Nidia to wait in the pickup, he jumped out. As she watched him disappear through the glass doors, Nidia was overwhelmed by a terrible feeling of aloneness.

She barely noticed the police cadet stick the parking ticket under the windshield wiper. When the young man passed her open window and saw her weeping, with genuine concern he stopped to ask, "What is the matter, Señora?"

"I am Joelito's mother," Nidia answered. Over the months, she had found that these four simple words said it all.

"Oh, Joelito's Mamá," the cadet replied, "I'm very sorry, Señora. Many in the police feel the same way." Before moving on, he retrieved the ticket. Through many such small acts of kindness, people expressed their sympathy.

Inside, the burly Investigaciones officer, Jaime Mattos, did not present a simpatico face. Coming straight to the point, he told Filártiga, "Peña made a tape recording while torturing your son."

Hit by the startling news, Joel managed to keep his composure only by focusing on how invaluable such a tape was. We needed evidence to convince Amnesty and the other NGOs that the *Caso Filártiga* was a legitimate human rights case. Never did we expect to find the proverbial smoking gun.

But Mattos refused to give Filártiga the tape recording.

"I tried everything," Joel told me. "I offered him money. Visas for him and his family to go to the United States. Everything. Anything!"

"Mattos wouldn't budge. He said that what Peña did to Joelito was so repugnant it disgusted even him. That it would inflame me beyond reason. That, in my fury, I might do something rash. That he bore a great responsibility and would not give the recording directly to me.

"I knew he was lying. 'Why have you deceived me?' I asked him. 'What is it that you want?'

"And then it came out. He said he would only give the torture tape to an appropriate person," Joel scoffed. "'That way,' he claimed, 'whatever he tells you, is on his head.'

"I laugh in his face. 'Is that it? Is that all you want? Why that's fine. Just fine,' I told him. 'Quite soon, very soon, a not very nice man will be here to see you.' Then I left. I just left."

Joel paused to catch his breath. "Nidia and I came straight back here. I have a plan. There's not a moment to waste! You must go right away!"

"Go where?" I asked, although I was pretty sure.

"To see Mattos," Filártiga replied. As if asking me to run an errand, he went on, "Just act like you're from the CIA and he'll give you the tape."

"Nonsense," I replied. "It's a setup to find out your international contacts. Or they're playing some psychological game with you. Or Mattos is pulling his own scam, like the others."

Since Joelito's murder, the Filártigas had been assailed by a string of slimy characters. One offered to produce an eyewitness, another promised a disgruntled policeman who really knew what happened—all for a price.

"I know, I know," Joel groaned. "But there *is* enormous revulsion over Joelito's murder. It's too much. Maybe this time. . . ."

Shaking my head, I said, "Joel, you're chasing phantoms."

"I'm not a fool!" Filártiga exploded. "You think I don't recognize what you say? It doesn't matter. I must know the truth."

Confronted with Joel's agony, I took a few minutes to think it all over. Stroessner had relegated the trial to the judicial back burner. By mid-June, even the press coverage had cooled. Clearly, the government's strategy was to leave the legal case simmering indefinitely and let public interest fade, until the Filártigas tired of banging their heads against the wall.

By casting the *Caso Filártiga* as a criminal matter, Stroessner muddied the waters enough to create doubt among the international human rights NGOs. Before risking their credibility and committing themselves, they would have to be sure Joelito's murder was politically motivated, and not a crime of passion.

Knowing full well that the odds against us were astronomical, we also knew that Mattos' torture tape was the only game in town.

2

Walking across the ultramodern black granite lobby, a pistol dug into the small of my back and a tape recorder whirled in the inside pocket of my suit coat.

I approached the security station. At first Mattos, engrossed in a paperback with his feet propped up on the desk, failed to notice me. Standing motionlessly, I studied the Investigaciones officer: thick forearms, a scowl under his grungy five-o'clock shadow.

We had never met or, for that matter, ever seen each other. Yet I *knew* this guy. Mattos, this police state thug, was just a grown-up incarnation of the schoolyard bully.

I stood motionlessly until Mattos became aware of my presence. Startled, he sprang to his feet. Glaring at me, he demanded, "What do you want?"

Wearing my diplomatic three-piece costume, I appraised the cop's unkempt appearance, my disapproval conveying his failure to pass muster. I said simply, "Jaime Mattos."

Mattos nodded his massive head, tentatively conceding the initiative.

In a marginally courteous manner, I said, "I am told, Señor Mattos, that you insist upon speaking with me."

Again, he nodded. And I could see him pull his temper under control. It was a revealing display of self-restraint. Here he was, an officer in Stroessner's secret police, accustomed to deference. Obviously, the cop had set up the meeting because he wanted something. Yet, that he would choose to play it safe, contrary to his every impulse, telegraphed his lack of confidence as plainly as if he had sent it over the wire.

Continuing the game of domestication, I dropped my voice. "My time is not unlimited."

To hear me clearly, Mattos either had to strain or ask me to speak up. The cop leaned forward to catch my words—another good sign.

Mattos suggested that we move to a more private place. When he stopped to withdraw his revolver from the desk, a copy of the OPM Wanted Poster caught my eye. Thick black crosses blotted out seven of the photos. Only the faces of Soledad, Salvador, and Francisco remained.

I reached into the draw and withdrew the paper. "Any luck?"

"No, sir. But I keep watching," he replied, sheepishly, almost as if ashamed.

3

From the building's ten-story rooftop, four centuries of Asunción architecture sloped down to the Paraguay River, so mighty that ocean-going vessels traveled its 1,200 miles from the South Atlantic. Just beyond the river's bank the arid, untamed Chaco stretched to the horizon, and on to the Andes.

Ignoring the spectacular view, I leaned against the parapet—positioning Mattos upwind, to catch his words on the cassette recorder—turned to the cop and demanded, "Give me the tape."

"But I don't have it," he protested. "It is in the desk of Pastor Coronel. The *jefe* of Investi—"

"Mierda," I snapped, cutting him off in my most arrogant SS Obergruppenführer impersonation. Strutting to the exit, I growled, "It is as I told Filártiga!"

"No! Please!" he called after me. "Sir. I have heard it myself. Many times. I know everything!"

I stopped. In a half-sigh that made it clear he did not have much time to make his pitch, I said, "Tell me."

"At first, many important people came to the office of Pastor Coronel to hear the recording of Joelito. Naturally, we wanted to hear it, too."

"Naturally," I replied, with a superior's tolerance.

Nervously shifting his weight from one foot to the other, Mattos explained. "Last week a colleague who works there borrowed it.

"We are accustomed to such things," the veteran hurried on. "But, what they did is different. It is repugnant."

"'Repugnant?'" I scoffed. "A routine procedure at Palma Street?"

"But it was not at the headquarters of Investigaciones. There we have proper facilities, experienced people," the cop indignantly protested. "If *I* had conducted the interrogation, it would not have happened. The fools took him to the station in Sajonia. Without even a doctor present!"

I gave Mattos an incredulous look, and nodded disapproval at such an unforgivable lack of professionalism.

"And what did they want from the boy?" I asked.

"Dr. Filártiga, the Christian Peasant Leagues, the OPM. But he knew nothing."

"He could have been protecting his father."

"Impossible! Everyone confesses," Mattos retorted. "He just kept screaming, 'Why are you doing this to me? I do not know anything. Why are you doing this to me?'"

"How long?"

"Well, it is all on one side. Joelito stops about halfway, and then they all begin yelling. So perhaps twenty minutes."

"You know Peña's voice?"

"He was called by name."

Again the cop began shuffling his feet on the heat-reflecting white pebbles of the roof. Mattos was working himself up to it. I gazed at the Chaco.

"It is a disgrace," he blurted. "Peña and his gang killed Joelito out of personal ambition. Not for the Fatherland. It is an insult to us."

4

I raised my finger in the just-a-moment signal. Like virtually every other Latin American country, Paraguay's constitution prohibits capital punishment. Yet everyone knew Investigaciones routinely served the dictatorship through torture and executions. And while the public's repudiation of Joelito's murder had caused an uproar, that could not be what was eating at Mattos.

No. But that his beloved Investigaciones was taking the heat for botching the job, that was something else. The professional derision—and most of all the ridicule—from their rivals in the military, now that would sting. Especially because Mattos and his cronies knew that it was a bum rap.

So, finding the torture tape, this ad hoc cabal of midlevel Investigaciones officers devised a scheme to repair their tarnished prestige and to pin the blunder where it belonged, on Peña and his gang. The riffling of Pastor Coronel's office, however, was a problem. That is where I came in: the appropriate outsider from the U.S. Embassy to blow the whistle. Then, it all could be handled in house, restoring Paraguay's premier institution of terror to its unsullied omnipotence.

"You were right to come to me," I told Mattos. "Such degradation of Investigaciones' authority is unacceptable."

At first Mattos looked perplexed. He had mentioned nothing about Investigaciones' loss of stature. Then he smiled.

"But we must move quickly," I insisted, "before some imponderable creates complications. How soon can you deliver the recording?"

"Well, Señor," he stammered, "that would be very difficult, not to say impossible. To attempt to borrow it again—"

"You failed to make a copy?" I shot back.

"But I have already told you everything. On the grave of my Mother, it is as I have said."

"Without the recording, it all amounts to nothing more than gossip," I berated him. "Do you think Stroessner doesn't already know everything? Without the torture tape, what power do I have to persuade him to sacrifice Peña?"

5

At 10:00 the next day, June 28, Joel charged into my upstairs rooms for the second time that morning.

"Horacio just called," he exclaimed. "Judge Martínez granted our amplification motion. Peña and Juana Villalba, and Jorge and Nery and Charo, have all been charged as codefendants with Duarte for killing Joelito!"

Three hours earlier, Joel had rushed in, and with an air of satisfaction plopped the morning papers on my desk. The International League for Human Rights was sending a fact-finding mission to Paraguay. Drs. Benjamin Stephansky—a Washington insider and JFK's ambassador to Bolivia—and Robert Alexander—the Rutgers University historian—would arrive in a week.

"Quite a coincidence?" Filártiga now said. "It appears that this human rights investigation has captured Stroessner's attention. To buy such costly insurance! Charging Inspector Américo Peña for homicide is not going to set well with the police."

This development had a double edge. It strongly reinforced the *Caso Filártiga's* facade as a criminal trial, further clouding the waters for the ILHR team to see Joelito's murder as a legitimate human rights case. Even so, charging Peña and the others as coconspirators expanded the scope of the legal proceedings.

Also, it was at this time we learned of another "blessing," as Nidia came to call the events and circumstances helping the struggle. Amnesty got out their briefing booklet ahead of schedule. In AI's meticulous fashion, *Paraguay* laid bare the regime's gross human rights violations, drawing worldwide attention to Stroessner's crimes.

And, as if all this was not enough, late the following night, June 29, yet another blessing arrived, literally, at my door. Answering the soft tapping, I found two volunteers from the church human rights group: Sister Graciela—a Paraguayan nun—and Father John Vesey—my missionary friend from the States. In fact, after meeting the OPM fugitives, John had become actively involved in our efforts to help keep them alive.

Father Vesey developed a special relationship with the Filártigas. In countless sessions—both individually and as a group—for years he offered spiritual guidance and compassionate counseling, helping the family work through the insidious web of survivor's guilt that ensnared them.

We exchanged greetings by the fireplace, as Padre Juan and Hermana Graciela chased away Paraguay's winter chill. Then, as if passing the potatoes at the dinner table, Graciela handed me a list containing the names of hundreds of political prisoners.

She, along with the other nuns at the convent, had secretly compiled the fifteen-page document, precisely the kind of information Amnesty needed. Methodically, they had noted the victim's full name, age, sex, profession, and family status, as well as the date and place of their arrest, the location and conditions of their imprisonment, and when available, other relevant facts such as their political affiliation or the self-help organization to which they belonged.

I looked over the material. "Graciela, where did this come from?"

In her unassuming manner, the petite nun explained. "As you know, we are a nursing order. What is not common knowledge is the long-standing arrangement between Archbishop Rolón and President Stroessner that permits us to attend to prisoners—provided we do so discreetly."

"Then why are you giving me this?" I asked, holding up the list.

"Not everyone," she replied, "thinks the suffering of these poor souls should remain unknown. Some have been imprisoned for more than twenty years. All but forgotten."

"Twenty years," I reflected. "Why now?"

"Well, before Padre Juan told us about Amnesty, we had no other way to help them. For the past month," she went on, as if they had done nothing special, "many of us have been working on the list. Every day, each of us memorized the facts about three or four people. Until we had them all."

In the soft firelight, at that moment, to me Graciela looked angelic.

"All? You mean this contains all the political prisoners in Paraguay?"

"Oh, no. Although, almost certainly, it does have everyone here in Asunción. But not in the countryside. And not the many hundreds at the Emboscada concentration camp. We are not allowed in there. Yet."

"Incredible," I mused. John and I momentarily exchanged a worried look.

Graciela must have noticed. "We must be careful," she said. "If the authorities find out, it could cause difficulties."

Now there was an understatement fit to be embroidered and framed.

"Hermana, this information is of incredible value. I'm sure it will be used in the best possible way to help the prisoners. And Amnesty is extremely responsible in handling just such delicate matters. But, they are not infallible. Would it not be prudent to discuss this further with the other Sisters?"

"We have decided," Graciela replied, "to trust in God."

The hour after they left I spent typing a cover letter. Though explaining how the nuns had obtained the prisoner list, I did not give the names of any individuals. I had thought AI's security measures excessive. Now, as I worried about a foul-up, I became a believer.

I removed the screws from the light switch cover and stuffed the papers into the pocket I had hollowed out in the masonry behind the wiring. With luck, first thing in the morning I would find Colonel LaSala and get the list on its way to London.

A few hours later, I swung open the tall metal driveway doors and sat for a moment in the car. It still sported Joelito's Playboy Bunny decal. No one, not even, or especially, Dr. Filártiga ever mentioned scraping it off. Suddenly, I heard the familiar sound of clapping that Paraguayans use, instead of knocking on the door, to announce their presence.

Glancing in the rearview mirror, on the sidewalk was a smiling Bob LaSala. As an act of solidarity—that qualified as another of Nidia's blessings—Bob stopped by the Filártigas about once a week. Always in uniform, driving an official U.S. military vehicle with diplomatic tags, he would arrive toting a bulging briefcase that was mostly filled with old news magazines.

Invariably, when Bob left, his attaché case was noticeably slimmer. The charade, we figured, gave the Investigaciones watchers stationed across the street and their superiors something to ponder.

Now, if we could get ahold of Joelito's torture tape, we could really get their attention.

6

That same evening, I marched through the lobby and took the elevator straight up to the rooftop. Presently, Mattos burst through the door.

"It is impossible to get the tape," he gasped. "Investigaciones is on full alert. Since the day before yesterday. After the news of that human rights mission. The charges against Peña. It is like the *jefes* expect a coup."

"Nonsense," I scoffed. "Get a grip on yourself Mattos."

It had crossed my mind that these new developments might very well cause a hitch. But a coup? No way. Maybe a purge within Investigaciones, a power grab by their institutional rivals. Bob LaSala had explained how Stroessner played the military off against the police, keeping them at each other's throats by rewarding one with a smuggling concession or a shipment of new weapons. By maintaining a rough parity of strength, it kept the traditional rivals too busy worrying about each other to indulge in coup plots against the dictatorship.

Still, the Amnesty pamphlet and the ILHR mission could be just the precipitant for a house cleaning, a way to rid Investigaciones of the zealots responsible for bringing on the troublesome international scrutiny.

The Investigaciones *jefes* knew that Stroessner was perfectly capable of such ruthless maneuvering to safeguard his international standing. After all, he'd just had Peña charged as a coconspirator. By no stretch of the imagination were they overreacting.

"Your *jefes* are overreacting," I told Mattos. "They're only concerned about a turf battle with the military. They've no interest in you or the torture tape. You're acting like an old woman."

Before leaving to meet Mattos, we had figured that at best there was a fifty–fifty chance of actually getting the recording. Everything would have had to click perfectly over the past few days.

But the dread in Mattos' face now made that all irrelevant. He wanted out.

"This is precisely the type of imponderable that I warned you about," I berated him, as if it was all his fault. "Now when will you make the duplicate?"

"We must wait. Two or three weeks," he equivocated.

"I am beginning to suspect that you are insincere," I replied with a menace that was coming all too easily. "If I become convinced of it, it will go badly for you."

More confused than concerned, the Investigaciones cop asked, "Why do you threaten me? It is not as if Joelito was a person of consequence."

I turned away, concentrating on the *SS Asunción* as two tugs nudged the Paraguayan merchant vessel into its berth, until I had it under control.

"That is not the issue," I said. "You see, I would prefer to take down Peña. But you will do nicely. Either way, it is an acceptable operation."

"An acceptable operation?" Mattos stammered.

"From the moment you disclosed your conspiracy," I told him, "the only question has been if it would be Peña—or you."

"Me? But why me?" he gasped. "You gain nothing."

"Do you think Pastor Coronel would be ungrateful to learn of your treachery?"

"You would do that to me?" the cop exclaimed, as if I owed him something.

"Ask yourself," I replied, "if you were in my position, what would you do?"

With a jerking motion, Mattos twisted, looking down and away.

"Jaime," I said, using his given name for the first time, "Jaime, you know my sympathies have always been with you. I am sure that in a week or two, you and your friends will solve this small problem."

As soon as I entered the Filártigas' house, they knew it had gone wrong. The postmortem took less than a half hour.

"At least the door is left open," Filártiga reflected philosophically.

7

After lunch the next day, Joel and I had just settled in with the afternoon papers when he roared, "Gorostiaga is Peña's lawyer!"

"Gorostiaga?" I asked.

"José Emilio Gorostiaga is the best-connected, highest-paid criminal lawyer in Paraguay. An important member of Stroessner's inner circle.

"On all major cases he 'consults,' with," Joel paused to get the wording just right, and went on to mimic the dictator's full, formal title as it was used to open the nightly news broadcasts, "with *His Excellency, General of the Army, Commander and Chief of the Armed Forces, and President of the Republic, Don Alfredo Stroessner.*

"Gorostiaga *never* loses. That is why he commands astronomical fees," Filártiga stormed. "And Peña does not have a peseta to his name."

"So that's how Stroessner's solving the credibility problem with the police," I said. "He set it up. Probably even before having Peña and the Villalbas charged."

Evidently, to impress the ILHR team with a show of activity, Judge Martínez ended the months of judicial purgatory by having Peña give a deposition the very same day he was named as a coconspirator. But the inspector merely repeated his original April 2 testimony: Awoken by the sounds of a fight, he reached Duarte's bedroom to find Joelito dead, so he called the police.

Charo had long since disappeared without giving her deposition. As for Juana Villalba and her sons Jorge and Nery, the court got around their depositions with transparent complicity.

On the day each was scheduled to depose, their lawyer would claim that his client could not appear because he or she had taken ill, or had to work that day, or some other nonsense. Accepting these pretexts, Martínez simply rescheduled for a later date, when the farce was played out again.

The International League for Human Rights team arrived on July 6. A few days later, Colonel LaSala and I arranged to spend an evening at Bob's house with Ambassador Ben Stephansky and Professor Robert Alexander. I explained the lengths to which the regime went to present the *Caso Filártiga* as an ordinary criminal matter, instead of the human rights case it really was. Giving them the color photos of Joelito's tortured body, I ran through a simplified version of the complex story. As expected, the evidence convinced them the police had tortured Joelito to death. And, as I had suspected, they refused to touch it.

Ambassador Stephansky candidly explained. "We can't include the *Caso Filártiga* in our report. It could jeopardize the overall credibility of the mission. The extent of the cover-up, and especially these new codefendants, creates too much doubt. I know that's of small comfort to the Filártiga family. But there you have it."

In contrast, they reacted to Bob's detailed exposition of Paraguayan Army human rights violations with the enthusiasm of a couple of gold miners who had struck the mother lode. They never expected such a bonanza of inside information. And, except for Colonel LaSala—the three-tour Green Beret who had come to oppose the Vietnam War—would not have come close.

8

For years, Bob had tried working within the system to cut off U.S. military aid to the thugs in Paraguayan Army uniforms. As LaSala related one atrocity story after the next, Professor Alexander took notes furiously.

In the Latin American tradition, Paraguay's Army divided its commands by provinces. "The provincial commanders," Bob told them, "wield life-and-death power. They are virtual warlords, with their own private graveyards."

He described how one colonel confiscated for himself thousands of acres of pasture and farmland, cleared from the jungle over five years by a cooperative of peasants families. "He simply sent in a company of drunken soldiers and massacred the 'communists.'"

Another example involved how three rum factories hired the local commander to assassinate the "subversive" leaders of another self-help group. "Traditionally," Bob explained, "the distilleries hold the peasants in perpetual debt. Fixing prices so low that they are forced to borrow at outrageous interest rates to be able to plant their sugarcane crop. The Christian Peasant Leagues stepped in and organized a half-dozen families. Taught them basic accounting, provided start up loans to purchase vehicles, that sort of thing. The cooperative broke the 'business' cycle by transporting their molasses to the neighboring valley, where they received 30 percent more. And that was it."

LaSala went on for several hours, ending with a scathing overview of U.S. military aid. "Stroessner manipulates our assistance programs for his own ends. And, we turn a blind eye to his atrocities because he plays the international communist card. I've been here three years, and I *know* that's bullshit.

"The Paraguayan Army isn't a military organization. It's an internal police force. Look at their wish list," the professional soldier pointed out. "They want police equipment, antiriot gear, plexiglass shields, CS gas grenade launchers.

"You know that Congress specifically prohibits the funding, equipping, or training of foreign police forces. Yet, that's precisely what we're doing, under the guise of our military assistance programs, for Stroessner's peasant beaters."

"So, Colonel," Stephansky asked, "what would you have us do?"

"The same thing I say every Monday at the embassy's country team meetings," LaSala told him. "Immediate and total termination of all military aid."

The ILHR representatives considered all that Bob had revealed. "We are in your debt, Colonel," the Ambassador finally said. "The material you have provided us on the Paraguayan military will immeasurably strengthen our findings. The matter of our military assistance, however, . . ."

The qualifier hung in the air.

"However," Stephansky continued a bit uneasily, "the corruption of U.S. military aid programs. That is a different animal. In a way, it is not dissimilar from the *Caso Filártiga*."

As he spoke, he discreetly flipped the photo of Joelito's corpse face down on the coffee table. Alexander, I noticed, had already turned his over.

"It's not that I question you. I know it's true," the Ambassador told Bob as he rose from his chair. "Hell, I've known about our support of your 'peasant-beating warlords with their private graveyards' all of my diplomatic career."

Bob shot a sharp, reappraising look at the diplomat.

"In fact," Stephansky continued, unperturbed, "it is one of our open secrets. Thousands directly participate in the hypocritical circumvention of our laws. Not only at State and the Pentagon, but Congress itself. And every occupant of the White House."

"Then why hasn't it been exposed?" Bob challenged.

"Oh, it has. Many times," he said. "Speeches, books, documentaries."

"So what's the problem?"

"What's the problem?" the Ambassador rhetorically repeated. "Propping up tyrants in the name of fighting communism is a cornerstone of U.S. foreign policy. Has been since before the cold war began. It's supported by the Democrats. It's supported by the Republicans. And that makes it state policy.

"*That's* the problem."

9

Stephansky and Alexander did not try to crack the U.S. military aid nut. In their press releases, congressional testimony, and the ILHR published report, however, they did do a first-rate job of unmasking many of the long-overlooked atrocities in Stroessner's fiefdom.

Indeed, when the issue of *Time* magazine reporting their findings arrived at the Asunción airport, the regime promptly confiscated every copy.

Actually, the General's troubles began even while the ILHR team was still in Paraguay. At first, the coconspirator charges against Peña and the others raised people's hopes that the truth of Joelito's murder would be clarified. Then, with the appointment of Gorostiaga as Peña's lawyer, it all became apparent for the sham that it was.

Stepping up their campaign, the Filártigas spoke out more fearlessly than ever. At the memorial Masses, and anywhere else they could draw an audience, they defiantly denounced the judicial corruption and the continuing cover-up.

The speed and fervor that public outrage escalated caught Stroessner off guard. Apparently to show there was nothing to hide, Stroessner lifted the press ban on the *Caso Filártiga*.

On Sunday, July 11, a few days before the ILHR team left Paraguay, *La Tribuna* came out with the full-page article, "The Questions That Await Answers." Touching off a fierce press war, other mainstream papers began publishing hard-hitting pieces of their own.

In the coming months, the turnaround in the establishment press legitimized the *Caso Filártiga*. The saturation coverage made it acceptable, almost required, that even the upper social echelons express an opinion. Of course, unlike the masses, they did not condescend to read *Aquí*—except while sitting on the throne, if judged by the regularity with which I found the tabloid tucked away in their bathrooms.

Two weeks after its initial story, *La Tribuna* again pulled off a scoop. Titled "When Drawings Speak," the centerfold feature in its July 25 Sunday supplement juxtaposed Filártiga's poems and drawings.

One showed two torturers—one bearing an unmistakable resemblance to Peña—whips at the ready, standing over a prostrate young man. Below, the caption decried how they killed not only the boy but also his dreams and hope-filled future. Alongside was a poem by Dr. Filártiga:

TO ANOTHER JOEL

On a Monday, 29 of March
the most sinister and blackest of nights
another way of being Joel
ceased to exist.
An endless journey of torment.
Youth cut off
cruelly ended
by the bearers of death and nothingness.
Others will be what you could not become:
Soldiers of a New Dawn.
Joel, your father, another Joel but
Joel just the same.

A fifth Filártiga drawing was Analy's Devil Drawing that Nidia had salvaged: a feathered demon, flying into the foreground on a mission of vengeance, its talons clutching a three-pronged killing spear. Overlaying the creature's otherwise emotionless features is a disturbing veneer of self-doubt that seems to question its grim task.

"What inspiration explains this devil's contradictory impression, captured by the sister of Joelito, Analy, a week after the death of her brother?" the caption asked. "There is something tremendously tragic in this monster, something that gives it a vengeful Fury that cries out for Justice in this brutal crime."

At fifteen, Analy's adolescent innocence—that not even the devil can abide such a travesty as killing Joelito—captivated people, embedding in their minds a haunting image of injustice.

But if Stroessner had lifted the wraps off the *Caso Filártiga*, any criticism that threatened to smear his international image remained strictly taboo. When the political opposition papers published excerpts from the ILHR report, soldiers marched into their plants, seized the offensive copy, and smashed the presses.

Only the Catholic weekly managed to get out some of the news. *Sendero* boldly summarized the ILHR findings in its article "International Interest in Our Prisoners." Reluctant to break the historical, if strained, ties with the church, Stroessner let it pass.

That, however, was the only exception. A friend's metaphor eloquently captured the oppression of Stroessner's obsession when she said, "Opposing injustice in Paraguay is like screaming in a locked room."

10

For two hours the tall, well-dressed man waited his turn among the peasants outside the Clinic of Hope. Only when his number was called did he enter Dr. Filártiga's office.

Once alone, he introduced himself as Señor Velázquez. Pointing out the window to a state-owned jeep, he explained that, although he worked for the government, his visit was personal.

"So, what can I do for you?" Filártiga inquired warily.

"Hopefully, it is I that can do something for you, Doctor," the stranger replied. "Purely by coincidence, I learned that certain high officials have decided your activities are no longer tolerable. If you continue, they are determined to stop you. One way or the other."

"And what does that mean? 'One way or the other'?"

"Please, listen," Velázquez pleaded. "If you withdraw now, there will be no further reprisals. Dr. Filártiga, you must drop the case."

"Or?" Joel asked.

"This is very difficult for me. I knew Joelito. So, when I heard what they intend to do, I came right away," Velázquez stammered. "Doctor, this is not a fight with Duarte, or with Peña, but with the entire police. You can never win."

The ritual complete, Joel rose and circled his cluttered desk. "Tell your masters you have delivered their message. Tell them it changes nothing."

Before Velázquez reached the door, his conscience got to him. "Doctor, if there was anything I could do, I would," he said honestly. "Believe me."

"I believe you, my son," Filártiga replied. "They gave you a dirty job."

In Stroessner's Paraguay, there existed a protocol for death threats. Those received over the phone or in the mail presented the least danger. Most often they were meant to instill fear, unnerve the target, disrupt the family's life.

The most serious of all came from the friendly messenger. With sympathetic commiseration, he would deliver the warning, attempting to convince the victim to capitulate.

As soon as Stroessner's emissary had left, Dr. Filártiga canceled the rest of his appointments and took off for Asunción. During the drive, he composed an open letter, which Nidia wrote down and edited. The next day, August 6, it ran as a paid *solicitada* in *ABC Color*:

TO THE PUBLIC

Once again I call upon the moral support of the people of my country.

We continue to receive repeated death threats. They usually come by way of anonymous letters and telephone calls. But recently, an unknown man confronted me face-to-face. He said that if I did not abandon the case, I would be killed.

Regardless of the mortal danger to me and my family, I will resolutely pursue these painful efforts until the truth is publicly known about the hidden circumstances of the sadistic torture and death of my young son. . . .

We still remain hopeful that those who exercise power will take the necessary steps to finally clear up this brutal crime.

We, and everyone else who knew Joelito, plead to God Almighty for such a resolution. Only by bringing down the full weight of the law upon the truly guilty, will the thirst for justice of countless mothers, anxious to know the truth of what happened, be quenched.

I also take this opportunity to ask for a guarantee of safety for Hugo Derlis Duarte, who is another victim of this tragedy. The murderers of my son are using him as an alibi to cover-up their actions. Even though he is in the Tacumbú Penitentiary, his death would frighten the other witnesses from testifying truthfully.

Moreover, we ask for proof that María del Rosario Villalba de Duarte [Charo], is still alive. We have a letter from her saying that she wants to tell the court what really occurred, and identify the true perpetrators of this atrocious crime.

Joel Holden Filártiga Ferreira
Identification Certificate #181,729

Why Stroessner decided to kill Filártiga at this time—four months after Joelito's murder, a month after rejuvenating the trial by charging Peña and the Villalbas, three weeks after the ILHR team departed Paraguay, and just when the establishment media coverage gave the *Caso Filártiga* a shot in the arm—became quite the topic of conjecture.

People argued their favorite theory. The prevailing one held that Stroessner had allowed matters to get out of hand, and was now repairing the damage. No one doubted the seriousness of a friendly death threat visit. What made this one especially interesting was Filártiga's refusal to cave in.

It was time to let Amnesty know what was happening.

11

Over the past weeks, Joel and I had spent countless hours sorting through the information surrounding Joelito's murder. Separating facts and reasonable deductions from rumors and unsubstantiated inferences, we ended up with something approximating an intelligible account of the *Caso Filártiga*.

The night after the Filártigas arrived in Asunción, I conducted a long interview with Joel. The whole family pitched in putting together the packet of materials: We dubbed Filártiga's ninety-minute taped interview, copied the *solicitada*, collected a selection of newspaper articles showing the court's corruption, and put together a full set of color photos portraying Joelito's brutalized body. First thing in the morning, Bob LaSala made sure it was sent.

Without Mattos' torture tape, though, we did not hold out much hope that Amnesty would actively take up the case. As when I sent them our résumés before coming to Paraguay, however, at least AI would have the basic information at hand in the event of an emergency.

12

The Filártigas stayed on in Asunción. Anxiously awaiting the showdown, it seemed like the capital held its collective breath. People overflowed the daily Masses celebrated for Joelito. Joel, Nidia, and Dolly denounced the latest outrages. With each day that the Filártigas pushed—some said provoked—the regime, the tension grew.

At last, precisely one week after Joel's *solicitada* appeared, the confrontation came to a head. On the night of August 13, three highly placed government officials arrived in Sajonia. Old friends of Filártiga's mother Lidia, they all had known Joel since childhood.

"My dear Joel," the leader of the delegation, a distinguished man in his fifties, announced with satisfaction, "we've come to put your mind at rest."

"All a dreadful misunderstanding," he assured Filártiga, "the unfortunate excess of an overzealous coreligionist. Nothing to concern yourself about."

And with this second, unheard of, friendly visit, it was over.

We did not complain, but it did cause us to wonder. As we gathered around the dining room table, Filártiga asked, "Why would Stroessner rescind my execution order?"

"Your uncompromising reaction?" I ventured. "The *solicitada*, your denunciations at the Masses, the enormous support of people?"

Joel pondered this for some time before speaking. "Yes. And to Stroessner such irrational behavior would be beyond his comprehension."

Picking up on Joel's line of thought, I added, "To a dictator who rules by terror, the idea of placing conviction above self-preservation wouldn't add up. It sure could have caused him second thoughts."

Filártiga nodded pensively. "Then, too, there is your unexplained presence, living here. Bob Garrison's trip to Ybycuí. And Colonel LaSala's visits. All tying us somehow with the U.S. Embassy.

"He might fear that our 'inexplicable' actions are in reality a show of strength. Of our international support. And that my disappearance or death would create a greater problem than it resolved.

"Yes," Joel concluded, "Stroessner's preoccupation with his international image could be sufficient for him to err on the side of caution."

13

Ironically, instead of resulting in death, the dictator's threat quite possibly saved two lives.

Normally, Joel and Nidia spent weekdays at the clinic, an eighty-mile drive from the capital. When the time came, the OPM was to place a call to the telephone kiosk in Ybycuí, telling Filártiga that his mother had injured herself. The coded message, of course, was to let them know that Soledad had gone into labor.

But everything happened too fast. It would have been next to impossible for the Filártigas to have made it. Only because they already were in Asunción did they manage to reach the safe house in time. Within minutes of arriving, they had sized up the situation and begun preparations for the cesarean section.

Previously, I had seen how Nidia coolly anticipated Dr. Filártiga's needs, allowing him to totally concentrate on an operation. This time, because of my minor role helping out, I had an up-close view of their display of superbly honed professionalism. Their symbiosis all but transcended working as a team; they almost seemed to function as a single entity.

"Richard, quickly bring two 300-milliliter packets of plasma from—" Dr. Filártiga began, breaking off to staunch a gush of blood.

"—the refrigerator," Nidia finished. "The ones on the bottom. They are no longer frozen. She's lost so much blood already. Tell Salvador—"

"and Francisco to come. Now!" Filártiga interjected, with no discernible interruption to his work. "We're going to run out of plasma and will have to use whole blood. They know what to do."

"Soledad is AB so there won't be any problem but—" Nidia started, stopping to slap a surgical clamp into Filártiga's outstretched hand, "she's going to need every drop," Joel finished, setting the clamp without lifting his eyes.

And so it went.

Soledad and the baby came through the operation in fine shape. In the following weeks, she rapidly recuperated while her daughter enjoyed robust health. We all spent the time in blissful ignorance of the curveball speeding our way.

14

It hit us near the end of August. About two in the morning, the sounds of conversation drifted up to me from downstairs. I stayed put. If it concerned me, they would let me know.

Fifteen minutes later, I opened my door to Soledad, Salvador, and Francisco, who stood in the shadows of the outside stairway. I hustled them in from the cold winter night. Soon Joel and Nidia joined us.

Coming to the Filártigas' house anytime, especially at this late hour, could only mean trouble. The only question was how bad.

"It's very bad," Soledad said. "Around eight tonight, I mean last night, I had to go out to get some personal things at the local store."

I suppressed a moan. In Stroessner's chauvinistic Paraguay, even wives would never think of asking their husbands to pick up sanitary napkins. Any man making such a purchase would attract notice.

"Anyway, a cop who knew me came in. A couple of years ago, I was taken in a general sweep by Investigaciones. They arrested so many people, we couldn't all fit in the downtown headquarters. So some of the women were sent to local police stations.

"For two days, we waited our turn to be interrogated. All the while, this strange cop kept looking us over. Not that he mistreated us." Soledad said.

"What's his name?" I asked.

"We never learned his name. Only that he's called Ganso. Because he looks like a goose, with his long neck and all.

"Tonight he pretended not to recognize me," she explained. "But I saw his startled look."

The fire lit the room. Oddly, the same soft light that gave Sister Graciela an angelic glow now harshly highlighted Soledad's worried face.

"Salvador was covering me from across the street," she went on. "I told him what happened right away and we followed Ganso to his house. Then hurried back to our place, packed up everything, took it to a safe place. And warned others to take precautions. And came here."

Soledad's mother took in the baby.

"The way we figure it," Salvador picked up, "the cop will do one of two things. If he informed Investigaciones, the barrio's already cordoned off and they're raking every house. Or, he may try to be a hero, and find our house on his own."

"Either way," Soledad spoke directly to me, "you are compromised. Eventually Investigaciones will find the house. It is leased to you. And, because you live here, Joel and Nidia will also suffer."

At that moment, more than the fear, I felt an irrational rage at the stupidity of it all: Sanitary napkins!

"There's no time to waste," she said in her *comandante* voice. "The police could show up here at any minute. First we must get Analy and Dolly to the safety of their grandmother's house. Then we'll find refuge."

The eight of us left immediately in Filártiga's two vehicles. After dropping off Analy and Dolly, we went to the house of an OPM comrade.

Instead of safe haven, though, we found there was no room at the inn.

15

David, an agronomist in his twenties, openly wrestling with his conscience, appealed for our understanding.

"It's impossible," he told Soledad, standing on his doorstep. "Your vehicles alone will give you away. And my children will tell their friends about the strangers who came in the middle of the night.

"Since the repression, people have changed. My neighbors never would have helped the dictatorship," he protested. "But now. Now just an anonymous call denouncing them for failing to inform any unusual occurrence, and—"

David stood squarely in the doorway, fingers brushing his uncombed hair, unconsciously blocking passage into his house.

"You can't stay here. Investigaciones will have us all before this day is half-over," he said. "Soledad, I have been an OPM militant for four years. You know that I'm no coward. If there was any way. . . ."

For no apparent reason, other than unmitigated frustration, he turned around in a full 360-degree circle. "If it were just me," David pleaded. "My family."

With forced resolve, he said, "Forgive me." And, turning his back on Soledad, he closed the door.

Before dawn, four more OPM comrades had turned us away.

The months of repression had taken a heavy toll on the OPM. The police had killed Soledad's husband, and hundreds more. And now five comrades-at-arms had abandoned us. After years of trusting each other with their lives, they had crumbled, betrayed their ideals. And us. For all knew that to give us refuge was tantamount to a death sentence— *and worse.*

Each refusal stripped away a layer of our own beliefs; each closed door squelched another part of the truths we counted upon. By the fifth time, it might as well have been the five hundredth: Beyond psychological devastation, our value systems collapsed.

It was in this mindset that, shortly before sunrise, we ended up at Asunción's central plaza. The Plaza Uruguaya—surrounded by the gaudy Hotel Guaraní, Paraguay's Baroque central bank building, and other garish monuments of the regime—sat in the very heart of Stroessner's capital. It would have been safer to stop anywhere else. It was also irrelevant.

16

Perception took on an almost supernatural lucidity. And knowing it would be us who determined the when, the where, and the how greatly simplified matters. To this final degree, we controlled our fate.

I had no desire to eke out an extra day or two by playing the fox in the Investigaciones' hunt. We all felt the same.

Other than the handguns we all carried, except for Nidia who always refused any weapon, our armory consisted only of two U.S. M-16 folding-stock rifles.

Calmly, we prepared. Dr. Filártiga reached into his medical bag and gave us each a yellow tablet.

"What?" Soledad asked with detachment.

"Cyanide."

"Thanks," she said sincerely. Everyone else nodded.

After a moment, Filártiga again reached into his bag and gave us each a second pill.

"Why?" Soledad queried, in the same distant tone.

"Keep them in opposite pockets. If one arm is immobilized," he said reasonably.

Again, we all nodded.

The predawn light began to illuminate the Plaza, vendors arrived to set up their stands. Still no sign of the police. Conversation had ceased, everyone enveloped in their own timelessness.

Abruptly Joel bolted upright. Looking at Nidia he cried, "Mirtha!"

"Mirtha! Yes, Papi," Nidia exclaimed, "Mirtha!"

"Follow us in the pickup," he ordered the OPM people in the back seat.

I knew Filártiga's cousin, Mirtha Ayala, who lived just three blocks from us in Sajonia. And while she frequently stopped by the house, she knew nothing of our OPM involvement.

At twenty-five, an attractive widow with two children, Mirtha despised the dictatorship. She also could be pretty spacey. No one questioned Mirtha's commitment, but the militant opposition groups mostly assigned her peripheral tasks, such as preparing and distributing leaflets.

When we reached Mirtha's house, the rest of us waited outside while Joel and Nidia went in. Filártiga began explaining our situation, "We are six people running from the police. The two of us, Richard and the three OPM leaders. It is very dangerous to—"

"Hurry Papi," Mirtha interrupted, "bring everyone inside."

17

Sunlight filtered through the light fabric of the drawn drapes. In our heightened state of awareness, the dimly lit living room radiated an intimate, nestlike aura of safety.

For the first time since the crisis hit, we let our guard down. However, beyond the welcome of Mirtha's refuge, everyone knew that it was far from over.

"Before we can even begin to develop a plan," Joel said to me, his meaning obvious, "we must know what is going on with Ganso."

Three hours later, furious with myself and everyone else, I was back from reconnoitering the barrio. I had learned that in good part we had fabricated the crisis ourselves. I had even stopped at the Archives, to fully think things through, before returning.

"Everything out there is normal," I announced. "No police—"

"That means Ganso's looking for the house on his own," Francisco broke in. "We can still stop him!"

"And just how are you going to do that?" I retorted.

"This is no time for sarcasm," Salvador said, backing up Francisco. "We must kill him. And you know it. If we move fast, you might even be able to resume your normal lives. Not as fugitives. Like us, surviving from day to day."

"I'll have no part of cold-blooded murder!" Joel's voice boomed.

While Filártiga's reaction caught the OPM leaders unprepared, to me it came as no surprise. I had seen him refuse offers to kill Peña. Most amounted to little more than bravado, expressions of spontaneous outrage. During a trip to Argentina, however, in an unsuccessful attempt to obtain identification papers for our OPM friends, there was no doubt.

The men we met with there, both distant cousins of Filártiga, had become hardened partisan fighters in the insurrection against the military dictatorship. They proposed sending a "technician" to Paraguay to kill Peña; there was no question of either their will or their ability. Assassinations on both sides had become routine in Argentina's "dirty war." The very insignificance they placed upon dispatching Peña made their proposition ring with the terrible timber of truth.

Francisco was the first to recover from Joel's outburst. "What happens when they find out about you and Nidia and Richard and Mirtha? And that's only to start. How do we justify the torture and death of the people we will betray? Because we ourselves will . . ." His voice died on his lips.

"Francisco's right," Soledad concurred. "We cannot condemn others because we lack the courage to prevent it. There is no other way."

"Ganso's not a threat anymore," I said. "If he ever was. In our stupid panic, we missed something big." Damn, that came out sharper than I had intended. "Look, there's no police raking. So he didn't tell Investigaciones. And it no longer makes sense for him to be looking for you."

"Why do you say that?" Soledad demanded.

"Because the train has left the station."

18

Filártiga picked up on what was going on. After protesting the killing of Ganso, he had withdrawn. Now, he keenly watched the action unfold.

I was about to show up our collective incompetence, a tricky proposition. But I was in no mood to coddle anyone, most of all myself.

"The train has left the station?" Soledad snapped. "What does that mean?"

"To our incredible good fortune," I replied testily. "Ganso is a very, very rare bird. Incidently, his name is Ramón Augustín Bautista."

Soledad offered an indifferent shrug.

"According to Alonzo—the owner of the store where you ran into your old friend—Ganso's quite an eccentric. A homebody who spends his time puttering around his house, doting on his three kids.

"Ganso is known for his lack of ambition." I turned to Salvador. "He is not part of Investigaciones. And in ten years as a precinct cop, he's been only promoted once. And, Alonzo says, other police never visit him."

Salvador showed no more interest than Soledad.

"Now, Señora Ganso is something else. She's full of ambition. Runs a small business out of their house, rip-off copies of designer clothes. Alonzo thinks it's disgracefully funny that a woman earns more money than her husband. Ganso's the laughingstock of the barrio."

In the hours since we settled in at Mirtha's living room nest, the initial sense of safety had slowly worn off. Yet, even among our tense exchange, there still remained something of a sedate residue.

"Interesting," Soledad conceded, settling back into the couch while remaining sharp eyed.

"I used the same story about delivering a package to Ganso from his brother in New York with the kids playing soccer in the street, that going to a cop's house made me a little nervous. They cracked up and ran off to Ganso's place, shouting insults."

"Interesting," Soledad replied, still unimpressed.

"Yes, well, there you have it," I told them.

Their irritability ratcheted up a notch closer to hostility. Except for Joel. A glint flashed in his eyes.

"And that is your 'something big?'" Soledad exclaimed.

"That's it," I assured her. "There it is."

Soledad shook her head, gave Salvador and Francisco a despairing look. Their patience as exhausted as their minds, they were in no condition to put the pieces together. It would not be long before they began to see my fractiousness as Yanqui arrogance. And I still felt like biting the head off a chicken.

Filártiga sidled up to me. "Joel, I don't think I can do it."

"No," he said, "I do not think you can."

19

Glowering at the world from behind my grump, I watched as Dr. Filártiga administered a dose of humility to the young revolutionaries.

"Assassinating Ganso now would be the biggest mistake we can make," Joel told them. "It will guarantee the full attention of Investigaciones."

"And if we do not kill him," Salvador countered, "what's the difference?"

"There no longer is any reason to kill Ganso. His only opportunity to benefit from spotting Soledad was last night, immediately after seeing her. Now he gains nothing. The train has left the station."

They stared stone-faced at him. I stared stone-faced at them.

Filártiga went on. "Because he is a cop, Ganso cannot claim the reward himself. But not so his Señora. If he had told her last night she would have told Investigaciones she had seen Soledad. And the police would be raking the barrio right now. But they are doing nothing. Ganso did not tell his wife. He did not tell anyone. And he is not going to."

"He still could be looking for the house on his own. To be a hero," Salvador said.

Filártiga shook his head. "He has no idea Richard leased it and would lead to us. So what could he expect to find? Another abandoned OPM safe house."

"No," Joel said. "I would not be concerned even if he had seen you sitting on the front porch. Because Ganso intentionally gave you the time to get away."

Filártiga's startling conclusion focused the full attention of our OPM friends. Good job old friend, I thought. Never could I have come close to establishing your nonthreatening rapport.

"Perhaps he is a truly contented man," Joel went on, "who treasures his family. And just wants to be left alone. Certainly he is not the fool people take him for.

"Ganso knew that by doing nothing, he was sending you a message."

"A message?" Soledad queried.

"Exactly. A proposal for a truce," Filártiga said. "That everyone forget the entire incident. That is the way our eccentric Ganso sees as the best chance to protect what he values most—his home and family."

The room broke out in a gaggle of cross-talk. When we finally wound down, Soledad summed up. "But to be certain, we must continue to watch the barrio."

20

"And until we are absolutely sure," Soledad reminded us, "we remain six hunted people without refuge."

"I will send my children to their grandparents' house," Mirtha offered. "You can stay here."

No one wanted to place Mirtha in such peril. Besides, if the Ganso hypothesis proved true, our situation amounted to more of an inconvenience than a crisis. Even so, as a basic security precaution we decided it would be best to split up.

The Filártigas stayed with the same friends who had sheltered Nidia and Dolly while they eluded Peña's arrest warrant. Soledad chose to remain with Mirtha for a few days. After months of hiding out with men, she welcomed the female companionship, especially that of another mother.

Salvador and Francisco asked me to bring them to the house of another OPM militant. Reluctantly, I complied. But their comrade took them in. Evidently, two people rather than six, arriving in the afternoon instead of the dead of night and without a vehicle, made all the difference. Sister Graciela arranged a place for me at the convent.

That first week, with the help of OPM comrades—including all five of the people who had turned us away—someone checked out Ganso's barrio several times a day.

With the passage of each uneventful day our confidence grew, until the last vestige of doubt vanished. Not long after, we found another house for the OPM leaders. By the end of August, as absurd as it may sound, life had returned to normal.

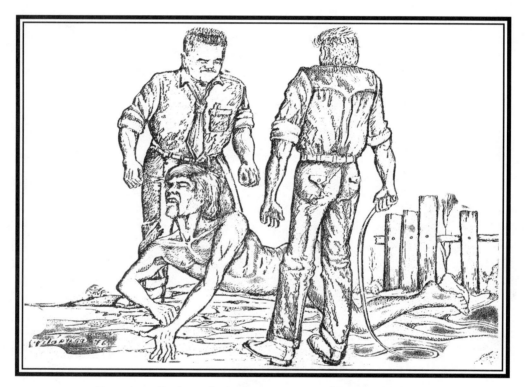

Inspector Peña and another torturer whipping Joelito.

SIX

EVEN IF DUARTE CONFESSES, so what?" I asked Horacio Galeano Perrone as we drove to the courthouse on the morning of September 1. "What does it matter?"

"Actually, from a legal perspective, it opens up quite a range of options," Filártiga's lawyer explained. "If Judge Martínez accepts Duarte's 'confession,' he could sentence him to prison. And drop the charges against Peña and the Villalbas.

"Or, I suppose, he could even rule Joelito's killing a justifiable homicide—and dismiss the charges against Duarte as well.

"You are aware that Paraguayan law exonerates a husband who encounters his wife with a lover, and kills either, or both, in a passionate rage," he mused. "Though I can't think of the last time any court made such a decision."

By the end of August, public disaffection had again brought the *Caso Filártiga* back to center stage, and Hugo Duarte was ordered to complete his interrupted deposition.

"But, if it's public pressure over the manipulation of the trial that's forced Duarte's deposition," I reasoned, "such a transparent ruse would only make things worse."

"Just so," Horacio agreed, "Which is why I think it probable Stroessner will not simply offer up Duarte as a scapegoat. Should the court not accept his 'confession,' the trial simply continues on, without dropping charges against the coconspirators. It would be unnecessary to sentence Duarte and alienate the police, who he is protecting. And yet, there would be a show of movement in the trial, soothing the public."

However, Duarte's team of lawyers—led by his father, Pedro Duarte—apparently sold Stroessner on a last-minute rewrite of the script. They contended that Dr. Filártiga's "disruptive insults" intimidated their client, preventing him from freely testifying, and refused to let Duarte be deposed.

Their argument was not without merit. Shortly after the trial began in April, while on the stand, Duarte boasted that through his prowess in hand-to-hand combat, he alone killed the physically larger Joelito. Filártiga angrily punctuated Duarte's testimony with loud shouts of "liar." Unable to control his rage, Joel ignored the judge's repeated admonitions and threats to expel him from the courtroom, until Martínez summarily ended the hearing.

This time, to avoid a repetition and give the defense reason for further delays, reluctantly Joel accepted Horacio's advice and stayed at home. Only Nidia, Dolly, and Analy attended the court hearing.

Nevertheless, Duarte refused to testify. Martínez' reaction reeked of a setup as he rescheduled Duarte's deposition for the following week. And, shocking everyone in the courtroom, he ordered that, "inconvenience forbade any member of the Filártiga family from attending the proceeding."

The sight of Nidia, Dolly, and Analy busting into tears at Martínez' ruling—forbidding them from hearing first-hand how their loved one allegedly died—visibly upset even the most seasoned reporters.

On the ride back to Horacio's office, we speculated that the media coverage could hardly be expected to calm public acrimony. Our conversation then turned to another courtroom drama when Filártiga's discipline failed him, one that came close to costing him his life.

"I hadn't arrived yet, so I've only heard Joel's side," I reminded Horacio.

"Well," he explained, "it truly was frightening. The taxi driver who brought Duarte from the Hotel Guaraní to Peña's house the night of Joelito's murder had given the police a statement. He had sworn that there were no sounds of a fight. It was one of our strongest pieces of evidence refuting the crime-of-passion cover-up.

"But two weeks later, at his formal deposition in court, he totally changed his testimony to support Peña's story. We presume they presented him the *plomo o plata* option. That is, the choice of the *lead* of a bullet or the *silver* of a bribe.

"Filártiga completely lost control. He leaped from his seat and charged the taxi driver, who was on the stand," Horacio recalled. "Six police beat Joel unconscious with their truncheons, and dragged him outside."

"That's just about what Joel told me," I confirmed. "Except his version's considerably more dramatic."

"For him," Horacio said somberly, "no doubt it was."

1

The press reaction to the latest episode in the *Caso Filártiga* surpassed our expectations. Again, *La Tribuna* led the pack, with three separate articles.

The above-the-fold article, "Duarte Arredondo Refused to Continue His Deposition," openly criticized the proceeding for the farce that it was.

The second piece, "The Humble of Ybycuí Have 'Their' Clinic," was a testimony to Dr. Filártiga's work with the poor. Obviously prepared in advance, it introduced its various sections with such titles as "Only Those Who Are Able to Afford It Pay at the Clinic."

"The Photo of a Tortured Corpse Raises Doubts Concerning Filártiga's Death" appeared on the front page next to the lead story. It featured a picture of Nidia, Dolly, and Analy on the courthouse steps, as the caption explained, "handing out photos of Joel Filártiga with visible marks of having been tortured."

A few days before, Filártiga had arrived at the house lugging a good-sized parcel. Dropping the heavy package on the dining room table, he excitedly called us in and proclaimed, "This will win us the support of the human rights organizations."

With his penknife Filártiga cut away the string binding the thick outer wrapper, revealing dozens of smaller bundles neatly packed in the same sturdy brown paper. Joel, Nidia, Dolly, and I each grabbed one and tore it open.

Out tumbled hundreds of three-by-five-inch, high-quality color reproductions of *the* photograph. In all, Filártiga announced, he had had 5,000 cards printed. The copies graphically showed the brutal torture wounds mutilating Joelito's body. On the back side appeared Filártiga's poem, "To Another Joel."

"We will spread these throughout Paraguay," Joel exclaimed. "We will send them all over the world. Everybody will see the truth with their own eyes! Then they will have to help!"

"They certainly are powerful," I said with admiration at Filártiga's latest initiative. After a pause, I went on. "But I'm not sure that, by themselves, they'll be enough."

"How can anyone deny the truth after seeing this!" Filártiga fumed, shaking a handful of cards in my face.

"They can't. They won't. You're absolutely right," I concurred, snapping a card with my thumb. "These prove that Joelito died of torture. But that's not the point."

"There. You see!" Joel cried triumphantly, so pumped that his mind refused to register any contrary input.

"Joel, Joel," I pleaded, "it's the same as when Stephansky and Alexander saw the original photo. It convinced them, all right. But they still refused to include the *Caso Filártiga* in their report. The criminal trial, the new charges against the codefendants, and the lifting of the press ban have impossibly confused things.

"The point is that just knowing the truth isn't necessarily enough," I said.

Suddenly, as if a hole had been punched into a life-sized blown-up replica, Joel's vibrancy burst. He lowered his deflated body into a chair.

"Hold on, Joel," I backpedaled. "I'm definitely *not* saying that Joelito's cards won't generate international support."

"How can that be?" he asked. "You said that they won't get the NGOs involved."

"And I still have doubts that they'll be enough to bring in the NGOs—as organizations. But institutions are made up of people. And we've seen the impact Joelito's photos have on people."

Joel's grunt held a spark of renewed interest, his eyes fixed on the cards scattered on the table.

"Damn it, Joel," I persisted, "you said it yourself. When people see these pictures, they *know* the truth. That Joelito suffered the most horrible death under torture.

"It'll be like all the people here who're helping us, because they believe in the justice of your cause. And so will many of the people at the NGOs. Even if on an individual basis, it's a sure bet, some *will* take action. And action leads to more action."

"What kind of action?"

"Well, we'll send them hundreds of the cards. At the least they'll spread them around, give them to others. You know the hardest part of organizing anything is getting people involved, getting things moving."

"So you do think Joelito's cards can serve to build international support?" Filártiga asked.

"Why not? Like you said, we'll get the cards out everywhere. After that, the momentum takes on a life of its own. Anything's possible," I assured him, suppressing thoughts of how our false medical report backfired.

After the morning Masses, at gas stations, among the market stalls, or simply on the sidewalk outside a restaurant, the entire family worked at passing out handfuls of Joelito's cards. Everywhere the Filártigas appeared, the news raced along the barrio grapevine. Literally, people came running.

As always, the image of Joelito's desecrated body appalled and outraged them. But we also saw how the wrenching photo could touch off an emotional backlash. Horrified by what assaulted them, and impotent to do anything about the inner terror it evoked, some people took out their anguish on the messenger.

One afternoon I gave a photo to Vicente LaGuardia, an archivist at the National Archives with whom I had become friendly over the years. He took one look and went into orbit.

"This goes beyond every sense of human decency!" Vicente exploded. "No one, not even the family, should have to remember that fine young man so defiled.

"And to publicize it with this! It's blasphemy! A travesty! It turns Joelito's death into an attraction for sick minds! Dr. Filártiga must be a sick man himself, to do such a thing," he said contemptuously, tossing the card at me.

I kind of lost it, too. "Tell me, Vicente, what would you do if the police did this to your son?" I shot back, throwing the photo back at him. "And then they covered it up, crushing your every attempt for justice? And you couldn't find out how he died, or where he died—or even why he died?

"I suppose you'd act properly and keep silent, in the name of decency. And that would make you a better man than Dr. Filártiga?"

Later that week, while working at my desk in the Archives, Vicente came over and asked me to step outside. "I have thought a lot about what happened the other day," he said. "I do not know what caused me to say those things. Please give Dr. Filártiga my apologies. Tell him that I admire him. Tell him that if they ever do to a son of mine, what they did to Joelito, I only pray for such courage."

2

That same week the hapless Duarte finally delivered to the court his tale of machismo: Unexpectedly arriving home from work, he caught Joelito and Charo in bed, flew into a blind rage, pulverized Joelito with his karate prowess, and finished him off with the kitchen knife.

Judge Martínez listened with sympathetic sagacity. The press treated Duarte's confession with contempt. Only *Patria*, the dictatorship's official propaganda rag, hailed Duarte's self-aggrandizing yarn.

The insatiable appetite for news about the Filártiga trial created a kind of self-sustaining loop. By keeping the *Caso Filártiga* in the forefront of public consciousness, the press fueled the people's interest, which translated into mushrooming circulation, making the competition all the more intense.

Filártiga's apprehension over mobilizing international human rights support, however, remained our single most important concern. By then, we recognized the hopelessness of Mattos coming through with the torture tape. Still, Joel insisted that I keep trying.

Perhaps once a week I would stop by to harass the defanged Investigaciones cop. Mattos would swear they almost had it worked out, and promise to have Joelito's torture tape in just another week or so. For four more months I kept after him. But, other than my therapeutic pleasure of bullying the bully, it all came to nothing.

The intense media coverage, however, did translate into even greater public support. It became socially acceptable, even somewhat fashionable, for Paraguayans of all social classes to openly repudiated the torture and murder of children, even of political dissidents.

And while Paraguay's upper strata relied upon the mainstream press, the masses scooped up the more flamboyant *Aquí*. Being closest to the people's pulse, the tabloid continued pounding away at the official line. *Aquí's* September 10 headline so exquisitely captured public sentiment that it became an instant classic:

DUARTE ARREDONDO SAID

"I KILLED FILARTIGA"
(But Nobody Believes It)

3

Joel and I sat on the patio after our lunch break. By early September, over a month had gone by since sending Amnesty the packet containing Filártiga's taped interview and other materials on the *Caso Filártiga*.

"Still no word," Joel said.

"It takes over a week for mail to reach the Secretariat in London," I replied, adding with an optimistic spin, "and they'll need time to evaluate the information. At best, it'll be a while yet."

Cutting to the chase, Filártiga asked, "What is your honest opinion? Have they been scared off? Like Stephansky and Alexander?"

"AI's an enormous organization, with hundreds of people working on dozens of projects. It's not as if this one case would jeopardize everything they're doing. Not like the single mission the ILHR put together.

"Stroessner's window dressing won't fool them for a minute," I predicted. "Other than that, I really can't say what they'll do. We can only wait."

That was the hard part. Waiting.

"Why don't you call them?" he asked.

Actually, I half expected to have heard something from Amnesty by then. And they had Filártiga's phone number. I had sent them several contact numbers before leaving the States.

By 1976, satellites had linked even remote Paraguay to the rest of the world. We could pick up the phone and direct dial London.

"Won't work," I sighed.

"And why not?" he persisted. "Sure, Investigaciones supposedly listens in on all international phone calls. But you know that's a joke.

"Half the time they are asleep. The other half, the equipment isn't functioning. And those idiots aren't really proficient in English anyway. Just be a little discreet, use idiomatic expressions. You can talk all day."

"Investigaciones isn't the problem," I conceded. "No one at the Secretariat knows me personally. My voice. With AI's penchant for security, I'd be surprised if they would even acknowledge me. The only way is for them to contact us."

"Mierda," Joel grumbled.

"Look, I'm getting off a report to Amnesty tomorrow. With a lot of clippings about Duarte's 'confession.' The three *La Tribuna* articles, and a bunch of others too. How about Joelito's cards?"

"Send them 500. And this too," he added, handing me an op-ed from *El Radical*, the weekly paper of Paraguay's largest legal opposition party. "I found it in the latest number."

In a sweeping analysis of five cases, the article laid bare Stroessner's corruption of the courts to persecute his political enemies. The *Caso Filártiga* merited but a single paragraph:

> While it has been many months since the unspeakably violent death of young Filártiga under extremely suspicious circumstances at the hands of unknown assailants (?), the administration of criminal justice is so absolutely controlled that the courts have not been allowed to proceed with the case, leaving it in legal limbo. And this is not a question of an isolated example of ineptitude, of one judge following orders instead of the law. The "Caso Filártiga" exemplifies, better than any other case, the degree of trust that society can place in the suitability of the magistrates charged with watching over its safety.

I had also seen the *El Radical* article but, since it contained no new information, had decided not to bother with it.

"Good idea," I told Joel.

As the months passed, we heard nothing from either our August or September sets of *Caso Filártiga* materials. Dismay turned to disillusionment.

In the vacuum of Amnesty's silence, reluctantly we came to accept that both had been treated with the same regard. As it turned out, we were absolutely right. And completely wrong.

4

"Dismissed it! My God, it electrified us! In all my years at Amnesty," Conrad Stuart told me, "except when we won the Nobel Peace Prize in '77, nothing, absolutely nothing, created so much excitement."

"And you can document this?" I challenged.

"It's all right here," Conrad said, slapping Amnesty's massive *Caso Filártiga* dossier.

"It all started with the first, August 1976, dispatch. Dr. Filártiga's taped interview, those ghastly photos of Joelito, the newspaper articles, especially his *ABC solicitada* about the death threats. Everyone knew we were onto something big. Really big.

"Immediately we began planning a leaflet on the *Caso Filártiga*," he went on. "Never before had Amnesty published a leaflet exclusively on a single case."

My marathon encounter with Conrad took place more than a decade later in 1989, over a three-day bank holiday weekend in London, as I was conducting research for this work. His flatmates had grabbed the chance to escape to the countryside, giving us the time and privacy to unravel the enigma that had perplexed the Filártigas all these years.

We scheduled periodic breaks, and I treated the underpaid idealist to several extravagant meals. Otherwise, for those seventy-two hours, we left Conrad's hovel only once.

"So why did Amnesty wait so long before doing anything? Were you scared off by Stroessner's crime-of-passion cover-up?"

"Hell no!" he protested. "That kind of thing is standard operating procedure for dictators all over the world. Even the coconspirator charges against Peña and the Villalbas, and lifting the press ban, didn't cause a qualm. They only reinforced our conviction."

"Then you doubted our information?"

"No. Not exactly," Conrad said. "But for such a high-profile campaign, we had to build the tightest possible case. No chinks in our armor, so to say, that Stroessner's counterattack could get through."

Somewhat mollified, I stretched out on the dilapidated couch. "So what was the holdup? You received our first packet of materials in August."

"Right," Conrad agreed. "Like I said, it touched off a maelstrom of activity. Right away we formed the *Caso Filártiga* task force, with two senior staffers heading it up. Inger Farhlander, the director of research, and Lia Fleming, from the Campaign Against Torture department.

"That's not what I mean," I grumped. "How come you didn't do something to help us in Paraguay? At least let us know what was going on."

"Sorry. Yes, I see. Well, you know how Amnesty is. We dealt with the *Caso Filártiga* in our cautious way. And there were some troublesome aspects. That did hold things up for a bit. About a month, until the second set of materials came in. The middle of September. That's what broke the deadlock.

"Actually," Conrad told me, "it was the *El Radical* piece that did the trick." From the dossier, he handed me a photocopy of the article.

It was the same op-ed piece Joel had insisted I send along to Amnesty. The one that I had dismissed as inconsequential. The one that I included at the last moment only to keep up his spirits.

5

"Sorry. Getting ahead of myself," Conrad said. "Here. Take a look at these memos between Inger and Lia."

Although written in turgid bureaucratese, there could be no mistaking their tremendous effort. The stilted style reflecting not a lack of compassion but a coping mechanism, the emergency room paradox. AI staffers unable to maintain a professional detachment soon burn out and leave. And those who do adapt to the emotional assault of dealing daily with Amnesty's human rights work often develop such a deeply reserved character that, only half-jokingly, they are often referred to as "Amnestiods."

"You see," Conrad explained, pointing to the memos, "in early September, before we got the second packet, Inger began having second thoughts. She wanted to find a way to make the campaign stronger. And she asked Lia to conduct a complete review of all of our *Caso Filártiga* material."

Reading Lia's memo back to Inger, I came to her pithy summation:

Hesitations:
- It is an **expensive leaflet dealing with one—sensational—case**.
- A lurid, very complicated story **based on one source. Is it possible to obtain corroboration?**

Pros:
- Arrest of mother/daughter.
- Threats to drop case.
- Disappearance of Rosario. [Charo]

Addressing Lia's first "Hesitation," in her return memo Inger queried, "Do we have more doc + info on torture in Paraguay that could be included and make it more comprehensive?"

"Inger's suggestions struck a strong chord in Lia," Conrad recounted as he located the fiery proposal she shot back.

"Lia wanted to drastically expand the leaflet, to make Joelito's death the centerpiece of a comprehensive indictment of Paraguay's violations of human and legal rights."

Lia advocated attacking the structure of Stroessner's thugocracy through exposing ". . . the widespread use of torture, lack of centralized control of law, enforcement personnel who dispose of their power at will, lack of the judiciary to operate impartially and independently. . . ." Within this context, she reasoned, they then could introduce ". . . the actual [Filártiga] story on the grounds that it depicts these very institutions and the way they operate."

Lia also addressed Inger's concerns to find some action by which AI could offer immediate support to the Filártigas. "In the meantime," she recommended, "and taking into consideration the time factor as noted by you, we could include a brief summary of the [Filártiga] case as an appeal case in the CAT [Campaign to Abolish Torture] Bulletin, in addition to the letter to Stroessner."

Lia's spirited proposal impressed Inger, particularly the idea of a Special Action CAT Bulletin. She came back to Lia agreeing that they do an extra mailing on the *Caso Filártiga* to the CAT subgroups of physicians.

At best, we had hoped that Amnesty might support our actions in Paraguay, much as I had explained to Soledad: Let Stroessner know they were monitoring the Filártigas' plight, and assign the case to an adoption group who would follow up with an ongoing letter writing campaign.

Never did it occur to us that Amnesty would consider employing the *Caso Filártiga* as the foundation of an international human rights offensive against the dictatorship.

6

"Let's move on to the second packet." Conrad organized another group of papers. "You'll find this interesting, I'm sure."

Our September dispatch had reached the Secretariat at a decisive juncture in their debate on how to deal with the *Caso Filártiga*.

"By the end of August, we had finished up with transcribing and translating Filártiga's interview and the draft leaflet. But like I said, the initial blow was out of the sails.

"And then this arrived," he announced, waving our second, September batch of materials. "It was like a shot of adrenaline. Broke the bureaucratic logjam.

"Well," Conrad amended, "perhaps not entirely.

"Lia was your biggest fan. She even pushed to get the go ahead for the leaflet right then."

I looked over Lia's memo. "It seems to me," she had argued, "that the article in *El Radical* gives that final push to go ahead with the leaflet (i.e., it corroborates the main issue, that the murder happened under the most suspicious circumstances, and it confirms that nothing much is happening at the official level)."

"Still there remained a number of unresolved issues," Conrad sighed. "But we did get right on the CAT action." Rummaging through the file, he pulled out AI's letter to Stroessner. "See," slapping it on the table he announced, "the day after your packet arrived, September 16, this was ready for Sherman Carroll, the codirector of Amnesty's Campaign Against Torture."

As always in such cases, AI's correspondence employed the most respectful language. Even so, there was no way the dictator could miss the message: Carroll laid out Amnesty's plans for a full-fledged international campaign, using the *Caso Filártiga* pamphlet as the fulcrum to excoriate Paraguay for its gross human rights violations.

With profound sorrow, Carroll informed His Excellency, AI had learned of the appalling circumstances regarding young Joelito's death and went on to say Amnesty sought only to determine the truth of the matter.

However, "In response to the world-wide interest stirred up by the events . . . ," the CAT codirector declared, "we consider it important to disseminate the details of the case. To that end, we are preparing to publish a pamphlet, in various languages, based upon all of the available material, including the photographs of the corpse depicting the torture wounds."

Slowly I read Carroll's missive to Stroessner a second time. Something about it bothered me.

"There's something about—"

7

"And see here," Conrad interrupted, "the next day, we stepped up the international pressure with the special CAT action. This went out to our global network of Amnesty groups with medical contacts."

Pointing to the September 17 date, he shoved the confidential *Special Action Request* across the table. In a moving account detailing the events of Joelito's death, it stressed the life-and-death jeopardy confronting the Filártigas: ". . . it is important that international concern be expressed without delay, to pressure the authorities to protect Dr. Filártiga and his family against coercion and persecution."

The CAT *Special Action* letter concluded on an enigmatic note. "Please also write personal letters to Dr. Filártiga (do *not* mention Amnesty in this case), expressing your support for his efforts to obtain justice."

"Why try to disguise Amnesty's involvement?" I asked. "Carroll's letter and the CAT bulletin already told everyone what Amnesty was doing."

"Amnesty's learned that it's best not to link people too directly with our actions. There have been cases when victims have told others, who have told others, until it becomes such a public big deal that it ends up provoking further repression against them. This way, it was less likely that the authorities would hold the Filártigas personally responsible, take it out on them."

"Yeah, well," I grumped, "it would have been nice to know what was going on. In Paraguay we didn't have a clue about the *Special Action Request*. Never mind Carroll's letter to Stroessner. Or that Amnesty was doing anything at all."

After cooling down, I explained, "Filártiga received dozens of letters. For months they poured in. We thought they were from an article written by Henri Nouwen.

"Henri Nouwen? The theologian?" Conrad exclaimed. "I didn't know he was involved."

"In a big way," I assured him. "Henri's an old friend. Became a Filártiga supporter during Joel's January '76 trip to the States. And that August he spent a couple of very hard weeks with us in Paraguay."

Right in the middle of the OPM crisis, I remembered. Henri had come to know Soledad and the others, provided the money to rent the new safe house, and run himself ragged futilely begging his contacts in the Paraguayan Church and the Papal Nuncio, even the Dutch Consulate, to give them political asylum. But it did not seem like something Conrad had to know.

"At the time, Henri was finishing up *Compassion*. Joel did some drawings for the book. And Henri wrote up the *Caso Filártiga* as its epilogue. When *Compassion* was published, it gave a terrific boost to the Filártigas' struggle.

"But before that, the October 8, 1976, *National Catholic Reporter* ran the epilogue as the cover story, with three or four of Joel's drawings, and called for letters of solidarity. And in December, *NCR* did a follow-up piece by Joel. So we figured that's what generated the letters."

When Conrad and I returned to the CAT campaign materials, that something about Sherman Carroll's letter to Stroessner still nagged at me. I read it a third time. Then it hit me.

8

"That must be it," I groaned.

"What?" Conrad asked.

"The explanation of a mystery that's confounded us all these years. As they say in Spanish," I said, holding out Carroll's letter to Stroessner, "this is the last drop of water that made the glass run over."

"What are you talking about?"

"The date on the letter," I replied. "The timing. It's the key to our worst setback."

"I still don't get it," Conrad protested.

"No way you could, without knowing what was going on in Paraguay in September 1976."

Just at that time, I began, the mainstream media coverage was becoming bolder than ever. Especially after *ABC Color* got away with its September 12 Sunday Supplement editorial, "Impresiones y Contradicciones."

ABC conducted a survey of people who knew both Duarte and Joelito, and then eviscerated Duarte's "unconvincing confession," reporting that it found that everyone "doubted" that the "self-declared karate expert" could have possibly overpowered the far stronger and athletic Joelito.

It was one of those instances where *who* says something carries as much, if not more, importance than *what* is said. *ABC*, Paraguay's most influential newspaper, was the first of the establishment press to cross the line from sympathetic news articles to an openly critical opinion-editorial piece supporting the Filártigas' struggle. The escalating press competition quickly led the other papers to follow suit.

"I'm surprised Stroessner didn't put a stop to it," Conrad said.

"That's what I thought too. But Filártiga saw it as our golden opportunity. He figured that Stroessner was on the defensive, caught in a political bind that forced him to make concessions.

"For instance," I told Conrad, "*ABC's* editorial among other things criticized the court for releasing Charo before getting her deposition. And within a few days Judge Martínez, along with his secretary and the court stenographer, recused themselves from the trial. They claimed "irreconcilable enmity" with Dr. Filártiga. But everyone knew Stroessner had ordered the whole gang out, as a conciliatory gesture to the public."

"OK. So what *was* going on?" Conrad wanted to know.

"First of all, His Excellency was up for 'reelection.' Naturally it was all a farce. Every five years the dictator holds demonstration elections.

"But, to keep up the fiction of democracy, this time to run again he needed a constitutional amendment. So he called a rubber stamp constitutional convention.

"The wrinkle came from the opposition parties' threat to shred the charade by boycotting the convention. And Stroessner was attempting to entice them into participating by loosening up, especially by easing up on the repression."

Leafing through the Amnesty dossier, I found my September 12 report. "Look here, on the same day as *ABC's* editorial I wrote AI that 'It seems as if the government is continuing to release prisoners, although a realistic estimate would place 600 people still

imprisoned. . . . Last week 80 of the 86 political prisoners being held at Investigaciones . . . were transferred to Emboscada.'"

"It was a major victory for the opposition," I told Conrad. "Conditions at Emboscada concentration camp didn't measure up to country club standards. But to be freed
from the secret police dungeons, from the around-the-clock screams from their torture
chambers. You can't imagine what it meant to the prisoners."

9

At this same time, I went on, Stroessner's international reputation was taking a pounding. Again I rifled through the dossier and pulled out a handful of publications for
Conrad.

There was Amnesty's pamphlet, *Paraguay*, and two scathing attacks that the Latin
American Documentation Center in Lima sent around the world in back-to-back news
bulletins. Also, that September, the ILHR published its findings, the *Report of the Commission of Enquiry into Human Rights in Paraguay of the International League for Human
Rights*.

"Then, as if that was not enough," I said, "the *Caso Filártiga* was propelled right
into the middle of the international blitz."

I told Conrad about Bob Garrison, the young diplomat who had supported Filártiga by accompanying us when he first returned to Ybycuí after Joelito's death.

"And Bob did it again. More than did it again. Bob took the initiative and organized a week-long art exhibition of Joel's work at the Paraguayan-American Cultural
Center.

"The excitement began opening night, September 23, when the overflow crowd saw
the well appointed brochure. The large bold letters of its dedication—IN MEMORIAM TO
ANOTHER JOEL—followed by Filártiga's poem "To Another Joel," set the rumor mill
buzzing.

"Ambassador George Landau, a savvy career bureaucrat, stopped by long enough
to establish his human rights credentials. The polls were showing Jimmy Carter handily
taking the U.S. elections, only six weeks away.

"Never before had the U.S. Embassy sponsored such a blatantly anti-Stroessner
event. The press jumped on it, played it to the hilt." From the AI file, I gathered a
collection of clippings. Invariably including a photo of the Ambassador shaking hands
with Dr. Filártiga, the press spent hundreds of column inches outdoing each other.

"Most of it's hyperbole. Like this," I said, reading a ridiculously laudatory sentence—" 'Filártiga's exhibition raised Paraguayan art to its greatest heights.' But it gives
you an idea of the big time hype that was going on."

Separating the feature article from *La Tribuna's* September 29 issue, I pointed to a
single paragraph. "Out of it all, Joel told me, these few lines best captured what he was
doing:

> No matter how hard one tries, it is impossible to find
> a dichotomy between the tragic loss of the artist's son

and his current work. And, most curiously of all, the drawings made before the death of Joel Filártiga Speratti and the ones done afterwards, merge together to create a thematic and emotive unity that is profoundly compelling.

"Speculation ran wild," I recounted. "What it all came down to was another gutsy act of solidarity by Bob Garrison. The exhibit took on enormous significance that had little relationship to reality."

"I can just imagine your efforts to set the record straight," Conrad laughed.

"They were appropriate," I conceded.

"Anyway, you couldn't convince anyone that the exhibition wasn't a deliberate political statement. The show's dedication to Joelito, the Ambassador's public participation, Joel's high-profile trip to the U.S. earlier in the year. It all fed people's hopes—or paranoia. Some even went so far as to insist that the Filártiga exhibition signaled a U.S. policy shift, towards Carter's human rights, stepping back from its traditional backing of Stroessner."

That brought to mind another incident. On the second day of the exhibit, Pastor Coronel telephoned Joel. Apparently, the *jefe* of Investigaciones phoned for no other reason than to assure Filártiga that his secret police had nothing to do with the murder of his son. Curious, we thought at the time.

"In any event, Stroessner reacted to this onslaught of domestic and international problems with compromise and concession—and not repression—for damage control."

"All this is very interesting," Conrad said. "But I still don't see what it has do with Carroll's letter."

Again I delved into the files, and came up with Horacio Galeano Perrone's Forty-Five Points petition. Passing the shelf of documents to Conrad, I asked, "You're familiar with this? The motion the Filártigas filed with the court. To expose the police involvement and the complicity of the judicial system in Joelito's murder?"

"Of course. It was Galeano Perrone's Forty-Five Points, his letter to the U.S. ambassador and, of course, everything that happened to him, that ended the doubts, convinced us to go with the leaflet."

"And what's the date of Carroll's letter?"

Taking a quick check, Conrad answered, "September 16. So?"

"So. With the Paraguayan mails, Carroll's letter telling Stroessner about Amnesty's plans would have arrived at the end of the month," I said. "And Horacio filed the Forty-Five Points motion on September 29."

"Oh shit!" Conrad blurted.

10

Galeano Perrone's Forty-Five Points petition threatened to turn the *Caso Filártiga* on its head. We understood the risk of provoking reprisals. But it was a calculated risk.

Of course, we were ignorant of Sherman Carroll's letter announcing AI's intentions to use the *Caso Filártiga* as the cause célèbre in an international campaign to rip apart the reputation of Stroessner and his regime.

As far as we knew, our position had never been stronger, the government's never so vulnerable. In good part, that is what finally convinced Horacio to file the Forty-Five Points motion. That, and Filártiga's persuasion.

About noon on Wednesday, September 28, I arrived home to find everyone in the living room, screaming at each other.

Filártiga, totally out of control, wildly waved the Colt .45 automatic pistol over his head, bellowing that it was not his fault. Nidia and Dolly circled him, making frantic leaps to grab the weapon, yelling that he was crazy.

I had no idea what it was all about, but I jumped in and began hollering at them to tell me what had happened. It took a while before everyone calmed down enough to learn they had just come back from Horacio's office, where Joel literally blew it.

"You know that for months we've been preparing this big motion," Filártiga managed to say, struggling to catch his breath. "Horacio's team of detectives put together a list of all the police on duty at the police station the night they killed Joelito. We're going to ask the court to subpoena every one of them. Make them give depositions.

"And have a completely honest autopsy on Joelito," he huffed. "To determine which wounds were inflicted while he was still alive, and which ones were made after he died. To match the stab punctures with the knife Duarte claims he used. And prove the *picana eléctrica* caused the burns."

Filártiga's breath still came heavy. "Also to require the police to produce the real matrimonial mattress. Not the single prison-style one they used to return Joelito's body. And make the Villalbas give their depositions.

"That's not all, either," he gasped. "Interrogate Dr. Molinas about his false death certificate. And why Judge Martínez validated Molinas' lies at Peña's house that night. And the disgraceful way he conducted the trial. With his entire staff. They all conspired to obstruct justice.

"There's more, too. Many more particulars to unmask the cover-up. For the first time a criminal case will be brought against the police. For the first time the police will be on trial, instead of the other way around."

Without relaxing his grip on the pistol, Joel plowed on. "Now. After months and months, all of the petition's forty-five points are properly prepared. It's ready to file.

"And this morning Galeano Perrone told me he wasn't going to submit it. Even though he promised to. He said we had to wait!

"I tried to reason with him. Everything is constraining Stroessner. That there would never be a better time. That—"

"OK, OK. I know all that," I interrupted. "What happened at the office?"

Nidia answered, giving Joel a badly needed respite. "Well, Horacio said that he was not going to present the petition. Papi became very impatient. He took out his gun and told Horacio, 'You are a perfect coward. You must present it. If you do not present the motion, I will kill you.'

"Well," she added, a little sheepishly, "that's when the gun went off."

"You shot Horacio?" I gasped.

"Oh no. Nobody was hurt," Dolly said, downplaying the incident. "Everybody was very excited and, you know, it just kind of happened."

"Not on purpose," Joel interjected. "Only one bullet escaped. That's all. I just wanted to frighten Horacio. And it worked. He's going to file the papers tomorrow."

According to Galeano Perrone, it was not quite so inconsequential. "Joel came to my judicial study in a savage mood," Horacio told me later that afternoon. "When I explained that we should wait a while, to give the new judge a chance to review the case file, he became so infuriated that he lost his mind. He savagely shook this large automatic at my chest, and threatened to kill me if I didn't file the Forty-Five Points immediately.

"What alarmed me most wasn't the threats, or even the pistol. I knew that he really wouldn't shoot. On purpose. But in his frenzy, his hand trembled violently. So I told him to watch out, to be careful, and slowly moved the gun aside with my hand.

"But he had a cartridge set in the chamber, with the safety off, and his finger on the trigger. That's when the automatic fired. The bullet blew through the door of the library, as you can see," he exclaimed, pointing to a pucker in the polished oak.

"Filártiga says he's going to fix that," Horacio said. "But that's minor. Only by the grace of God, he didn't kill someone. One of the lawyers who works for me was interviewing a client in the library. The bullet just missed them and lodged in a book above his head!"

Divine intervention aside, it was damn lucky no one was hurt. Even before I had heard Horacio's side of the story that morning, I berated Joel for his recklessness.

"I only took out the pistol like this to frighten him," Filártiga protested, waving the gun to demonstrate. With a roar the big Colt exploded, smashing a round into the living room ceiling, showering us with plaster.

Just at that moment, Father John Vesey pulled into the driveway. Hearing the blast, he thought someone had been shot and rushed into the house to help. As the door burst open, Joel spun around; the cocked pistol in his outstretched hand pointed directly at John, not ten feet away.

Everyone froze. Then the reality of what happened set in. Joel had come within a breath of killing Padre Juan. Slowly, Filártiga lowered the weapon. Without taking his eyes off the still stationary priest, he handed the pistol to me. Joel crossed the short distance to his friend, and overwhelmed with gratitude at being spared the terrible consequences of his manic hubris, emotionally embraced John.

11

Horacio filed the Forty-Five Points the next day. Every newspaper ran it as their lead story, most publishing the entire text of the brief. The following morning, September 30, the police arrested Galeano Perrone. Not a word was found in the press.

Although any arrest by the Paraguayan police can be nothing less than harrowing, perhaps because we moved so rapidly on Horacio's behalf, he got off comparatively easy. A few days later, I sent a full report to Amnesty.

"Actually, the arrest itself was something of a spectacular performance. The police surrounded the court building at 10:00 A.M. (the hour of most activity) and secured the central plaza inside. They then searched out Galeano Perrone and dragged him off in front of the judges, lawyers, and all the other people present."

Horacio ended up spending a little more than one terrifying day in their clutches. The night of his release, we all got together at his home.

"I can't adequately express my appreciation for all you did," Horacio told us. "I know it must have been difficult."

"Not anything like it was for you," Joel said. "Richard called me in Ybycuí about noon. Right after your wife and mother went to see him in Sajonia."

"I'm not sure how much good I did," I told Horacio. "I spoke with Philip Gill. The head of the political section. And the CIA station chief, McGuire.

"They let me know the embassy 'remained unconvinced' that Joelito was murdered for political reasons. But, they did say they would 'make some inquiries' about your arrest. Who knows? With everything else, maybe it did help."

"Well, something changed the intentions of the police. I'm sure it was the pressure all of you put on the government ministers that saved me," Horacio said sincerely, even humbly.

"Tell us what happened when you got to police headquarters?" Joel urged. Having gone through it himself, he knew Galeano Perrone needed to externalize his terror.

"I was frightened. I didn't know what would happen. What came to mind was the possibility of being tortured. Like Joelito. Remember that time I told you of the feelings I had, of being at the mercy of people capable of torturing you? That's what I felt."

Horacio went quiet. After a while, he began again.

"They shackled me to the wall. Inside of a box made of bars, so small I could only sit. A cage, like for animals in a zoo. Then, one by one they came, the officials I named in the Forty-Five Points.

"The chief of police. The director of the police hospital. The commissioner. The subcommissioner. They didn't say a word. They stood over me, looking down at me for a little while, and then left. I always had visitors.

"They looked at me just like you look at an animal in the zoo."

"They put you on exhibition," Filártiga said.

"Yes, on exhibition," Horacio agreed. "And I thought, how bad for the animals in the zoos."

"No one talked to you at all?" Joel asked.

"Only Peña. He said, 'It is going to be very hard for you to get out of there.' And that they were going to kill me and anyone else involved in pushing the case.

"That's why," Horacio said, "I'm sure something disrupted their plans."

12

The following morning, October 1, we learned that within hours of Galeano Perrone's arrest, Duarte's lawyers appealed the Special Appeals ploy: Since Joelito could not be interrogated as the law required of both participants involved in mutual combat, they insisted, all charges against Duarte should be dismissed. Evidently, with Horacio imprisoned and unable to respond within the requisite three days, they expected their petition would be granted by default.

After his release, however, Horacio moved quickly to prepare the countermotion. And once again the Appellate Court rejected Duarte's Special Appeal.

Otherwise, Stroessner buried the trial in judicial purgatory, where it remained entombed for years.

13

Horacio did get off one last shot. From the Amnesty dossier I retrieved his appeal to the U.S. ambassador.

In his October 12 letter to George Landau, Galeano Perrone reviewed the facts of the *Caso Filártiga*, and he offered to provide a detailed file "of the many flagrant inconsistencies, irregularities and aberrations." His real concern, he explained, was the "rogue DEATH SQUADS in Paraguay . . . that operate with the support of a powerful sector of the police."

He described how, "While imprisoned, my 'visitors' told me specifically that my life, those of every member of the Filártiga family, and even the life of the family's friend, the North American historian Dr. Richard Alan White, were in 'serious danger.'" And added with conviction, "I assure you, Mr. Ambassador, they are more than capable of carrying out this threat and killing any one, or all, of us."

Horacio's letter went on, "I would ask that you authorize your intelligence agencies to conduct an investigation of the *Caso Filártiga*, and make their findings known to the people of Paraguay and the world." And he concluded "that once the 'Death Squads' become entrenched, it will be next to impossible to root them out. Therefore, it seems now is the time to combat, and eliminate this evil, before it takes hold and is too late." He cited the provisions of the new Amendment to the Foreign Assistance Act—that had become U.S. law with the beginning of the 1977 fiscal year a few weeks earlier—requiring the termination of all aid to any nation that systematically violated its citizens' basic human rights.

Horacio gave me a copy of his missive to the U.S. ambassador to forward to Amnesty, and asked what I thought. I thought about Ambassador Stephansky's lecture on "state policy," how our government had enacted similar laws to stake out the moral high ground, only to make a mockery of them by following its cold war agenda of supporting *our* tyrants. I thought Galeano Perrone's plea was futile.

I also thought that, if Stroessner ever found out that Galeano Perrone had asked for a U.S. investigation into the crimes of his mafioso regime, he would treat it as an act of treason. In my report I cautioned the Secretariat that his information "should not be made public unless you are specifically authorized to do so by us, or in the event that any of us disappear or are arrested."

I told Horacio his letter looked real good, and I would get it off to Amnesty right away.

14

"I swear," Conrad insisted, "when we received the news of Galeano Perrone's arrest, and his letter to the ambassador, no one linked it with Carroll's letter."

"The connection is obvious," I said.

"Now, sure. But truthfully," Conrad confided, "I'm still not entirely sure I understand what happened."

"All right, here's the way I see it," I fumed. "What didn't add up was Stroessner's utter ruthlessness. For no reason we could fathom, he abandoned all restraint. Busting Horacio and unleashing Peña and his thugs. It was irrational. And one thing Stroessner is not, is irrational.

"The Forty-Five Points motion wasn't enough. Such total contempt of international pressure, and Paraguayan public opinion, was completely out of character. Counterproductive. Unnecessary. Like killing a fly with a cannon!"

Conrad retreated to a grimy window. I paced about the dingy flat.

"Now Stroessner's viciousness makes sense. Look at it from his point of view," I said. "By the end of September he was under siege." I raised my index finger. "Devastating international condemnations." Second finger. "Unprecedented criticism in the press, public and political parties at home." Ring finger. "Even his traditional U.S. patronage seemed in question.

"And don't forget the international hysteria about state terrorism back then—hijacked planes, Kadaffi running around dropping off millions to terrorist groups, all that. And Stroessner had plenty to hide. He was up to his neck in the 'Human Wrongs Network.' Like Operation Condor, the pact among Latin American dictatorships to help each other hunt down and kill their enemies around the world."

I stopped, pulled a folder out of my briefcase, checked to make sure. "Remember the 1976 assassination of the former ambassador from Chile to the United States? When Orlando Letelier and his assistant Ronni Moffitt, a U.S. citizen, were blown up in downtown Washington, D.C.? Remember that when the FBI caught up with the Chilean hit squad, they were traveling on phony Paraguayan passports provided by Stroessner's Investigaciones?

"It was less than two weeks after the D.C. car bombing when *jefe* Pastor Coronel called to assure Filártiga they had nothing to do with Joelito's murder, to distance themselves from the *Caso Filártiga*. The day after Joel's U.S.-sponsored art exhibition opened, September 24. Before Carroll's letter would have reached Stroessner."

Spreading little finger and thumb. "Then he gets hit with the *Caso Filártiga* double whammy. In the same week Stroessner finds out that Amnesty's going to tear him apart internationally, and Horacio files the Forty-Five Points to blow the lid off the police cover-up."

Conrad moved back to the cluttered table.

"And all of a sudden, he's looking at potentially the biggest scandal of his rule. No way would paranoid Stroessner believe it a coincidence. He'd see it as a coordinated assault by the international communist conspiracy.

"Stroessner must have feared that it might all come out. Surely there was a lot more, not only the Letelier-Moffitt assassinations in D.C. And that Paraguay would be branded a pariah-nation.

"He couldn't do anything about Amnesty, out of reach here in London. So, just as he's always done when things get bad, Stroessner unleashed his police and hunkered down to ride out the storm."

Conrad shook his head in dismay. "At least, Galeano Perrone's letter bloody well put an end to our reservations."

"Yeah, ironic, isn't it? If we had known about Carroll's letter to Stroessner, maybe Horacio wouldn't have filed the Forty-Five Points at that time. Or been arrested. Or written the letter to the ambassador. And there would have been no Amnesty pamphlet."

15

Emotionally wrung out, Conrad and I took a major break. Relaxing on the upper deck of the tour boat making its way along the Thames, the *Caso Filártiga* was not mentioned. Indeed, after leaving the Westminster Abbey dock, cruising to Greenwich and back, we hardly spoke at all.

When we got back, I wanted to see how Amnesty had dealt with the Horacio mess. In Inger's October 25 memo, I was gratified with the seriousness with which she took my request for confidentiality. "Attached is the letter that makes me at last convinced that this is for us," she told Lia. "Can you work the contents in without it being seen as coming from this letter?"

However, even with Galeano Perrone's corroboration at last driving a stake through the heart of their "one source" hesitation, Inger continued to worry. "It is an **expensive leaflet dealing with one—sensational—case,**" she insisted. "I still would prefer [the *Caso Filártiga*] be worked into other torture material on Paraguay and made the **central piece**."

With her colleague's conversion, Lia wasted no time. In her memo back to Inger two days later, she explained that incorporating Horacio's information had required yet another complete rewrite.

True to Amnesty's meticulousness, Lia found several overlooked ambiguous, even contradictory, facts. Most perplexing of all was a medical conundrum—both the police and Galeano Perrone reported that Joelito's body showed signs of rigor mortis. But by Amnesty's reckoning—after having Sherman Carroll "check about the rigor mortis with his father (who happens to be an MD in charge of 'declaring people dead')"—not enough time had elapsed for that to be feasible.

It took another month before Amnesty decided to contact us. With conflicting memories, I reread Inger's November 24 letter to me.

"Our dossier about the Filártiga case is now almost complete. However, there are some contradictory points we urgently need to clarify. . . ."

This was the first, and only, communication I received from Amnesty while in Paraguay. That they were preparing a dossier on the *Caso Filártiga* was news. The depth of their inquiries was even more surprising:

(1) One of the main arguments put forward by the lawyer [Galeano Perrone]," Inger explained, "is that when the body was delivered at 4 A.M. on 30 March, it already

presented signs of rigor mortis. These symptoms, according to the lawyer, could not have developed since 2:30 A.M., time at which the boy died according to the police version (this argument is scientifically correct, for these symptoms do not in fact appear before 8/10 hours after death). However, this argument presumes that Joel would have died some time on 29 March, which is not possible in the light of the testimonies. In fact, both the official and the private versions coincide that Joelito died some time around 2 A.M. on 30 March. It is very important that this point is clarified. (2) Can you clarify the actual course of events?

"Ah yes," I said, laughing. "The infamous rigor mortis panic."

"You may think it's funny," Conrad retorted testily. "But when it suddenly popped up, it was no joke. Unless we reconciled the discrepancies, the entire project could very well have been scrapped.

"Damn infuriating. Galeano Perrone's letter convinced us we were on solid ground. Then Lia finds these problems and sets us back to square one. It took us two months to work it out."

"Poppycock," I chided. "You know that Amnesty didn't figure it out. That's why you guys finally broke down and asked us for help."

"Well. I expressed myself poorly. It's been a long time. All somewhat hazy."

"It's no longer clear in my mind either," I agreed, searching for the report I had sent back to Inger. "Here it is. Actually, it was Dr. Filártiga who worked it out for you.

"To begin with, Carroll's father's eight-hour estimate may be true in merry old England, but it doesn't hold up for someone being tortured to death in tropical Paraguay. And, the old boy seems to have confused total rigor mortis with the time it takes for the initial symptoms to appear."

Joel had explained how the heat in Paraguay causes rigor mortis to start setting in quickly. An unexpected death, such as an auto accident, could delay it for up to four or five hours. Whereas, during the extreme and prolonged torment of torture, the body secretes adrenaline and other chemicals that accelerate the onset of symptoms. But from Filártiga's experience, the stiffening never began in less than two hours.

I did not need this scientific explanation. Both Dolly and Bernardino Ortíz, as well as the helpful neighbor, had told me how Joelito's partially rigid body would not settle into the mattress, how it kept sliding to the side, as they carried him back to the house.

So, while Horacio's argument rested upon a rather precise calculation, he was right. Rigor mortis could not possibly have begun in the hour and a half between 2:30 A.M.— when Duarte came home and the police claimed he killed Joelito—and 4 A.M., when Dolly recovered his body.

According to our reconstruction, Joelito probably had been lured from the house between 10 and 11 P.M. and had died between midnight and 1 A.M.—after suffering excruciating torture—and those three to four hours were enough for the rigor mortis to commence.

With the rigor mortis crisis put to rest, at last the Amnesty pamphlet took off. But in Paraguay, we were left no better off.

16

"You know, Conrad," I said, "it's really a shame we weren't working together from the beginning."

"You'll get no argument from me."

I held up Inger's rigor mortis letter. "This didn't arrive until December, a week or so before I left Paraguay. And even then, there is no mention of Carroll's letter to Stroessner, the CAT campaign, or the *Caso Filártiga* pamphlet. Yes, in those last days we found your answers. But not enough reasons for me to stay."

"Since August we'd been waiting to hear something from you. Every day of every week of every month, we waited. It's almost impossible to describe the feeling. Out there alone, the emptiness like an icy hole in your chest. That's where it lived. In its cold, hollow cavity. It never went away."

Conrad said nothing. Into the awkward silence, I confided that had we known what AI was doing, we would have been overjoyed, enthusiastically approved. At that crucial juncture, though, the lack of communication and our ignorance made any attempt to coordinate our plans impossible.

As 1976 came to a close and I prepared to leave Paraguay, the trial had been at a dead stop for over three months. And, while Stroessner renewed his campaign of repression with a vengeance, he left us alone.

In October, the nuns finally had gotten into the Emboscada internment camp to inoculate the population against typhoid. They brought out a list of 409 prisoners. By November, the local jails had filled up again, with the police even rearresting some of the recently released prisoners. We also got most of their names. I sent it all to Amnesty, together with several long reports detailing the latest developments.

The regime also renewed its WANTED notices in the newspapers. And while our OPM friends retained top billing, they also remained free.

With the *Caso Filártiga* hopelessly stagnated in Paraguay, and unaware of what, if anything, was happening on the outside, we decided I should return to the States and try to organize international support. In a month the Carter administration would take office. I had kept in touch with Ambassador Stephansky, as well as making a number of other promising contacts.

Nidia did not want me to leave, and she tried to devise ways of getting me to stay longer. But Joel understood that now, with the *Caso Filártiga* clamped down under Stroessner's boot, international pressure was the best chance of breaking the impasse. We reassured Nidia with promises that I would be back soon—in three or four months, most likely.

On December 16, I boarded a flight to the States. With profound remorse at leaving my friends behind, I felt ashamed at the warm relief that swept through me.

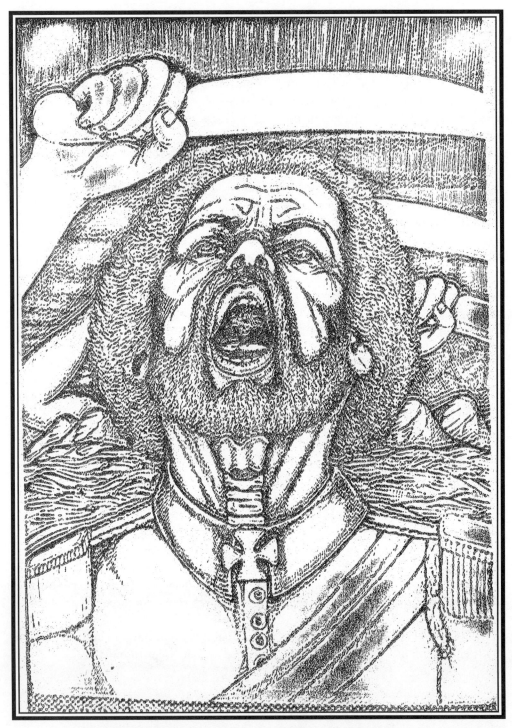

Black-and-white perception of Paraguayan reality.

SEVEN

COMING BACK to the States after a prolonged stay in an underdeveloped country, most everyone goes through some degree of culture shock. It can be unsettling, disorientating, even frightening. And the deeper one has lived under the oppression of that life, the greater the psychological reentry trauma.

Human rights activists often return with a razor-sharp, black-and-white developing-world perception, where no shades of gray muddle their thinking. They shout out their truth: how institutionalized injustice debases people to an endless struggle for existence; how, for many, the measure of success is survival.

But all too soon, the sharpness begins to lose its edge, the clarity of vision dims. Their insights become mired in complacency, their best punches absorbed by the matrix of affluence that molds our society—and us. And in a week, two at the outside, this matrix—what I've come to think of as a "giant marshmallow"—has sucked us back in.

The blizzard that lashed New England that Christmas of 1976 helped smooth my transition. For a time my mind bounced all over the board. I could neither push aside the jumble of random thoughts flashing through my head nor get a grip on the free-floating rage that threatened to explode at the slightest provocation.

December marks the height of Paraguay's summer. Only weeks before, I had lived with 110-degree heat and the fear of Stroessner's secret police. Now, in the comfort of a Boston suburb, mesmerized by the tons of ice and snow burying my world, there could be no question that all that had been left behind.

Sure enough, little by little, my laser-like perception slipped away. By New Year's Eve, I took a nap. For the first time in seven months, I totally lost consciousness and slept.

1

On the way back from Paraguay, I had stopped in Lima to arrange with friends at the Latin American Documentation Center (LADOC) to do a feature piece on the *Caso Filártiga*. Fortunately, before adjusting to life on the dimmer switch, I had completed the long article in a smoldering three-day work snit.

In those first days of January 1977, I sent off the manuscript to LADOC. And to Inger Farhlander at Amnesty's Secretariat in London went 300 pages of official *Filártiga* trial proceedings. Adopting the ways of the dictatorship, a generous gratuity had persuaded the clerk of courts to lend me the complete file—transcripts, depositions, rulings, reports, the whole works. An afternoon with a photocopier finished the job.

I then began phoning people along the East Coast, lining up contacts to begin the work of building support for the *Caso Filártiga*. My antiwar organizing had been directed against the establishment, but operating within the system was quite something else. And my nearly nonexistent understanding of what mobilizing support for the Filártigas' cause entailed only deepened my ambivalence.

So, after calling Inger to arrange with the Washington Amnesty office to help with an orientation and introductions, I set out on my baptismal foray into this new universe of international human rights.

By the time I returned in February, not a vestige of intimidation remained. The frenetic pace of the trip, however, left me exhausted. Driving back to Boston, I had been daydreaming about sleep. Stumbling through the door of my parents' place, I dropped my bag in the hallway and headed for bed. The neatly stacked pile of letters on the pillow put an end to that fantasy.

On top was a large manila envelope from Father John Vesey. Somehow his Paraguayan Church group had pulled together four updated lists of political prisoners, including Emboscada, Investigaciones, and several local police stations. Incredibly, they had compiled a detailed description of the conditions, and pinpointed the locations, of the majority of Stroessner's victims in Paraguay.

Next was a packet from Filártiga. The optimism that filled his long letter helped allay my anxiety for the family. Joel enclosed a batch of articles from among the year-end media hullabaloo over "The Trial of the Decade," declaring them "proof" that the Paraguayan press had not been cowed. Enthusiastically, he went on with the heartening news of the flood of support that kept coming in—including petitions signed by twenty-six Swiss and fifty-three Swedish physicians—which he insisted showed my activities to build international support "had already yielded positive results."

A letter from Lia Fleming filled me in on the CAT medical bulletin. So while some of the letters had come from Henri Nouwen's *National Catholic Reporter* article, I learned it was Amnesty's campaign that had generated the physicians' petitions. Certainly none of the outpouring of international solidarity was the result of anything I had done.

Acknowledging the *Caso Filártiga* court documents and Joel's rigor mortis treatise, Lia offered their thanks "for sending us so complete and useful information on the Filártiga case, and for clarifying our doubts on the sequence of events."

She also sent along the list of people who had died under torture in Paraguay, which Amnesty planned to use in the Filártiga booklet, and asked me to review it. And so I finally learned of AI's plans to publish a pamphlet. As it turned out, Amnesty's request for assistance portended an about-face in their policy of strict in-house security. From then on, it seemed they wrote whenever they needed help. Not that I minded in the least. Quite the contrary, working closely on all aspect of Paraguayan human rights turned out to be the best thing that could have happened.

Thoughtfully, Lia also sent along an article from the January 2 *London Sunday Times*. The sharply written "Mystery Killing of Artist's Son" showed how the *Caso Filártiga* indeed had begun to attract international attention.

On the bottom of the shelf of correspondence keeping me from my bed, I found a dozen copies of my January 20 LADOC cover story. As usual, the article was published simultaneously in their *Notícias Aliadas* as well as their *Latin American Press*. Taking copies of both the English and Spanish language versions of "Murder of Son Prompts Paraguayan Doctor to Combat Repression of Stroessner Regime," I explained to Lia that I had written it under a pseudonym, Alberto Cabral—to shield my friends and associates in Paraguay from paying the cost. Also in my note to Lia, I apologized for Filártiga mistakenly crediting the letters and petitions to me. Adding that my work hopefully might soon start showing results and that our efforts would now reinforce each others, I pointed to the concluding paragraphs of my Alberto Cabral article:

> Every mention of the Filártiga case in the foreign press is another stain on Paraguay's bloody record of human rights violations. Every petition sent to General Stroessner demanding justice is another reminder that the world is watching. Every letter or telegram expressing solidarity with Dr. Filártiga's struggle sent to Ybycuí, Paraguay, is another weight placed on the scale in his favor.
>
> Even if the balance has not yet tipped, every indication shows that the international pressure building up will be the deciding factor in who survives the Filártiga–Peña confrontation.

And that was it. I crammed everything in an envelope, begged a friend to get it in the mail to London, and collapsed into anesthetic darkness.

2

It is not uncommon while traveling to wake up not knowing where you are geographically. But that next morning, February 11, as I came to consciousness, I had no idea where I was in my life's trajectory: I could have been eight years old, or fifty, or any place in between.

Not that I had time to think about it, because I had overslept and barely had time to make it to the airport. During the flight from Boston to Los Angeles, I wrote a full report of my East Coast trip for Joel and Inger. And just for the hell of it, I began a private tally of Filártiga's supporters.

Beginning with my first stop in New Haven, Connecticut, where Henri Nouwen taught theology at the Yale Divinity School, I explained that at my January 19 talk some fifty people signed a petition to Stroessner, and that the students were making plans to invite Joel to give a series of speeches and an art exhibition at the university. Moreover, during the following days a group of thirty-five students revived the Amnesty International Yale chapter, which had only eight members on the central campus, and moved it to the Divinity School.

Of course, I did not say anything about my personal accounting, but in my mind added Yale's AI chapter to the Secretariat. Neither did I mention the plans we worked out at Henri's place with Walter and Jeannette Gaffney.

"If the Peace Corps already's accepted you both," I had asked Walt, whom I had known for years since he began as Henri's assistant, "why do you want to work with Dr. Filártiga?"

"Because," Jet answered, "with the Peace Corps there's no telling where they'll send us, or what our assignment will be. But by assisting Dr. Filártiga in his work at the Clinic of Hope, we'll be certain of spending our two years in Latin America doing something meaningful. And, from everything you say, he can use the help."

"That's for sure," I agreed, "but there are other things to consider if you're going with the Filártigas.

"Make no mistake," I warned. "They're prepared to die in the struggle. Apart from the death threats, don't forget how the police threw Nidia and Dolly in jail—on trumped-up charges. And just a few months ago, their lawyer spent an extremely unpleasant day being psychologically tortured—on no charges at all.

"Also, there's something else you must know. The Filártigas are risking their necks trying to save the lives of the few remaining OPM leaders. And they're the most hunted people in Paraguay. At any moment, it all could blow up again into a deadly crisis. And I'm not using 'deadly' as a figure of speech.

"Henri, tell them. You were there during the worst of it."

"Already I told them," he said. "How you always carry guns. Even in church, when we would celebrate the Eucharist in memory of Joelito. What more is there to say?"

"We picked up Henri at the airport when he came back," Jet cut in. "We saw what a nervous wreck he was. That told us everything."

For hours in Henri's sparsely furnished living room we sipped wine and explored the pros and cons. What we did not know, as we discussed the Gaffneys' plans to join the Filártigas, was that a squad of soldiers was raiding the Clinic of Hope.

That same morning the police had hit the latest OPM safe house in Asunción. Fortunately, after a brief exchange of fire, our friends all managed to get away. But in making their escape, they had to abandon everything in the house—including Mirtha Ayala's wallet. And because Mirtha was Joel's cousin, the Army mounted an operation against the clinic, searching for Soledad and the others. Or anything else to incriminate the Filártigas. They found nothing. But that did not stop them from hauling off Joel.

At the Army barracks in Ybycuí the comandante, receiving instructions and questions by radio from military headquarters in Asunción, grilled Filártiga about his subversive activities: "What is your schedule of fees?" he demanded. "I do not have one," Joel confessed. "It is known that you give medical attention to enemies of the Fatherland," the comandante accused. "All of my patients are patriots," Filártiga responded. And so it went for six hours.

Unaware of the drama being played out at their future home in Paraguay, we talked over the Gaffneys' plans in Henri's New Haven apartment. "So you've really thought this out?" I asked.

"Completely," Walter said. "Joel won our admiration exactly one year ago. When you sent Henri all the information about him and his California trip."

"That was only a year ago?"

"January 1976. Then you stopped here at Yale, on the way to Paraguay, with the terrible news about Joelito. We prayed for you. We wanted to do more, especially after Henri came back."

"And now here you are again," Jet finished excitedly. "Just as we're getting ready to go to Latin America anyway. It's almost providential!"

The Gaffneys could hardly be considered kids naively blundering into harm's way. Both Walt and Jet were in their late twenties, and they knew the score. Well, as much as possible from the giant marshmallow.

"Of course, there's still a lot to do," Jet said. "Anyway, we haven't even written Joel to ask if he'll take us."

"That's the least of your worries," I assured them. Indeed, Filártiga accepted the Gaffneys' offer with "joy and delight." Two more allies to add.

"I spoke with Joel and the family on Christmas Day." The call picked up the Filártigas' spirits, I explained, but what they really wanted to know was when I would be coming back. "They're doing fine. But feeling a little vulnerable, isolated, not having the protection of a gringo around. And two will be even better."

Looking at Jet, I added, "Especially since one of them is the favorite niece of Mo Udall, a most senior member of the U.S. House of Representatives."

3

In my reports to Joel and Inger, I moved on to New York. Roberta Cohen, the director of the International League for Human Rights, took charge of the arrangements. At a briefing with the UN correspondents of the *Christian Science Monitor* and the *New York Times*, I gave them a packet of materials on the *Caso Filártiga*, and fielded their questions.

But, as would be the case all along, it was the torture photo of Joelito that did it. When we broke up three hours later, as one of them colorfully put it, he was "righteously pissed."

The next day, after spending an afternoon with Mort Rosenblum at the Council of Foreign Relations, he decided to expand his work on repression in the Southern Cone to include the *Caso Filártiga* as the primary case study.

My brief address at the human rights symposium at the Carnegie Endowment for International Peace proved less satisfying. However, it did give me the chance to size up these elite policymaker types, and I met a few decent human beings among them.

4

My time in Washington turned out to be most educational and productive. The people at Amnesty's office set up the first dozen or so appointments, which led to other contacts. In three days of back-to-back meetings, I spoke with twenty-seven people.

At the State Department my appointment with George Lister, a human rights officer in the Bureau of Inter-American Affairs, turned into a conference with four other bureaucrats. The only question their condescending attitude left was whether they found me, or my presentation, more distasteful. I wondered why they had even bothered.

Over the course of several late-night sessions with Jack Michael, an associate of the columnist Jack Anderson, the veteran muckraker explained the facts of political life in our nation's capital. What it boiled down to was that no one knew how far Jimmy

Carter intended to push human rights. After all, the week before he had taken office vowing that "our commitment to human rights must be absolute." So, just in case, the careerists of official Washington were missing no chance to get their good intentions on record.

Even Stroessner, Jack pointed out, was hedging his bets. Earlier that month, his chief of protocol arrived in town on a special mission. Conrado Papalardo assured anyone who would listen that Paraguay held the highest respect for human rights—but if by some off chance there should be any complaints, to just let them know and the government would straighten it all out.

After extolling to Inger and Joel the news of Paraguay's conversion, I got back to reality. On the official level, the most significant results came out of my meetings on Capitol Hill. In a long session with John Salzberg, the staff director of the House Subcommittee on International Organizations, he got it all down, taking pages of notes. John made no promises, but he felt that the powerful Filártiga material stood a good chance of influencing their deliberations to cut off aid to Paraguay. And, in fact, when the United States did finally tighten the financial screws on Stroessner, the *Caso Filártiga* played a good part in it.

It did not take nearly that long for the State Department to feel the congressional pressure. On February 1, Edward Kennedy entered my entire Alberto Cabral article in the Senate *Congressional Record*. Soledad's hero, Edward Koch, did the same in the House of Representatives on February 9. Both legislators sent their Cabral *Congressional Record* entries to the State Department. At the same time they "requested" that the U.S. Embassy in Asunción keep them apprised of Paraguayan human rights developments in general, and specifically of any changes in the status of the *Caso Filártiga*.

Nothing so rattles the cages of the pallid denizens of Foggy Bottom as a "request" from the Hill. Congress controls every penny of the State Department's budget, and all appointments above the ambassadorial level must be confirmed by the Senate.

Chalk up two more for Joel.

5

As much as possible, while away I had kept up a flow of information to Filártiga's many friends and admirers in California. Now, my welcome home to Los Angeles quickly merged into their mobilization for Joel.

Because of my OAS-sponsored research, UCLA's department of history offered me the position of postdoctoral scholar. Not incidentally, the appointment also provided a platform to carry on my *Caso Filártiga* activities. On university stationery, I followed up with the State Department bureaucrats and every other official I had met in Washington, confiding to them the profound concern Dr. Filártiga's supporters in California felt for his safety, especially after reading Alberto Cabral's alarming LADOC article. For their convenience and immediate reference, I enclosed copies of both the Spanish and English publications.

As I explained to Inger and Joel in my report to them, by far the greatest help in Washington came from the human rights NGOs. At the Washington Office on Latin

America (WOLA), Juan Ferreira dove into the treasure trove of human rights documentation. Impressed by the *Caso Filártiga*, he was awed by the comprehensive data on the political prisoners and set up a special Paraguay section at WOLA. Further, if I would continue sending them copies of the prisoner materials as they arrived from Paraguay, Juan proposed an exchange of information with Amnesty's Washington office.

It struck me as a great idea, but I was worried about a conflict of interest. During the trip, I learned a good deal about the strengths and weaknesses of the NGOs. Typically, I had known, each carved out a specialized niche. What came as a surprise was the zeal with which they guarded their turf. WOLA's focus was influencing human rights legislation in Congress, while Amnesty concentrated on promoting human rights using more direct action. In any event, we had talked it out and came to an agreement.

Then Tom Quigley, head of the Latin American division of the U.S. Catholic Conference (USCC), jumped in. Through the USCC, Tom offered WOLA and Amnesty's Washington office access to the extensive set of publications they received from Paraguay, as well as free use of their photocopier.

The *Caso Filártiga* absorbed Juan. He wrote Joel offering his personal condolences and urging him to pursue the struggle to uncover the truth. And, at the professional level, he pledged WOLA's institutional support and solidarity.

Rack up several more big ones for Filártiga's international support.

6

The most byzantine part of the Washington trip began when a young intern at WOLA saw Joelito's torture card. With spontaneous indignation, she demanded that a human rights abuse complaint be lodged with the Organization of American States.

Sure—except that the OAS is one of the least respected institutions in Washington, notorious as a plum tree in whose shade well-connected international bureaucrats with Potomac fever laze about. And, if possible, the Inter-American Commission for Human Rights (IACHR) of the OAS ranks even lower, lacking any ability to enforce its recommendations.

Everyone knew that the IACHR could not actually sanction the government of Paraguay. However, the official mandate of the commission is to investigate human rights abuses among the OAS member nations. And, just every once in a great while, the commission had been known to take the bit in its teeth and run with a case, pursuing an especially egregious human rights violation.

It might be worthwhile to charge Stroessner with the torture-murder of Joelito, if for no other reason than to further tarnish the dictator's reputation and generate international publicity for the *Caso Filártiga*. But first, of course, an official complaint would have to be lodged. After asking at least a dozen people, and not just ordinary people but also human rights activists from several NGOs, I could find no one who had a clue about how to do it. Obviously, filing the complaint with the IACHR, we all agreed, was no simple matter.

Walking into the IACHR's office, I took a few moments to study the setup before spotting a kind-looking white-haired gentleman reading the newspaper. I introduced myself properly and politely said, "I'm unfamiliar with the commission's procedures, and I was wondering if you'd be kind enough to help me do something about this?" And then I dropped Joelito's torture card on the desk and slid it under his nose.

It was kind of a dirty trick, putting the old boy at ease with my affable demeanor to maximize the shock, but remorse was not among the emotions I felt waiting for him to recover.

The horror of Joelito's mutilated body, right there on his desk, sullying his comfortable surroundings, stunned him. Perhaps a minute passed before he tore his eyes from the photo.

"It is strictly forbidden for a staff member to influence a potential complainant in any way," he croaked unsteadily.

"Unless I know what to do, there won't be any complaint," I said, abandoning my milquetoast pretense and slapping another Joelito card in front of him. "I need a place to start!"

"As I said, I cannot coach you in any way," he replied. "However, it is common knowledge that anyone can file a complaint."

"Yes, but can't you see that I don't—"

"I repeat, young man," he interrupted, and said in a quarter-beat cadence, "our-charter-decrees-that-*anyone*-has-the-right-to-file-a-complaint-of-human-rights-abuse. We-then-are-required-to-conduct-an-investigation-to-determine-its-merits."

"*Anyone?*"

"Anyone."

Then, as if just entering the room, I said, "Excuse me. I'm here to petition the Inter-American Commission for Human Rights to investigate the torture and murder of Joelito Filártiga in Paraguay."

"Please be seated," he said. "We will require as complete details as you are able to provide. It may take some time."

For seven years, guided by the able Amnesty attorney Harold Berk, IACHR Case 2158 was a thorn in Stroessner's weathered hide. More than simply one of those rare instances of standing up to injustice, the *Caso Filártiga* became the commission's stellar human rights offensive.

At the time, however, my report to Joel and Inger merely related that I had filed a complaint against the government of Paraguay—and that, with the opening of an official IACHR case, the OAS had initiated an investigation to determine if the police had violated Joelito's human rights.

The follow-up among the NGOs, however, was a lot more exciting. The simple procedure of filing a human rights complaint with the commission was one of those overlooked pockets of Washington's institutions. Learning how routine the process actually was, Juan Ferreira took it one step further and contacted Tom Quigley and Roberta Cohen. Combining the weight of their three NGOs—WOLA, the USCC, and the ILHR—they expanded the complaint to request that the IACHR conduct an on-site investigation of the *Caso Filártiga* in Paraguay.

In my informal reckoning, I added Tom and Roberta to Joel's growing list of backers. And in all fairness, I also threw in the OAS Inter-American Commission for Human Rights.

7

WOLA and the USCC did not forget Stroessner's other victims. Employing the most recent list of political prisoners, they formally filed separate cases for all 330 people with the IACHR.

On February 4, the commission cabled Stroessner requesting permission, ". . . TO VISIT PARAGUAY IN ORDER TO CONDUCT AN INVESTIGATION *IN LOCO* ON THE SERIOUS AND CONTINUING ALLEGATIONS OF VIOLATIONS OF HUMAN RIGHTS IN THAT COUNTRY RECEIVED BY THE COMMISSION."

To no one's surprise, the government of Paraguay replied with its usual stalling tactic, informing the commission that it would take their request under consideration. To everyone's astonishment, rather than letting it go, the IACHR openly challenged Stroessner's evasions. In a heated exchange of communiqués, it tenaciously demanded a straightforward answer. Finally, on March 18, Stroessner flatly asserted that "for reasons of domestic politics, an official visit by the IACHR is not at present advisable."

And so, by refusing to allow the commission's on-site visit, the master manipulator had been manipulated into a big-time blunder.

A month later, Juan Ferreira wrote me in California with even better news. In February I had sent him the Paraguayan Church network's four lists, and in March, an additional four, even more extensive compilations of the regime's political prisoners that I had just received from another network. WOLA and the USCC filed more than another 650 individual cases of human rights violations with the IACHR. And, for each and every person, they asked for an in loco investigation into the fate of the victims.

Stroessner, completely missing the power shift in the human rights community, insolently dismissed the commission's request to carry out its on-site visit. To our delight, the government of Paraguay's arrogance so rankled the IACHR that it touched off one of the most gratifying feuds ever between the OAS and a member nation.

The commission set to work on its *Report on the Situation of Human Rights in Paraguay*. The final document, a ninety-page booklet, published in Spanish and English, tore into Stroessner's crimes with all the vituperation of offended bureaucrats. Reproducing the complete exchange of cable traffic leading up to Stroessner's refusal to allow the on-site investigation, the *Report* detailed a dozen or so complaints we filed to demonstrate Paraguay's "violation of the most basic human rights, such as those that protect life, liberty, and personal security."

Prominently including the *Caso Filártiga*, it drew special attention to several cases under active investigation because, "In view of their seriousness, a decision was reached to include them in this document, by way of example." Then, to assure maximum exposure, the commission held off releasing its condemnation until the 1977 OAS annual conference in Washington. One week before the convention opened in July, the IACHR spared no effort to make sure copies of the *Report* reached every one of the Latin American ambassadors and their staffs, the NGO observers, and the expanded press corps members who had been tipped off. The controversial *Report* was a big hit, going a long way to establishing Paraguay as the most discredited and despised regime in the hemisphere.

All in all, by then I was feeling pretty good about the international pressure that was building up. Not that I had mastered the intricacies of the international human rights system; no more than I understood the function of every part in my car. But I had learned how to make it move.

8

My first night in California, Friday, February 11, as I looked over the auditorium filled with many old friends and other friendly faces, went a long way to dispel the residual reentry trauma. The premiere of Jim Richardson's film *Filártiga* was as much a home-coming as a fundraiser.

After all, I had lived in Los Angeles for six years, and many of these people had befriended Joel, making his California visit such a success. My talk went over well, as did Jim's moving explanation of why he had spent such effort producing *Filártiga*. People contributed generously, signed the petitions, and joined the new letter-writing campaign.

It was all a great success. Still, I could not shake a feeling of off-centeredness.

For the next three Fridays, Jim and I repeated our presentation. People responded with the same enthusiasm. In early March, I took the film to San Francisco for a few weeks, and I found the same solidarity in the Bay Area.

Lia Fleming wrote Jim asking for a copy of *Filártiga*, to be used by AI's National Sections around the world in publicizing the *Caso Filártiga*. With the Los Angeles Amnesty chapter handling the publicity, they raised enough funds to make an extra print of *Filártiga* for my own work.

The afternoon I got back to Los Angeles from the northern California trip, I found an enormous pile of correspondence. As I plowed through it, the sensation of déjà vu was almost spooky. Just as when I returned to Boston from the East Coast tour, there was a letter from Lia expressing AI's thanks for the Paraguayan documents I had sent them before leaving for California. And again she saved her greatest enthusiasm for the photocopied *Caso Filártiga* legal materials, "They are," she insisted, "most impressive and—apart from the useful details for our dossier on the [*Filártiga*] case—some documents are of particular interest. An example are the medical certificates, which will be used by our forensic medical group, currently working on medical ethics in this specific field."

She even ended on the same general note, asking if I "have any suggestions regarding ways of corroborating the data in the [leaflet] list," and specifically if, by any chance, I could help in their work "trying to gather as much reliable information as possible on cases of deaths in custody, for use during our future campaigning activities."

And it got weirder. Last time, in Boston, the Paraguayan Church network's four lists of prisoners was just what AI needed to double-check and fill out their information from other sources. This time, in the volume of correspondence waiting for me, not only did I find another impressive list from Father John Vesey, but three other rosters sent by Congressman Domingo Laino as well.

Two of Domingo's lists, compiled by his opposition political party's Paraguayan Youth for Human Rights group, contained the names of more than 300 people each. Astoundingly, one of them detailed a complete inventory of the Emboscada concentration camp's population—catalogued cell by cell. And then, as if made to order for Lia, the third list was of "Political Prisoners Either Killed or 'Disappeared' after Detention."

The bonanza was off to Lia and Juan Ferreira in a matter of hours. In my cover letters I also let them know that the Kennedy and Koch letters to State, together with their Alberto Cabral *Congressional Record* entries, had arrived at the U.S. Embassy in Asunción. According to my source there, I reported, the congressional inquiries had "precipitated anxious discussions among the Ambassador and his senior staff." To take advantage of the momentum, I urged them to step up their efforts and generate as much pressure as possible. Thankfully, in light of the approaching troubles, they got right on it.

Lia's reply to the information coup was not unexpected. Predictably, after all but magically receiving the precise information Amnesty needed, she tried it again. I sure would have.

After offering AI's gratitude, Lia explained how the material "helped us to revise our list of deaths and disappearances," and went on, "I enclose a copy of this latest compilation for your information and in case you have more detailed information about any of the more poorly documented cases."

Unfortunately, at the time her letter reached me, I had no new information. Worse yet, there would not be any good news coming out of Paraguay for quite some time.

9

In his letter of April 3, Joel told me how the death threats had started up again and described what quite possibly had been an attempt on his life. While traveling from the clinic to Asunción, a huge, long-haul truck suddenly swerved, blinding him with its halogen driving lights and forcing his pickup into a ditch. Miraculously, Joel and Nidia ended up only badly bruised.

Furious, Filártiga drove directly to the ambassador's residence and denounced the incident as an *atentado*—an assassination attempt—while making it look like an accident. The ambassador immediately called the minister of the interior, Sabino Montanaro, and demanded the minister's guarantee that Filártiga's life was not in danger. Naturally, Montanaro denied any knowledge of an *atentado*, assured the ambassador no such threat existed, and wrote it all off to Filártiga's paranoia.

While the *atentado* leaves room for doubt, there is no question about the dictatorship's political persecution of Horacio Galeano Perrone. Continuing their interrupted plans to punish the attorney for his audacious Forty-Five Points motion, Horacio found himself facing trumped-up charges of criminal misconduct. On May 9, after being disbarred by the Supreme Court, Galeano Perrone was forced to withdraw from the *Caso Filártiga*.

In Joel's letter to me after losing his lawyer, he took a remarkably philosophical view of his predicament. "In other words," he wrote, "from the viewpoint of constitutional justice, we are a lost cause. Fortunately, another forum still remains—the people's tribunal, which is even more severe. Slower, but more severe."

Filártiga showed similar equanimity when reporting Horacio's disbarment to the OAS. Normally, the lack of legal representation automatically would have meant the end of the trial, with all charges dropped against Duarte, Peña, and the other codefendants. Apparently, Stroessner did not quite dare take it that far, and simply allowed the case to continue languishing in legal limbo. As Filártiga informed the commission, "because at that time an international campaign had made the *Caso Filártiga* known around the world, it prevented further injustices against our persecuted family."

Even so, as the International League for Human Rights would later explain in its 1980 mission report, *Mbareté: The Higher Law of Paraguay*, after laying bare the government's frame-up against Galeano Perrone:

> In proceeding against Dr. Galeano [Perrone] the Chief Justice and the Attorney General distorted and subverted the law in order to achieve two purposes; to punish him for his temerity and to warn all other attorneys that the Filártiga case was untouchable. They succeeded in both purposes. Dr. Galeano [Perrone] has been and continues to be punished, and from the date that he was forced to abandon the Filártiga case no other attorney has been willing to take it on.

10

In his letter, Joel went on to explain that the possible *atentado* and Stroessner's vendetta against Galeano Perrone had finally moved the embassy to action: "Due to security considerations," Ambassador Landau strongly urged evacuating the entire Filártiga family to the United States.

Not that Landau had come to accept that the killing of Joelito was a legitimate human rights case. Rather, with Carter's human rights policy still in flux, by May 1977 the international campaign had elevated the *Caso Filártiga* to the point where it no longer could be brushed aside. Should Joel, or any member of the family, come to harm because of the embassy's indifference, the political fallout might very well amount to considerably more than a road bump on the ambassador's career path.

Adding to the pressure, during a visit to the embassy, Joel had been shown several publications that seemed to be causing more than a little concern about the growing notoriety of the *Caso Filártiga* in the U.S. press. In late April, the influential Jesuit magazine *America* republished my Alberto Cabral piece, giving it feature play and the new title "Political Murder in Paraguay."

As upsetting to the embassy staff, Filártiga wrote, was Jerry Helfand's cover story that came out a week later in the nationally circulated *Los Angeles Free Press*. Jerry's article contained several of Filártiga's drawings, as well as the torture photos of Joelito. "Two Versions of a Murder: Paraguayan Dictatorship Eliminates Dissent" raked the State Department and embassy in Asunción over the coals for not standing up to Stroessner. The magazine sold out so quickly that the publisher sent several hundred extra copies to the nation's capital overnight.

In any event, Filártiga sidestepped the embassy's offer to evacuate the family, saying he would have to think about it. Scuttling off to safety in the United States was not even a consideration; nothing was going to force him to abandon the struggle in Paraguay.

My three months in California had been busy and productive. I had given dozens of presentations, helped organize petition drives and letter writing campaigns, spread the word, and raised financial support for the Filártigas' cause at countless receptions, given interviews on National Public Radio, written a half-dozen newspaper and magazine pieces, and shepherded through as many more electronic media stories and print articles on the *Caso Filártiga*.

By the time Joel's letter arrived in May telling me of the latest troubles in Paraguay, I had already reached my decision. The uneasiness that continued to bother me in California, I realized, was a matter of geography—political power resided on the other side of the continent.

Reluctantly, I decided to return to the East Coast, where my efforts to build international support would have a more direct impact. By the middle of the month, I had firmed up invitations to speak with the *Filártiga* film in Washington, followed by other presentations along the seaboard up to Boston.

I was all set to go. Then, on May 14, fate stepped in.

On and off over the years my chronic back pain had been the source of considerable inconvenience, though for some time it hardly had been a matter of interest, never mind the center of my life. But that sunny Saturday morning I awoke, gave a gratifying stretch, and heard a loud crack in my neck. Every movement seemed to send bolts of electric pain shooting up my spine, yanking my head backward in savage thrusts. And just like that, the axis of my world shifted from moving and shaking to shaking to move.

11

"Have you seen this?" I asked Henri Nouwen as I burst into his apartment at Yale. Flipping a copy of Joelito's long-awaited Amnesty pamphlet on the coffee table, I said, "It arrived from London this morning, just before I left Boston."

A lot had happened in the four months since my lesson in humility. It had taken a month of physical therapy at the UCLA Medical Center before being able to pick up even the most limited schedule, and it was still pretty slow going.

"So, at last. We have it," Henri declared. "They certainly gave it an impressive cover." Set against an all-black background, in striking contrast the large white lettering read *Deaths under Torture and Disappearance of Political Prisoners in Paraguay*.

"How many languages?" he asked, leafing through the oversized twenty-page booklet, which contained summaries of about three dozen cases.

"I'm not sure. As I understand it, the Secretariat sends it to the Amnesty National Sections. They then translate and publish editions for their own countries. I imagine it'll come out in all the major European languages, at least."

"Oh, look here!" Henri exclaimed, coming across the centerfold section on the *Caso Filártiga*. Along with the write-up, it showed two pictures of Joelito—the first with him alive and smiling, the other of his tortured body—and a full-page drawing by Filártiga. "My, my, this will really be a great help."

"Yes. It's a real boost to the campaign. The job now is to take advantage of the attention it generates. Keep up the pressure. Build momentum," I thought aloud. "Good thing Filártiga will be here soon."

"When did this come out?" Henri asked, fascinated by the pamphlet's presentation.

"As I said, it arrived this morning," I replied. "So, maybe about a week ago, early September."

"Too bad you missed Walt and Jet. They would like to see this. And you too, of course."

"I'll send them a copy. At least we had a good visit when I was here."

In June, with a lot of help from my friends and Tylenol 4, I had managed to give a presentation at the Latin American Studies Center at Yale. The students took the opportunity to push through Joel's formal invitation, officially requesting him to begin his lecture series and art exhibition on November 15.

During my stay, Henri had arranged for yet another battery of tests with a neurologist friend of his. Other than a few herniated discs, nothing conclusive showed up. I could try a second back operation. Alternatively, he recommended building up my upper body strength with a disciplined regimen of physical exercise.

12

In 1969 I had bought an abandoned house on a beautiful, deserted island in the Bay of Fundy, only a few miles off the coast of Maine, but in Canada. At the time, the height of the antiwar movement, more than a few people saw no reason to pester U.S. Immigration when they were forced to leave, or come back into, the United States. Over the years, I and the many others who passed through Wood Island fixed up the 100-year-old nine-room house into a very special, if somewhat rustic, retreat.

So, after a few weeks in New Haven with Henri, I took my Paraguayan research and headed for the island. The splendor of the place never failed to work its healing magic, no matter how bad the state of my physical or psychological wreckage. After wrapping up a few loose ends—forwarding another long list of prisoners from the Paraguayan Church network to Amnesty and WOLA, offering a few suggestions to Roberta Cohen about the ILHR's second mission to Paraguay, and generally touching base with the other East Coast people working on the *Caso Filártiga*—I escaped to my refuge on the outer fringe of civilization.

Now, back at Yale with Henri, it no longer existed.

"By the way, when did the Gaffneys leave?" I asked him, coming back to the present.

"About a month ago. You still were in Canada. Before the fire." Then, he got straight to it. "Richard," he said, "it is time now. Tell me everything."

We still had a lot of important *Caso Filártiga* matters to cover, but Henri knew why I had come to see him just then. I needed to share my loss and grief with my friend.

"Well," I began hesitantly, "I'd been on Wood Island for five weeks or so. Pushing myself physically and working on my research, feeling 100 percent better.

"One morning I took the skiff over to Seal Cove on the big island, Grand Manan, to pick up supplies and have the chain saw repaired. August 23. I planned to return before dark, but the saw couldn't be fixed until the next day.

"I ended up spending the night in Seal Cove, playing poker with friends, while someone turned that big old house into eighteen inches of ashes on the bottom of the cellar. The Mounties and fire marshal said it was arson."

"How could they be sure?" he asked.

"I never used the front door. Always the side entrance, into the kitchen. They found the front door lock outside the foundation. Key still in it, but the mechanism was in the unlocked position. They figured someone had opened the door for ventilation. Same with the windows. Smashed out from the inside.

"And my car had been searched. Door panels ripped off. I'd left it at the Seal Cove pier. At first I thought it was just kids. But when I asked around, people told me about Rocky—a Cuban American who'd been hanging around Seal Cove and asking about Wood Island."

"Your research?" Henri asked.

"Gone. Burned. Or stolen. Like everything else. Hundreds of note cards, columns of figures from the historical financial ledgers. Same as my first book on Paraguay. Once I organized the figures into charts and tables, there was no reason to ever look at the raw data again. So I saved a lot of unnecessary work and didn't bother photocopying the note cards. Good thinking, huh?"

Henri shook his head.

"And then there's the assassination of Ambassador Letelier and Ronni Moffitt in Washington last year. Remember how Operation Condor used anti-Castro Cuban Americans to set it up? So I asked a former student of mine from UCLA, who used to work for the CIA, to check it out.

"Pat got back to me right away," I went on. "Couldn't say definitely if it was the Human Wrongs Network. But she was adamant about how 'incredibly lucky' I was."

"She?"

"Yeah, she, you sexist pig," I retorted with feigned irritation.

"'Lucky? Shit!' I told her. 'Another week and I'd have had it all on paper. Then, I'd have left a copy with someone for safekeeping. Like always.

"And you know what Pat said?" I demanded. "She said, 'Hold on, Prof. You say you needed another week?' I said, 'That's right! Just one more week!' And she said, 'So stop your pissing and moaning. And thank God you weren't at home. I know these people. You didn't have one more day!'"

Nodding in sympathy, Henri gave me a few minutes to cool down.

"And when I called Joel to tell him what happened, you know what he said? He said he wasn't surprised."

"Joel wasn't surprised that your home was burned down!" Henri gasped.

"His exact words," I groused. "Then he told me he had been waiting for my call. Hoping it wouldn't come."

"What did he mean?"

"In August, there was a false fire alarm on his house in Sajonia," I explained. "All at once, almost like a show, a parade of fire trucks and police cruisers arrived, sirens screaming, disrupting the entire neighborhood.

"Joel couldn't remember the exact date. But we pinned it down to a day or two of when they torched my home. One more *Caso Filártiga* enigma."

"Losing your home and possessions like that is very much like a death," Henri said calmly. "Now you are filled with anger and grief. And pain. But in time you will heal."

I did not want to hear it.

"I know how much Wood Island meant to you," Henri said. "You will always feel the loss. That will never go away. But in time, perhaps a long time, you will heal. It is much worse for the Filártigas. But they, too, will heal. Of that I am sure. Because life heals."

13

After a good meal, and a better bottle of Henri's wine, we got back to it. Filártiga had a lot of other news. Stroessner seemed to be cleaning up his act.

I skipped through the notes of our conversation. "Right. Joel says that on September 11, the OAS was informed," I paused to find the exact wording, "'. . . the Paraguayan government is willing to receive your visit on a date to be determined by common agreement.' Filártiga's hoping the commission's investigation could force some action on the legal case."

"But you are not so optimistic," Henri said.

"We'll see," I replied. "Most likely it's another stall. Until Stroessner actually sets a definite date for the visit, it means nothing."

Indeed, Stroessner repeatedly put off the on-site OAS visit, until the change of U.S. administrations in 1981 made even the pretext unnecessary. During the intervening years, however, the commission's grudge match with Paraguay roiled on.

"But there has been a letup in this wave of repression," I said. "Quite a few prisoners have been released. His Excellency even deigned to grant the ILHR's investigators an audience, during their June mission. I spoke with Ben Stephansky. They're writing up the formal report now, *Denial of Human Rights in Paraguay*. Should be out in December.

"Anyway, Joel feels Stroessner's promised OAS invitation was all part of setting the stage for the warm reception he received at the White House last week."

"Stroessner was here? He met with the president?" Henri blurted.

"Sure did. Along with every other Latin American dictator. For the signing of the Panama Canal Treaties. And as President Stroessner is the senior head-of-state, he was given the place of honor at the ceremonies. Protocol. But something of a contradiction with Carter's Christian morality, his 'total commitment to human rights,' wouldn't you say?"

"But why?" Henri asked, indignantly. "Why? To compromise your most basic beliefs. Why would he do it?"

I found Father Nouwen's naiveté so refreshing, I opened another bottle of his wine.

"Because," I replied, "the president's job is to be the president. Because the presidency is always more important than the president. Always."

The hard-ball reality of U.S. foreign policy offended Henri's compassion and morality. He did not like it, and would not acquiesce to it, but that never blinded him from understanding it. Which is one of the reasons why you could always count on Henri.

"Joel did have some good news," I announced, moving on. "The embassy's taking him seriously now."

"How is that?"

"Stroessner's trying to stop him from coming up here again. Guess he remembers the fallout from Joel's California trip. Anyway, they refused to renew Filártiga's passport, so he took his Yale invitation to the ambassador. And Landau said not to worry. They'd give him a passport waiver."

"A passport waiver? How does that work?" Henri asked.

"Paraguayans can go to a neighboring country using only their *cédula*, the national identity card. Then, say from Rio de Janeiro, he flies to the States on the special passport waiver."

"That sure is preferential treatment. I have never heard of anything like it."

"Neither had I. Just goes to show how having friends in Congress will open hearts at the State Department."

"Oh, yes," Henri said, refilling our glasses. "Bless their souls."

I couldn't tell if he was referring to Filártiga's supporters in Congress, or the bureaucrats at State. Henri could have meant either. More likely, both.

"And there's better yet," I finished. "Joel and Bob Garrison pulled off the biggest coup of all. Got the ambassador to OK another art exhibition at the Paraguayan–American Cultural Center. Same as last year.

"Filártiga's already had two other shows this year in Asunción," I said. "But this is the big one. Starts next week. Can't imagine the press missing such a golden opportunity."

"Oh no. They won't do that," Henri agreed reflectively. He understood all too well how the game was played, having grown up in Nazi-occupied Holland.

The same as in any police state, the media stood no chance of getting away with directly criticizing the regime. Only through more subtle means could they get their message out. Like giving spectacular play to an ostensibly apolitical cultural event. And Filártiga's exhibition, the second U.S.-sponsored show by the dictatorship's most outspoken critic, now held that promise.

14

A year had passed since Joel's big exhibition, Horacio's Forty-Five Points, and Stroessner's heavy-handed reaction. Yet, instead of withering away, the *Caso Filártiga* had flourished into a worldwide sensation. The story was more important than ever.

If Joel had felt the coverage went overboard in 1976, he found that it paled beside the gusto with which the media seized upon his 1977 exhibition.

The press didn't even wait for opening night, September 20. Two days before, the leading papers kicked off the supercharged campaign with double-page, centerfold Sunday Supplements. *La Tribuna's* eulogy, "His Drawings Are His Being and His Testimony," featured an enormous photograph of Dr. Filártiga framed by eight of his most striking works. They had been chosen from the ninety new pieces to be displayed because "in these drawings can be seen the dualism of placid chaos and bucolic suffering that comprises the world surrounding him in his practice of medicine . . . a vision formed by his constant struggle against humanity's misery that is sickness, death, and poverty."

The refusal to renew Joel's passport and prevent him from traveling abroad again had spread through the Asunción grapevine. Adding to the political drama, in a prominent sidebar *La Tribuna* drove home how Filártiga had trumped the dictatorship.

After recounting the enormous success of Joel's California visit, the article heralded Filártiga's upcoming East Coast tour. "Such trips are eloquent proof of the Paraguayan artist's prestige," it brayed. "His travels also explain how, through perseverance and dedication—but without neglecting his profession as a physician for an instant—this man from the virtually unknown village of Ybycuí has become known in the far-off places of the planet."

And so it went. All through Filártiga's week-long exhibit, the press vied in its quest for superlatives.

The people loved it.

Joel, however, had mixed feelings. In his next letter he acknowledged that the media hype caused him "genuine personal embarrassment." But Filártiga, never one to let false humility cloud his judgment, clearly saw how the limelight's intensity refocused public attention. Despite Stroessner's best efforts to kill the case, it refused to die. Yet again, the *Caso Filártiga* rose as the symbol of people's discontent, and hope.

15

All that day at Yale, as Henri and I reveled in the Amnesty pamphlet and the media blitz Filártiga's exhibition would set off, he had said nothing about his own latest contribution. With typical modesty, Henri waited until the following morning, as I was preparing to leave, before bringing out "Compassion and the Seven O'Clock News."

The five-page cover story in *Sojourners* magazine centered on the frontispiece Joel had composed for Henri's *Compassion* book. In his uncluttered prose, Henri drew a graphic word picture of the Filártigas' saga, gave his university address to write for more information about Joel's "art, invitations to him to speak and exhibit his works," and ended by reminding his enormous readership that "letters of encouragement are welcomed."

Judging from the steady flow of letters that arrived mentioning Father Nouwen, Henri's solidarity played no small part in the ever more effective international campaign. In fact, from the start, Henri was a pillar of support, always there; from traveling to

Paraguay to helping others come, from arranging for free medical supplies to making generous financial contributions himself. Even before I started keeping tabs, Henri ranked among the strongest of Filártiga's friends.

From Yale, I made a quick trip to Washington. It was the first chance since my inaugural East Coast foray to meet with the human rights activists who had taken up the Filártigas' cause. I filled them in on the latest developments. They invited me to help in the flurry of activity it touched off, especially the preparations for Joel's visit. But I had to get back to my rehabilitation program. Until picking up Filártiga in New York, the daily grind of my life consisted of cutting, splitting, and stacking cord after cord of firewood at my brother's place in rural Massachusetts.

There was one thrilling interruption to my masochistic existence. On October 11, Amnesty International won the Nobel Peace Prize for 1977. It is next to impossible to properly convey the impact of winning The Prize. Overnight, it conferred a quantum leap of prestige, respect, and celebrity; and Amnesty's soaring status took the *Caso Filártiga* right along on the ride.

Precisely one month later, on November 11, Joel and I exchanged a welcoming *abrazo* at LaGuardia Airport, vaporizing the eleven months since our farewell at Asunción's Aeropuerto Presidente Stroessner.

16

"The letters keep coming in. Dozens every week!" Filártiga exclaimed once we settled in at the Manhattan apartment of a vacationing friend. "And the way the embassy treats me now! It is like I am a favorite son!

"I never imagined so much support. And it continues to grow. How is it possible?"

"It's just as I've told you. Many people and organizations have taken up the cause. My role has been mostly a facilitator, providing information on the *Caso Filártiga*, and Stroessner's repression."

"That still fails to answer my question. You only describe what has been done," he countered. "That does not account for such extraordinary results."

The outpouring of solidarity far exceeded anything we had hoped for when I left Paraguay with the uncertain prospect of building international support. Then, within a few short months, it had happened.

"You're right," I replied. "It finally came together for me last month when Amnesty won the Nobel Peace Prize. It's been building for years. And Jimmy Carter's administration put it over the top. International human rights has come of age.

"Just about when I came back, the game changed radically. All in our favor. There's never been a better time to be advocating human rights. And that is the reason behind the otherwise inexplicable support for the *Caso Filártiga*."

"So two or three years ago, no one would have paid attention?" he queried. Filártiga is remarkably knowledgeable about world events. Instead of sleeping, he spends his nights listening to news over the short wave radio.

"I wouldn't go that far. But it wouldn't have been anything like this. Look," I said, "during the '60s, civil rights and the Vietnam war tore at the traditional consensus of our body politic. Then, events in the '70s shredded it."

I ran through the Pentagon Papers revelations of government lies to escalate the war; how its expansion into Cambodia and the killing of students at Kent State and Jackson, Mississippi, brought the antiwar protests to a zenith in 1971. And then Nixon illegally ordering the mass arrests of demonstrators in Washington, herding them into the RFK sports stadium.

I mentioned some of Nixon's other abuses of power, like his Red Squads that manipulated the federal grand jury system to persecute opposition groups, sending people to jail without even a trial, and the racist attacks on the black militants, killing dozens of their leaders.

"But what brought it home to the Eastern Establishment was when they found themselves on Nixon's 'Enemies List,' harassed by income tax audits, their mail intercepted."

Joel leaned back into a big leather chair, adopting his Buddha-like pose.

I had forgotten the Mai Lai massacre whitewash, but decided to leave it and jumped to the Watergate scandal, Nixon's 1974 resignation, and his pardon a month later by his hand-picked successor Gerald Ford. And Senator Frank Church's 1975 release of the devastating *Church Committee Report*, which documented how the long history of official lies and illegalities, especially by the CIA, were not aberrations but the way things really worked.

"I've left out a lot," I said, "but by the 1976 presidential elections, people were deeply divided and thoroughly disillusioned. And the stature of the United States around the world had plummeted to an all time low."

"These facts are not new," Joel said, "but the context you place them in is. Even so, I have yet to see their relation with 'human rights coming of age.'"

"I'm there," I said. "Jimmy Carter ran as an outsider, vowing to instill high ethical standards. Right the wrongs. Restore respect for the United States. Human rights became the most popularly respected issue of his campaign.

"It served to dissipate people's cynicism, something everyone could get behind. Feel good about. Abroad, it held the key to regain the moral high ground, reestablish a respected foreign policy. Over and over Carter hammered away at his 'absolute commitment to human rights.'"

"And he has kept his word?" Joel asked.

"It's still too soon to tell," I replied. "But one thing's for sure. It's put teeth into the international human rights community.

"And that is the answer to your question, of how and why such support has been possible. And which opens up a world-class opportunity for you."

Unconsciously, Joel massaged his temples.

"During this trip you're going to be meeting the people who have been organizing support for the *Caso Filártiga*. You know how solidarity has helped keep the case alive in Paraguay. From here on, it's you who are going to make things happen."

Filártiga rose from the recliner and paced around the large apartment.

"God knows," he said, "Stroessner has hermetically sealed down the lid on the *Caso Filártiga*. International pressure is not simply our best chance to pry it open. It is our only hope."

That afternoon we met the people at the AI/USA national headquarters in New York City. Just as with the Amnesty offices in Washington and Los Angeles, the London Secretariat's introduction opened the door. But it was Joel who won their hearts.

Within hours, plans that would make AI/USA one of Dr. Filártiga's most energetic and effective allies had been laid. On the spot, Larry Cox, the head of publicity, conducted interviews with Joel and me for radio broadcasts on Spanish and English stations throughout the country. We left loaded down with hundreds of the newly released U.S. edition of the pamphlet *Deaths under Torture and Disappearance of Political Prisoners in Paraguay.*

On top of Joelito's torture cards and Jim Richardson's *Filártiga* film, our weapons included a number of magazine articles on the *Caso Filártiga.* Now, with the addition of the powerful Amnesty booklet, backed by the prestige of The Prize, we possessed an impressive arsenal.

But just as during the UCLA visit, at Yale it was Filártiga's charisma that mobilized the dozens of spin-off activities. A host of eager volunteers set up Joel's art exhibitions and screenings of *Filártiga*, publicized the lecture series, arranged media coverage, circulated petitions, and organized the letter-writing campaigns.

And more. Several of the assistants used their personal and family contacts to put Filártiga together with individuals able to make generous financial contributions, and arranged to have free medical supplies sent to the Clinic of Hope. Everywhere we went, it seemed, people could not do enough for the crusading doctor from Paraguay.

Shortly after beginning our month-long travels, I had an insight that went a long way in explaining Joel's ability to inspire people. Filártiga's life, spent among the harshness of underdevelopment and the persecution he endured as an active opponent of Stroessner's police state, had immunized him from the giant marshmallow's seduction.

Even though Joel's limited English required that someone serve as an interpreter, in no way did it hamper him and his art from conveying the truth with the full force of developing-world clarity. From Boston to Washington, the lucidity of Filártiga's unvarnished presence never failed to move those who really listened; hundreds in an auditorium, or one-on-one face-to-face, it made no difference.

17

Joel and I arrived a little early for our appointment. Peter Fenn, "special assistant/ scheduler to Senator Frank Church," greeted us warmly, explained that the senator would be with us presently, and disappeared into the inner sanctum.

Despite his lofty title, Peter showed a down-to-earth sincerity when we had met the previous afternoon. The anger that grew as he listened to Filártiga tell his story burst into a scarlet rage at the sight of Joelito's torture card. As keeper of the gate to Senator Frank Church, the second senior member of the Senate Committee on Foreign Relations—outranked only by the chairman, John Sparkman—Peter exercised enormous influence. And, to have arranged this conference with the powerful senator so soon must have taken every bit of it.

Simply getting to Peter had been no simple matter. We worked it out during Joel's visit to Wellesley College, over breakfast at the Worsthaus in Harvard Square with Forrester Church, a Harvard Divinity School student. Actually, the whole thing began with Terry Esther and David Cobb, old friends from Berkeley with whom I stayed during my trip through the Bay Area in February. Like the Gaffneys, they also became interested in working with the Filártigas at the Clinic of Hope, and had come to Boston to meet Joel. It was a classic old-boy connection: David introduced Joel to his friend Forrester, who called his father Frank, who had Peter meet with us.

And now, on the morning of December 1, we waited to see the senator himself, a tremendous opportunity for the *Caso Filártiga* because nothing, absolutely nothing, we might do would approach the pressure Church could bring to bear on the State Department. It was, after all, his Committee on Foreign Relations that confirmed all their high-ranking nominees—from ambassadors to the secretary of state.

The way things functioned at this rarefied level, we knew, all would be decided in a few hurried minutes. And there would be no second chance.

At precisely 8:30, Peter ushered us into the exquisitely appointed office. He reminded us to get right to the point.

Sitting behind an elegant walnut desk, flanked by flags set against a backdrop of framed awards and photographs, Senator Frank Church cut an impressive figure. He exuded authority—and power.

Peter did the introductions and it was on. The senator's assuring smile animated his melodious voice. "I've seen the materials you left with Peter," he said. "What can I do to help?"

Filártiga began speaking as I simultaneously interpreted. "Our only hope for justice is to apply maximum international pressure on Stroessner. Because he fears the financial and political consequences. By exposing his crimes and damaging his reputation.

"In Paraguay we have enormous support for our struggle. But the dictatorship is so strong that—"

Church's fantastic transformation stopped me in mid-sentence. Maybe he chose me because I was the one speaking directly to him. Or because he wanted to avoid offending Dr. Filártiga. Or because I was a fellow American. Or the youngest. Or whatever.

It is not that I missed the shift. From the moment I began interpreting, not for a nanosecond had we broken eye contact. It just happened: There was no transition.

One instant Church was radiating his famous charisma. The next, his face was a mask of stone. Not a trace of emotion. Except for the fearsome orbs of hostility that were his eyes. Literally, without a blink, that chilling stare sliced through me, cutting straight to my core. It was indescribably intimidating. I have never experienced anything like it.

At first I did not understand. Then I did. The incessant demands on Church's time left none to waste on charlatans. He was testing us. Making sure we were the real thing. There is absolutely no doubt that had we been pulling a scam, I would have crumbled. As it was, I felt like an insect splayed open for microscopic inspection. I met his glare straight on, with a vulnerable honesty. Knowing that we *were* the real thing, I relaxed a bit while Church made up his mind.

His eyes hardened into accusing slits of suspicion.

He didn't believe us! With seven minutes remaining on the clock, it was over.

18

I awaited the politicians' stock platitude of dismissal; thanking Filártiga for bringing this important human rights matter to his attention, assuring him that every effort would be made to investigate the family's tragic loss.

Instead, Church tightened the screws. His eyes emitted the searing accusation of the inquisitor. With open hostility he was impugning our good faith, degrading the Filártigas' entire struggle for justice as a sham.

All told, the assault lasted perhaps a minute. About twice as long as it took me to thoroughly despise the arrogant bastard. And long enough to scrape away the scales of the Giant Marshmallow. Free of the blinders for the first time since being sucked back in after returning to the United States, the force of what defined my life in Paraguay broke through. It was like coming home.

That same black-and-white perception put this smug politician's rebuke into perspective. We had not lost. The struggle would go on. Not that it lessened my ire. No longer the least bit concerned with what Church thought, I shot a bolt of raw disdain at him. The flicker in his eyes, a barely perceptible touch of alarm, was enough to know he got the message: Screw you. We are so real that the only way we can be stopped is to kill us.

Joel had taken it all in, had not missed a beat.

Personages of Church's stature do not apologize. Again, without a noticeable transition, he morphed back to the gracious host.

"So," the senator said to Filártiga, "tell me your story."

19

Showing a thorough grasp of the *Caso Filártiga*, Church probed for flaws and inconsistences. Filártiga flushed out the facts, filled in the gaps, cleared up the complexities. By the end of the senator's tutorial, all hard feelings had passed. Somewhere along the line, we even began calling each other by our given names; a matter of seeming insignificance—except to Washington insiders. In fact, it is one of those carefully watched for indicators that bespeaks status, to be missed at the careerist's peril. For them, the implied accessibility and influence translate into newfound respect.

While it is true that the four of us slipped into a first-name basis, to leave it at that would be misleading. For the most part, Peter concentrated on taking notes and jotting down Frank's suggestions. I remained mostly a talking machine.

As Joel and Frank went at it, I simultaneously interpreted. In computer mode, my mind switched languages with no conscious effort. And, like any smoothly functioning instrument, I was quickly taken for granted. All but forgotten, soon they even stopped looking at me when I spoke.

The meeting went on until Church had to leave for a pressing matter. For all intents and purposes, Frank and Joel spent that time speaking directly with each other; interrupting for clarifications, loosening up with witticism, adding gestures for emphasis, asking probing questions that elicited insightful answers, expanding into a free-wheeling exchange of ideas that ventured beyond the political into the personal, finding they had many similarities—from little things (both were forty-eight-year-old workaholics) to big ones (they shared virtually identical political beliefs)—discovering each other to be interesting and likable, and ending up establishing a rapport that laid the foundation for a solid friendship.

20

In the dignified surroundings of a small conference suite, the polished oak paneling and studded leather furniture providing an aura of senatorial substance, Peter, Joel, and I dined on a mushroom pizza. But it was the after-lunch show that was the real treat.

Before leaving, Frank had worked up a list of people he wanted to meet with Joel. We sat back and watched Peter at work. To him it was routine. To us it was a fascinating demonstration of political arm twisting.

"The senator's friend Dr. Filártiga showed up rather unexpectedly today. They spent the morning talking things over. Really rather shocking, what's going on in Paraguay right now. . . .

"Indeed. Well, it occurred to the senator that you'd appreciate the opportunity to meet him. Only problem is Joel, ah, Dr. Filártiga, is in town just through next week, so . . .

"Right you are. It did seem quite impossible. He's already on a tight schedule. But the senator did think that speaking with a few special people . . .

"That should work. I'll confirm that with Dr. Filártiga and get back to you. Thanks. Have a good one."

And the portals were open. Trouble was, we really did have a jam-packed schedule; another art exhibition, a major lecture followed by a reception at Sweetbriar College, an appointment with the OAS Commission, interviews with the press. Most important, though, were the human rights activists. All wanted to meet Joel, and he wanted to meet them all.

Still, Filártiga could not pass up these opportunities. People understood. They readily canceled their own appointments, freeing up time for Joel to confer with ranking officials at the State Department and members of Carter's National Security Council at the White House.

But after the close of the business day, they came. Not only the people from the NGOs who had been working on the *Caso Filártiga* for months but also others who had more recently learned of the struggle. They met with Joel at the home of a Paraguayan exile we had commandeered. Night after night, sometimes until dawn, Filártiga's inspiration cemented ties with old allies and brought in a whole new cadre from the human rights community.

Adding to the whirlwind of activity, a few days before Joel's departure on December 12, another report and updated list of political prisoners arrived from the Paraguayan Church group. The news was not good—many new arrests in an upswing of repression. But with plenty of volunteers, we got the time-sensitive information out quickly. The extra strategy sessions it touched off took somewhat longer.

Going around the clock left no time to sleep. Not that it bothered Filártiga. He had not slept in years. I, however, slogged through the last week of his 1977 tour on catnaps. At last, joining the group of well-wishers seeing Joel off at the airport, with trepidation and relief I watched the plane carry him off to Stroessner's Paraguay.

The agony of oppression in Paraguay.

EIGHT

AFTER THE HOLIDAY BREAK, when the people and organizations supporting the Filártigas picked up our solidarity activities, no one could have guessed what lay ahead. In fact, it took the better part of the year before we began to see the true impact of the tumultuous, often violent, chains of events that began in January 1978.

Imagine a half-dozen trains, coming from different starting points, but heading for the same station. Later, we called these fateful vehicles the January Trains.

From the start, Stroessner put up obstacles, hoping to divert their course, or at least slow them down. Yet with each passing month, events continued rolling along, picking up momentum. Finally, as the paths of the January Trains converged, the dictator pulled out all the stops. Throwing every switch at his command, Stroessner tried to derail the juggernaut coming down on him. And that is when the *Caso Filártiga* took some truly astonishing turns.

1

As soon as Congress reconvened on January 5, Senator Frank Church got the first train under way. In a long letter to the new U.S. ambassador to Paraguay, the senator made sure he understood that this one was personal.

"I am deeply concerned by the state of human rights in Paraguay and, particularly, with the Filártiga case," Church wrote Robert E. White, who only weeks before had taken up the ambassador's post in Asunción. He went on, "I would greatly appreciate it if you could keep me informed periodically of any developments in the Filártiga case and notify me immediately of any reprisals taken against the Filártiga family or our citizens residing with them."

Routinely, U.S. embassies around the world seek "guidance" from their masters at the State Department in Washington on how to deal with inquiries from members of Congress. And here was a fuss being kicked up by a ranking member of the committee that oversees State's finances, and confirms the appointment of its top officials. That would have been bad enough. But, as certainly as Foreign Service officers had nightmares about being hauled before Senator Church's own career-wrecking subcommittee hearings, Washington's reply to Ambassador White contained more substantial orders than a "tread lightly" warning.

Even so, as everyone knows, legislative staffers write letters. Senators sign them. On occasion they even read them. Just the really important ones, though. Only those warrant expending a dollop of that most precious, finite commodity—time.

Frank, a master at the game, ensured with one short sentence that Joel would receive more than sympathy from the embassy. In understated diplomatese, he informed Ambassador White, "I appreciate your assistance and look forward to the opportunity to meet with you upon your return to the United States next month."

To the uninitiated, Frank's invitation would appear to be no big deal. To the careerists at State, though, it conveyed an unmistakable threat: Either comply with my demands or be prepared for a face-to-face confrontation with my wrath.

Everyone knew that Church wielded enormous power. But in itself, that is not necessarily enough to convince cynics that he actually would go to all the trouble of exercising it. In reality, the senator had not simply asked the ambassador to stop by his office during his home leave; Church had checked on White's schedule and ordered him to report in person.

For a man whose days are budgeted in ten-minute intervals, whose normal agenda revolved around superpower politics, to insist upon a personal meeting said it all. The senator's extravagant expenditure of time—with an ambassador to a country of virtually no economic, political, or strategic significance to the United States—served notice of Frank's commitment to back his friend Joel.

2

Peter Fenn sent me a copy of Frank's letter to the ambassador. I replied with an encouraging "atta boy" note.

The following week, again I received from Peter a copy of a letter the senator had written, this one to General Stroessner. But instead of being delighted, I felt sick. After going through it a second time, I felt really sick.

They had taken Church's original letter to Ambassador White, and tailoring it with a few minor alterations, sent it off to Stroessner. In fact, the most alarming part—the opening paragraph—had not been changed at all.

"Recently, Dr. Joel Filártiga, the Paraguayan philanthropist and internationally renowned artist, met with me to explain the circumstances of the brutal murder of his seventeen-year-old son last year," the missive read word-for-word. "Furthermore," the senator informed the dictator, "I enclose an article which details the complex events surrounding Joelito's death, written under a pseudonym by Dr. Richard Alan White, a postdoctoral scholar from UCLA and Paraguay specialist, with whom I have also discussed the case."

Of course, just as with the 1976 crisis that hit us when Amnesty sent Stroessner the details of their upcoming campaign, there could be no question of malice. Even so, the screw-up did blow my cover, and potentially endangered a lot of people in Paraguay.

How could these foreign affairs experts fail to see why I had disguised my identity by using a pseudonym when attacking the Paraguayan dictatorship? It was the same old story, I supposed. From their insulated citadel of power, the potential for disaster of their well-meaning actions simply never entered their minds.

About eighteen months later, events required me to make a quick in-and-out visit to Paraguay. Realistically though, after I had been exposed as the author of the infamous Alberto Cabral piece, the chances of openly returning to Paraguay safely were less than promising. Even so, stranger things have happened.

So I asked the embassy to check it out. In July 1979, a letter from the political officer confirmed my suspicion that I was not on Stroessner's Christmas list. "There is always the chance," Andrew Kay informed me, "that the reactionary elements in the Government of Paraguay, which you have most deeply offended, might try to retaliate against you if you visit Paraguay."

"The reactionary elements in the Government of Paraguay?" Who, I wondered, were the nonreactionary elements in Stroessner's police state? The garbage collectors? Maybe.

3

The crises that engulfed the Filártigas in mid-January 1978 soon chilled my indignation. In fact, it turned out to be a damn good thing that Church had put the pressure on just at that time.

The second January Train was on the move. The same day the senator sent his letter to Stroessner, the Army raided the Clinic of Hope. They arrested everyone, including the Gaffneys. So, traumatized by all that followed, by the end of the month Walt and Jet felt they had no choice but to leave Paraguay. Even though they had been driven out of their home at the Sanatorio la Esperanza in Ybycuí, the Gaffneys had no intention of abandoning their solidarity with the Filártigas. Once back in New Haven in February, Walt wrote and widely distributed an insightful account of what had happened.

He began by explaining how the day before the round-up, January 13, the police had attacked an OPM safe house in Asunción, "which resulted in the death of a young man and the wounding of several police."

Later, Joel filled in the details. Salvador held off the assault long enough for Soledad, Mirtha, Francisco, and several others to get away. According to eyewitnesses, he then tried to escape himself. Salvador made it only a few blocks before being shot down. At the age of twenty-seven, Jorge Agustín Zavala died in the gutter of a poor Asunción barrio.

"Caught in a general wave of repression and the continuous harassment inflicted upon the Filártigas," the Gaffneys' saga continued, "the Paraguayan officials obviously took the opportunity to investigate and intimidate us.

"They were successful. Mature, responsible, and rational people, we began to live the nightmare of many Paraguayans. We spoke in whispers, lay awake at night listening for marching feet, and became even more discreet around the informants and secret police who shadow the Filártigas. The stories of imprisonments, tortures, disappearances, murders became ever more real to us. We now understood more clearly the fear on the faces of the Paraguayans who came under cover of darkness to be treated by this courageous doctor and advocate of human rights. . . .

"The web of intrigue and suspicion which had been spun around us affected all our relationships," Walt explained. "The politics of fear, of which this regime is a master, had worked. We were now living under the tranquil surface of life in Paraguay. The air is noxious.

"While I could control my own fear," he concluded, "I could not withstand the fear I saw reflected in the woman I love. The same phenomenon was true for her. Rumors persisted that we and the Filártigas would meet with a well-planned 'accident' on the road. Reluctantly, sadly, we informed Dr. Filártiga that we could no longer live in his tragic country."

4

Ambassador Ben Stephansky had predicted the start-up of another of the January Trains. Because of Paraguay's dismal record, and in light of the international beating our campaign was giving Stroessner, Ben speculated that the Carter administration might target Paraguay as a showcase for its human rights policy. And indeed, Ambassador Robert White arrived in Asunción with a mandate to kick His Excellency around—but not too much.

By this stage in his career, Bob had distinguished himself as the State Department's gutsiest envoy, the mirror image of his bland predecessor George Landau. As a practicing Catholic who was influenced by the works of Father Henri Nouwen, Bob's innate sense of morality clashed with Stroessner's Paraguay. Even so, no one makes the long climb up the bureaucratic ladder to ambassadorial rank without proving to be a Foreign Service team player. Bob would carry out State's instructions, regardless of how personally repugnant he found them.

In short, White's complex character uniquely qualified him as the instrument of the United States' contradictory foreign policy. On the one hand, he would be sure to pressure Stroessner's regime to improve its human rights record. On the other, he could be counted on to implement our "state policy" of propping up anticommunist governments.

During fiscal 1978, Washington held up some loans and grants to Paraguay. Several were canceled outright. Yet, during these same twelve months the United States bestowed $98.1 million in direct aid, and it approved many millions more in loans from international financial institutions like the World Bank and the Inter-American Development Bank.

For just over two years, Bob tap-danced along a fine line, whenever possible championing human rights, giving dissidents more support than any other ambassador before or since. And while he did push the envelope of his authority in opposing Stroessner's repression, at times his loyalty to the State Department led him to carry out conflicting activities. Still, when judged on his overall record, Ambassador White, and the job he did, must be respected.

5

Not surprisingly, the Filártigas became the first beneficiaries of the ambassador's human rights activism. Promptly responding to Church's letter, White informed the senator that he had spent over an hour discussing the *Caso Filártiga* with the family.

"I share your concern over the unresolved murder of Dr. Filártiga's son," Bob made clear in his January 23 reply. "The case has many unanswered questions and contradictory allegations. The embassy has urged the Paraguayan officials to investigate the matter fully and make all facts public. . . . I will continue to urge that the case receive thorough examination and that justice be done." The ambassador ended with a promise that "I plan to visit the Filártiga clinic soon in order to demonstrate to the Paraguayan authorities my interest in the clinic and those who work there."

White's letter to Church came at a crucial juncture for the people in Paraguay. Following the raid on the Clinic of Hope, the Army was looking for something to pin on Joel. The Gaffneys, working through their ordeal, still had not left. And David Cobb and Terry Esther, the friends of Forrester Church, who had set up the initial meeting with his father, would be arriving in a few weeks to begin their stay with the Filártigas.

So, on February 14, when Frank turned up the heat, the timing could hardly have been better. The "Dear Colleague" letter he sponsored—cosigned by twenty-one other senators—announced to Stroessner that, "as Members of the Senate of the United States, we would like to express our deep concern over the infringement of constitutional rights and denial of basic individual freedoms for some Paraguayan citizens."

Specifically, the senators urged the dictator to lift the state of siege, account for the people who had disappeared, and restore the constitutional rights of prisoners detained without trial. By way of conclusion, they "strongly requested" that he allow the on-site OAS investigation to begin immediately.

Such high-powered scrutiny, the object of nearly one-fourth of the world's most powerful deliberative body, certainly must have given Stroessner second thoughts about harassing the Filártigas and their friends. By the time Ambassador White returned to Washington a few weeks later, the full glare of the international spotlight exposed decades of neglected tyranny in Paraguay.

Bob invited me to get together. No sooner had we settled into an ambassadorial suite at the State Department than his refreshing candor set the tone of our meeting.

"Keep up the good work," he encouraged, "it makes my job a hell of a lot easier."

"How's that?" I asked.

"The more Congress pushes the administration," he said, "the bigger the stick I have to rattle their cage—to show that gang of thugs that we're serious about human rights.

"You know international pressure's the only thing Stroessner responds to. And the avalanche these past six months has catapulted him right up there along with Idi Amin as the poster boys for cattle prods. The bastards are really worried."

"Now that warms my heart," I replied. "How's everything at the clinic? You did make it out there?"

"Not yet," he said, catching the implication. "But the enormous attention on the Filártigas puts them right in the middle of it all. It's the first thing everyone points to."

"Why's that?"

"It's the human angle people latch on to. The *Caso Filártiga* gives a personal face to Stroessner's human rights violations. There's always been a certain amount of quiet sympathy for the Filártigas' drive to bring Peña to task for killing Joelito. Now, with its high profile, criticism of protecting Peña and his cronies has become more outspoken. Torturing kids just doesn't go down that well, even among some of the regime's top dogs."

Bob's last comment sparked my interest. It must have showed.

"Oh, no. No," he quickly said. "There's no danger of a coup. Still, there is a small, but definite split in the Colorado Party, and the upper class."

"So why doesn't Stroessner disappear Filártiga? Get rid of the problem?"

"First of all," Bob said, "Joel's international prominence gives him a special kind of immunity. Also he comes from an old and respected upper-class family himself. You know how in Latin America, more often than not, friendships survive political differences. Joel has a lot of childhood friends, in and out of government. No. Should something happen to him, it wouldn't sit well at all. Moving against Filártiga is just too costly." Then, after a pause, he added, "For the time being, at least."

I knew how the campaign was going, that the solidarity work already under way soon would bring to bear much more international *Caso Filártiga* pressure. I decided not to get into it.

Instead, in what appeared to be a non sequitur but that Bob understood perfectly, I said pointedly, "In the coming months, what you do is going to have a big influence on what Stroessner does."

"Don't overestimate my importance," he cautioned.

Of course, I thought, White is a career diplomat. Regardless of his personal morality, the ambassador was far too savvy to place himself in position that later might prove awkward; especially with someone on a first-name basis with Senator Frank Church and who was apprised of his dealings with the senator, like his promise to visit Filártiga's clinic. Even the inference of a tacit agreement could open him up to a backlash if things did not work out.

"But," he emphasized, "the Embassy will continue to use every legitimate means to promote human rights and assist the victims of Stroessner's persecution."

"Might that include the APO?" I asked casually. Actually, my request was a good deal more urgent than I let on. Our access to the diplomatic mail would run out in a few weeks, when the person helping us would be leaving Paraguay.

"Well, that would be stretching the rules a bit," Bob said with a grin. "But perhaps not all that much."

6

The first test of Bob's sincerity came sooner than expected, as yet another of the January Trains prepared to get under way. Juan Ferreira had been trying to arrange for Congressman Domingo Laino to come to the States to lobby for Paraguayan human rights. But as Stroessner had done with Joel when he was planning his last trip, the government refused to renew Laino's passport.

In early March, I forwarded WOLA's official letter of invitation to Bob White, asking that it be delivered to Laino; and by the way, Domingo also needed a passport waiver. Sure enough, the ambassador took care of everything.

In fact, by this time, Bob White's family had developed a friendship with both the Lainos and Filártigas. In April, and again in May, Bob and Mary Anne sent the rumor mill into a frenzy with visits to the Clinic of Hope. And on their weekend trips to Asunción, Joel and Nidia reciprocated by regularly stopping by the ambassadorial residence.

Utilizing the APO, and helped out by the translating services of David Cobb, Filártiga kept in touch with his friends in the States. To Frank and Peter, Joel sent each a strikingly poignant portrait that he drew from memory.

We assumed that the embassy in Asunción perused all our letters before passing them on—it was considered bad form to seal correspondence. So, when Frank sent along an autographed photo of himself, he made sure to pen a few lines to "Dear Joel": "Just a note to let you know how much I appreciate your sending along the paintings of us. You did a marvelous job, and I appreciate the thought very much. I hope you are fine and that the clinic is going well."

7

A fifth train departed from Boston on January 24. Loaded down with our full arsenal— Jim Richardson's *Filártiga* film, a stock of Joelito's torture cards, bundles of Amnesty's *Deaths under Torture* pamphlet, heaps of the Alberto Cabral "Political Murder in Paraguay" reprints, piles of AI's "Matchbox" news magazines, and stacks of "Amnesty Action" materials to keep up the letter writing and petition campaigns—that morning I set out on an AI/USA-sponsored speaking tour.

From the first stop at Rensselaer Polytechnic Institute in Troy, I dodged blizzards across upstate New York into northern Pennsylvania and back again to Cornell University in Ithaca. In each of the six cities along the way, the local Amnesty chapters, determined to make the best use of my short stay, awaited my arrival with merciless schedules; from morning TV shows to university lectures, meetings with Amnesty Adoption groups and church-based activists. Invariably, the sessions went on into the small hours, only to begin all over again, it seemed, moments after I finally collapsed onto the nearest couch. In ten days I gave fourteen radio interviews, made seven television appearances, delivered eight formal presentations, addressed the Syracuse United Nations' Support Organization, and spoke with hundreds of other people at informal gatherings.

In early February, I straggled back to Boston to find the customary pile of correspondence. On January 25, Joel had written with the latest. "We received your check [from the sale of his drawings during his East Coast tour] with much gratitude," he began. "Thank you, my friend. One more time I am using you in the name of the struggle." That's nice, I thought, so what's new?

It was the "very bloody event," that Filártiga went on to describe, the first I had heard of the police confrontation with the OPM. Salvador had been killed. And while Mirtha and Francisco had found asylum in the Mexican Embassy, there was no word of Soledad.

"Now," Filártiga wrote, after telling about the raid on the clinic, "I must appear at the government delegation in Paraguarí next Friday. We will see what happens. But in short, we continue with our quota of apprehension. It has become our way of life." Almost in passing, Joel ended by mentioning that "it would be a great help if Ambassador White received more letters from people there. The additional international pressure could save my life."

Yet again, our timing was great. The day before Filártiga had sent his plea for help, I had started the Amnesty tour. Dozens of petitions and hundreds of letters were already on the way.

The nuns who ran Pax, the Christian Center for Non-Violence in Erie, Pennsylvania, circulated a petition signed by scores of people. Several weeks later, one of the Sisters wrote Dr. Filártiga to let him know that she had "first heard of your noble work when I read the story by Henri Nouwen in the September issue of *Sojourners*. Since that time I have heard Richard White speak on Paraguay—and especially you and your son, Joelito."

Assuring Joel "that many people are in sympathy with you," Sister Marlene Bertke went on to say, "I love what I have seen of your art work—I am deeply impressed by what I have read and heard of your Christ-like service to others."

And after noting that they had sent copies of the letters and petition to Stroessner, she informed Joel that "we are reprinting Henri Nouwen's story in the January–February issue of the paper we publish—*Erie Christian Witness*—so at least 1,000 more people will read of your plight."

And the many other letters from well-connected people who had received the Alberto Cabral article were also sure to help.

"Dear Dr. Filártiga," James G. van Koolburn of Rochester, New York, wrote, "I have just recently read an article in *America* magazine describing the inhuman repression of the people of Paraguay, and in particular the frightful murder of your son Joelito and the efforts of the government to cover it up.

"Please accept my prayerful sympathy and promise of support," he assured Joel, "of your efforts to regain human rights for yourself and the people of Paraguay."

And he ended by adding, "I shall write to General Alfredo Stroessner to express my concern; and attempt to enlist the support of United States Secretary of State Cyrus Vance and Senator Frank Church on behalf of human rights for the people of Paraguay."

8

After a day's recuperation, the idea of life after the Amnesty International Death March began to seem less improbable. So when I read Walt and Jet's letter, with its cry that "we are home, as you can see, and feel a deep need to talk to you about our experience," it got me on the road.

That evening, at Henri's New Haven apartment, the Gaffneys purged their demons. Sitting around the kitchen table, I asked, "Following the shoot-out with the OPM, did the police take other reprisals?"

"Of the worst kind!" Jet declared. "At first, they claimed that the OPM had set off a bomb, killing ten officers. It turned out to be a total lie. But Investigaciones used it as a pretext. They arrested and interrogated over 400 'suspects,' trying to find the people who'd escaped."

"Did they get anyone?"

"No. According to the papers, no OPM people were captured. But they didn't let anyone go either," Jet replied. "Then, after midnight, the morning after the shoot-out, Nidia woke us. Soldiers had surrounded the clinic. My immediate emotion was that a dreaded evil had arrived. And I was right."

"Had you been harassed before that?"

"No. Not at all. It was just like we hoped," she said. "We expected to love the Filártigas. And we did. And we still do. They loved us, too. And they still do."

"How did you spend your time?" I asked.

"You know how Joel is," Walt took over. "He didn't assign us any specific work. The first few months we spent studying Spanish and picking up a spattering of Guaraní. Then we created our own jobs at the Clinic of Hope. Like most Yanquis we're list makers, information-gatherers, and organizers.

"We wrote a couple hundred letters, mostly soliciting medical supplies for the Sanatorio La Esperanza. Now we've found out only a handful got through.

"The other thing we did was to catalogue some 700-odd medicines. Most of them had been donated by religious organizations from eleven countries. We'd finally settled into a routine. And we felt good about it."

"But all that came to an end on Saturday, January 14," Jet cut in, "when we stepped out into the tropical night and saw the moonlight grotesquely silhouetting twenty-five soldiers pointing burp guns at us.

"They brought us to the Army barracks and took our passports away. But the interrogation wasn't hostile. Actually, the comandante was stiffly polite. He asked us only the most basic questions. But we just couldn't come up with answers that satisfied him."

"Because of the language?" Henri suggested.

"Yes. No. Well, in part," Walter said, and looked at Jet, her face taut with bewilderment. "No, that really wasn't the problem. We still don't understand it."

"Can you describe what happened?" he prompted.

"Well, he asked us simple things. Just simple things," Walt said. "But nothing made sense anymore! Nothing!"

Walt shook his head in frustration. "Nothing, nothing made sense anymore!"

It took a minute or so for Walt to regain his composure. "We'd been waiting about three hours while the colonel interrogated some of the other people. Finally, they brought us into his office. The first thing he asked us was, 'Why have you come here?' That's all, just 'Why have you come here?' And, and, we just didn't know anymore!"

"You did not know why you went to Paraguay?" Henri asked softly. "Why you were at the clinic?"

"Yes. That's exactly it," Walt gasped. "What had been so clear to us before, that we wanted to make a meaningful contribution to help Dr. Filártiga in his work serving the poor. It all seemed so lame. It didn't even sound convincing to us."

There it was. Desperately, they sought some explanation for their incomprehensible loss of commitment.

"Giving up our safe, comfortable lives in the United States—the impossible dream of almost everyone else in the world—traveling thousands of miles to live in this little Paraguayan village. The middle of nowhere. All the hardships, under a brutal dictatorship. It simply didn't add up."

Jet nodded her bemused confirmation.

"At that moment," Walter cried, "being interrogated in that sweltering office, surrounded by soldiers with guns, we didn't know why we had come to Ybycuí! What we were doing there! It no longer made any sense!"

Nodding his head, Henri said, "The Stockholm Syndrome."

9

"That is what happened to Patty Hearst," Henri explained, "when she was kidnapped by the Symbionese Liberation Army a couple of years ago. It is a survival mechanism. The victim adopts the beliefs of their captors.

"I would say," he went on, "that is what began to happen when they arrested you, took away your passports, stripped you of your identity as United States citizens. You were prisoners, at the mercy of Stroessner's police state."

Walt and Jet looked at each other.

"The first stage is to lose your own values. Next comes accepting theirs," Henri said. "But it did not get that far. What happened next?"

"Well," Jet picked up, "after a while, they said we could go. And we went straight to the embassy in Asunción. They were very responsive and reassuring. They got our passports right back in just a couple of hours. And with an apology. That it was all a terrible mistake of the local military commander overstepping his authority.

"That's right!" she realized. "That's when we regained our perspective and went back to the clinic."

"But by then it was too late," Walt bemoaned. "When they had asked us, 'Where do you get money? Who pays you?' we told the truth. That friends here in the States had contributed some, but mostly we lived off our savings.

"That had cinched it. It made everything all the more unbelievable. Even to us," he said. "They claimed we had 'no visible means of support.' So, with their constant suspicion of Joel, we became objects for investigation, too."

"Then they poisoned the well," Jet interjected. "They spread the rumor that we were CIA. People who had been warm and friendly became standoffish. It ruined all our relationships. Except with the Filártigas, of course.

"But the hardest part was seeing each other's fear." Jet paused for a breath. "Maybe if it had been just one of us alone—either one of us—it would have been different. But the fear and paranoia changed everything. Everything that had been normal; our lives, ourselves."

I sure could understand that. Living on that edge, I knew, it was best to be alone. Only your own life was on the line. But that the one you love might be killed—*or worse*—is a profoundly human vulnerability.

"Finally, we couldn't bear it anymore," Jet said. "Always afraid when they would come again. And what they would do. Knowing, as they did, that our only protection was the embassy, three hours away from the Sanatorio La Esperanza. We just couldn't go on."

10

Outside, a light snow fell on New Haven. As we strolled along, I lobbed a high, arcing snowball at the Gaffneys. It was a measure of their reentry trauma that they fell for the childish trick. They watched the missile's arcing descent, casually moving out of its way. That's when Henri and I drilled Walt and Jet with the straight-on shots.

Dashing apart, they set up a cross-fire, and with a barrage of snowballs pummeled us into submission. As a tension reliever, the snowball fight worked wonders. We returned to the apartment, made coffee, and lit candles.

"It's only been two weeks since getting home," Jet told me, "but already we've established La Esperanza Fund to help Dr. Filártiga and the clinic. We're going to invite Joel up here this fall for another series of art exhibitions and lectures. We can handle the up-front expenses. Do you think Amnesty might sponsor his trip?"

"Next week I'll be seeing the people at the AI/USA office,' I replied. "Have to talk with them about the way they schedule speaking tours anyway, something of a personal human rights matter. It might take a while with the red tape, but sure, it's a good bet they'll go for Filártiga's trip."

After making the rounds in New York, I moved on to Washington. By then, several of Filártiga's supporters had joined the Carter administration's beefed-up Bureau of Human Rights and Humanitarian Affairs at the State Department.

Mark Schneider, Senator Edward Kennedy's former chief legislative assistant, who had arranged for the senator to put my Alberto Cabral article into the *Congressional Record*, became the second-in-command, after Patt Derian. And Roberta Cohen, the former director of the ILHR, joined the team as an assistant deputy secretary of state.

Given Senator Church's personal efforts on behalf of Joel, the extraordinary respect I now found in official circles was hardly unexpected. The meeting with Ambassador White was just the beginning. Bureaucrats who previously had been unreachable suddenly had developed remarkable interest in the *Caso Filártiga* and Paraguayan human rights.

The power of Washington's tribal customs over the local chieftains, however, did come as somewhat of a revelation. Almost invariably, the stodgy old boys responded to such offhand comments, such as how Frank would appreciate their cooperation, with yet greater assurances of sincerity. I took it for what it was, trying to leave them happy, and their doors open.

The State Department invited me to participate in its first National Foreign Policy Conference on Human Rights. After enduring most of the morning in a plenary session listening to the dignitaries blab, we broke into working seminars. The purpose of these smaller groups was to evaluate the conditions in the various regions of the world and to come up with recommendations for improving human rights.

The NGOs pooled their influence to elect me chair of the Latin American seminar; I was to report our findings to the full conference when it reconvened in plenary session. Not surprisingly, the prestigious State Department conference had attracted considerable international coverage. The media focused on the major speeches and each rapporteur's formal presentation. And our Latin American seminar's condemnation of the worst human rights abusers, denouncing them by name and presenting Paraguay's *Caso Filártiga* as a prime example of their brutality, proved to be a favorite of the news-hungry press corps.

The fast work of the NGOs distributing copies of the Alberto Cabral article and Joelito's torture cards served as a magnet for the herd of journalists competing with each other to file the most sensational stories. So, while the conference officially ended at 5:00 P.M., not until three hours later did I finally wrap up the last of the interviews with a national Brazilian television network.

Of course, what made the Latin American Seminar's condemnations so newsworthy was that they had been announced at the vaunted United States Department of State. Virtually all the reports blurred over our unofficial status, presenting our recommendations as if they were bona fide Carter administration policy.

11

The State Department's human rights conference coincided with events in Paraguay. On the same day, March 15, the Paraguayan–Argentine Cultural Center in Asunción opened a month-long show of Dr. Filártiga's art. The coincidence provided a terrific new angle to build up the already hyperbolic coverage that the press normally bestowed upon Joel's exhibitions.

Because the media dispatched their stories from Washington via satellite, articles began appearing in daily newspapers the next morning. Some TV and radio programs aired the same night. Editorials, feature pieces in newsmagazines, biweekly publications, and monthly journals stretched out the publicity. Accounts of our stinging denunciations of Stroessner and the rest of the Human Wrongs Network continued throughout the entire month of Joel's exhibition.

By 1978 inexpensive battery-powered short-wave radios had become a major source of information in the developing world. Tapping this new technology, Joel had a friend record Spanish and Guaraní broadcasts about the human rights conference from the Voice of America to Radio Havana.

12

March 30 marked the second anniversary of Joelito's death. Just as they had the year before, in 1978 people showed their solidarity by flocking to the memorial Masses. This year, however, after the services, the Filártigas passed out cassettes of the radio programs along with Joelito's torture cards. The cassettes circulated around Asunción, and long-haul truck drivers made sure more than a few reached towns and villages in the countryside.

Even in the United States, the *Caso Filártiga* began taking on a life of its own. At last, our Paraguayan campaign penetrated the media's habitual disregard of things Latin American. It was like some ephemeral barrier of disinterest dissolved—which in good part accounts for my return to California.

13

"So what are you doing here? I thought you'd defected to the East Coast power elite?" Susan Cloke chided when I arrived at her home in Santa Monica.

"Just passing through your no-smoking zone to stoke the Filártiga embers," I quipped. "Only for a couple of months. Got to be back in Washington in June for the OAS annual conference. They're planning a Paraguay spectacular featuring the *Caso Filártiga.*"

"How goes my friend Joel's struggle?" she asked. Susan was a dear friend and one of Filártiga's ardent supporters.

"You wouldn't believe it," I said, filling her in on all that had happened in the year I had been gone. Susan's quick mind absorbed every detail, leaving only the question of how she could help.

"Same as before," I explained. "Solidarity. Press. Talks to get the petitions and letter-writing campaigns into high gear again. Receptions to raise funds and medical supplies for the clinic. You know the drill."

"There's more behind you coming out here than the drill," she said.

"Yes. Well, there are a few other things," I conceded. "A couple of courses at Cal State. Since losing my historical research in the Wood Island fire, I really can't justify keeping the postdoctoral fellowship at UCLA. So the teaching's a way of maintaining an academic standing. And credibility.

"It's set up so I'll be on campus only two days a week. Be traveling quite a bit. First is the AI/USA annual meeting in San Francisco in early April. They've programmed a special briefing on the *Caso Filártiga* and human rights in Paraguay for local Amnesty chapter heads from around the country. It's a good opportunity to spread the word and maybe break through the bureaucratic logjam holding up Amnesty's sponsorship of Filártiga's visit this fall."

In fact, once everyone got together at the AI meeting in San Francisco, the endless memos to coordinate scheduling, arrange publicity, and all the other details delaying Filártiga's formal invitation were quickly worked out.

"And there's a couple of other things, here and there. Like the Amnesty chapter at Iowa State University in Ames has asked me to stop by."

"And . . . ?" Susan said, raising one eyebrow, not about to let my levity get me off the hook.

"And right," I said, smiling. "There's a real good shot at serious national publicity. It would appear the press has discovered Paraguay. Mercedes Lynn de Uriate at the *Los Angeles Times* has asked me do a piece for their Sunday opinion section."

"That's nice," Susan said, "but what's the big deal? Another article."

"Actually, more like a couple of hundred. Well, it'd be the same piece, but carried in newspapers all over the country."

"Now that is interesting. How does it work?"

"First they publish here in the *Times*, as a Sunday feature op-ed. Then, it's sent out on the *Washington Post / Los Angeles Times* wire service, to its 400-plus subscribers."

"And they're the papers that pick it up, reprint the article?"

"That's it. And not just this one. Paraguay's hot. Might lead to doing a series of occasional op-ed pieces. When I've got something to say, follow-up developments, different angles. So, with everything else on my plate, I'm going to need all the help I can get."

"Let's do it," Susan said, grinning.

And so it started. And with the help of Dr. Filártiga's cadre of friends in southern California, we did it. Barely.

Before dawn on Sunday, May 28, with my car packed and ready to go, I waited in the parking lot of a Ralph's supermarket for the *Los Angeles Times* delivery truck. Already behind schedule because publication had been delayed a week, when the papers arrived I culled out a dozen copies of the full page op-ed, tucked $20 in an unopened bundle, and took off for Washington.

I made great time crossing the country. Even so, it didn't come close to the mileage that "Paraguay: Latin America's Neglected Chamber of Horrors" racked up in the coming months.

14

Another of the Paraguayan January Trains had left the platform crammed with Investigaciones heroes, trumpeting their prowess as if they had raised the Kremlin. On the heels of the OPM shoot-out, even by Paraguayan standards, the wave of repression that swept the country was ferocious. Imposing yet harsher conditions on political prisoners, torture and extrajudicial executions became even more routine, and arbitrary mass arrests and disappearances became the order of the day.

Spouting the official line, the Paraguayan press rolled over, becoming the government's propaganda arm. Even the marginally independent papers offered their tacit approval of the terror unleashed on the people. As *ABC Color* reported on January 17, "In numerous towns throughout the interior, police brigades . . . are detaining and interrogating countless people in order to determine their association with the [OPM] group."

Once again, Dr. Nidia Antonia González topped the list of the most wanted. But even the massive hunt for Soledad by Stroessner's finest, backed up by another run of WANTED posters offering nearly $5,000 "compensation" for turning her in, failed to reveal her whereabouts. In fact, no one seemed to know what had become of Soledad. Except for Salvador, however, everyone else somehow had beat the odds and reached safe haven.

Responding to Paraguay's latest wave of repression, the Amnesty Secretariat mounted a worldwide Campaign Against Torture action. In March 1978, AI released a new pamphlet protesting the human rights abuses inflicted upon young people around the world. The booklet, titled *Children*, juxtaposed the same two photos of Joelito— alive and smiling, dead and desecrated—used in the international edition of the 1977 *Deaths under Torture* pamphlet.

By May, the growing international revulsion against Stroessner's regime convinced AI in London to reprint its 1976 briefing booklet *Paraguay*. Further, AI/USA printed a second U.S. edition of the *Deaths under Torture* pamphlet. Sending copies of all three publications to its local chapters, they called for a rejuvenated campaign against the Paraguayan dictatorship.

Still, it is doubtful that Amnesty's May offensive would have taken on such intensity had not Soledad's disappearance remained a mystery. People feared the worst. By early April, Mirtha Ayala had reached Mexico City and joined up with a group of exiled Paraguayan political activists. A few weeks later, I received from them a draft of their pamphlet *To Save the Life of Nidia Antonia González*.

On the basis of police sources, they said in the pamphlet, the Paraguayan press reported that Soledad had been captured along with a group of other suspected OPM members. A few days later, however, the newspapers "published a statement by Police Inspector Alberto Cantero (a known torturer), claiming that the report of Señora González' detention was a lie. Nevertheless, the imprisonment of these people has been confirmed.

"Stroessner's dictatorship frequently denies having custody of political prisoners," the pamphlet explained, "so they can brutally torture them physically and psychologically, and later kill them with impunity. It is now known that Nidia González has been barbarously tortured. We cannot permit the dictator Stroessner to continue murdering Paraguayan patriots. We must save the life of NIDIA ANTONIA GONZÁLEZ."

The draft ended with a plea for an international telegram and letter campaign to force Stroessner to admit that the police had Soledad. Then, at least, the government could be held responsible for her well-being, perhaps even forced to file formal charges, giving Soledad the chance to present a public defense in court.

Hours after receiving Mirtha's prepublication pamphlet, I got a copy off to Inger in London. A few weeks later, a letter from her arrived thanking me "very much indeed for the excellent material. We have used this case as part of the follow-up to the Paraguay Campaign and we will send it to the CAT [Campaign Against Torture] network for action and publicity."

Moving on to another matter we had been working on, Inger advised, "Regarding Domingo Laino: he attended our conference on the death penalty in Stockholm. I believe it is a good precaution that he should visit the States. I imagine you and the [Amnesty] Washington Office will be able to give him advice about approaches to the U.S. Congress, the State Department, and the Organization of American States."

Checking with the other NGOs, everyone agreed that Domingo's visit was an excellent idea.

15

The last of the January Trains of 1978 got under way not long after the Carter administration's first anniversary. Filled with the people and organizations pushing Paraguayan human rights, instead of occupying its customary seat in the caboose, the OAS sat in the first-class coach.

It is all but impossible to instigate any conflict with the toothless OAS; to whip up a confrontation reaching all the way to the top unheard off. But Stroessner managed to do it.

In late January, already stung by the Inter-American Commission for Human Rights' charges, His Excellency made an incredibly inept attempt to forestall further damage to his international reputation. Prodded by repeated OAS requests to begin its on-site investigation, the government of Paraguay made a show of renewing its invitation and again pointedly refused to set a date.

The IACHR took Stroessner's ploy for the insult that it was. And while the OAS lacked the authority to compel the dictator to make good on his word, it did have the power to make him wish he had never opened his mouth.

Standing on the terra firma brought about by the human rights sea change, on January 31 the commission struck back by releasing its revised *Report on the Situation of Human Rights in Paraguay*, perhaps the strongest attack it had ever leveled against any nation. And that was just the opening shot.

Normally, the IACHR staff alone prepares the human rights reports for the OAS annual conference. But infuriated by Stroessner's arrogance, bureaucrats from throughout the organization responded to the public humiliation.

Some months after I filed the original 1977 *Caso Filártiga* complaint, Amnesty assigned a U.S. attorney to join the case as a cocomplainant. While Harold Berk actively followed the commission's inquiry, I had concentrated on other aspects of the campaign. So, not until early 1978, when a friend at the Secretariat sent me a copy of a letter written by the secretary general of Amnesty International did I learn of the vendetta Stroessner had provoked. In February, Martin Ennals, answering a request from the OAS executive secretary, forwarded to Edmundo Vargas Carreño "additional information on the case of Joel Filártiga (Paraguay). The material consists of a photograph of the corpse, the official death certificate, and a report of the examination carried out at the request of Dr. Joel Filártiga on his son's body.

"We have sent," Ennals went on, "additional information on this case to another complainant, Dr. Harold Berk, who will undoubtedly pass on the relevant material for your files."

Such correspondence between the secretary general of Amnesty International and the executive secretary of the OAS, in what amounted to routine staff work, spelled serious trouble for Stroessner. Trouble that Stroessner took seriously.

16

Like so much of the *Caso Filártiga*, it took years before we fully understood many of the pieces. Only a full decade later, when in 1988 I slipped into Paraguay to conduct research for this book, did this part of the story finally fall into place. By then, Horacio Galeano Perrone had more than recovered from his years of persecution.

"Look, Horacio," I began, "I just got a hold of the rest of the *Caso Filártiga* court files. They cover everything since the documents I left with, when I was living here in '76. And, frankly, I find some perplexing matters—around the time the OAS was preparing its Paraguay Report for the 1978 annual conference."

"I shouldn't wonder," he replied. "As I recall, there was some very dicey legal maneuvering that took place around then. What, precisely, is it that concerns you?"

"Before we get to that, first let's make sure of the facts," I proposed.

"Always a sound procedure."

"In '77 you were disbarred. After the Forty-Five Points balls-up. Everything came to a dead stop on the *Caso Filártiga*. You couldn't practice law until Stroessner let you get your license back in '84."

"Just so," he said.

"Then how were you able to conduct a twelve-week flurry of legal activity in early 1978? These court records show motions, countermotions, appeals, and rulings. And it all coincides with the months leading up to the OAS annual conference that June."

Galeano Perrone nodded.

"And everything began on April 26. When you resubmitted the Forty-Five Points petition," I said. "The exact same motion that got you thrown in jail and ended up with you getting disbarred!"

Horacio continued nodding pensively.

"And the court didn't waste any time. A week after you filed, the judge granted you everything. All the Forty-Five Points. He ruled to expand the scope of the trial. To investigate the discrepancies between the police reports and the depositions. To find the true perpetrators of Joelito's murder. To uncover all the other lies!"

"Quite right," Horacio said.

"Well then, damn it," I demanded, "how the hell could you practice law without a license? Why did the court capitulate to the Forty-Five Points?"

"Now I see your dilemma. As I said, it was a tricky piece of business. One that could only happen in Paraguay. You know how Stroessner controls the courts."

It was not a question. I offered no reply.

"I resubmitted the Forty-Five Points brief. The courts disregarded the fact that I did not have a license to practice, and the judge granted the motion, you see."

"No, I don't see," I said. "That's just what I don't see."

"Well, it really is not so mysterious," Horacio said matter-of-factly. "Although I can understand your confusion. The fact that it all occurred preceding the conference was as irrelevant as intentional.

"Certainly the OAS intended to use the *Caso Filártiga* complaint to make a scandal at the international conference. Stroessner's concern was the extraordinary efforts the OAS was making to investigate the *Caso Filártiga*. He believed that if the court granted me, the attorney of record, the Forty-Five Points, it would discredit the accusation of a judicial cover-up."

"And you obliged him?"

"I believed that the transparency of Stroessner's plan stood no chance of deceiving the OAS—even should the legal proceedings in Paraguay ever reach that point. Which I considered negligible. As proved true.

"I judged that in his panic, Stroessner had provided us a unique opportunity," Horacio continued. "I chose what I considered best."

I chose not to reply.

"On one hand," he elaborated, "at worst we ran the minuscule risk of possibly helping him mitigate an embarrassment. An international embarrassment, to be sure. But still only an embarrassment.

"On the other, I decided the importance of a judicial ruling validating the Forty-Five Points outweighed whatever advantage Stroessner was unlikely to gain."

"But, just as easily as he ordered the court grant the Forty-Five Points, he surely would have it reversed on appeal," I protested firmly.

"But not so long as the international pressure kept him on the defensive," Horacio countered. "And, as things worked out, can you say that I was wrong?"

"No. I suppose not."

Indeed, Stroessner presented the Forty-Five Points manipulation to the OAS to defuse the charges. Predictably, the court never conducted the promised investigation. And, eventually, the ruling was reversed on appeal. Even so, as far as the commission was concerned, Stroessner's legal ploy did not help in the least.

"In any event," Horacio added wryly, "no doubt it did not fail to escape your attention that a few days after the OAS conference, the Paraguayan Supreme Court passed a resolution banning me from any further participation in the *Caso Filártiga*. And it was another six years before I regained my license.

"Perhaps it could be said that Stroessner co-opted me into resubmitting the Forty-Five Points petition. But to what end? The OAS still gave him a more severe drubbing than he feared. True?"

17

Paraguayan congressman Domingo Laino landed in Washington on May 22, a month before the OAS conference. It did not take that long, however, for Domingo to ignite a roaring controversy, fueling the commission's vendetta with Stroessner.

Three days after his arrival, at the National Press Club, Paraguay's leading opposition politician chastised the OAS, challenging it to pass an unequivocal condemnation of Stroessner's human rights violations. Laino declared that the only way to rehabilitate the OAS' impotent reputation, and become a truly respected institution, "was to cease aligning themselves with the dictatorships of the hemisphere."

Laino went on to call for the total cut-off of U.S. economic aid to Paraguay, declaring that "we are not asking for your help, only that you stop backing the dictator. We can win the struggle against the regime, but not if at the same time we are forced to fight outside powers supporting it."

And three days after that, Stroessner played the patriotism card, accusing Laino of "soliciting foreign intervention." In Asunción, the Colorado Party's tightly controlled student and professional organizations broke into demonstrations of "spontaneous popular rejection," denouncing Domingo for his unconscionable attacks against the Fatherland. Most ominous of all were the reports in the Paraguayan press that upon his return, Laino would be arrested and tried for treason.

Domingo countered with another press conference. Denying any call for foreign intervention in Paraguay, he elaborated on the real results of economic aid. Even programs specifically designated to help the poor and needy, he pointed out, become patronage for Stroessner's corrupt political machine. They end up serving "to bolster the repressive apparatus, whose greatest cruelty is employed against the most impoverished and destitute classes. For example," he said, "90 percent of the people who die in Investigaciones' torture chambers are campesinos."

As the campaign against Laino heated up in Paraguay, the international human rights community prepared for the worst. Stroessner rarely made public threats, and he virtually never broadcast them.

18

Laino spent the following weeks speaking with many of the same members of Congress and Carter administration officials who had heard Dr. Filártiga. At meetings with the National Security Council's Latin American director, Robert Pastor, and the deputy secretary of state, Warren Christopher, he lamented the hypocrisy of continuing to support Stroessner, while proclaiming a foreign policy of total commitment to human rights.

Even as Domingo pushed on with his killer schedule, he made time to lend a hand in the preparation of the NGOs' information packets for the approaching OAS conference. To my chagrin, along with such substantial information as the prisoner lists and field reports on human rights violations, Laino and the organizers at WOLA insisted on including my *Los Angeles Times* article lambasting Stroessner's Chamber of Horrors. I protested that it was the most biased piece of writing I had ever done. I had thrown in the whole works—not only the *Caso Filártiga* and Paraguay's massive human rights abuses but also the economy of smuggling, drug trafficking, harboring Nazis, the systematic massacre of Aché Indians, and anything else I could think of to smear the dictator. It was a piece of smut. They all happily agreed, which was precisely why, they predicted, the OAS delegates would love it.

During the preceding month, I had learned from friends around the country that newspapers had picked up my foray into yellow journalism. Even WOLA reprinted the *Chicago Sun-Times* version, sensationally retitled "Paraguay: The Uganda of Latin America," in their *Latin America Update* magazine. And sure enough, at the OAS conference it did help set up Stroessner as a target of derision, and better yet, the object of international ridicule.

19

At the June 21 opening session of the 1978 OAS annual conference, Jimmy Carter addressed the General Assembly, delivering one of his most forceful speeches. The president's pledge—"we will not be deterred from our open and enthusiastic policy of promoting human rights"—and his threat—"where countries persist in serious violations of human rights, we will continue to demonstrate that there are costs to the flagrant disregard of international standards—" established a new respect for the commission's human rights work.

The sequence of presentations at the General Assembly roughly coincides with the importance that they hold within the OAS. Diplomacy, trade, military affairs, culture, and all other matters came first. Customarily, the last spot on the agenda, when the weary delegates only wanted to wrap things up and go home, was reserved for the Inter-American Commission on Human Rights.

Normally, the IACHR presented the General Assembly with a single *Annual Report*, covering human rights in all of Latin America. This time, however, building upon its new status, the commission broke with tradition. Instead of the single report mandated by the General Assembly, on its own initiative it prepared special county reports on Paraguay and Uruguay.

Not until June 30, the day before the OAS conference ended, did the commission get its turn. By then the *Special Paraguay Report* had been circulating for a week, so everyone knew what was coming.

The *Report* hammered away at Paraguay's institutionalized human rights abuses. Accusing Stroessner's regime of imprisoning hundreds of political prisoners without any charges or trial, it lamented that "some have spent as much as 19 years in this manner."

Moreover, charging that "the use of physical and psychological duress and of every form of cruelty in order to extract confessions or to intimidate detainees is a constant and continuing practice in Paraguay," it added that "no information whatsoever has been received by the Commission regarding the application of sanctions against even a single individual responsible for such inhuman treatment."

But what gave the *Report* its ring of truth was the example after example of human tragedy. And Case 2158, the *Caso Filártiga*, became its centerpiece.

20

Before a Special Country Report reached the General Assembly to be formally voted upon, the nation under fire first had a chance to refute the allegations at a commission hearing. Domingo and I used our NGO observer passes to get front-row seats at the IACHR Paraguay meeting. A half hour before the action began, we settled in next to the thick red cord that ringed the twenty-foot oblong table where the main event would be fought out.

The commission chair, Andrés Aguilar, calmly sat at the table's head. Many of the twenty-three delegates, flanked along its sides, furtively glanced at the new face among them. Replacing the regular representative, Stroessner had dispatched his favorite hatchet man, Paraguayan senator Luis Maria Argaña, to take care of matters.

"At last Stroessner's crimes are going to be displayed for the world to judge," Domingo whispered in my ear. "And all the better he sent that fool Argaña."

We had a clear view of Argaña across the conference table, fifteen feet away. At first impression, he kind of reminded me of a pit bull at a Tijuana dog fight. Closer inspection confirmed that he indeed was of the same breed.

Argaña was about ten minutes into his defense of Paraguay's human rights record before he blew. "This whole thing is a farce. Pure calumny," he raged, alternatively waving a fist and the *Special Paraguay Report*, "despicable sensationalism containing not a single word of truth.

"Only lies, lies, and more lies." Argaña whacked the report on the table. "Without any concrete evidence. Just false allegations fabricated by mercenaries to defile the Fatherland. Part of their criminal campaign of lies to defame our president."

Stroessner's boy was carrying on as if to cower the Paraguayan Parliament, instead of addressing an international forum. Aghast at the breach of protocol, some embarrassed delegates concentrated on doodling on their notepads, one actually edged his chair away from Argaña, and many discreetly positioned a hand to block their line of vision.

Domingo and I watched with wonder and disbelief as Argaña alienated the commission delegates and had no idea that he was doing it.

The show went on for perhaps fifteen minutes before Chairperson Aguilar had had enough. Raising his own voice beyond propriety, he lit into Stroessner's special envoy. "Paraguayan human rights are a chronic evil," Aguilar thundered. "We have displayed a Franciscan patience with Paraguay's stalling. And now, after fifteen years, you finally agree to our request for an on-site investigation, only to deceive us with a worthless promise, because you refuse to set a date. When," he demanded, "will the government of Paraguay allow the commission's visit?"

Ignoring Aguilar's question, Argaña continued his harangue. "The biggest lie of all is your accusation that young Filártiga was kidnapped and tortured to death by the security police.

"The so-called *Caso Filártiga* 'tragedy' is a total fabrication," he stormed. "In reality, the boy's death was nothing more than a Romeo-and-Juliet comic opera. Just another victim of failed romance.

"The husband of his mistress caught them in bed together and in a jealous rage stabbed him. And that is God's truth. I have proof.

"I have proof that all your cases are lies too," Argaña roared, "not just this one, but every one of them!"

Argaña's mean-spirited characterization of Joelito's murder, and his ludicrous boast of proof that every OAS complaint was false, raised a chorus of derisive hoots from the audience. In a frantic attempt at damage control, Paraguay's ambassador to the United States, Mario López Escobar—who normally also doubled as the ambassador to the OAS—desperately tried to salvage something short of complete disaster. Invoking his superior rank, López Escobar abruptly dismissed Argaña and offered the IACHR a profuse apology.

But it was too late. The bully tactics of Stroessner's special envoy had not only showed him up for the ass he was but had also wiped out any sympathy for Paraguay among the delegates.

The following day, at the General Assembly's formal vote on the *Special Paraguay Report*, not even the other seven Latin American dictatorships supported Stroessner, choosing instead to abstain. Paraguay cast the only dissenting vote. The remaining sixteen countries all voted approval of the devastating report. Further, in an unprecedented rebuke, the General Assembly ordered the commission to prepare an updated revision of its *Special Paraguay Report* on human rights for the following year's OAS annual conference.

Never before had the OAS so emphatically censured a member state for its human rights violations—just as Laino had called for.

The resounding condemnation dealt Stroessner's international reputation a mortifying blow. It was not just news; it was big-time news on a hemispheric scale.

21

Wednesday evening, July 5, I took Domingo to the airport, wished him well, and promised we would do all that we could if anything happened. Two days later, it happened. As Laino walked along a downtown Asunción street in the middle of the afternoon, four men dressed in plain clothes beat him to the ground, kicked and dragged him to the curb, threw his bloody body into the back of their car, and sped off.

Several bystanders got the plate number—11888—a police vehicle. Within the hour, Ambassador White was on the phone to the Paraguayan authorities expressing "Washington's deep concern over Laino's abduction." It is all but certain that Bob's fast and decisive intervention spared Domingo from becoming yet another victim, disappeared into the night and fog of the Investigaciones murky police state.

Stroessner's flunkies categorically disavowed any involvement in what had happened to Laino. But the immense international outcry—involving virtually every human rights organization; the U.S. State Department and members of Congress, as well as many of their European counterparts; the United Nations and the International Red Cross; the solidarity coalition formed by all of the Paraguayan political opposition parties; and the enormous press coverage, including another op-ed I did for the *Washington Post / Los Angeles Times* wire service—finally forced the dictatorship to admit that Congressman Domingo Laino had been "detained."

Although saved from Investigaciones' worst tortures, Laino hardly escaped unscathed. "The first days were the hardest," he told me later. "They refused to give me any food or let me sleep. They made me stand erect, facing a blank wall—for seventy-two hours. If I so much as touched the wall, or even bent my knees, they'd hit me with their truncheons until I stood up straight again. The ache in my legs and back was tremendous."

"Why didn't you just collapse and end it?"

"It doesn't work that way. They'd just have beaten me unconscious. And then I'd have to start the three days all over again."

Other than conceding that they had Domingo, the regime did its best to ignore the mushrooming international protest. As threatened, the Paraguayan Ministry of Justice charged Laino with treason. And, to intimidate anyone else from similarly besmirching Paraguay's good name, Stroessner had a bill introduced in his puppet parliament to revoke the citizenship of anyone criticizing the regime from abroad.

22

By the middle of 1978, the January Trains had come together into a potent political force. Indeed, second only to the Jewish lobby, the *New York Times* called the "human rights lobby" the most powerful in Washington.

It took several more weeks for the *Caso Laino* to build up full steam. And while never diverted from demanding Domingo's liberty, the solidarity movement soon drove over the full landscape of the regime's depravity—from its mafia-type organization to its Gestapo-like Investigaciones police.

With his reputation in a shambles, Stroessner attempted to mollify the international outcry. After allowing a representative from the International Red Cross to visit Laino in prison, he forgot about the treason charge, and no more was heard about the draconian citizenship-revoking legislation. And, in early August, releasing Domingo from the Investigaciones hell hole, Stroessner banished him to internal exile in Mbuyapey, a tiny hamlet so remote that it didn't even have Coca-Cola.

Stroessner's public consumption of crow did little to placate the *Caso Laino* solidarity campaign. Indeed, filled with optimism, we pushed on with the general's forced feeding. But the dean of Latin American dictators held out longer than anyone guessed.

Five months later, on December 10, Domingo rose to face yet another boring, sultry Paraguayan summer day in Mbuyapey. Leaving his shack, listlessly he meandered along the dusty street when a military officer he had not seen before approached him. After exchanging the customary pleasantries, the captain said, "I have been sent here to inform you of the latest developments in your case."

Instantly on guard, Laino took a step back.

"Don't be alarmed. My instructions are to tell you that all your problems have been resolved." He smiled and added, "If you would like a ride to Asunción in my Jeep, we can get started whenever you're ready."

23

Several months before, however, with Domingo still banished to internal exile, the *Caso Laino* raised troublesome questions about Filártiga's upcoming trip. I knew that Domingo's plight stood little chance of influencing Joel's decision. His commitment to expose the regime's crimes and publicize the *Caso Filártiga* fell far beyond concerns for his personal safety. Even so, during a phone conversation that September, I gave it a try.

"Look, there's no telling how long Stroessner will continue punishing Laino," I told Joel. "Even if he does gain his liberty by the time you go back, that's no guarantee." Then, assuming an authority that I probably did not have, I assured him, "Don't worry. We can always reschedule your tour."

"There is nothing to worry about, Richard," Joel replied. "Tell Amnesty and the Gaffneys I am definitely coming. I will be there October 22. Just as we plan."

"But there's no rush! There's plenty of time to decide, over a month," I persisted. "Let's wait and see how things work out with Domingo. There's nothing to lose. And it might just save you from another vacation in Mbuyapey, sharing a hovel with Laino."

"There is no danger of that," he insisted. "There is no danger at all. I can do or say anything."

"Joel, listen to me, you know how we've kept up the enormous pressure on the *Caso Laino*. And except for backing down a little after the first few weeks, Stroessner hasn't budged. It's just plain stupid not to hold off making a final decision."

Filártiga did not say a word. No doubt, as he intended, his silence forced me to ease up.

"OK," I asked, "just out of curiosity, what's behind your attack of audacity?"

"Don't you mean arrogance?" he chided. "No matter, you're wrong on all counts. My decision is based on logic."

"I'm listening."

"It is really quite simple," Joel went on, switching to lecture mode. "The *Caso Laino* has caused Stroessner incalculable problems. You know well the influence of international pressure on him.

"This indifference he projects is a facade. Laino will be released. But not too soon. That would undermine his authority. Such a loss of face is unacceptable.

"The last thing he wants is to compound the international assault with another protest campaign. And he knows that is what would happen if he arrests me. Stroessner's already so inhibited that my trip presents no risk."

"Well, perhaps," I conceded. "You're the one on the spot, best able to judge the situation. But people here don't see it that way. And they have the final say. For your own good, of course, they could pull the plug and cancel the trip."

"That is what I worry about the most," Joel confirmed. "We have suffered well-meaning stupidities before."

"It is unnecessary to remind me."

"But it is necessary that you do not let it happen again."

24

With the whirl of activities that began as soon as Filártiga arrived, it took over a week before we found the chance to really talk. At last, in early November, Joel and I were alone at the Gaffneys' home in New Haven. Everyone else had left to wrap up the final preparations for the Yale exhibition.

Piling pain upon pain, the bill that had built up over the years of the Filártigas' struggle had come due: the cost was the family's close-knit bond. Survivor's guilt and post-traumatic stress fractured their unqualified trust into passionate love/hate relationships. And while everyone suffered from the bewildering debilitation that to varying degrees wreaked dissension between every member of the family, it hit Dolly the hardest.

"Her reaction was frighteningly self-destructive," Joel told me. "We came to fear for her life. Not because Dolly tried to 'kill herself' with sleeping pills. That was a cry for attention.

"It was her physical and psychological deterioration that alarmed us. And when she miraculously escaped being killed by the truck, we became absolutely desperate. So then—"

"Whoa," I interrupted, "this is too confusing. Back up a little. How did it all start?"

"Three or four months ago, about when Laino was arrested, Dolly rebelled. In just a few weeks she lost interest in everything. The struggle. Becoming a physician. She said that her school transcripts had mysteriously disappeared, so she couldn't continue her studies. Anyway, she dropped out of everything—even refused to come to the clinic anymore."

"So where did Dolly live?"

"In Asunción. There was no way we could control her during the week. She fell in with a bad crowd. It became their place to have parties. Loud music and lots of liquor, marijuana. They even pilfered some pain medication from my medical supplies."

"Did Dolly work?"

"No," Filártiga explained. "Part of her psychological disorder was an inability to concentrate. At times, she had trouble remembering her own name. It was impossible to maintain employment. At first she borrowed money from boyfriends. The relationships never lasted. Always they ended in vicious fights.

"Another of her psychological dysfunctions was abusiveness," he sighed. "Dolly's erratic, aggressive personality swings drove away all of her friends. She was socially ostracized. She became clinically depressed. That is when she made her cry for attention. A handful of Valium.

"And antagonism between Dolly and me became insufferable," Filártiga elaborated. "Every time we saw each other we had a violent argument. Maybe it was another way to get attention. I am not certain. But I am sure my intolerance provoked her attacks against me. I came to loathe our weekends in Asunción."

Joel suddenly stopped. His last remark reminded him of something else he wanted to tell me.

25

Brightening a little, Joel hefted his bulk from the couch and paced around the room as he spoke. "Except for one thing. Sometime in July, I noticed that Peña's house was shut down. I asked the neighbors what had happened. No one knew—only that one day they were all gone.

"Peña's vanishing intrigued me," Filártiga went on, "so I asked some old friends to look into it. In the government, but sympathetic to us. They told me that Chief Inspector Américo Peña had been kicked out of the police. In May, maybe early June."

Right around the time it was all coming to a head, I thought; pressure from Congress, the letter-writing and petition campaigns, unrelenting international press criticism, the embassy's human rights activism, and especially the ambassador's personal intervention on behalf of the Filártigas, Laino's trip, the OAS conference, and the rest of the January Trains.

"My friends said that the other people who had lived in the house were still around town. But Peña and his woman, Juana Villalba, had disappeared. That is all they knew. Or all they would tell me."

"It was no mystery to me," Joel said. "Peña posed a threat. Like Charo, right after they killed Joelito. And why not Villalba, too? They all knew the truth.

"Stroessner was thrown into a defensive terror. Paranoia. Panic." Joel exhaled a bushel of air. "With the *Caso Filártiga's* international prominence? The OAS condemnation? The explosion of the *Caso Laino?* What was next?

"What if they were forced to permit the OAS on-site investigation? Then Peña would not be only a *potential* threat. He would be an *actual* peril. I was sure that the government got rid of them."

Even though at the time we knew nothing of the Galeano Perrone's legal maneuvering during these months, Filártiga's reasoning was right on the mark. His conclusions, however, had missed the target altogether.

26

"I'd like to hear the rest of Dolly's story before everyone gets back from the exhibition hall. What's this about her almost being killed by a truck?"

"She was running across the Avenida when she suffered an epilepsy-type attack. Perhaps the amphetamines. No matter," Joel said. "She collapsed not ten meters in front of a truck. People called it a wonderment. The way the driver swerved, missed crushing her head by centimeters.

"The thought of losing another child was unbearable. Nidia and I were terrified. Even Dolly recognized her life had become untenable. And she sought our help. Dolly, Nidia, and I decided something had to be done. But we did not know what. We lacked a specific—"

Just then the gang came bursting in.

"Papi, it's perfect," Dolly excitedly announced. "Everything's ready for your show tonight."

27

"Thank you, my daughter. Could we have a few more minutes? We are almost finished."

With Dolly and the others out of earshot in the kitchen, Filártiga finished up. "And not a week later they intercepted the letter. You cannot imagine the effect on Dolly. Overnight her lethargy and depression dissipated. She became determined, even obsessed, to come on this trip.

"You know how strong-willed she can be," he concluded. "There was no choice but to agree. That is when I phoned to see if Dolly might stay with you."

"You shouldn't have bothered," I replied, "what with all the other things you were dealing with."

On top of everything else, Filártiga had to produce scores of new drawings for his third U.S. visit. Even before he arrived, the superb organization of Amnesty, WOLA, the Gaffneys, and a host of others had created an air of heightened expectations. Once here, the almost daily press interviews they set up turned out people everywhere Filártiga went.

Even so, as always, it was Joel who made it happen. Spontaneously, invitations flooded in, bringing even more financial contributions and medical supplies for his Clinic of Hope. And as before, Joel's inspiration recruited a new legion of volunteers eager to help out.

Beginning with the two exhibitions in Manhattan, a dynamism surrounded Filártiga that eclipsed anything that had come before. Swelling the opening day crowd at the great hall of Riverside Church, hundreds of people—some of whom initially had come to hear Father Henri Nouwen talk on the spiritual meaning of Joel's art—became enthusiastic converts. Unexpectedly, their numbers grew when dozens more wandered over from the next-door chapel, after the memorial service for Nelson Rockefeller. And, drawn by the announcements in the Spanish-language media, Filártiga made contact with a small group of activists from the Paraguayan expatriate community living in the New York area. Two weeks later, at Saint Peter's Lutheran Church, a delegation of compatriots greeted their visiting celebrity.

Adding to Filártiga's successes, the shows at Yale and Harvard, and the cocktail party fundraisers that followed, surpassed all expectations. From Boston to Washington, Joel revitalized *Caso Filártiga* solidarity with talks to church organizations and Amnesty Adoption Groups, meetings with members of Congress and administration bureaucrats, and endless strategy sessions with old friends and new allies. Also, bringing additional documentation to the OAS, Joel spent hours working with the commission on their ongoing inquiry into Joelito's case and Paraguayan human rights.

By early December when Filártiga returned home, his 1978 tour had stoked the support movement to full steam. And a damn good thing, too, for the January Trains had forced a bizarre twist in the course of the *Caso Filártiga*.

The first hint had come six weeks before, when I met Joel and Dolly at the airport. Everyone arrived grumpy after the miserable overnight flight from Paraguay. But the Filártigas bounded through the gate. Catching sight of me across the crowd, they broke into irrepressible smiles, radiating excitement.

We made our way through the throng and exchanged family-close *abrazos*. I was about to suggest that we collect their luggage, but Joel could not hold off.

"Américo Peña and Juana Villalba are here!" he burst out. "They're living right here. In Brooklyn!"

Joelito

NINE

"It was a Saturday afternoon last September," Dolly told me as we waited at the JFK baggage claim. "A man came to the house in Sajonia. My aunt Coca was there and asked him what he wanted. The man told her that he was trying to deliver a letter for his boss. Coca didn't remember his name, only maybe he was the owner of a foreign car dealership, something like that. Well, his *patrón* had just come back from a business trip to the United States and a friend gave him some letters to be hand-delivered when he got back to Asunción.

"Anyway, there was something wrong with the address on this letter, the driver said. He couldn't find the house. For more than an hour he'd been going around the neighborhood, talking to people, asking them where Señor Victor Fernandez lived. Finally, someone sent him to our place."

On the conveyor belt, the Filártigas' luggage arrived. People scrambled for their bags. We paid no attention.

"That name rang a bell," Dolly went on, "so Coca said that the Señor was not at home, but she'd take the letter and give it to him when he returned. Then, right away, she and Analy boiled a pot of water and steamed it open. It was from Blanca Fernandez, Juana Villalba's teenage niece, telling her father how lonely she was."

"Peña and Juana took Blanca with them as a slave," Joel put in. "To do housework and babysit their three-year-old son. Blanca said they lock her in the apartment all day when they are at work. At night, too, when they go out."

Around the carousel their suitcases came and went.

"Blanca begged her father to write her. And she gave him their address in Brooklyn!" Dolly exclaimed. "I had been at the movies. And when I came home, everybody was very excited. Coca had rushed out to make a photocopy of the letter. But they didn't have any glue to reseal the envelope, so we used the white of an egg to put it together. We got everything finished before the driver must have realized his mistake. Because a little later he came back to get the letter."

As Dolly finished up, their baggage circled around again. "That night Papi and Mamá came from Ybycuí, like they always do on weekends. We were all so happy. We had always dreamed that something like this would happen!"

Peña in Brooklyn? A jumble of half thoughts, half emotions, looped through me. The whole idea was too enormous to take in. Besides, just then, we had more immediate business.

"We're going to have to deal with this later," I told them, grabbing the Filártigas' luggage. "Right now we've got to get you and these drawings to Riverside Church. The exhibition opens in a couple of hours and there's a dozen people waiting to finish setting up."

1

It wasn't so much that we dropped the ball; more like we never quite got a grip on it. Not in our wildest fantasies had we imagined that the twists and turns of the *Caso Filártiga* would land Joelito's murderer within our grasp. Yet, Peña was here. And that raised some very serious questions.

Not until almost two weeks into the tour, however, did we have the chance to take them head on. It was late, well after midnight, by the time we made it back from the Yale exhibition's opening night. After the others had shuffled off to bed, Dolly, Joel and I got together in the Gaffneys' living room in New Haven.

"He's not a big shot under Stroessner's protection anymore," Dolly began from the big arm chair across from us. "Now we have the power."

Next to me on the sofa, Joel seemed relaxed. He puffed on his pipe, a sketch pad balanced on his lap as he absently worked on a drawing. In fact, now that we were into it, Filártiga appeared almost detached.

"It's not that simple," I told Dolly, "Peña isn't the only one who's found a home in the United States. And not just Latin American torturers either. Look at all the Shah's Savak secret police roaming around as if they still were in Iran. And then there's Adolf's boys. Real old Nazis who skipped out of Europe one step ahead of the hangman. World War II mass murders, enjoying their retirement here for more than thirty years.

"It's one of our nastiest open secrets," I fumed, remembering Ambassador Stephansky's lecture on U.S. state policy. "The United States is a haven for just about any of our cold war, anticommunist 'sons-of-bitches.' The authorities turn a blind eye. It's not as if there's a Ten Most Wanted List of International Torturers."

Dolly's expression fell somewhere between disbelief and defiance. Staring hard at me she said, her words measured, their meaning unmistakable, "Mamá says you can do anything you want to to Peña."

Without looking up, Joel nodded in confirmation. We all knew how Nidia felt. I have never known a more compassionate person, anyone who lived a more giving life, than Nidia. Yet, in the primordial depth of her mother's vengeance, she could never forgive Peña for taking away Joelito.

"And Nidia's right. She's absolutely right," I agreed. "We can kill Peña."

This was a flat, unqualified statement of fact—there it was. From the moment of their arrival, it had been the Filártigas' heaviest piece of baggage. Now, it was open, laying upon us its inescapable weight of decision.

Only the light scratching of Filártiga's pen marred the heavy quiet. Turning to Joel, I said, "You could have had Peña killed in Paraguay. There were several offers. One very serious, I remember. From the Argentine guerrillas, to send a 'technician.' Is that what we want now?"

Filártiga took another puff, his attention fixed on the sketch pad. I glanced down to see the profile of Joelito, an ancient hand-fashioned iron spike—like those often depicted in the crucifixion of Christ—half driven into the top of his head. With each stroke, Joel's steady hand created the macabre etching.

A knotted rope stretched around Joelito's neck. Another spike, its shaft grotesquely left protruding from his temple. A stream of tears fell from his eye.

I looked up at Joel. Filártiga's head methodically moved from side to side, like the arc of a metronome, his air of serenity undisturbed.

"Well, maybe not kill him," Dolly backed up. "But make him tell the truth. How they killed Joelito. Where they took him. Everything."

A balancing of the scales: Abduct Peña, force from him all the hidden facts surrounding Joelito's death that had never stopped haunting the Filártigas, cauterize their psychological wounds with a measure of closure.

"It could be done," I said. "It would take a lot of planning, a lot of time. After all, I can't just invite Peña over to my place for dinner so we can throw him in the cellar."

Filártiga laid the sketch book aside, rose from the sofa, and paced around the room. After several slow circles, he stopped, his back toward us, to gaze through the old-fashioned frame window. In each of the six darkened panes, the glow of lamplight reflected the tableau. Over and over, Dolly anxiously leaned forward in her chair. And there I was, cast in half shadow, my multiple selves trying to read Joel's faces, his stare absorbed in the inky night.

An interminable time passed before Filártiga, still without uttering a syllable, settled back in the couch and picked up the pad. I watched as a tranquil panorama of the Ybycuí countryside, peasant huts scattered among palm trees, filled in the background.

There then appeared a bloody butcher knife, stuck into Joelito's throat. Down his face a second stream of tears dripped to a heart, which burst apart in a violent spray.

Belying Filártiga's exterior calmness that November 1978 night, after adding his signature to the drawing, he unconsciously wrote in the date '76, the year Joelito had died.

2

The Filártigas' 1978 Amnesty tour was a marathon from October when they arrived until Joel crossed the finish line six weeks later. Especially that last week in Washington; our days were crammed with nonstop meetings lined up by Filártiga's supporters, the flow of people passing through my apartment half the night. Even after Joel returned to Paraguay in early December, Dolly and I still had to wrap up the myriad loose ends he left behind before official Washington shut down.

When the holiday doldrums set in, we crashed. For me, the punishing pace ended in a fierce attack of back pain that took the festivity out of the season. For Dolly, it was a lot worse.

As the excitement of the Amnesty tour wound down, Dolly's traumas resurfaced. In the same day, sometimes in a matter of hours, she would swing from manic buoyancy to the pits of depression. At twenty-three, Dolly found herself spending her first Christmas away from the family, jobless and with few friends, in a foreign country whose language she had yet to learn. Of course, she had come to the States as much to get away from the mess her life had become in Paraguay as to find her brother's murderer. Even so, our failure to come up with a plan to move against Peña worsened Dolly's troubles.

We had rejected the idea of killing Peña, or even ringing the truth out of him, but that hardly meant that we would let it go. During our East Coast travels, the idea of Peña living in Brooklyn fired people's ire. With the same noncommittal good grace he accorded those back home, Filártiga patiently heard out the spontaneous vows of vengeance.

On the surface, busting a torturer-murderer on the lam, so internationally infamous that even the sleaziest of Latin American dictators had cut him loose, might seem a pretty straightforward proposition—especially in light of Peña's notoriety in the *Caso Filártiga*, the cause célèbre of the Nobel Peace Prize–winning Amnesty International campaign.

In a brainstorming session with Bob Maurer at the AI/USA office in New York, we discussed the possibilities. Backed by Amnesty's prestige, it was a safe bet that the press would jump on a torturer lying low in the United States. But then Peña would disappear, and that would be that. How about some legal action first? Have him arrested for the torture and murder of Joelito? Bob reminded us he was not a lawyer, but he doubted that the U.S. courts had jurisdiction over a homicide in Paraguay. He was sure, however, that no torturer had ever been brought to trial here.

In 1978 there existed no official interest in bringing to task human rights violators living here. It would be another two years before the Department of Justice established its Office of Special Investigations. And even then, OSI refused to prosecute war criminals. Only when shamed by enough publicity, and forced to take action by a formal extradition request, did the government deport a few particularly infamous Nazis back to the old country to answer for their crimes.

In January 1979, when Washington came back to life after the holidays, again our NGO friends began looking for something, anything, to move on Peña. For the next frustrating month everything we tried, everywhere we turned, led nowhere.

And on top of everything else, Dolly's tourist visa had run out. At any time she could be deported back to her dead-end existence in Paraguay.

3

Michael Maggio first met Dr. Filártiga the year before, during the Washington leg of Joel's 1977 tour. By December 1978, when they renewed their friendship, Maggio had finished law school, been admitted to the bar, and opened a storefront legal practice specializing in immigration law.

"The way to do this," he explained to Dolly in Spanish, "is political asylum."

"I didn't come here for political asylum," she protested. "Maybe right now I'm pretty covered up, and not doing very much. But I'm not running away from them. I came here to find Peña. Anyway, I don't have any of my papers with me."

"It doesn't matter," Mike insisted. "Just the facts of the *Caso Filártiga* I already have should do it. The trial transcripts show the court's corruption. How the police arrested you and your Mamá, throwing you in jail, the charges still pending. All we have to demonstrate is that you have a reasonable fear of political persecution in Paraguay. We've got more than enough."

"But what if it isn't," Dolly persisted. "And they make me leave?"

"They won't," Maggio assured her. "Look. The way the system works is once you file for political asylum, the Immigration and Naturalization Service can't deport you until they give you an official hearing to evaluate your case. And reach a final decision. The INS review procedure takes months, years sometimes. In the meantime, you can get a work permit—a job to support yourself."

"Well, what if they refuse and send me back anyway?" Dolly worried. "Then I'll really be in trouble."

"That won't happen," Mike told her. "Even if they rule against you at first, which I really doubt, we'll find new stuff. And appeal. And there's lots of appeals and motions we can play. We'll keep it up forever if we have to."

Regardless of Mike's assurances, Dolly decided against applying for political asylum. Taking her under his wing, Maggio gave Dolly a part-time job at his law office interviewing Spanish-speaking clients. Not long after, Dolly found an apartment to share with another Paraguayan woman, and she also began working with the woman cleaning houses a couple days a week. Even though she was still illegally in the country, Dolly was on track, pulling her new life together.

Best of all, in February 1979, after all the months of banging our heads against officialdom's stone wall, we got a break in the Peña impasse.

4

About six months before, in mid-1978, I had taken a job as a senior fellow at the Washington-based Council on Hemispheric Affairs (COHA). Well, not what my mother would consider a real job. Rather, it was what is known as an institutional affiliation, a common practice among human rights NGOs.

The way it worked, since COHA did not give me a regular salary, I was not tied to a normal work schedule. With the freedom to pick and choose my own projects, I spent most of my time on the *Caso Filártiga*. Moreover, the position at COHA gave me a respectable base of operations, and a prestigious title to use when applying for grants. In turn, COHA put my name on its letterhead, gained a fresh face to chair its press conferences, and reaped further publicity from my public speaking, interviews, and publications. All in all, it was a very satisfactory, mutually beneficial arrangement.

Lately, I had stepped up the pressure on Larry Birns, the brilliant if decidedly eccentric director of COHA, to get something moving on Peña. The *Caso Filártiga*, as a simple human rights case, was one thing—a clear-cut moral issue that any person of good conscience could get behind. But bring in a former high-ranking police official from a hard-line anticommunist ally slinking about New York, and it became something else altogether.

Peña's presence here recast the *Caso Filártiga* into a political hot potato, steaming with embarrassing fallout for our cold war foreign policy. If the calculating bureaucrats in official Washington had been wary of helping us out before, now they would not touch the case.

At first, just as with Filártiga's other friends scouring the system for a solution to the Peña quandary, Larry's efforts were stymied. But Birns had an ace to play, one that just might trump the Peña wildcard.

Leonel Castillo, the Chicano leader from Texas, had been a member of COHA's Board of Trustees for years. During the 1976 campaign, Leonel worked to rally the Mexican American vote for Jimmy Carter. And just that month—February 1979—President Carter appointed Castillo to be the commissioner of the Immigration and Naturalization Service.

Although coming to Washington as an outsider, the longtime human rights activist could hardly be unaware of the government's unspoken policy of overlooking our disreputable anticommunist friends in residence. So when Larry finally got the chance to explain our Peña problem to Leonel, it presented the new INS chief with a moral dilemma.

On the one hand, Castillo had no doubt that he stood on solid legal ground in ordering an INS investigation of Peña. On the other, as a federal bureaucrat, he knew that doing so would do his career no good. In the end, his decision had little to do with any pragmatic political calculation. What settled it, as Leonel told me later, was his respect for Larry Birns and a gut conviction that Peña was guilty.

And so, at last, we had found a crack in the system, someone to whom the idea of a Paraguayan torturer hanging out in Brooklyn somehow did not seem right.

5

"So what happened to Peña's address?" I fumed at Dolly. "Finally, finally, after all these months we've got something concrete. But nothing can be done if the INS can't find Peña. I thought you had the letter with his address. Now you say you don't. And I don't. So how the hell did we lose it?"

"We haven't really lost it," Dolly replied. "It's just that we don't have it."

I collapsed into the armchair, my head dropping in frustration.

"Let's start from the beginning," I said. "At the airport, you told me about Peña. Then we rushed off to Riverside Church."

"And right after we got to the exhibition," Dolly recalled, "four Paraguayans came up to Papi and me. They said they'd read about our struggle and came from Brooklyn to offer their solidarity.

"Ah, I said to them, we think the murderer of Joelito is in Brooklyn, and asked if they knew Peña. They told us there was a man called Américo Peña there, but weren't sure he was the same person.

"So I gave them Peña's address, and we asked them to watch him and let us know, because we had to travel on the Amnesty tour. Candito Arbo, he was the one who talked most, said they would help us find Peña. Papi gave Candito your telephone number. Candito gave us his address and number, and we promised to keep in touch."

But, in our muddle during the past months, we had not stayed in contact. In fact, we had not so much as spoken with the Paraguayan expatriates since the New York exhibitions. Worse yet, not only had we failed to make a photocopy of Blanca's letter; incredibly, none of us had even thought to write down Peña's address.

"Did you give Candito the letter, too?" I asked.

"No, no. I kept it in my wallet. Until," she reflected, "until we came here to Washington. That's right! Papi took it to the OAS!"

"The OAS? What for?"

"To prove to them that Peña was in the United States. Yes, now I remember!" Dolly exclaimed. "Papi gave Blanca's letter to the OAS!"

6

With bureaucratic righteousness, the OAS stood firm. Under no circumstances, they insisted, could they release any information concerning an investigation in progress. My plea that surely an exception could be made in this case, as I had initiated their inquiry in the first place, was the original complainant in the case, met with indifference.

After a week of trying to reach our Paraguayan friends by phone, I went to New York and finally got together with Candito Arbo and Nora Vega. At the exhibition, they had told the Filártigas that Peña was a soccer fanatic who never missed the Sunday afternoon Paraguayan games. Hoping to pick him up, after leaving Riverside Church they had gone straight to Flushing Meadows Park. But Peña had dropped off the radar screen. For the previous week or so, since the publicity of Filártiga's tour, no one had seen him.

After that, their hunt for Peña just kind of petered out. And when Candito and Nora explained that they had also misplaced Peña's address, I half expected it. However, they did promise to renew the search. Meanwhile, they suggested that it might be a good idea to talk with Gilberto Olmedo.

It was not so easy to contact the furtive anti-Stroessner activist, who had developed an impressive paranoia during his thirteen years of sniping at the Paraguayan dictator from his New York exile. Everyone seemed to have his phone number, yet no one knew where the secretive Olmedo lived.

Gilberto had spoken with Joel at the Saint Peter's Church show, but the crush of people demanding Filártiga's attention cut their conversation short. A few days later, though, Olmedo learned the full *Caso Filártiga* story when *El Diario de la Prensa* published a delightful word-for-word plagiarization of my Alberto Cabral piece. In turn, Olmedo reprinted the article in the November issue of his newsletter, *Paraguay Libre*, adding dramatically that the torturer Peña was hiding out in the New York area.

It took until late February to reach the elusive political exile.

"It was around the middle of December," Gilberto told me over the phone, "when this guy came up to me. At the Casa Paraguaya. That is the cultural and political center of the Paraguayan community here. We went down to the men's room, in the basement, so we could talk alone.

"He said he was Francisco Reyes, an Argentine. But that he worked in Brooklyn at Gampel & Stoll, a furniture-finishing shop owned by a Paraguayan. All the other people who worked there, they were also all Paraguayans. One was called Américo Peña. Reyes saw my article about the *Caso Filártiga* and thought this was the same Peña, because everyone at the shop was pro-Stroessner and was protecting him."

I exchanged a glance with Dolly, who was on the extension in my apartment.

"I told Reyes to be careful, that we should look into this with caution," Olmedo went on, "but he had such a hatred that a week later he confronted Peña. Reyes showed him my article and asked if he was the same man.

"Peña got very angry. He said, 'Yes, I am. And I am still collecting my police salary. I just had to get out of the country for a few years to let things cool off.' Then he bragged, 'When I return, not a hair on Filártiga's head will be left. He is going to be hamburger.'"

Dolly shot me a worried look.

"Well, then Reyes became very mad also," Olmedo continued. "They yelled at each other some more, and he took my article to the boss and denounced Peña as an assassin. In a little while, the *patrón* came over to Peña with my paper in his hand. He was not angry. He was scared. He told Peña, 'This is very serious. It is just a question of time before someone comes to get you.' And then he fired him."

"You mean that Peña's gone?" Dolly gasped.

"No. I do not think so. He is not at the furniture shop anymore. But I do not think so," Olmedo replied. "Others say they have seen him at the same building where he lives in Borough Park. Everyone there is also pro-Stroessner, even the super, López Morán."

"You wouldn't happen to have that address by any chance?" Dolly asked. We heard the shuffling of papers as we waited.

"Right here," Gilberto said, "1865 Fifty-Second Street."

7

"My dear Birns," I greeted Larry when he answered his phone around midnight," you've had your chance. It's been a month since I gave you Peña's address. That's when you promised it'd be a week, two at the outside. It's now the end of March, and Peña's still strutting around Brooklyn—if he's even in the country."

"Indeed, I quite see how in your ignorance you might be annoyed," Larry retorted. "But COHA isn't exactly in the business of rolling up death squads. These things don't always follow a bloody schedule, you know. Or you would if you spent less time trotting about doing God knows what, instead of condescending to drop by the office as the whim strikes you.

"By the way," he squawked, "where the devil are you? Frolicking about some rancid cat house in Buenos Aires, calling collect as usual?"

"Not at all, old boy," I laughed. "Actually, I'm passing a quiet evening at home. Sharpening my machete."

Normally, Larry and I enjoyed our exchange of irreverent quips. This time, though, a decidedly sharp edge marked our conversation.

"I realize it's late, but under the circumstance, it seemed the decent thing to do. Couldn't have you wearing out your worry beads. You're going to be needing them."

"And what drivel are you spouting now?" he demanded.

"Time's run out," I shot back. "Our contacts in New York tell us Peña's ready to split on a Paraguayan freighter. The *SS Asunción* is berthed at the Brooklyn docks. Shame to let that happen, wouldn't you say?"

"And?" he said.

"And the day after tomorrow—Thursday, March 29—the good people at Columbia University have asked me to give a chat for their human rights lecture series on the *Caso Filártiga*."

"No," Larry groaned, seeing where it was heading.

"Yes," I countered. "No doubt you find my dissatisfaction at Joelito's murderer living the good life just across the East River demonstrates a lack of refinement. But there you have it."

"You can't be—"

"But I am," I interrupted. "It's a '60s thing. Remember? The exhilaration of marching a swarm of Columbia students across the Brooklyn Bridge, chanting, 'Hell no, Peña's got to stay! This time he won't get away!'"

"Listen to me, White," Larry exploded. "You're going to ruin everything. Leonel's people are ready to move. Any day now, they're—"

"They're going to do nothing," I retorted. "Same as all the others."

"What's wrong with you, White? You're raving like the Gingerbread man," Larry sputtered. "Don't be a damn fool!"

"See you at the barricades, comrade."

On the extension Dolly had overheard my exchange with Larry, but her English still had not reached the point where she could follow it all. After we went over it in Spanish, she could not suppress a chuckle. It was not the first time Dolly had seen me play the "light a fire and see who comes out with the hose" game.

But I did not join in with her laughter. Since the holidays, I had increasingly been relying on painkillers to deal with the back pain. At last, my physician warned that I was getting a greater amount of narcotics from the pharmaceutically pure drugs than a street junkie. I assured him I understood the risks, but that he had to keep me going. Reluctantly, he prescribed more and stronger medication, under the condition that once we wrapped up Peña I would go into the hospital—quite possibly for another back operation, certainly to dry out.

With the pain and drugs beating me down, I had become more frustrated than ever with the endless inaction. Time was running out. My fear was that I would not make it, that I would collapse before we got Peña.

"You're not really going to do it?" Dolly asked. "Are you?"

"I don't know. I just don't know," I told her. "Maybe it'd get something moving, throw the dice, hope that it will make something happen."

"But what about ruining everything?" she insisted. "Like Mr. Birns said."

"What? I don't see anything to ruin. Do you?"

8

When we recovered Peña's address from Olmedo in February, I had given it to several other people besides Larry. Bob Maurer at Amnesty had not been able to come up with anything, though he was still working on it.

On March 1, Jo Marie Griesgrabber at WOLA had shot a long memo to Diana Lang, one of Senator Edward Kennedy's top aides. Kennedy, the chairperson of a Senate Judiciary Subcommittee, certainly was the right person for the job. As an arm of the Justice Department, the Immigration and Naturalization Service fell under his purview.

In her memo, Jo Marie gave a summary of the *Caso Filártiga* before pointing out that "even though in Paraguay [Peña] was forced to leave the police and has charges pending against him for his activity as a torturer." She ended by querying, "Would Peña's admission to the U.S. be cause for a congressional hearing?"

Some days later, we received word that the senator wanted more substantial information before convening a hearing and issuing subpoenas. And that was it. Cut out of the loop, we received no more feedback from the Kennedy people.

9

Needless to say, we hardly rated the confidence of the Department of State either. Actually, Kennedy did send a request to State asking for an explanation of how the consulate in Asunción could have given Peña a visa. While completely in the dark at the time, years later through the Freedom of Information Act, I obtained a fairly complete copy of the State Department cable traffic. Although censured with angry black redactions, they paint a clear-enough picture of the behind-the-scenes action.

One week after receiving the initial query from State, on March 14, Ambassador Robert White cabled back to his masters in Washington that "AS STATED ASUNCION 10/13 POST HAS NO RECORD VISA APPLICATION AMERICO PEÑA DURING PERIOD CITED."

The reference to the embassy's October 13, 1978, cable refers to the standard inquiry made by State when Peña failed to return to Paraguay from the United States after his tourist visa ran out. Now, however, with Senator Kennedy breathing down their neck, no one was treating it as a routine matter.

Going on to review the *Caso Filártiga*, Bob first offered the official line: "POST FILES CONCERNING CASE OF JOELITO FILÁRTIGA . . . SHOW ONE AMERICO PEÑA WAS POLICE OFFICER ALLEGEDLY DIRECTLY INVOLVED IN MURDER . . . SUPPOSEDLY IN CRIME OF PASSION." And so on and so on.

Then, after summarizing my Alberto Cabral article, Bob went on: "PROFESSOR RICHARD WHITE . . . PUBLISHED A DIFFERENT VERSION OF THE EVENT . . . THAT COMBINATION PERSONAL AND POLITICAL FACTORS CAUSED PEÑA TO 'KIDNAP' JOELITO WHO WAS THEN TORTURED TO OBTAIN A CONFESSION OF HIS FATHER'S AND HIS COMPLICITY IN THE OPM." And so on and so on.

Finally, in a dazzling display of bureaucratic ass covering, the ambassador skirted the visa issue. "PEÑA," he stated, "HAS NEVER BEEN ARRAIGNED OR TRIED IN THIS CASE. LACKING A CONVICTION, EMBASSY IS UNAWARE OF ANY GROUNDS OF INELIGIBILITY AGAINST PEÑA."

Wiggling about at the sharp end of the stick, the career diplomat tread a very fine line to shield his embassy and the State Department from the embarrassing consequences. The *Caso Filártiga* was a snake pit that not even Dr. Filártiga completely understood. Still, it did not take an international jurist to know that, unlike U.S. common law, there existed no procedure of arraignment under Paraguay's Napoleonic legal system. And, the press had carried story after story of the formal criminal charges placing on trial Peña and the others as conspirators in Joelito's ongoing murder case.

About the only factually correct statement Bob made was that Peña had not been convicted. In fact, there had been no convictions in the *Caso Filártiga* because Stroessner had derailed the proceedings, consigning the trial in a legal limbo.

Perhaps careless advice from his legal staff accounted for Bob's hair-splitting cable to Washington. Or maybe it was a smoke screen to cover for their blunder. Be that as it may, it begged the question of Peña's visa.

While Peña may not have technically violated any of the consular guidelines, citizens of foreign countries possess no right to come to the United States. The way things work, U.S. consulates around the world have the most sweeping power to grant, or deny, visas. They can, and routinely do, turn down anyone that fails to meet their unwritten discretionary criteria.

I know a Latin American student who, because he had signed a petition protesting the Vietnam War, was refused a visa to attend a Columbia University–sponsored conference in New York. Another friend from France could not understand why he had been denied entry, until a kindhearted secretary at the consulate explained that someone had floated the suspicion that he might be gay. Surely, Peña's June 28, 1976, inclusion as a coconspirator in such a heinous act as the torture and murder of Joelito was more than enough to deny him a visa.

Some years later, during a candid talk, Ambassador White explained what had happened. Had Peña's visa application come to his attention, he would have canned it in a heartbeat. There existed no diabolical plot to help Stroessner's minion escape to a new life. More than a bit chagrined, Bob admitted that the applications of Peña and his party "simply fell between the cracks."

Blanca Fernandez, Juana Villalba, and Peña and their son had signed up with a tour group organized by a reputable Asunción tourist agency. As a matter of course, the consulate approved the two dozen or so visa applications. They slipped through, Bob told me, because the embassy had Peña filed in their Filártiga dossier instead of red flagging him under his own name.

On July 11, 1978, the tourist agent picked up all the U.S. visas, and ten days later Peña's party arrived in Florida. The Miami Immigration official stamped their entry permits, and welcoming them all to the country, wished the torturer a pleasant stay. Forgoing the pleasure of their Disney World vacation, Peña cashed in their return tickets before hopping a flight to New York.

Eight months later, pressured by Kennedy and the INS for the Peña paperwork, the embassy staff stepped up their search. And just one week after insisting that no visas had been issued, on March 21, they found the elusive documents. Immediately, Bob cabled the details to Washington; but State stalled, holding back the information from the INS.

As for us, completely iced out, we remained even deeper in the dark. Kennedy's office had not let us know about his State Department inquiry. State would not even acknowledge that they had an interest in the matter. The INS would tell us nothing about their Anti-Smuggling Unit's investigation.

10

On the afternoon of March 9, INS commissioner Leonel Castillo sent the Peña case to his director of anti-smuggling activities—with a move-on-this-one-at-once directive. The call to the New York Anti-Smuggling Unit (ASU) came in a little after eight o'clock, that same Friday evening. The secretary explained to Burt Moreno that all the agents were still in the field, or had already gone home. Only the rookie, Frank DiConstanzo, was in the office. Put him on the line, the boss ordered.

"Listen to me DiConstanzo," Moreno barked, "we've located this guy in Brooklyn. Américo Peña. A cop laying low from a torture-murder rap back in Paraguay. No telling what he's up to. Political death squads. Drug smuggling. White slavery. No telling."

That Peña could be running a gang of thugs to intimidate Stroessner's political enemies here was not out of the question. Not eighteen months earlier, a Chilean hit team had carried out the Letelier-Moffitt assassination in downtown Washington. And, just the month before, the FBI had revealed that Stroessner's Investigaciones had provided the Chilean assassins with phony Paraguayan passports.

And the infamous French Connection, which during the 1960s channeled heroin from Marseille through Paraguay and on to the States, made the drugs a natural.

Then too, the ASU already had got wind of a possible white slavery operation out of Paraguay. During the preceding few years, oddly, the U.S. Consulate in Asunción had issued hundreds of tourist visas to young women from the small town of Caraguatay, few of whom returned from their "vacations." Indeed, because of the dollars they send back to their families, Caraguatay had become known as an oasis of prosperity among the poverty of rural Paraguay.

After talking with Burt Moreno, DiConstanzo drew a surveillance van from the pool, drove to Brooklyn, and set up down the block from Peña's place. As the new guy in the ASU, Frank still had not been teamed up with a regular partner. Alone, watching the action on the street, the vulnerability of his situation began seeping in. From all that Moreno had told him, Peña was a thoroughly dangerous character.

Half-spooked, Frank spent a half hour nestled in the van before abandoning its safety to finish the job. After checking out the alley behind Peña's building, he worked his way into the apartment house vestibule. Tucked into the mail box slot of apartment 9A, the cardboard strip announced in large, hand-printed black letters, "A. Peña."

11

Except for the occasional help from other ASU agents, at first DiConstanzo worked on his own. Hoping to turn up a lead on the drugs or the human trafficking operation, he spent his nights on a dockside parking lot overlooking the *SS Asunción*. He even hung out at the local bars, striking up conversations in Spanish with the freighter's crew. Nothing.

"So how long did you work the Peña case by yourself?" I asked him years later, after the dust had settled and we were on speaking terms.

"Couple of weeks, until Bill wanted to be part of it," he said. "Kerins put his name on as co-case agent, which never, ever happens. You have to understand that this guy is the best friend I have at ASU. He's the head of ASU, the best man in the unit.

"What finally happened was that everybody got caught up in it. Kerins' interest developed over the white slavery. Because that was a big rap, a good criminal case.

"Nocella's interest grew when he saw the pictures. He was in 'Nam, a war veteran, a real hard-bitten war veteran. I think he was captured and escaped. Anyway, when he saw that picture of the boy's tortured body, something snapped. He wanted this guy."

That I understood. Over the years, I had seen the power of Joelito's savaged body move people.

"There was other stuff too," Frank went on. "How they take Indians out. Three, four hundred at a time, and machine gun them. And these bastards just walk away. Like in Nazi Germany."

Dr. Richard Arens, a law professor at Temple University, had exposed the massacres of the Aché Indians in his book *Genocide in Paraguay*, and he was feeding ASU more details.

"But what got us first," Frank finished up, "we kept getting all those Amnesty International articles and pamphlets, and stuff that you wrote. About the torture methods they used down there. The excrement baths, cattle prods, truncheons.

"Your name was on the original orders. They said Dr. White could be contacted for further information."

"Yet you ignored me, treated me as the enemy," I shot back, surprising myself that ten years later the anger could still boil to the surface.

"Well, you have to understand," DiConstanzo replied. "People at ASU have a natural fear of talking to outsiders."

12

The day before my Columbia University lecture, Larry Birns, bless his conniving soul, hit the panic button. As I drove to New York on Wednesday, March 28, the news broke of trouble at the Three Mile Island nuclear plant. At the same time, Burt Moreno was on the phone from Washington warning ASU of their own potential disaster heading into town.

No sooner had I arrived at my friend's Manhattan apartment than Waldo handed me a message: "URGENT YOU CONTACT US IMMEDIATELY. DICONSTANZO."

At last, after all these months, here was something tangible. Sure, Castillo had made sympathetic noises. Even so, the INS commissioner played it close to his vest, never giving us anything concrete. Only now, with DiConstanzo's frantic messages, did I receive official confirmation that ASU actually might be doing something about Peña.

Crushing the note into a ball, I tossed it into the trash can. "He's been calling every hour," Waldo said.

"Good for him. Let's get a beer and a pastrami sandwich."

When we got back two hours later, the phone began ringing.

"Dr. White," an agitated DiConstanzo implored, "please don't go through with the Columbia demonstration. It'll blow everything."

"Everything?" I shot back. "Not a peep from you guys. And now you expect me to believe there's something to blow?"

"But there is. The case is ready to break. Won't you at least talk with us before your lecture tomorrow?"

"Impossible. The talk's on at ten. And I'm not a morning person. Hell, as far as you're concerned I've been a nonperson. And now, all of a sudden, you're falling all over yourselves."

"So what does that tell you?" he said. "Isn't that reason enough to at least sit down with us, hear what we have to say?"

"All it tells me," I told DiConstanzo, "is that you guys want to keep control. You don't want to talk with me. What you want is to talk me out of talking. Why should I believe you?"

"Because it's the truth!" he exploded. "If you do this thing, we'll lose Peña."

DiConstanzo's outrage did not impress me. The fear in his voice, though, was persuasive.

13

Arriving at 26 Federal Plaza Thursday afternoon, I found the gang waiting. The receptionist hustled me through ASU's ninth-floor headquarters, straight into an interrogation room. Soft-spoken, reasonable Frank DiConstanzo began the dog-and-pony show by offering coffee. From across the table, physically imposing Bill Kerins shot me a look that was in no way benign.

"Thank you for coming by like this," DiConstanzo started. "It'd help us to know why you're so interested in the Peña case."

"Because he murdered my friend," I said, tossing a bulging manila envelope on the table. "Américo Peña tortured Joelito Filártiga to death in 1976. It's all there."

Another agent took the batch of *Caso Filártiga* documents and hurried out of the dismal little chamber.

"You're telling me you've been after this guy for three years?" Kerins scoffed. "And now, when we've got him by the balls, you're going to screw it up. Because your feelings are hurt? Bullshit! What are you really after?"

I had not expected them to believe the truth, so I was ready with a story that they would buy. Dismissing Kerins with a scowl, I spoke to DiConstanzo. "A half hour alone with Peña. Eighteen months ago, someone torched my house. All I want is a private talk with him, to clear things up. That's the cost of my cooperation."

It was, I knew, an outlandish demand. No law enforcement organization, particularly the imperious Feds, would go for such a deal. DiConstanzo retreated to scribbling on his yellow legal pad. Kerins, his Irishman's beefy face as grim as ever, stomped out with a snort of disgust.

14

Frank DiConstanzo remained fixated on his doodling, his mind racing. That first call from Washington had cemented Burt Moreno's directions in DiConstanzo's head. Moreno had been emphatic. Go for the criminal charges—the girls, death squads, drugs—make sure Peña ended up in a federal penitentiary for a good, long stay.

But the investigation had bogged down, brought to a halt. The ASU did not have a photo of Peña, or even a good physical description. Frank tried to get a copy of Peña's visa application, which contained his picture and other important information, from the State Department in Washington, only to be bumped to the U.S. Consulate in Paraguay. Then the bureaucrat in Asunción informed him that they released such information only upon receipt of a formal request, directed through proper channels. It took another couple of days before DiConstanzo worked out a way to send an official cable from the U.S. Mission at the United Nations.

At the time of my getting-to-know-you chat with the ASU boys, they still were waiting for an answer from Paraguay. Even though by then the consulate had located Peña's documents, instead of cabling back the urgently needed information, they decided that a reply by mail would do.

In the lull that followed the blowup with Kerins, agents scuttled in and out of the room, whispering into DiConstanzo's ear. They had been combing the *Caso Filártiga* documents, searching for anything to identify Peña. I could have told them they would not find it. I also could have given them a pretty good description of Peña. I guess they did not feel all that comfortable asking me for help just then.

"Look, Dr. White, this isn't Paraguay," DiConstanzo sighed. "We can't just give you Peña like that. We don't operate that way."

Of course, I could have cared less about the half hour alone with Peña; such a dicey international operation involving arson and possibly assassination was out of the league of a cop who could not even torture a kid into betraying his father. I had only thrown it out to give ASU a reason that they would accept for my interference.

Up to that point, no one had even addressed me by name. And here was DiConstanzo bending over backwards, stroking me by using my formal title. A good sign.

"Well, I guess that's it, fellows," I said, getting up. "Probably be running into Peña around town anyway."

"Please!" DiConstanzo stood, and he held up his hand like a traffic cop trying to stop a runaway eighteen-wheeler. "You're a human rights activist. Of all people, you value the rule of law. Personally, I'd like to let you have your talk with Peña.

"I know it isn't much, but what I can say is," he went on, "is once we have Peña in custody, I'll ask him about your house. Sorry. It's the best I can do."

It was, I knew, all that he could honestly say. If he had promised anything more, I would not have believed it. Not that I trusted him or anyone else at ASU.

"Already too many people are involved," DiConstanzo continued. "Peña's going to know we know where he lives, because you guys know where he lives, and it's going to get back to him."

"So arrest him?"

"We haven't got a criminal case," he admitted. "If we raid the house or grab Peña off the street, and he isn't the right guy, he's gone. And we won't have any idea where to find him."

Until then, I did not know for sure that ASU's investigation was stymied. Now, DiConstanzo was letting me know that they had nowhere left to go. It took another hour to hammer out the deal.

They would keep me up to date on the investigation's progress. I would set up a meeting with Gilberto Olmedo the next day, Friday, March 30.

15

The Filártigas spent that Friday very much as they had the first two anniversaries of Joelito's death. At a half-dozen memorial Masses spread out over Asunción, the family joined the overflow crowds—peppered as always with Stroessner's *pyragués*. After the services, they handed out cards to the people who surrounded them, and they denounced the government's continuing cover-up.

During the past year, the press had regularly put out sympathetic stories on Dr. Filártiga; the opening of a new exhibition, an interview about the influence of art in Paraguayan society, his philanthropic work at the Sanatorio La Esperanza, and Joel's third triumphal tour to the United States. And while fear of government reprisals tempered what the media came right out and said, everyone understood the subtext of solidarity for the Filártigas' struggle.

In what had become an annual ritual, the press began resurrecting the *Caso Filártiga* weeks before. Beginning on March 11, *La Tribuna* adorned the cover of its weekend Cultural Supplement with a full-page color Madonna drawing by Filártiga. One week later, the Sunday editorial in *Hoy* opened, "In the clear dawn of the March 30, 1976. Joelito Filártiga set out on his endless journey, and today, nearly 3 years after his death, a cloak of darkness still enshrouds the mystery of his death." That following Thursday, as I sparred with the ASU in New York, the story in *El Pueblo* prophetically ended, "But Justice, real justice, never forgets."

As much as anything else, Paraguayan popular religiosity kept Joelito's death alive. Far from fading, the legend of Beato Joelito flourished. In desperation, Paraguay's dispossessed came to the cemetery to pray for miracles. With the anniversary *Caso Filártiga* media blitz and the approach of Holy Week, the flock of pilgrims to their martyr's crypt blossomed into a congregation.

16

Before the Filártigas had taken their seats at the first Mass of the day in Asunción on that morning of March 30, the ASU team was set up in Brooklyn. They had organized the operation overnight.

Inside the ConEd van parked across from Peña's place, DiConstanzo focused his camera at the doorway. When Peña came out, there would only be a few seconds to get a clean shot. He would try for as many as possible, but it was the first one that really counted.

At 6:30, there he was. But not coming out. Moving fast along the sidewalk, Peña headed straight for his building and disappeared inside before anyone could react. An hour later, Peña and a woman appeared at the entranceway. Carrying a large black satchel, he turned left, retracing his steps. DiConstanzo's shutter started clicking.

"It's cloak-and-dagger stuff," Frank told me later. "When Peña gets out of sight of the surveillance van, Kerins and Burk peal off and tail him on foot. He takes the subway from Brooklyn to Manhattan. They followed him to a train stop, Fifth Avenue near the cathedral. You come out of the subway into a little plaza with a fountain. It's like walking into Grand Central station, only outside. Thousands of people. It's impossible to follow anybody into that kind of stuff. He's lost.

"You've got to remember these are guys in a new organization, doing stuff like this for the first time. But now we're sure Peña's a real pro. He's got eyes in the back of his head. When we go after him, we're going in with shotguns.

"And, well, like you know, the pictures weren't all that great," Frank went on. "Shit equipment. No tripod. No bayonet. The camera wasn't even motor driven.

"Anyway, we rushed the film to the FBI on Seventy-Second Street. Did us a favor, developed it right away."

17

It was a red-eyed DiConstanzo who showed up in Queens for our noon meeting. Gilberto Olmedo had insisted that we meet at the outdoor Latin American market on Jamaica Avenue. People jostled us as the cacophony of exotic birds, screaming from their cane reed cages, vied with the rumble of passing trains on the elevated track. I felt right at home. Frank seemed less at ease.

I spotted two ASU guys from headquarters, the only other Anglo faces in the crowd, pretending to make a call as they hung around a sidewalk phone booth. The best they could do for back up, I supposed. ASU had no Latino agents.

We went into a nearby restaurant for lunch. "Mr. Olmedo," Frank said, "too many people have become involved in the Peña case. They are a danger to our investigation."

"It is true," Gilberto replied. "I have spoken with a correspondent from the *Village Voice*. She said she had visited the building of Peña. And only the day before yesterday Mr. Jeff Nesmith telephoned. He works in Washington for a newspaper called the *Atlanta Constitution*."

Frank pressed, "We must find out something that even they don't know. You couldn't give us Peña's current place of employment? Or be able to find out?"

"That, Señor," Gilberto replied, "is a problem. At first he worked at the furniture-finishing shop on President Street—before we exposed him as an assassin. Many months ago they fired Peña. Now he hides."

DiConstanzo took out an envelope and spread on the table a set of the pictures they had taken that morning. "Perhaps you can identify him from these."

"In this matter," Olmedo said, barely glancing at them, "I can be of no assistance. I do not know Peña. It was an Argentine coworker who denounced him to the *patrón*."

I took my time studying the blurry black-and-white images. It could have been Peña. There was a definite resemblance. And I sure would have loved to nail him.

"The guy looks a lot like Peña, but there's no way I can say from these," I grumbled.

Frank picked up the photos and stuffed them in his jacket. "If anyone can tell, it'd be Dolly Filártiga," I told him. "I'll take a set back to Washington this afternoon for her."

With a noncommittal shrug, DiConstanzo turned back to Olmedo. "You say it was your friend who found Peña? Then he could give us a positive identification?"

"Without doubt. For three months, this man worked with Peña. Each day he saw him face-to-face."

"Could I speak with your friend? To have him look at the pictures?"

"Well," Olmedo hedged, "that might be difficult."

Frank understood. "Let me assure you," the immigration officer said, "we have absolutely no interest in his legal status here in the United States. On that, you have my word."

"In that case perhaps it could be arranged," Gilberto replied.

"It's of the utmost importance." Giving Olmedo his card, with the ASU's Federal Plaza address, he pressed, "Tonight. My office? Nine o'clock?"

"I will bring him myself."

18

On the way back to Washington, I listened to the radio updates on Three Mile Island. Forty-eight hours before, driving to New York on the day the story broke, I had not paid much attention. Now, the reports said that 150,000 people had been evacuated from their homes around the plant. The news that we might face a full-blown nuclear meltdown took my mind off our own little disaster-in-the-making.

After the meeting with Olmedo, again I had offered to take a set of the surveillance photos to Washington for Dolly to check out. Kerins would not hear of it. I argued that to expect an undocumented immigrant, subject to arrest and deportation, would voluntarily saunter into the INS lair was fantasy. Kerins assured me that they knew what they were doing.

Frank called me at home around ten that night. Olmedo and Francisco Reyes had not shown up. They would wait another hour or so, but it did not look good. Maybe it was not such a bad idea for Dolly to take a look at the pictures.

By then, I had pretty much put Three Mile Island into perspective. There was not a damn thing to be done about the China Syndrome. So I had spent the past few hours stewing over how the testosterone-bloated ASU had reneged on our deal.

"Get real!" I snapped. "You don't really think that a beautiful, single young woman is sitting around on a Friday night waiting for you. If only I'd called her before leaving, like—"

"OK," Frank cut me off. "You've made your point."

"Call tomorrow," I said a bit smugly. "Just hope Dolly's not out of town for the weekend."

Saturday afternoon, DiConstanzo called. No, the Paraguayans did not show up. Yes, I had spoken with Dolly. Kerins would be on the next shuttle.

Like Francisco Reyes, Dolly had her own immigration worries; but there was never any question about what she would do. At nine o'clock, there was a sharp rap on my door, a cop's knock. Since I had seen him the day before, Kerins had done nothing to polish his social graces. Skipping the amenities, the taciturn ASU agent got right down to business.

Dolly hunched over the coffee table, scrutinizing the grainy photos. "I can't say for sure," she said at last. "Maybe. It kind of looks like him. Maybe a relative. But this man is a lot older. And Peña always stands straight up, and looks right at you with his hard green eyes. It could be, but I can't say for sure."

Kerins grunted.

"But the woman," Dolly burst out, tapping her finger on a photo. "This woman. This is Juana Villalba."

"You're sure?" Kerins demanded.

"Oh, yes. Yes. That's Peña's woman," Dolly told him. "I know her well. They live together in Asunción. We are neighbors. All of us children are friends. This is Juana Villalba."

Kerins scooped up all the photos and was gone before I could thank him for stopping by.

19

Monday morning, April 2, now pretty sure they had the right guy, the ASU team went at it again. This time they got Peña through the packed plaza, and a few blocks further on. The agents tried to stick close as he pushed his way through the rush hour crush of people. Then Peña ducked into one of two adjacent office buildings—they could not tell which—and they lost him.

About noon, I caught Kerins at ASU headquarters. It struck me as odd that Bill took my call. Even more surprisingly, with what for Kerins amounted to outlandish expansiveness, he mentioned that his boss Burt Moreno had already called three times that morning to check on their progress. Perhaps the ASU director's interest had something to do with Mike Maggio spending Sunday afternoon at a cookout talking about the Peña case with Commissioner Leonel Castillo. The political pressure, it seemed, was working its way down the INS food chain.

Kerins also told me that ASU staff had received some news from their Miami Immigration colleagues that morning. Following normal procedure, after issuing the tourist group's visas, the U.S. Consulate in Asunción notified the INS officials at their designated port of entry. However, entry cards do not contain a physical description of the visitors. All the ASU men learned was that Peña entered the country on July 21, 1978, and his date of birth. Not much, but it fit. What they really needed was the detailed information and photograph on his visa application, and ASU still had not heard from Paraguay.

The next day, Tuesday, the surveillance team leapfrogged Peña, picking him up in front of the Midtown office buildings. Several agents surrounded him as he entered the lobby, for the first time getting a close look at their quarry. But, waiting until the last moment to push his way onto a packed elevator, again Peña gave them the slip.

Returning to ASU headquarters, the team began their gloomy postmortem—until one of the agents began describing Peña.

"Green eyes!" Kerins blurted, remembering what Dolly had told him. "That cinches it."

20

"Give me fifteen hours." Frank pleaded. "That's all I ask."

All day Tuesday, April 3, the ASU boys had been ducking me. I had made a dozen attempts to get ahold of someone at headquarters. Finally, around eight, I left a message for DiConstanzo: "REQUEST OFFICIAL STATEMENT FOR COHA PRESS RELEASE TOMORROW A.M." A half hour later, Frank called.

At last, ASU had a positive ID of Peña, and even if he moved out of his apartment, they knew where he went during the days. Still, at any moment, they feared it all could come apart. More reports had come in about Peña leaving on the *SS Asunción*, which was getting ready to sail. And from Washington, Director Moreno ratcheted up the pressure: "Don't lose this guy. I don't want any surprises. Understand?"

It had been a long, frustrating day for me, too. And now, again, ASU had clammed up. Instead of filling me in on what was going on, Frank skirted my questions. Taking too much medication for the back pain, and fed up with ASU's one-sided idea of cooperation, I was in a thoroughly foul mood.

"Shame you guys have been so busy," I admonished DiConstanzo. "So much happening at this end. It's not just Senator Kennedy anymore. More members of Congress have signed on. Representatives Robert Drinan and Bill Schuerer think a subcommittee hearing's not such a bad idea. Have a hard look at consulate corruption handing out visas in Paraguay. ASU's less-than-impressive performance taking our resident torturer off the streets. That sort of thing."

We had managed to get Drinan and Schuerer involved, and they were looking into the whole mess. Like Kennedy, though, they also insisted on more specific information before they could convene a congressional inquiry.

"But the real reason I wanted to talk is the story's going to blow. All day, that old muckraker Jack Anderson biting at the bit. And here I am, without any new ammo to hold him off. Then Selwyn Raab from the *New York Times* kept it up until pestering me into an interview tomorrow."

DiConstanzo took a sharp breath.

"Can't help feeling like a bit of a heel, though," I laid it on, "reneging on our cooperation agreement. Failure of communication, I suppose. You see what a tough spot I'm in, what with my own *Washington Post / Los Angeles Times* op-ed set to go. So, if you have anything to—"

"Give me fifteen hours," Frank interrupted, his voice two octaves higher than normal. "That's all I ask. That's all I can say. Whatever I can tell you, I will. But please, trust me."

He was not asking for twenty-four hours, or thirty-six, the standard stall times. Sure, DiConstanzo was holding back. Still, he had never come straight out and lied to me.

"Two questions. Are you sure Peña's still in the country?"

"Yes."

"Is he going to get away?

"No."

"OK. The balloon goes up at noon."

21

"Everybody was there," Frank exuded when he later told me the full story, "the entire Anti-Smuggling Unit. It's a bright, shiny day. The sun is shining. It's early in the morning.

"We didn't have to wait very long because we knew what time he left, more or less. Like fifteen minutes. Peña comes out of his house with Juana and the kid. He's dressed well, jacket and tie. I jump him. You can imagine, walking down the street, going to work, seven o'clock in the morning. We jump out of the cars and the van, all nine agents."

Sure enough, years later, studying ASU's official paperwork, I saw just how badly everyone wanted in, to get the big bust on their records. Two of them, however, must have been disappointed; the space for the arresting officer on the form only allowed room for seven agents to cram in their names before the list ran off the page.

"But I jump Peña," Frank went on. "He was real scared. Now he's being exposed to what he does in Paraguay. But he doesn't realize American policemen don't operate that way. He thinks he's really in for it. Nine men jump him, from all sides. Like a blanket was thrown on him.

"Juana Villalba was terrified. She's crying, 'Don't kill me! Don't kill me. I have children.' She turned in the super of their building for not having papers. 'Course we weren't interested in that kind of crap.

"I establish alienage deportability on the spot. In Spanish I ask him, 'Is your name Américo Peña?' He says yea. All the while he's backing himself against the wall of the building. Like a wild animal that's been cornered. He's like a bull, bull guy, a short, stocky guy.

"Then he reaches into his pocket. This is the moment of truth, because now this is where we can make a case on him. He's going to bribe me. But he's only got six bucks. Six bucks! He didn't have enough money to make a criminal case. This isn't going to stand up in court for bribery."

I shake my head in sympathy.

"If he'd had a hundred, said, 'Well, let's work something out,'" Frank continued, "I could have said, 'Oh, you want to bribe me?' But without enough on him to substantiate that kind of a deal, you can forget it. We almost got him on bribery. But he didn't have enough pocket change.

"Cuffed him. Took them back to the apartment and looked for documents. Anything to make a case. All we found was a dildo in the closet. I asked him, 'What's this for?' Asked him if he had any truncheons, or rubber hoses. I just wanted to hit him with questions like that."

DiConstanzo paused, collecting his thoughts. "We got to headquarters, brought him into the interview room. At first Peña was kind of subdued. Then, when he realized he wasn't going to be mistreated, he once again became the dominant figure. Probably saw it as a sign of weakness. Freaked out. Threw a tantrum. The interpreter refused to stay alone with him. She was too frightened.

"Juana Villalba was still crying. Still trying to bargain. Kept telling us López Morán, the super at their building, was here illegally. But Peña thought he was the chief. Arrogant, very vociferous and loud, moving around fast, yelling. He acted like a nut job. Picked up a chair and threw it against the wall. I got the feeling that he thought he was in Asunción, in command, at his station house.

"We didn't bring up the drug smuggling or prostitution. He's on their side. Why would you ask him that?" Frank reasoned. "He'd just end up letting the bad guys know what you know. We don't see him as having any potential for cooperation. Her either. They're bad people."

22

"But we let him know he wasn't in Paraguay. Verbally, not by coercive action."

"That's not what he was expecting," I said. "In the least he'd have threatened you, and a lot worse. With a little theatrics he could have bellied up."

"We'd have had to use props. At least gestures and body language," DiConstanzo said dismissively. "Gave him a 214. Let him know he has the right to remain silent, to an attorney."

When Frank had called me at the Council on Hemispheric Affairs that Wednesday morning, April 4, 1979, he'd not been so expansive. Still pumped, he did proudly tell me they had arrested Peña, but he would not offer much more.

"What did Peña say about burning my home on Wood Island?" I had asked him.

Frank hesitated. "We haven't got to that."

"Sure thing."

"Look," he had sighed, "right now, they're at our holding facility. Under a big bail. Normally it's $1,000. But we got Peña's set for $75,000. Villalba's at $25,000. I've filled Moreno in on everything. He's really pissed at the State Department. They're still stonewalling. There could be incriminating evidence on their visa applications. False statements. Felonies.

"And Moreno's already got an INS lawyer asking the U.S. district attorney for a deportation postponement—"

"Deportation postponement?" I blurted. "What for? What about—"

"We have to," Frank interrupted. "At this point, the only thing we've got is that he stayed here for longer than his visa permitted. So they're entitled to a first hearing before an INS judge right away. Tomorrow. It's standard procedure."

"Tell me that you guys aren't going to let Peña off for overstaying his tourist visa! Buy him a ticket and send him home in a couple of days."

"I've already told you," Frank said. "There's the criminal leads to follow up. Peña's not going anywhere. Not before we know how an indicted torturer got a visa to take a vacation at Disney World. This is an ongoing investigation. Don't worry."

23

But I was worried, really worried. Larry Birns happened to be out of town when it all came down, leaving me to deal with the office. In between telephone interviews, I cranked out a press release and dispatched a troupe of COHA interns around town delivering copies to the national news bureaus.

The next day, Thursday, April 5, it hit big.

The *New York Times* and the *Washington Post*, in what for them approached sensationalism, gave the story full play. "A former Paraguayan police official and his mistress, who are charged with a torture-murder in Paraguay, were arrested in Brooklyn," the *Post* article led off. Plucking one of the juiciest quotes from the COHA press release, after running down the bust, the piece noted "that it was generally understood in Paraguay that Peña was involved in drugs and prostitution, and predicted that further investigation of Peña 'will very likely reveal a sordid story of drug sales and the bringing into the New York area of unsuspecting Paraguayan teenagers who were immediately forced into prostitution.'"

The traditionally staid *Times* offered an equally dramatic account under the headline "Paraguayan Alien Tied to Murders in Native Land." It read: "Political groups opposed to the current government in Paraguay have identified Mr. Peña as a member of a police 'death squad' that investigated and tortured opponents of the government of Gen. Alfredo Stroessner." And, apparently also unable to resist a snappy line, the *Times* reported in its scrupulously proper fashion the COHA accusation "that Mr. Peña was 'among the most detested and feared government officials in his nation.'"

Drawing upon the documents we had included in the press packets, both papers gave good summaries of the *Caso Filártiga*. "Américo Peña, 45, and Juana Bautista-Fernandez Villalba, 41," the *Post* explained, "became the center of a controversy in Paraguay following the March 1976 death of Joelito Filártiga, 17, the son of a prominent philanthropist, doctor and painter. . . .

"Sources said that there had been personal animosity between Peña and the Filártiga family for some time before the murder. The victim's father was known as a dissident in a country where little dissent is tolerated. Peña and Filártiga lived two houses apart in Asunción."

The *Post* went on to explain that "initially, Peña was not charged with the kidnapping, torture or murder of Joelito Filártiga. Peña held the rank of inspector at the time of the killing, and the government of Gen. Alfredo Stroessner declared that no police participated in the crime. . . . Peña was promoted to chief inspector, but the international publicity organized by the dead youth's well-known father apparently led to Peña's being charged and forced to leave Paraguay."

The *Times*, recounting most of the same material, pointed out the role of Amnesty and other human rights groups in the international campaign. "A confidential report prepared by the Inter-American Commission on Human Rights of the Organization of American States contended that Mr. Peña and three other policemen kidnapped the Filártiga youth on March 29, 1976, with the intent of forcing him to incriminate his father falsely in sedition charges. The report, obtained by the *New York Times*, asserted that the boy had died of a heart attack after being beaten and receiving high-voltage electric shocks."

By any standard, the *New York Times*, which in 1979 was the only newspaper with a truly national circulation, marked the pinnacle of credibility and exposure. Three years before, we'd had to depend on the Paraguayan tabloid *Aquí* to get out the *Caso Filártiga* story.

24

"So where does it go from here?" Bob Maurer had asked me. Within hours of Peña's bust on Wednesday, April 4, the news had spread throughout the human rights community.

"I'm putting together a press packet. Working the phones," I replied in the pandemonium at COHA. "Haven't had a chance to think it through."

"You know they've only charged Peña with overstaying his visa," Bob said from Amnesty headquarters in New York. "They're planning on hustling him out of the country as soon as possible, after the deportation hearing tomorrow."

"Don't worry. The hearing's just a formality," I said sarcastically. "That's what DiConstanzo told me a couple of hours ago. He was insulted I could even think they'd do such a thing. Promised that absolutely no way was Peña going anywhere, not before ASU finishes its investigation."

"This one's way over his head," Maurer said. "We've been calling around. Peña's arrest is an international relations problem. There's a lot of political pressure coming down to get him out of here. Now."

In fact, Filártiga's friends and NGO supporters, Bob explained, were so worried that they had mobilized something like a Super Urgent Action Campaign to counter the government's intention to whisk Peña out of the country. Already telegrams, letters, and phone calls were pouring into Congress, Justice, State, and the INS—even the

White House—demanding Peña's detention until all the questions about his tourist visa in Paraguay, and his possible criminal activities here in the United States, were cleared up.

"What about that legal action we talked about, the arrest warrant for Peña torturing Joelito to death?" I asked Bob. "Anything there?"

"Maybe," he said. "This morning Gerhard Elston from Amnesty spoke with a lawyer friend at CCR. Peter Weiss. Can't say anyone's optimistic, but—"

"What's CCR?"

"The Center for Constitutional Rights. Here in Manhattan. It's a high-powered legal advocacy NGO. Goes back to the '60s. Civil rights, anti–Vietnam war stuff, women's issues. Good people.

"Anyway, Peter's called an emergency meeting at CCR," Bob said. "On the long shot they do come up with something, they're going to need Dolly's help. Asked me to get a hold of her."

"Haven't had a chance to talk with Dolly today," I told him. "She's just moved and I don't have her new number. Might catch her at Mike Maggio's law office. Works there part time, sometimes. I'll give it a try, but I'm busy as hell. Better take down Mike's number."

Dolly was not there, so I explained the situation to Mike. And while CCR meant nothing to me, it sure did to Maggio. He would get right on it.

At the time, it was just one more thing, and not an especially important one at that. I did not give it another thought.

Dr. Filártiga's images of his son.

TEN

ALL RIGHT, HOW CAN we hold him?" Peter Weiss asked the half-dozen attorneys and law students gathered in the library. As the emergency meeting got under way that Wednesday afternoon, discouragement hung over everyone in the group—except maybe for Peter.

Over the years, the successful trademark law attorney had found the simple making of money less than fulfilling. Especially as Weiss entered middle age, it was his pro bono work at the Center for Constitutional Rights that held greater meaning.

"So what do we do about Peña?" Peter pressed, turning to Rhonda Copelon. Although only in her thirties, Rhonda was CCR's star trial lawyer.

"Well, what about that ancient statute you're always bringing up?" she suggested.

"Of course," Peter replied. "It's been a while. Let's have another look."

At the bookshelf, Copelon leafed through a legal tome. "OK, here it is. The Judiciary Act of 1789, Title 28 of the United States Code, Section 1350."

"Indeed. 28 USC 1350," Peter replied. "The Alien Tort Claims Act."

If Copelon had earned the reputation as CCR's hard-driving litigator, the scholarly Weiss was thought of as something of the center's wise man. And everyone knew that Peter had a passion, a vision in which the federal courts would enforce U.S. law in a way that put teeth into international law.

Twice before Weiss had explored the prospect of using the Alien Tort Claims Act (ATCA). The first time for a young Vietnamese woman, who had lost her entire family in the 1968 My Lai massacre. And again he had floated the idea after the 1973 assassination of President Salvador Allende, during the U.S.-sponsored coup in Chile. But Peter's colleagues did not share his enthusiasm. In fact, they felt that any such suit would be laughed out of court.

No matter. Whenever the center had a case that in any way touched upon the possibility of expanding the role of the courts, Weiss wanted to bring in some international law angle. And while nobody really believed the federal courts were about to become champions of international justice, out of respect for their resident "rabbinical strategist," they would throw his ideas into the brief with a quip of "that's for Peter."

1

Now, as Copelon reviewed the Alien Tort Claims Act, it still struck her as a crazy idea. Barely able to hide her skepticism, she read aloud the one-sentence federal statute: "The district court shall have original jurisdiction of any civil action by an alien for a tort only, committed in violation of the law of nations or a treaty of the United States."

For hours the team pored over the law books, digging into the legal history, searching through ATCA cases, kicking around interpretations, brainstorming for anything that might offer an opening.

"Look here," a frustrated law student groaned, "1795, *Bolchos versus Darrell*. Their countries are at war. The Spaniard captures the Frenchman's ship, brings it into Charleston, South Carolina, and claims ownership of the cargo as a prize of war. Bolchos sues in federal court under the Alien Tort Claims Act to get his merchandise back. Argues that seizing his property's a violation of the Treaty of Amity and Commerce between the United States and France. The judge agrees with the Frenchman. Settles the squabble between these two gentlemen by ruling that Bolchos is the rightful owner of the slaves! So how does that help us?"

"Hopefully, with a full measure of ironic justice," Weiss replied dryly. "It's the legal principle, not the specifics, that matters. A U.S. federal court accepted jurisdiction in a suit brought by one alien against another alien for a tort—a wrongful act that carries provisions for civil damages. And the decision rested on a treaty of the United States.

"Today," Peter went on, "the idea of slaves being 'merchandise' is reprehensible. But for purposes of interpreting the law, it is also irrelevant."

Slumping into his chair, the intern glanced around the conference table. No one was convinced. Then slowly, the more they got into it, Rhonda began to wonder. It still seemed pretty farfetched, yet on some levels it kind of made sense.

"With the deportation hearing tomorrow, the Alien Tort Claims Act is our only hope," Weiss said. "Dolly Filártiga sues Peña for the torture-killing of her brother. It is getting late, but maybe we can still get ahold of Mike Maggio."

"I assume," Rhonda asked wearily, "torturing Joelito to death is a violation of the law of nations?"

"Well, we have the Universal Declaration of Human Rights," Peter replied, "the International Convention on Civil and Political Rights, the American Convention on Human Rights, and the UN Declaration on Torture. Yes, I would say torture is a violation of international law."

"Fine, that's your part," Rhonda told him, and to herself, "this one's for Peter."

2

Mike and Dolly stumbled into the Center for Constitutional Rights the next morning, Thursday, April 5. It had been close to midnight before Dolly could make it to Maggio's office. Peter had explained that CCR needed the basic facts of the *Caso Filártiga*, from the night of Joelito's death to the imprisonment of Dolly and Nidia, from the arrest of their lawyer Galeano Perrone to the stagnation of the case in Stroessner's courts, and everything else. Pushing straight through—Dolly going over it in Spanish, Mike scribbling notes in English—they broke off at dawn to catch the first shuttle to New York.

At CCR, dealing with cases on an emergency basis came with the job. After the meeting adjourned Wednesday evening, some of the crew stayed on. They had also worked through the night; the others had come in hours ago. So when Mike ushered Dolly into the buzzing conference room, waiting for them were the all-but-legendary legal celebrities. Heady stuff for the young lawyer.

There's Rhonda Copelon, Mike later recalled thinking, this unbelievably accomplished litigator. And Peter Weiss, the meticulous legal theorist of guru stature. And here I am, four months out of law school, working out of a storefront. And overnight, he realized with awe, I'm in the mitts of a high-powered international case with some of the best legal talent in the country.

"Don't just stand there," Peter said, cutting short Mike's reverie, "we need your help."

With the single-minded intensity of the legal activists that they were, the team focused on pulling together the complaint. Peter took charge of the overall picture, particularly the international law aspects. Mike dealt with immigration law and the specifics of the *Caso Filártiga*. Rhonda concentrated on tying it all together.

Which left Dolly pretty much off to the side. And everything was happening so fast. Yesterday at this time she had been cleaning houses with her Paraguayan roommate in Washington, had not even learned of Peña's arrest until Mike got ahold of her not ten hours ago. Now, with the feverish activity at CCR swirling around her, Dolly was scared to death.

Yet, in a way, she had been through it before: the frenzied meetings with lawyers in Paraguay, the endless legal maneuvering. Most of all, though, Dolly recalled her father's strength, leading the family through those terrifying times.

"Michael," Dolly suddenly spoke up, summoning the words in English, "Michael, we must call Ybycuí."

3

"Papi! Papi, we have Peña arrested!" Dolly cried the moment she got Joel on the phone. Caught off guard, Filártiga's exhausted mind simply was unable to take in the news.

Joel had returned home in early December to find the nation swept by a momentous protest movement. Beginning in November 1978, the Amnesty-supported hunger strike by political prisoners at Emboscada shocked Stroessner into closing the concentration camp and releasing most of the prisoners. By year's end, an emboldened coalition led by Paraguayan human rights activists—backed by the Catholic Church and opposition parties, along with representatives from several European NGOs and members of the diplomatic corps—organized an unprecedented display of defiance to the dictatorship. Filártiga got back just in time to throw himself into the activities of Paraguay's historic First National Human Rights Congress.

Following up on Ambassador Bob White's new policy of giving jobs at the embassy to released political prisoners, Dr. Filártiga ran newspaper *solicitadas* announcing that he would be honored to provide free medical treatment to any torture victim. Only after weeks of rushing around Asunción participating in the ongoing human rights activities generated by the Congress did Joel make it back to Ybycuí. The backlog of patients, especially the flow of torture victims clandestinely coming to the Sanatorio la Esperanza, was overwhelming.

"10:30 P.M. doctor went to O.R. First was a woman, early 20s, irregular heart beat," began the December 21 diary entry of Chris Hager, a volunteer who had just arrived from the States. "Strapped on a cardioscope from UCLA. She'd been tortured. Electric. Not well since. Psychologically especially. He prescribed medication.

"2 A.M. Doctor operating on Justino Caballero, early 20s. Six months in prison. Whole system inflamed from foul water. He said that was the result of the bathtub torture where they eat shit and it does a job on them."

Stealing time away from the clinic in Ybycuí to participate in the human rights activities in Asunción, by March Joel had run himself ragged. And, bogged down in our own problems, Dolly and I had not kept in close contact either. So when Dolly called, at first the news did not register. In fact, fatigued to the point of stupor, Joel had all but forgotten about Peña.

4

"Papi? Papi are you there?" Dolly asked, "Are you all right?"

"Yes, my daughter, I am fine," Joel replied, "Just a little tired."

"Listen to me Papi," Dolly insisted, "Peña is in jail. And we are making a legal case against him for killing Joelito."

It took an hour for Dolly to run through it. Then Mike cleared up some legal points, bringing Joel into the case as a coplaintiff with Dolly.

"We'd given up hope," Nidia later told me. "Then, right away we called all the family to tell them of Peña's arrest, and ran into the street to announce the news to the neighbors. Everyone was laughing and crying at the same time, embracing each other, jumping up and down.

"We learned about it on Thursday, at eleven in the morning. I wanted to celebrate so I opened a bottle of wine. I didn't even know what was really happening to me," Nidia exuded, remembering how her emotions ran wild. "Papi didn't want to drink, but I said 'Take it Papi, it's as if we won a thousand million dollars!' Maybe we got a little drunk. The truth is, I got crazy, crazy. Really crazy. My thoughts were very ugly."

That night as they lay in bed hugging each other, too excited to sleep, she whispered to Joel, "They should not just shoot him. He must die slowly. Not just two or three hours like Joelito. It has got to be six or seven hours.

"Now that they have him," Nidia's tormented soul calculated, "Richard will make sure he tells everything. Put him in an underground cell, make him confess everything. And I will be looking him right in the face. At last it's over."

"No, *mi querida*," Joel answered. "No, my dear. It is true, our prayers have been answered. Now it is God and Joelito who are in charge. They, who will make justice. This is an enormous thing. But it is not over. It is going to go on. There will be much more to do."

5

That afternoon of April 5, as the Filártigas celebrated on the streets of Ybycuí, in New York, INS Judge Anthony DeGaeto ordered Peña deported to Paraguay.

"Five days!" Copelon cried in a generic burst of outrage. "People regularly waste in jail for months, and they're going to deport a torturer within five days!"

"Technically," Mike said, "DeGaeto gave him voluntary departure."

"Voluntary departure?"

"Yeah. Means they're deporting Peña all right, but 'without prejudice.' If he wants he can even get another visa later. Come back to finish his Disney World vacation."

"But what about the promise of Mr. DiConstanzo," Dolly asked. "He said Peña must stay until they complete their investigation?"

"Well," Mike replied, "officially they've only got him for overstaying his tourist visa. And at the hearing Peña said they wanted to return to Paraguay as soon as possible. The INS lawyer offered no objections, so the judge ordered their voluntary departure right away. Routine."

"Sure, routine," Rhonda said. "Well, we've got one day. One day to bring the lawsuit."

"Today's Thursday," Maggio said. "Five days takes us to Tuesday."

"*Within* five days," Copelon shot back. "Think they don't want him hustled out on the first available flight? No. Friday's it. Else we're into the weekend."

"Rhonda is right," Peter said. "We have to file tomorrow."

6

Normally, even at the activist Center for Constitutional Rights, to prepare a major test case would take months. Faced with the INS ruling, though, they only had twenty-four hours to throw the complaint together. Calling in extra staff, the CCR team cranked up from emergency to crisis mode.

Mike occasionally called upon Dolly to clarify points about Peña and the government persecution in Paraguay. They also took a hard look at the repercussions of bringing the lawsuit. As they explained in the brief, because of the threat of reprisals if she returned to Paraguay, Dolly now was forced to seek political asylum in the United States.

Even so, there really was not all that much for her to do. Again, in the midst of the center's activity, Dolly was all but forgotten, her fear and sense of isolation gnawing at her. Neither Peter nor Rhonda spoke Spanish; from the start, their direct communication had been all but nonexistent. Even Mike, the only person Dolly knew at CCR and on whom she could always count, was absorbed in getting the complaint ready.

Dolly fought to maintain control. "Don't let your emotions interfere with the professionals, just answer their questions," like a mantra she repeated over and over, "Don't let your emotions interfere. . . ." Around noon, finding Dolly crying in a corner of the library, Mike made time to take her out for a coffee and a talk. No one noticed them leave, or return.

"I wouldn't call it the perfect complaint," Rhonda announced a little after four, but it's what we've got." Picking up the scanty six-page document, they raced down the stairs and piled into a taxi.

"We've got to be at the Brooklyn Federal Courthouse by five," Copelon urged the driver. With a New York shrug, the cabby took off through downtown, screamed onto the Brooklyn Bridge, and straight into the Friday afternoon traffic jam.

"We should've taken the subway!" Rhonda broke out in frustration as they crept along the bridge. "Damn. Damn. Damn. Why didn't we take the subway?" In their mad scramble, they all had forgotten about the weekend exodus from the city.

"The doors slam shut in twenty minutes," Mike groaned. "We're not going to make it."

The driver leaned on the horn. With maniacal aggression he wove in and out between lanes of traffic, tailgating the vehicles in front to force them to move over. As a testament to that heart-pounding dash, the whole carful of lawyers uttered not a word until pulling up in front of the courthouse a few minutes before five. The cabby accepted their monster tip as if he had been handed his daily mail.

In yet another of those coincidences that gives a certain symmetry to the Filártigas' saga, Dolly and Nidia had brought the first case against Peña in Paraguay on April 6, 1976. Three years later to the day, CCR filed charges in U.S. Federal Court against the cop for violating Joelito's human rights through "the wrongful torture and murder of the decedent." *Filártiga v. Peña-Irala* asked for "compensatory and punitive damages to be paid by the defendant Peña to plaintiff Joel Filártiga . . . and to Dolly Filártiga, in the sum of $10,000,000 plus interest, costs and disbursements."

7

"People are losing their fear," Joel told me Sunday evening. "No longer do they speak of the *Caso Filártiga* in whispers, afraid of being overheard and denounced to Stroessner's Gestapo."

"How's the family?" I asked.

"Nidia is very strong," Joel replied. "Before we left Ybycuí, a gang of local thugs paid us a visit. Yelled obscenities at us and threw rocks. Smashed out the front windows in the clinic.

"Thank God Katia and Analy are safe with their grandmother. And for Dolly's political asylum. Best that she stay away for a while. Yesterday we arrived in Sajonia. A butchered pig was in the driveway. The telephone threats have begun again."

Simple statements of fact requiring no comment from me. As Joel got into the press coverage, his excitement resurfaced.

"*Hoy* has started a series," Filártiga explained. "The entire history of the *Caso Filártiga*, from the beginning. Horacio says more than thirty articles."

"Galeano Perrone's writing it?"

"Secretly," Joel confirmed. "All his files. Everything he prepared for the case against Peña. Now it's all going to come out.

"The newspapers, radio, TV. It's like nothing before. Not even right after they killed Joelito. It started Friday. The international wire services sent the story right away. And everyday, more and more. No one talks of anything else."

I had already given a couple of phone interviews to the Asunción press, so it came as no surprise that this latest episode of Paraguay's "Crime of the Century" was being hyped with world-shaking gravity. Even so, I hardly appreciated its full magnitude.

Like the 1963 JFK assassination or the 1986 *Challenger* disaster in the States, Peña's arrest hit Paraguayans with mind-setting impact. People remember where they were, and what they were doing, when they first learned the news.

"I was drinking coffee at the breakfast table," Heriberto Alegre, a leading human rights lawyer, told me some fifteen years later. "I picked up *ABC* and read that Peña was apprehended in New York. I just sat there, I don't know how long, wondering. How could they have found him after all this time, half a world away, in such a big city? It was then that I saw the Filártigas' cause with new eyes. I wanted the case very much."

8

With everything in flux during those first days after Peña's arrest, we were still trying to get a grasp of the situation. In fact, at that time Joel and I had the chance for only one brief conversation. On Sunday evening, however, he wanted a full report.

"Best press ever," I began. "Our newspaper of record, the *New York Times*, has catapulted this new U.S. Filártiga case into a national story. Along with the articles in the *Washington Post*, they put out another feature piece this morning. The high-profile coverage has definitely focused the attention of our politicos. And there are a couple more big stories coming out tomorrow, that'll kick up the pressure even more."

"And what about the Anti-Smuggling Unit's investigation?" Joel asked.

"My contact there says they're still trying to pin down criminal charges," I said, checking my daily log. "ASU needs Peña's visa application, and State's still stalling. Anyway, they're getting pretty antsy with the constant calls from NGOs and the press. Yesterday DiConstanzo snapped at me, 'Every time I talk to you, the next day I read about it in the *New York Times*.'

"And the urgent action campaign's really taken off," I told him. "Amnesty, CCR, and WOLA have organized a full-blown mobilization. Letters, telegrams, phone calls to State and members of Congress.

"It's only been five days, so things are still gearing up. But I've got a letter here from Representative Robert Drinan to the head of Consular Affairs. Wants to know just how they could have given Peña a visa. He wants to know if the assistant secretary of state for human rights, Patt Derian, was consulted."

"What else?"

"There are factions in the government, both for and against holding Peña. It's all still pretty chaotic. Blame gaming between the different bureaucracies. Splits and ass covering within the same agencies." Reading from my notes again, I went on, "Peter Fenn at Senator Church's office told me, 'State and Justice overruled ASU's attempt to postpone Peña's deportation. He's a human rights embarrassment. There are some very powerful people who want him gone. Fast.'"

"Will they win?"

"Too soon to tell. But a lot depends on the court hearing tomorrow."

9

"We got Judge Nickerson!" Rhonda exclaimed to Mike and Dolly at CCR Monday morning, April 9. "I've been having nightmares we'd end up with one of the Neanderthals over there."

After filing on Friday, Mike taxied to the INS detention center and served Peña with the complaint. The next step would be Peña's deposition: to get on record his position in the police, the chain of command, others who were involved in Joelito's murder.

"Is he still here?" Mike wanted to know.

"Yeah," Rhonda said. "I've been jousting with the U.S. attorney all weekend. Jensen kept saying, 'Well, I don't know, Peña could be deported anytime before Tuesday.' Maybe they don't want to risk crossing a federal judge. In any event, as of this morning, he's still here."

Along with charging Peña with torturing Joelito to death, the Filártigas also had to sue the INS. At the court hearing they would ask Nickerson for a temporary restraining (TRO) order staying the deportations.

"Judges almost never give a TRO to keep aliens in jail," Mike said, "because it violates their civil liberties. And the ACLU backs them up."

"So do we," Rhonda replied. "CCR has always been against people rotting in prison while the INS bumbles along with some bureaucratic procedure, or simply forgets about them out of incompetence."

"But the INS wants to get rid of them," Mike pointed out. "And they want to go."

"That's precisely the point," Copelon replied. "This time it's us who want to keep them. If they're deported, we can't get their depositions."

"*Their* depositions?" Mike asked. "Plural?"

"Juana Villalba, too," Rhonda explained. "Like Peña, she's also charged as a coconspirator in the Paraguayan criminal trial. She was at home when they killed Joelito. And the Paraguayan court ordered her to be deposed, but she skipped out. Anyway, we need Villalba's deposition as a material witness.

"It's all in the supplemental memorandum of support we're working up, filling out the original complaint. Along with some more documentary exhibits—reports from Amnesty and the OAS human rights case. Other stuff, too. Better spend some time going over it before we see Nickerson this afternoon."

10

Since federal district courts assign cases to judges on a random basis, only the luck of the draw had landed the suit before the liberal Eugene H. Nickerson. Not that anyone expected a cakewalk, but at least they could hope for a fair hearing. When the proceeding began Nickerson, in his soft-spoken manner that masked a sharp legal mind, demanded to know on what grounds plaintiffs proposed delaying the defendants' immediate release from detention and deportation.

Defendants Peña and Villalba, the Filártigas' lawyers replied, possess many of the facts essential to the matter before the court—the wrongful death by torture of Joelito Filártiga. Their deportation will cause irreparable injury to the plaintiffs, because the Filártigas would be denied access to Peña's information and resources. Most important, without these witnesses, they lose all possibility of ever learning the truth.

Why then, Nickerson probed, should not he order depositions and allow their deportation? Why not employ the usual procedure of deposing defendants after they return home, as is common practice in civil suits?

Because that assumes the good faith of the Paraguayan judiciary, the CCR team argued. The impunity with which the government has denied the Filártigas justice leaves their only chance for a fair trial here, before an impartial court.

As documented in the exhibits detailing the OAS charges against the government of Paraguay, from the start General Stroessner's regime has shielded Peña. After their "crime-of-passion" cover-up failed, the police coerced the fall guy Hugo Duarte to falsely confess that he alone killed young Filártiga. But evidence like these photographs showing that Joelito died under professional torture caused a popular outcry in Paraguay and gained the active support of international human rights organizations, as demonstrated in the Amnesty International reports and pamphlet.

Then, reacting to this pressure, the police arrested the Filártigas' lawyer on trumped-up charges, forcing him to withdraw from the case. And the Paraguayan judiciary, which is no more than a docile appendage of Stroessner's dictatorship, squelched further proceeding in the lawsuit. From 1976 to this day, the Filártiga case continues to languish in this officially imposed legal limbo.

The Filártigas' lawyers concluded that a simple court order for Peña and Villalba's depositions—without a temporary restraining order staying the INS's intention to deport them to Paraguay where they would be inaccessible to plaintiffs and free to disappear again—would be meaningless.

The judge agreed. Granting a one-week TRO preventing their deportation, Nickerson ordered Peña and Villalba to give depositions.

Leaving the bench, Nickerson paused halfway to the door, turned back to the courtroom, and said, "Interesting case."

11

"Dolly has already explained how for now the court has ordered that Peña remain in jail," Joel began our Monday night conversation.

"A few more days anyway," I confirmed. "The way I understand it, once they give depositions it'll be next to impossible to stop the INS from deporting them."

"That is another thing," Filártiga said. "Michael said that Leonel Castillo is also a defendant in the suit. How can that be? Did not Leonel start the Anti-Smuggling Unit's investigation because of Larry Birns?"

"Right. Castillo's even on COHA's board of directors. But he's also the INS commissioner. That's why you're suing him."

"I'm suing Leonel!" Joel gasped.

"Sure. As a plaintiff you had to name Castillo as a defendant to stop the INS deportations. And not only that, WOLA's already got Representatives Walter Fauntroy and Tony Hall sending letters to him, asking to keep Peña here. As commissioner, Leonel has discretionary authority to hold a deportable alien in detention for up to six months. In fact, the INS does it all the time."

"Strange way to treat a friend," Joel said.

"I don't think Leonel minds all that much," I replied. "There's a front-page blockbuster in today's *Atlanta Constitution*: 'U.S. Probe of Visas Resisted: Embassy in Paraguay Target of Investigation.' Looks like there's a major scandal brewing. Goes on about how the INS is complaining that the State Department 'is refusing to provide documents sought in the probe or to make its employees available for questioning.'

"And it's not just Peña," I skipped ahead. "Says some 500 people, half the adult population of rural Caraguatay are up here; and 'have transformed the town into an island of prosperity.'"

"That white slavery operation was in the newspapers here six months ago," Filártiga replied. "The young women send millions back. They do the same as Peña. Tourist visas to Miami. Then disappear in New York. Some work as maids or baby-sitters. But many are forced into prostitution. The U.S. consul here, William Finnegan, was involved. Then suddenly they sent him to Hong Kong. And for months it was covered up. Only now has the press picked up the story again."

"Yet another reason State's running scared," I said. "Anyway, the article ends with a classic Larry Birns quip: 'How could a person who has been officially charged with complicity in a widely publicized murder simply sashay up to the counter of the U.S. consulate and routinely be issued a visa?'"

Filártiga let loose with a hearty chuckle. Then he asked about the ASU investigation.

"Frank DiConstanzo says they're still working on the criminal charges. But it sure looks like Peter Fenn was right. DiConstanzo told me the INS had already booked the Peña party on Braniff's five-o'clock flight to Asunción."

"You mean for today?"

"Yeah. For right after the hearing. So, if CCR had failed to file last Friday, or if Nickerson had denied the TRO this afternoon, at this moment your old neighbor would be halfway back to Sajonia."

12

The *New York Times* pegged its Tuesday, April 10, article to Nickerson's decision. The headline, "Judge Rules Peña Can Be Sued Here on Death in Paraguay," however, was not quite on target. Certainly, for the first time a federal court had stayed a deportation to take depositions in a suit for a violation of international human rights. Still, while allowing the case to go forward, Nickerson did not actually accept jurisdiction in the case.

Blowing it all into an "international legal controversy," as the *Times* reported, was the INS investigation of visa corruption in Paraguay, and State's stonewalling. No one else was talking either: Peña refused to be interviewed and the Paraguayan Embassy had no comment. Apparently, though, there was no lack of communication with their masters in Asunción.

"Fragano, Rebollo & Barone?" Rhonda announced Wednesday afternoon at CCR. "How did that half-baked Staten Island law firm get into this?"

"It kind of makes sense," Mike suggested. "On such short notice, maybe that's all that Somoza's congressman could come up with."

"General Anastasio Somoza? The dictator of Nicaragua?"

"Sure," he said. "The Honorable John Murphy and Anastasio are old pals. They were classmates at LaSalle Military Academy, both West Point grads. Happens that Murphy's the Representative from Staten Island, and Somoza's biggest booster in Congress. So, when one of Stroessner's people has a legal problem in New York, who do you call to get a line on how to fix this thing?"

"Well," Rhonda sighed, "somebody's coughing up big bucks for senior partner Robert Rebollo to represent Peña."

"Be that as it may," Peter said, "Nickerson has ordered their depositions tomorrow. First thing in the morning, Mike, best pay your friend another visit."

13

"The stenographer and I are all set up to take his deposition," Maggio reported to Peter when he called from the INS Detention Center Thursday. "Peña comes into the waiting room, recognizes me from when I served him last week. Tells us to get out. Pleads the Fifth, won't even give us his name, won't accept Rebollo as counsel. Got nothing to say until he talks with his Paraguayan lawyer."

"His Paraguayan lawyer?" Peter asked.

"Right," Mike replied. "Peña's heavyweight lawyer from the Filártiga trial in Paraguay. Peña says Stroessner's sending a guy named Gorostiaga up to defend him."

"Get back here right away," Peter said. "We'll call Judge Nickerson's office."

Arriving at the center, Mike found everyone ready to leave for the courthouse. "You're not going to believe this," Peter told him. "Nickerson ordered Peña be brought to court immediately, and some INS idiot said they couldn't because there wasn't any transportation available. Nickerson told them to take a taxi!"

14

They had just passed through the courthouse portals when Dolly took off running. By the time Mike and Peter caught up, she had raced across the lobby and was pushing onto the elevator with her brother's murderer.

The sight of Peña and Villalba triggered an emotional implosion in Dolly. Storming in on her came the years of persecution, devastating the family, backing their lives into a corner of fear and suffering. Not since the night of Joelito's murder, when the police dragged her out of bed to take away Joelito's body, had Dolly spoken to Peña. And now, there he was, being hauled into a U.S. federal court by two marshals, the center of an international legal controversy. Dolly remembered Peña's last words to her: "Shut up. Nobody has to know."

Now I am the one looking for trouble, Dolly thought, as they began the ascent to the sixth floor. Juana Villalba turned aside, unable to meet her fury. But pressing to inches of Peña's face, Dolly forced him to look at her, their eyes locking into a staring match.

"Why did you do this thing to us, to Joelito? Why? Tell me why," she demanded. "We were such a beautiful family!"

Peña stiffened and glared back. Mike pushed in between them, his back to Peña, his arms around Dolly. "It's OK," he assured her. "Don't worry, I understand."

And so did Dolly.

While she stared at Peña over Mike's shoulder, suddenly he broke eye contact, his Adam's apple trembling. Now he was the one gripped with fear. And at that moment Dolly realized that he is nobody, this is another him, really.

The elevator doors opened. The marshals escorted Peña to Nickerson's courtroom. Dolly crumpled into Mike's embrace, bursting into a cathartic flood of weeping.

15

The hearing itself proved as anticlimactic as it was consequential. Again Peña refused to say anything until speaking with Gorostiaga. To allow his Paraguayan lawyer time to travel from Paraguay, Nickerson extended the deportation TRO until April 30.

"Naturally, Stroessner must protect him," Joel told me a few days later. "Just like he gave Peña the best lawyer for the *Caso Filártiga* trial here. And this is a much bigger international scandal."

"Damn good thing Peña didn't give the deposition," I said. "Otherwise, they likely would have let them go."

"What do you mean?" Joel asked.

"The judge's order staying the INS deportation is only to get his deposition. After a foreign defendant deposes in a civil action, the rest of the suit can be handled through the established legal procedures, when he's back home. Keeping him locked up would violate his civil rights. In fact, once Peña gives a deposition, CCR probably won't even try to hold him any longer."

"So why not just tell the same lies he did in his deposition here?"

"Because he's not in a corrupt Paraguayan court," I speculated. "And most likely, Rebollo explained that perjury is a felony, and that means jail time.

"And speaking about felonies," I went on referring to my log, "today I spoke with Burt Moreno, the D.C. head of ASU. He's furious because the State Department is still refusing to give them the paperwork on Peña. Told me, 'I need that information. Just one lie on his visa application is a five-year felony!' "

On this same day, Friday the thirteenth, we later learned State had cabled the U.S. Embassy in Asunción asking for the "preferred language to use in answering congressional inquiries." Repeating much of the same information found in his March 14 cable, Ambassador White replied that the embassy had "no alternative" but to issue the visa since "no legal charges stand against Américo Peña in Paraguay. He is not under indictment."

True enough, technically Peña was not under indictment. But only because in Paraguay's Napoleonic legal system there is no formal indictment or arraignment; no presumption of innocence exists that requires a grand jury to determine if the charges are sufficient to hand down an indictment. Instead, from the start, the court simply accepts the prosecution's accusations—the rough equivalent of a U.S. indictment—thereby initiating the inquisitorial process of the legal proceedings. That also is why under Paraguayan law there is no need for an arraignment, for the defendant to enter a guilty, or not guilty, plea. In 1976 the prosecutor had charged, and the judge had accepted, Peña and the others as codefendants in Joelito's murder trial.

Further, just before the 1978 OAS annual conference, during Galeano Perrone's flurry of motions, the Paraguayan appellate court had confirmed that decision. So, in 1979, even with the suit stagnating in Stroessner's Supreme Court, Peña stood charged as a codefendant in the criminal *Caso Filártiga* trial.

In his cable, Ambassador White also suggested other "preferred language" to placate congressional concerns. Referring to Peña's visa application, Bob reported that "his financial status, the fact that his family was remaining behind and his position in the family firm satisfied the consul." In all fairness, the Consulate staff cannot closely scrutinize every tourist applicant. They can hardly be blamed for failing to discover that there was no family firm—nor that Peña's true financial status could more accurately be determined by the fact that he had just sold his house and car. Even so, it is not unreasonable that the photo on his passport—that had been issued for this trip, showing Peña with his toddler son sitting on his lap—might have tipped the consul that his family was not remaining behind.

16

Picking up our conversation that Friday, Filártiga said, "So Moreno is still unable to get Peña's visa application through official channels. Perhaps the lobbying campaign will persuade them to release the documents."

"Well, not as yet," I replied. "But the campaign is putting enormous pressure on the State Department. Here's another 'request' to Consular Affairs, from Representative James Scheuer, with copies shot-gunned up the bureaucracy. Real strong, raises the stakes to a foreign policy issue. Says 'that our commitment to human rights demands' a review of the entire procedure for issuing 'controversial visa requests.'

"And the chairman of Amnesty USA is throwing his prestige behind the suit. David Hinkley sent a telegram to the second-ranking State Department official, Warren Christopher, urging him to use his authority to hold Peña for trial. And referring to the same treaties CCR uses in their legal complaint, he insists they 'require that U.S. authorities should not hinder the Filártiga family from access to that legal remedy before a U.S. court which they were in practice denied in Paraguay.'"

"Good," Joel replied. "Very good. This is this just the kind of international pressure that Stroessner fears most. We must make sure he learns all about the campaign, every letter and telegram from powerful people supporting us."

"Right. From now on the Paraguayan ambassador here will be receiving copies of everything. I'll let CCR and the others know."

But it was not anything so impersonal as political tactics that occupied the people at the center that Friday evening.

17

Among activists it is not uncommon to get lost in the cause, fighting for humanity while overlooking human beings. During that first chaotic week, absorbed with legal principles and constitutional questions, the CCR team had lost sight of their client. Then, the dramatic elevator confrontation with Peña brought home to them Dolly's personal struggle.

"You've got to understand," Mike explained to Peter and Rhonda, "as bad as things were in Paraguay, Dolly always had the support of her family. And here she is, the first time away from home, only six months in a new country and just beginning to learn English, fighting this gigantic battle."

"I had always seen Dolly as this incredibly strong person," Peter reflected. "Never complaining, always there, answering our questions. And then there is the language barrier. I just assumed that the women here at the center—Rhonda, Nancy, Audrey—were taking care of her."

"Dolly's not letting on how tough it is," Mike said. "But look what she's going through. She's even had to seek political asylum. Along with everything else, Dolly's afraid she may never be able to go home again. The truth is, she's scared to death."

Rhonda started to say something. The demands of her other, ongoing cases had limited the time she could put in on the suit, by and large leaving the everyday work to the others.

"I've missed it too," Rhonda finally reflected. "Of course I saw Dolly steeling herself. One side saying, 'I just want to forget about the whole thing and get on with my life.' The other side saying, 'I owe it to Joelito, and I owe it to Paraguay and I owe it to myself. I *will* do this.' But truthfully, I didn't understand how enormous a thing this was for her, either."

"I do not think any of us realized how insensitive we've been," Peter acknowledged.

"The way Dolly put it," Mike said, "was she felt that 'nobody sees my face.'"

"Until yesterday," Peter replied. "Yesterday, in the elevator with Peña. That really shook me up."

18

Not until that weekend, however, back in Washington at the home of Malena Rodríguez, did the depths of Dolly's inner turmoil truly come to the surface. About a year earlier, Mike had befriended Malena when she arrived from Paraguay, another victim of Stroessner's gangster regime.

Along with several girlfriends, Malena had accepted an invitation to meet Stroessner and some other Colorado big shots. For nearly a week, behind the guarded walls of a government party house in Asunción, a rotating pack of revelers held the young women captives, repeatedly forcing upon them their sexual pleasures. When finally allowed to leave, instead of keeping silent as she had been warned, Malena went public, denouncing the lurid details to everyone who would listen. Of course, none of it appeared in the press; nor did Malena's arrest a few days later. Only after months in an Investigaciones cell was her influential father able to get her released—on the condition that she leave Paraguay.

"I feel horrible about myself," Dolly told Malena. "My life is all screwed up, my emotions. When I saw Peña and Villalba in the lobby I felt this terrible anger, a fury. I wanted revenge, to hurt him. And now I have to go to court and talk bad about him, attack him. Why do I have to give it back to them?"

"Because they are the enemy," Malena told her.

"And in the elevator, when we were face-to-face, I really wanted to kill Peña. They murdered Joelito, put me and Mamá in jail. And lots of other things. I mean, anytime they can come and break up the flow of our lives. I have to defend myself and my family. If somebody touches my family, you know, human nature is very strong."

"I know," Malena said. "They let Marisol and Vivian come with me. But they made my son stay in Paraguay, like a hostage, so that I would keep quiet. But after a while I had to speak out. I told everything, in the two Jack Anderson columns. So far, there've been no reprisals."

Through whipsawing emotions Dolly took in Malena's words. "I didn't want any of this to happen. Why did it have to happen? I feel so sorry for the whole situation, for me, alone away from home, for their children."

"At least they're safe in the foster home, away from Peña yelling at them all the time. And Blanca doesn't have to be afraid of him beating her anymore."

"But I'm so confused. I feel awful. What should I do?"

"You must be hard," Malena told her. "They don't teach you how to hate the enemy. But the only way to win against the enemy is hating them."

Hate. It was like a magic word. Desperate and scared, it hit Dolly with the impact of an epiphany. Hate made it all so simple, so clear.

What could I have been thinking? Dolly wondered. It's like our lives don't belong to us anymore. They can do anything, even kill us. I am in danger. My family is in danger. I must be strong, make them stop.

19

In Paraguay too, little emotional ambiguity remained. With the media daily stoking public feeling, Peña's fate had become something of a national obsession.

"So many peasants come to the clinic, pretending to be sick," Joel told me during our Monday night conversation. "They come to show their solidarity. And to ask about Peña. Their hate for Stroessner now is all against Peña. He should be killed, they say. Or left without arms or legs, to suffer for the rest of his life."

"You know that's not the way things work here."

"Of course not," he replied wearily. "It is the primal hatred of the powerless. The profound desperation of the oppressed.

"And in Asunción. Our house is always filled with people. Everyone now openly talks about the crime. In restaurants, on buses, walking down the street. Never before has there been such open public defiance. And it is hard to tell who is more surprised—the people or the dictatorship."

"Have they been giving you trouble?"

"Except for the death threats, nothing. So far," Filártiga said. "It is like they are in shock. Lots of rumors, but no action. In fact, only this morning did a small article appear in Stroessner's official newspaper, *Patria*. Just that we are using the suit against Peña to attack the government, not to seek justice."

Although by then, my back pain had me spending most of the day in bed, I had managed to finish the *Washington Post / Los Angeles Times* op-ed. "Yesterday my article, 'In New York, Suspect Faces U.S. Justice,' came out in Los Angeles. So for the next few weeks we can expect the usual run in papers around the country. Might even be picked up internationally."

"The favorable press coverage here also continues to grow," he said. "But that may change. With Peña remaining in jail until the end of the month, next week the newspapers are sending reporters to the States."

"Mike Maggio's going to love that."

20

Since first learning Malena's story, Mike had been looking to pay back Stroessner. Now, with the publicity exploding around the *Filártiga v. Peña* suit, he rarely missed an opportunity to rattle the regime with the most outlandish taunts.

On Wednesday, April 18, COHA held a press conference at the National Press Club. As the Washington-based correspondents fired questions at the panel, Mike outdid himself.

"Right now," Mike announced, "we are preparing the subpoenas for witnesses to be brought from Paraguay to prove the dictatorship's routine use of torture. And yes, President Stroessner is on the list."

That tore it. On Sunday, April 22, the dictator's propaganda machine launched its offensive to whip up nationalistic fervor. Denouncing Maggio's "infamous declaration," *Patria* charged that "sinister Paraguayan opposition figures in the U.S., aided and abetted by U.S. human rights zealots, were attempting to use the Peña–Filártiga case as the means to mount a political assault on the Paraguayan government."

The long editorial went on to decry the "legal monstrosities" that threatened Paraguay's sovereignty and defiled the Fatherland's international stature. And perhaps most revealing of the regime's private fears, *Patria* ended by warning that the case "endangered all Paraguayans who apparently could be tried abroad for alleged crimes committed in Paraguay."

Mike could not have been more delighted. "Here I am, just out of law school, and a head of state knows my name and hates me," he exulted. "It's always nice to, not just feel, but know that you actually are on the side of the angels. To see that you're against the devil. And what better devil than Alfredo Stroessner?"

The day after *Patria's* broadside, Monday, April 23, the devil's advocate arrived in New York to defend his master's honor.

21

José Emilio Gorostiaga, Paraguay's preeminent criminal lawyer, quickly sized up the situation. During that last week before the court hearing on April 30, Gorostiaga realized that Robert Rebollo was out of his depth, and hired Murry Brochin—a senior partner in a high-powered New Jersey firm with expertise in international law—to head the defense team.

Coincidentally, two Paraguayan journalists arrived at the same time, and went straight to the INS Detention Center. *Hoy* and *Ultima Hora* soon began entertaining their readers with jailhouse human interest pieces such as "Peña: 'Why So Much Hatred?'" and "Why Do They Persecute Me?" and "Peña Said, 'I Am Pure and Innocent.'"

Not so coincidentally, given Gorostiaga's close coordination with the Fatherland, on Friday, April 27, another prison interview prominently ran in the Asunción press. Parroting his 1976 "confession," from the National Penitentiary Hugo Duarte insisted that he alone had killed Joelito, had not even seen Peña that night, and accused the Filártigas of mutilating the body for their own political purposes.

On top of all this, the bureaucrats at State and Justice undercut the ASU investigation. "They're still holding back on the overall visa irregularities at the Consulate," Frank DiConstanzo called to tell me, "but State finally sent us Peña's visa application. We found at least one lie, that he wasn't bringing his family. But the U.S. attorney refuses to prosecute."

"That's preposterous," I fumed. "You know that any false statement is a felony."

"Yes, well, Jensen says it's not enough," a disheartened DiConstanzo said. "And that's not all. Word's come down to drop the Peña criminal investigation."

22

The stooped-shouldered Peña who had cringed before Dolly's ire in the elevator did not appear before Judge Nickerson on Monday morning, April 30. Instead, it was Chief Inspector of Police Américo Peña who stood defiantly, surveying the courtroom. Stroessner had protected him throughout the *Caso Filártiga* machinations in Paraguay. And now Gorostiaga's assuring presence at his side again left no doubt that he still counted with the regime. I'm an important Paraguayan official, Peña's brazen body language announced, you can't touch me.

The hearing lasted seven minutes. Murry Brochin requested a postponement to prepare the defense brief. CCR agreed. Nickerson extended the TRO until May 14. And that was it. Almost.

In the hallway as Peña and Villalba left the courtroom, one of the Paraguayan reporters attempted to snap a photo of the couple. The chief inspector's temper flared. The marshals blocked Peña's lunge, but as the journalist stumbled backward, Juana Villalba reached out and slapped his camera to the floor.

23

Joel was in high spirits when we spoke the following evening. By then, *Hoy* had published most of the series Galeano Perrone had ghostwritten, and popular opinion was gelling stronger than ever behind the Filártigas. Several editorials even called for reopening the *Caso Filártiga* trial. Because of the Paraguayan judiciary's lack of credibility, they reasoned, to defuse the escalating international clamor the court's investigation should go forward honestly, letting the chips fall where they may.

"Yesterday *Ultima Hora* ran the story about Peña's tantrum against its reporter," Joel told me. "And there have been several interviews with Dolly. How Peña threatened to kill us all after Galeano Perrone's arrest in 1976. And another saying he must be tried there, because here justice is impossible. The churches are filled with people lighting candles and praying for Dolly to maintain her courage, her strength to carry on the struggle."

I mentioned how Dolly seemed a lot steadier, centered. Perhaps her talk with Malena helped, and the CCR people were making her feel more accepted, part of the team.

Getting back to the Paraguayan journalists' dispatches, I asked, "So not all of their articles are pro-Peña?"

"Many do play into simpleminded nationalism," Filártiga explained. "You know, the international human rights conspiracy persecuting our countryman, disparaging Paraguay's honor.

"But you know my brother César," he went on. "How he always supported Stroessner? Would warn us to be silent and not cause trouble? Yesterday he came with congratulations, to encourage us.

"I have even had to print more cards of Joelito. People take dozens as they leave the house. To hand out at the universities, stores, Masses, gasoline stations, everywhere."

Here, too, I told Joel, solidarity was growing. Not only had his California friends joined in the lobbying campaign, the Gaffneys had mobilized the Esperanza Fund network. More members of Congress were climbing on board. Only that morning Representative Elisabeth Holtzman shot off a letter to State supporting us. And the Kennedy people had told us that the senator was still pressing his inquiries, "requesting" information about Peña's visa.

"Best of all, though," I reported, "is what your friend Frank Church pulled off. Frank's now chairman of the Senate Foreign Relations Committee. Just this afternoon he got a motion approved putting Paraguay on the list of the most intractable human rights violators. And then, the committee unanimously voted to cut off all military and economic aid. The bill still has to work its way through Congress before it becomes law, but Stroessner will get the message right away."

"And I have some good news, too," Filártiga said. "We spoke with Ambassador White. The government denies us passports, so he gave us visa waivers. There is still much to do before we travel. But Nidia and I will be with you Friday night."

24

The Filártigas were not the only ones busy making travel arrangements that week. On Thursday, May 3, Gorostiaga submitted an affidavit to Judge Nickerson reviewing the history of the *Caso Filártiga* trial in Paraguay. Pointing out that several appeals were currently before the Paraguayan Supreme Court, his brief assured Nickerson that "the criminal case is now proceeding against both Mr. Peña and Mr. Duarte."

The next day Gorostiaga returned to Asunción "for consultations." That following Monday, the Paraguayan Supreme Court issued two favorable decisions in the *Caso Filártiga*. The first denied Peña's appeal to be dropped as a defendant in the trial. The other upheld the Filártigas' appeal for the lower court to conduct a full investigation into Joelito's murder.

Even so, as Bob White cabled Washington, the rulings were meaningless. As he explained, Gorostiaga had convinced the regime that unless the *Caso Filártiga* appeared to proceed in a normal manner, "his efforts to defend Peña, and indirectly the honor of Paraguay, could run into difficulties in the U.S."

Sure enough, Stroessner's judicial ploy provided a crucial link in the defense's legal stratagem. Murry Brochin's tightly crafted motion argued that allegedly a crime had been committed by a Paraguayan against another Paraguayan in Paraguay; therefore, the U.S. courts had no jurisdiction in the matter.

Brochin then brought in the *forum non conveniens* argument. The U.S. courts were a "nonconvenient forum" to try Peña, he contended, because of the inaccessibility of evidence and other practical problems. Moreover, the *Filártiga v. Peña* suit should be dismissed since, as demonstrated by the recent Supreme Court rulings, Paraguay's judiciary was actively administering justice in the *Caso Filártiga*. It was, therefore, the Paraguayan courts that constituted the proper and only "convenient forum" to litigate the case.

With his mission accomplished in Asunción, Gorostiaga scuttled back to New York to pursue Peña's vindication and debunk the international calumny bent on desecrating the Fatherland.

25

Beefing up their complaint during these last weeks before the big hearing, CCR had the Filártigas bring from Paraguay stacks of legal documents and press clippings. Further adding to the supporting materials, they collected full sets of Amnesty, OAS, and International League for Human Rights reports, as well as affidavits from Malena Rodríguez, Dr. Filártiga, and others who had suffered firsthand the persecution of Stroessner's police state.

Mike drafted CCR's *forum non conveniens* rebuttal. Stroessner's courts were too corrupt, the brief argued, to be considered a legitimate forum to try Peña; therefore, because the Filártigas stood no chance of justice in Paraguay, the U.S. courts constituted the only "convenient forum" for the suit.

Peter and Rhonda tackled the jurisdiction question. For over thirty years, the world had paid lip service to the many treaties protecting human rights. Yet, in 1979, no nation had employed its domestic law to put an alien torturer on trial.

Unlike domestic law, international law evolves through agreements and principles recognized by nations, the acceptance of international customary practices, and along with judicial decisions, the teachings of learned commentators.

To buttress their case, the center's strategy counted on supporting amicus curiae briefs—"friend of the court" briefs, which are the written opinions of specialists and other interested parties who, although not principals in the suit themselves, offer the court their advice.

Drawing on his extensive contacts, Peter lined up a half-dozen amicus briefs from eminent law professors and legal scholars. With painstaking reason, they tied in historical analysis with current interpretations of international law and federal statues to support CCR's fundamental argument: The treaties adopted by the modern community of nations, and the evolving norms of customary international law, clearly recognized that gross human rights abuses, including torture, were a violation of international law. By torturing Joelito to death, therefore, Peña had become subject to U.S. jurisdiction under the Alien Tort Claims Act.

In this politically loaded test case of putting a foreign torturer on trial for the first time, virtually all of the human rights groups also weighed in. One of the earliest amicus briefs from five NGOs—including Amnesty, WOLA, and COHA—urged Judge Nickerson to accept the suit so as to announce to human rights violators "not to expect refuge from justice in the United States [because] our courts are open to the persecuted who find themselves shut out of their homeland."

In an ironic twist, that amicus put Leonel Castillo on both sides of the case. As a COHA board member, it placed him on record arguing to put Peña on trial. And, as the INS commissioner, of course, he was also a defendant. Not in the least put out, Leonel's heart was with the Filártigas. But, as he later acknowledged to me, being new at the job, the legal heavyweights at the Department of Justice had bulldozed him into going along with the official INS position to deport Peña. In fact, U.S. attorney Jensen submitted a memorandum requesting that all charges be dismissed against Peña, because in the Department of Justice's legal opinion the court even had lacked the jurisdiction to stay the INS judge's order to deport him.

On Friday, May 11, CCR filed its briefs. For the Filártigas, it began a very long weekend as they awaited the Monday-morning showdown in Nickerson's courtroom.

26

A week earlier, the previous Friday, Joel and Nidia had visited me at my apartment in Washington. More than two years had passed since the three of us had been together.

When I left Paraguay in December 1976, with the *Caso Filártiga* in a shambles, it was beyond conceivability that events ever could have reached this point: Peña charged with the torture-murder of Joelito in a U.S. federal court, the potential landmark human rights case touching off a foreign relations controversy generating publicity that spanned the hemisphere, and Stroessner scrambling to control the damage from the worst international crisis of his twenty-five-year dictatorship.

Even as we spent the afternoon catching up, the sheer magnitude of it all cast a sense of awe over our reunion. The complexity of the new dynamics in play—rife with imponderable twists and turns—left us at a loss to reach any informed opinion as to how it might all unfold. As we continued our speculation, the initial air of celebration was overshadowed by this unfathomable latest phase of the *Caso Filártiga* struggle.

Yet, even through their own worries, and fatigue from the overnight flight, from the moment she walked into my home, Nidia picked up our relationship as the surrogate son that I was to her. Taking my hand and asked, "Richard, you look terrible. What is wrong?"

"Nothing that a little rest won't take care of,"

"No," Dr. Filártiga said sternly, "you are on the verge of collapse."

There are some things your family has a right to know. "Yes," I relented, "my back's been pretty bad. The doctors are keeping me going with some rather strong painkillers. But as soon as Peña's wrapped up, I've got a reservation at the Washington Hospital Center. They'll wean me off the narcotics, fix me up, and everything will be fine."

Joel gave me a nod of acquiescence, and the knowing look of a physician who had seen it all and knew my true medical condition. Nidia was also far too experienced to accept my fib. She gave me a long, warm, motherly hug, and we let it go at that.

Later, Dolly and Mike stopped by, and we spent the rest of the night talking about the case. When I got up the next morning, Joel and Nidia had already left for New York.

27

The Filártigas entered Nickerson's courtroom on Monday, May 14, to find Peña seated at the defense table, deep in conversation with Gorostiaga.

"I am going over there," Nidia said, her voice a bit shaky, "and look him in the face. To see into the eyes of the man who killed Joelito."

"Yes. Go look at him," Dolly agreed, "but you must not tremble, Mamá. Don't tremble. Remember, people love us, but they don't love that idiot."

Glancing up, Peña saw Nidia approaching. The cocky police inspector had not expected to see Joelito's mother here in the States, much less striding across the courtroom straight at him. Nidia stood, staring down at her son's murderer. Peña lowered his head.

At the court hearings following the elevator confrontation with Dolly, Peña had avoided speaking with, or even looking at, her. And now, as she came to her mother's side, he concentrated even more intently on the papers on the table, refusing to face the women. Throughout the proceeding, whenever any of the Filártigas tried to catch his attention, Peña averted his eyes.

With an icy contempt, Joel watched Peña cower before his wife and daughter. At first, he had no intention of joining them. Considering the animosity between them, even though they had lived only a few houses apart, Filártiga had never actually had a conversation with the man responsible for his son's death. While they often caught sight of each other from a distance, their limited communication was carried on through the children. Indeed, not once in all the years did Filártiga and the cop exchange a word; unless one counts that encounter on the boulevard, when Joel pulled up next to Peña and, over the barrel of a pistol, yelled, "Face me, *cabrón*, so I can kill you right."

At last, Joel decided to confront the person who had so devastated the lives of his family. But before he could act, Judge Nickerson's court was called to order.

28

The media coverage and public interest had attracted an impressive audience to the *Filártiga v. Peña* hearing. People from human rights NGOs and the Paraguayan expatriate community mixed with representatives from the Paraguayan and U.S. press.

This suit had to be filed here, Peter Weiss began, because there is no rule of law in Paraguay. With the courts absolutely controlled by the dictator Stroessner, and the special protection Peña has as a former police chief inspector, for the Filártigas there exists no legal remedy in their homeland.

Nonsense, Murry Brochin retorted, it is Peña's rights that are being violated in what amounts to a show-trial, in this attempt by plaintiffs to propagandize against political conditions in Paraguay. Consider the outcry if one of our citizens were detained and tried in a foreign country—say Paraguay—for a racially motivated killing perpetrated against another American in the United States!

Peter was well acquainted with this "parade of horribles" ploy, a standard lawyer's tactic to attack a new legal principle brought before a court. By marching out all the horrible things that conceivably *might* occur at some point in the future under speculative circumstances, Brochin was trying to discredit a perfectly valid principle in *Filártiga v. Peña*.

In the real world, Weiss answered, such hypothetical situations rarely are legitimate concerns. First of all, down the line, these projected horribles probably will never happen. And if they do, we will deal with them one at a time.

In this racially motivated homicide scenario, for example, we would ask that the person be returned for trial. It is difficult to conceive that any nation that attaches importance to its relations with the United States, or that has an independent judiciary, would deny that our courts constitute a proper forum.

Brochin next tried the "floodgate" theory. This suit, he warned gravely, would open the door for any alien who chances to catch an official of a foreign government in the United States against whom he thinks he has a claim. The court should not set a precedent that would encourage every Kurdish rebel, every West Bank Palestinian, every

Soviet dissident, to seek redress in our courts for politically motivated injuries they claim to have sustained at home.

That is nothing more than another artificial twist of the theoretical "parade of horribles," Peter countered. In the past thirty years, human rights have emerged as a central concern of international law. And they now constitute a fundamental tenet of U.S. foreign policy under the Carter administration. Together with our responsibilities under domestic law, the defense of human rights is based on our obligations under the United Nations Charter and other international commitments. The time has come, Peter summed up, that our courts should be available to victims when redress is impossible in their own country.

It was precisely this principle, of course, that was Peter's dream; establishing the precedent of federal courts enforcing U.S. law so as to put teeth into international law.

With his customary civility, Judge Nickerson thanked both sides for their spirited presentations and adjourned the hearing. They would be notified of his decision.

29

Everyone was gathered at CCR when Nickerson's written decision arrived the next afternoon.

"It's not over yet," Peter tried to assure the Filártigas.

"But how could the judge dismiss the case against Peña?" Joel demanded.

"It certainly seems that Nickerson didn't want to," Peter said. "He goes so far as to say we made a very strong case showing that torture is condemned by the international community, that the proscription of torture has emerged as a norm of customary international law."

"Then why did he rule against us?"

"He relied on an earlier Appellate Court decision that interpreted the Alien Tort Claims Act very narrowly. It said that a crime in a foreign country violates international law only if it affects U.S. relations with that nation. So, despite our strong arguments that ATCA should apply to torture, he feels bound by the Circuit Court's decision. In other words, he ruled that he does not have jurisdiction in the suit."

"So what do we do now?" Joel asked.

"Appeal," Peter said. "Nickerson's decision extends the TRO staying Peña's deportation for forty-eight hours, to give us a chance to appeal his ruling.

"Actually, we're going to do two things. First we'll appeal Nickerson's ruling and ask the Circuit Court to order him to accept jurisdiction, and try Peña for the torture-murder of Joelito. Of course, it'll take months for them to reach a decision. But once there is an appeal pending before the Appellate Court, that gives us grounds to move to extend the TRO staying Peña and Villalba's deportation until they give their depositions."

30

After working all night, the CCR team filed their Notice of Appeal to the Second Circuit Court to review Nickerson's decision. That same day, Wednesday, May 16, they submitted the second motion, asking the court to order the defendants' deportation postponed until they gave depositions.

CCR did not object to the deportations. In fact, once Peña and Villalba were deposed, they had no intention of further opposing their return to Paraguay. However, as they stated, their motion not only reflected the widespread public interest in the case but also Nickerson's recognition of the merit of their argument. Requiring the defendants to give depositions before leaving the United States, CCR's brief contended, was the minimal necessity for the Filártigas to pursue the case. For, should the Circuit Court overturn Nickerson and grant him jurisdiction, the depositions would be needed to adjudicate the case.

Since the INS could not now deport Peña and Villalba because of the pending appeal, and Stroessner's backing did not go so far as springing for their $100,000 bail, the couple found themselves back in the Brooklyn Detention Center.

That Friday, counsel for both Peña and Villalba and the INS submitted their briefs in opposition to CCR's appeal. Allowing the Filártigas to continue their campaign of waging "a propaganda war against the government of a foreign state," Brochin insisted, "would be to countenance a totally unwarranted intrusion into the diplomatic relations of the United States." And the U.S. attorney reiterated the INS's argument that U.S. courts had no jurisdiction to stay the deportation order, and asked the Circuit Court to allow the defendants to leave as scheduled on Wednesday, May 23.

By this stage of the *Filártiga v. Peña* proceedings, the factions within the government were in open disagreement. In a long letter to the secretary of state, the director of the Human Rights Office of the National Council of Churches summed up the sharpening divisions. On the one side, the Reverend William Wipfler reminded Cyrus Vance that the INS "seems to be saying: Don't bother us with human rights issues—get these aliens out of the country as soon as possible." However, "Human rights specialists in the Department of State and civil rights specialists in the Department of Justice," he pointed out, "seem sympathetic to plaintiffs' position and aware of the precedential importance of the litigation."

Wipfler went on to emphasize the "transcending importance" that the case had in Paraguay, and that a decision against the Filártigas would be interpreted by Stroessner as a "victory," undermining "how seriously the United States takes its human rights policy in this particular instance." Consequently, he concluded by urging the secretary of state "to use your powers to the fullest" to convey to the U.S. attorney the strong support of the State Department to stay the deportations until the defendants could be deposed."

31

Tuesday morning, May 22, Weiss and Brochin presented their oral arguments on the deportation issue before a three-judge panel of the Second Circuit Court. A few hours later the court, without further comment, handed down its one-word decision: DENIED.

Again the CCR team pushed through the night, this time preparing their petition to the court of last appeal. With the sun coming up over Manhattan on Wednesday,

Mike hurried out of the center to catch the seven-o'clock shuttle to Washington. Waiting outside the office of Justice Thurgood Marshall, when the United States Supreme Court opened for business on May 23, Mike filed the emergency motion to stay Peña's deportation.

Everyone knew it was a long shot, if the only shot left. Such applications to individual Supreme Court justices are extremely rare, and it is rarer still for them to be granted. Even so, CCR hoped that by presenting Marshall with the complete history of the Filártigas' struggle, they might persuade him that this was one of those exceptional cases that merited special consideration. And they did. That afternoon, Marshall issued a temporary stay until the full Supreme Court could consider the matter.

The following day, Thursday, May 24, all nine Supreme Court justices met at their weekly conference and dissolved Marshall's stay. Wasting no time, the INS hustled the Peña party out of the country on an early Friday morning flight.

Filártiga's self-portrait on a Clinic of Hope prescription pad.

ELEVEN

DURING MOMENTS when they had let their hopes soar, the Filártigas allowed themselves to imagine that Peña would truly be brought to justice, complete with a confession finally revealing to them how Joelito had died. At the least, winning meant holding onto Peña, getting his deposition, keeping the initiative and publicity, especially since the *Caso Filártiga* had been reopened in Paraguay. But now, with Peña safely back in Paraguay, as everyone gathered at the Center for Constitutional Rights, they confronted a whole new set of concerns.

"Oh Mamá, Papi," Dolly worried. "What will they do to you, after all the trouble we've caused. Peña will seek revenge. Like when they arrested Mamá and me."

"Perhaps not," Joel reflected. "The dictatorship rescued him only because of national pride. To the regime Peña is not important. No longer does he count with the kind of backing that he had after Joelito's murder. In fact, he is a much worse embarrassment than when they kicked him out of the police, after the *Caso Filártiga* became an international scandal. No, I do not think Stroessner will allow Peña to create further problems by indulging his vengeance."

"Well, anyway," Nidia said, "all is lost."

"I realize it may be of little comfort at this moment," Peter told them, "but the legal battle is not over. Our Supreme Court's ruling permitting Peña's deportation does not prejudice the rest of your case.

"We have not yet begun litigating our basic appeal to the Circuit Court, to rule in favor of jurisdiction and allow Peña to be tried for torturing Joelito to death. Even Judge Nickerson recognized the strength of our argument. And we are lining up more amicus briefs from international law experts. We even have been talking with some sympathetic lawyers in the State Department. It is not inconceivable that they, too, could submit an amicus brief supporting us."

"Yes, of course, you are right. That is very important," Nidia said. But only out of politeness, for in her heart learning the truth about Joelito's murder and punishing Peña was what really mattered.

"All that will take months and months," Dolly protested. "Mamá and Papi can't stay here, like me. They have to go back to their work, to the clinic."

"Of course, we will do all that we can from here," Rhonda Copelon promised. "And in Paraguay, from what we've heard of Ambassador White's recent public statements, I'd say it's safe to say he's on our side."

"It's true," Dolly acknowledged, "Ambassador White has always helped us. But what are we going to do here, right now?"

"We are going to Washington," Joel said. "Richard is in the hospital."

1

On Thursday, May 24, I had already packed a bag before leaving for the annual COHA board of directors meeting. As their coup of the year, the Peña case topped the agenda, and the board members were looking forward to a firsthand account of the inside story. Yet, even after arriving late and delivering a somewhat disjointed presentation, everyone understood when I begged off early to catch a cab to the Washington Hospital Center.

Joel and Nidia came Monday afternoon. Even though emotionally wrung out, before anything else they insisted on a detailed update of my medical condition. Only after listening to me gripe about the sadistic spinal tap technician, and the night nurses' truly evil delight at my detox miseries, did we turn to their situation.

Peña's deportation had transformed the already-bewildering events into a morass. The complexity of the crisis made any attempt at long-term planning futile; at best, we could deal only with the next, immediate steps.

"It seems to me," Joel said, "that Stroessner must realize now is not the time to take reprisals against us. Consider the cost to Paraguay's international reputation he paid for arresting Domingo Laino."

"And," I agreed, "you've built up an enormously influential base of supporters. Among university and religious groups, the human rights NGOs, in Congress, and now the legal community with all their contacts."

"Yes, even before we left New York to come here," Joel added, "Amnesty, CCR, and the others already began organizing the campaign. Letters to the State Department and the embassy in Asunción. And to Stroessner's mafia. All seeking guarantees of safety when we return."

As we ran through these developments, my friend Richard Claude slipped into the hospital room and caught the last of our conversation. Although a longtime supporter of the *Caso Filártiga*, this was the first occasion that the University of Maryland professor of constitutional law actually met the Filártigas in person.

"It's doubtful that the embassy needs any further encouragement," Richard announced. Pulling out a manila envelope Larry Birns had asked him to deliver, he went on, "Seems that State has given Ambassador White a green light to speak his mind."

For a week we had been hearing how the diplomat in Paraguay had kicked up a ruckus with his outspoken opinions about the *Filártiga v. Peña* case. Now, reading the full text of Whites's controversial interview in Asunción's *ABC* Sunday Supplement of May 13, we were impressed by his pronouncement that the Filártigas had every right to sue Peña in the United States. Moreover, the ambassador insisted, our courts possessed jurisdiction over this human rights case, because "international law is in a constant state of evolution; and one of the principal vehicles of this evolution is daring and imaginative decisions by judges which open new fields of action."

Further rankling the dictatorship, Bob drew an analogy between pirates and torturers. Pointing out that under international law the courts of any nation that captures pirates has jurisdiction to try and sentence them—regardless of their nationality or where the piracy took place—he contended that these same laws should properly be applied to human rights violators.

Finally, Richard showed us Ambassador White's note to Birns for us to appreciate. "I send you the enclosed article," Bob told Larry in his cover letter, "to reassure you that we do something in this embassy in addition to giving visas to torturers who sashay into our consular section."

2

During that perfectly miserable two weeks in the hospital, the Filártigas made time in their schedule to visit every few days. "I feel rather useless stuck in here," I told them. "After all these years, it's as if suddenly I'm on the outside, looking in as the struggle goes on. And when I get out tomorrow, I go right into treatment at the pain management clinic, and physical therapy every day. So I don't know how much use I'll be even then."

"Don't worry about such foolishness," Nidia admonished. "Besides, now there are so many people helping, we can't do everything they arrange for us."

Squeezing in appointments with White House, State Department, and OAS officials, the Filártigas met with many old friends at the human rights NGOs, as well as their more recent advocates at the legal NGOs. On June 4, the Letelier-Moffitt Memorial Fund for Human Rights sponsored a symposium at the American University Law School, followed by a formal reception and fundraising exhibition of Joel's drawings. And the following day, WOLA held an ecumenical memorial service at their Capitol Hill office for Joelito, attended by the Filártigas' supporters and congressional staffers, some of whom were inspired to set up further appointments with members of Congress.

Representatives Tom Harkin and Tony Hall deepened their admiration for Joel and Nidia, and strengthened their commitment to their cause. Concerned with what awaited the Filártigas in Paraguay, both followed up by exercising their congressional authority with official letters—with copies to State and Stroessner—announcing that in the future they would be closely monitoring developments. Harkin went so far as to remind Dr. Filártiga that he "looked forward to visiting your clinic in Ybycuí" during his "fact-finding mission to Paraguay later this year."

I was able to participate in the June 13 COHA-sponsored press conference on Paraguay and the Peña case at the National Press Club. As the room full of correspondents scribbled notes and the TV cameras rolled, Dr. Filártiga, Richard Arens, Mike Maggio, and I sat on the stage doing our very best to skyrocket Stroessner's blood pressure.

Later, we agreed that Professor Arens had made the best of it. Elaborating upon the general's most unconscionable human rights crime, he began with a condemnation of the Paraguayan government's policy of systematically exterminating the Aché Indians. Then, calling for a congressional investigation into the indecent haste with which Peña had been deported, putting him beyond the reach of American law, he insisted on an explanation of why the U.S. government had declined to prosecute the torturer for fraudulent misrepresentations on his visa application. Finally, wrapping up his criticism of the tawdry handling of the Peña affair, Arens demanded to know why the INS had failed to interrogate Peña concerning his contacts with known Nazi war criminals in Paraguay, particularly Dr. Josef Mengele.

Arens' preoccupation with Mengele, known as the Angel of Death because of his "scientific" experiments on human subjects at Auschwitz, was no gratuitous swipe at the dictator. In fact, in the most offensive charge made in his *ABC* interview, Ambassador White said that giving Mengele Paraguayan citizenship was just the kind of act by which Stroessner's government discredited itself in the eyes of the international community. "Are you sure Mengele is a Paraguayan citizen?" the interviewer challenged. "Yes," White came back, "I've seen the documentation myself."

3

After the COHA press conference, Richard Claude invited the Filártigas and me to lunch. From his briefcase, the constitutional law expert extracted the current International Law Association's monthly publication. "See here," he said, tapping the June *Practitioner's Notebook's* front page. "This one article, 'Torture as an International Tort,' takes up the whole issue analyzing *Filártiga v. Peña*. It's barely been two months, and as it says, the case "has already attracted a huge following among international legal scholars and human rights activists."

He then showed us a notice from the International Human Rights Law Group; invitations for lawyers, legal scholars, and law students to attend a special teaching seminar in July, to discuss "the complex legal and foreign policy issues and the precedent setting implications raised by the suit."

"Regardless of how the appeal turns out," Richard told the Filártigas, "just by bringing the first real case against a torturer, you've forced the U.S. federal courts into a historic legal battle over international human rights."

Joel recognized the suit's enormous potential. But behind Nidia's ever courteous expressions of appreciation, there remained her mother's inconsolable pain: For her, all else came in a distant second to Peña escaping punishment for murdering her Joelito.

As for myself, the legal community's involvement left me conflicted. Rationally, I welcomed the efforts of all the new people and organizations in the struggle. Yet, I felt a touch of indignation, perhaps even resentment, at the recent converts, jumping on board now that the Filártigas' struggle had made the quantum leap from just another human rights case to a career-making international legal controversy. Strongest among my emotions, though, was a deep sense of relief. Now that the lawyers had taken over, the cause had acquired an irrepressible momentum of its own—no longer were the contributions of any individual needed to keep the struggle alive.

Two days later, we said our good-byes to Joel and Nidia at Dulles Airport. Easing our fears for their safety, upon arriving in Paraguay, in a demonstration of solidarity the

Filártigas' friends met them with warm welcome—quite unlike the reception that had awaited Peña.

4

Upon debarking at Aeropuerto Presidente Stroessner three weeks earlier, his former colleagues arrested Peña for passing bad checks before he had skipped off to the States. After the ex-cop's one night in custody, apparently he worked out an arrangement with the dictatorship; Peña spent the day taking care of odds and ends before leaving for Brazil.

At this same time, moreover, the regime took out of circulation others who might encumber its plans. In a wave of repression against opposition figures, Investigaciones paid special attention to the leadership of the human rights movement. In a few days, Stroessner's political police arrested hundreds, including, yet again, Domingo Laino.

Among history's lessons is the ease of the state to rally its citizens against any external threat—whether real or manufactured—in an emotional defense of their nation. With the troublesome Peña not around to complicate matters, Stroessner cranked up his propaganda machine, accusing the Filártigas of exploiting Joelito's "Romeo and Juliet" death to promote their political agenda. In a series of articles inflaming nationalistic indignation, *Patria* went on to level far more grievous charges. Claiming that by bringing the *Filártiga v. Peña* suit in the United States, with the help of international human rights organizations and other known enemies, not only did they besmirch the Fatherland's good name, but threatened the very sovereignty of Paraguay. By the time the Filártigas returned home in mid-July 1979, the propaganda campaign had created something of a nationalist backlash that divided popular opinion.

Still, the international media coverage and pressure—widespread articles including a prominent photo of Joelito in Amnesty's August *Newsletter* and the mass of letters generated by the Filártigas' trip—gave Stroessner cause to steer clear of direct reprisals. The dictator's restraint, however, did not extend to throwing up obstacles in the rejuvenated *Caso Filártiga* sham trial.

On June 19, Mario Melgarejo, the lawyer Joel had just contracted to take the case, was snatched off the street by plainclothes Investigaciones police. Notified of his arrest by Filártiga, WOLA mobilized a support campaign. Among others, Tom Harkin shot off a protest letter to Stroessner, and Tony Hall issued a news release publicizing the persecution of Filártiga's new lawyer. After his release, Melgarejo apologized to Joel, explaining the police had threatened him and his family if he did not drop the case.

Otherwise, life for the Filártigas went on as usual: At a court hearing, the tires on Joel's car were slashed; a dead cat, with the head of a duck stuffed in its mouth was thrown onto the upstairs balcony in Sajonia; and of course the ubiquitous letters and telephone death threats.

5

For the dictatorship, though, it was a long way from business as usual. Prompted by Joel's visit to Washington, on June 13 the OAS renewed its request for Stroessner to set a firm date for its promised on-site investigation. Moreover, forwarding a supplementary brief prepared by Joel's Amnesty lawyer, the OAS now asked for a response to the many inconsistencies that contradicted the regime's official line.

While failing to mention the on-site visit, on August 3, the government replied with a nine-page, point-by-point rebuttal denying everything. Not only had Horacio Galeano Perrone never been arrested, any claim of harassing the Filártigas was absolutely false. In fact, it was the Filártigas who inflicted Joelito's massive wounds in order to politically use his death to attack the government. And, as something of a final proof of the Filártigas' intention to smear Paraguay's international reputation, the report pointed to "the false suit in New York against Peña, which was set right by North American justice, by sending their citizen back to Paraguay."

All of which still left Stroessner with the U.S. Circuit Court's *Filártiga v. Peña* appeal.

6

On July 13, CCR filed its motion in support of the Filártigas in the Appellate Court. A few days later, Rhonda stomped out of what should have been a routine scheduling conference with the counsel for the Circuit Court.

"That jerk Fensterwald, or whatever his name is," Rhonda told Peter when she got back to the center, "tried to browbeat me out of filing the suit. I went into the meeting thinking Brochin and I'd set up the schedule. No big deal.

"Then Fensterwald starts out by saying we're wasting the court's time, the case is ridiculous. Of course Brochin jumps in, and I have to basically argue the whole theory of the case. Finally, the jerk threatens me, says that court costs would be high for bringing a frivolous appeal. That's when I said we're going ahead and walked out."

"I have never heard of anything so out of line," Peter said. "Do you think it was his idea to intimidate you, or could he have received instruction from the court?"

"Don't know," Rhonda said. "But Kaufman's one of the three judges on the Appellate panel that will be hearing the case."

"That's not good," Peter groaned. "Particularly just now that his past has come back to haunt him again."

If the CCR team had lucked out at the District Court proceedings by drawing Eugene Nickerson, they were less than thrilled with Circuit Court judge Irving R. Kaufman. Since presiding as the trial judge in the factious Ethel and Julius Rosenberg trial at the height of the early 1950s cold war hysteria, Kaufman had carried the reputation of a "loyal government man." Since then, numerous books and articles had presented compelling accusations that Judge Kaufman conducted illegal ex parte communication during the trial, secretly collaborating with the prosecution to manipulate the evidence. The charges against Kaufman centered not so much upon the guilt or innocence of the defendants but on the fact that his alleged behavior violated their constitutional rights to due process, so as to assure their conviction. Moreover, the critics insist, the death sentence he handed down was part of J. Edgar Hoover's anticommunist crusade to railroad the Rosenbergs.

Indeed, over the years the FBI director maintained a close relationship with Kaufman. In a November 17, 1964, tape-recorded conversation with Lyndon Johnson, Hoover recommended Kaufman for an appointment to the U.S. Supreme Court, pointing out Kaufman's handling of the Rosenberg case. However, with the stain on Kaufman's past still sullying his reputation, Hoover's pitch failed to impress the president.

The controversy surrounding the allegations of Kaufman's judicial sycophancy refused to go away. On the eve of the Filártiga appeal fifteen years later, yet again he was dragged into the national limelight. "The Hidden Rosenberg Case: How the FBI Framed Ethel to Break Julius," published in the *New Republic* on June 23, 1979, touched off a furor in the electronic and print media that made news around the country.

Exactly one month later, July 23, the CCR team submitted their *Filártiga v. Peña* brief, together with an elaborately reasoned amicus brief prepared by Amnesty, to the Circuit Court.

7

As his first line of defense, Murry Brochin asked the court not to accept the amicus from Amnesty and two other NGOs who had signed on to support CCR's case. His brief protested that the Filártigas and their supporters were attempting "to create a Don Quixote role . . . through Amnesty International and its affiliates, to enlist this Court in a crusade to define and assert norms of international law condemning torture." He went on to say that the amicus was "superfluous and immaterial" on two grounds. First, the defense had already conceded Judge Nickerson's finding that international law condemns torture. Moreover, the brief did not answer the central question of jurisdiction within the meaning of the Alien Tort Claims Act; that is, whether the court should accept the case in the first place. The only purpose of the amicus, Peña's lawyer concluded, "is to divert the Court from the narrow statutory question of jurisdiction which confronts it."

By August 10, when CCR sent the court its rebuttal of Brochin's motion, COHA and two more NGOs had filed a second amicus brief, further refining and strengthening the Filártigas' complaint. Refuting Brochin's arguments, CCR's reply showed that only a small part of these amici briefs addressed the conceded point that torture violated international law. Rather, the amici offered scholarly analysis examining case law and other statutes, essential aids in interpreting international law as it applied to ATCA. The defense's "brazen and unfounded suggestion that amici briefs be rejected," CCR insisted, "is both an affront to the intelligence of this Court as well as to the judicial process itself."

Evidently, ruling to accept the amici, the Circuit Court also thought so.

8

As the October 16 date approached for the Appellate Court hearing, both the defense and the plaintiffs filed their final briefs. Central to Brochin's thirty-five-page brief, was that Judge Nickerson had properly dismissed the suit; that by interpreting the Second Circuit Court's precedents—whose narrow scope restricted the use of ATCA only to cases in which violations of international law affected international relations— Nickerson had correctly ruled that federal courts lacked jurisdiction in *Filártiga v. Peña*.

The center's rebuttal brief, now sixty pages plus addenda and amici briefs, contended that Nickerson had misunderstood the Circuit Court's ruling. Citing the court's 1975 *ITT v. Vancap* decision, CCR noted: "The international condemnation of torture is both in theory and fact among the 'standards, rules or customs . . . affecting the relationship between states or between an individual and a foreign state.'" Further, the Filártigas' lawyers pointed out that human rights violations have triggered sanctions, such as the recent Senate Foreign Relations Committee's recommendation to eliminate economic aid because of Paraguay's human rights record. It is precisely because of such foreign policy implications, they argued, that the organic growth of international law now makes torture enforceable under ATCA, thereby giving U.S. courts jurisdiction in *Filártiga v. Peña*.

Continuing to push the outdated interpretation of the Alien Tort Claims Act argument, Brochin claimed that the separation of powers provision in Article III of the Constitution did not authorize using ATCA in such cases. Further, even if it was constitutionally permissible, it should be rejected because when Congress enacted ATCA it could not possibly have intended the expansive application proposed by the Filártigas.

Nonsense, the CCR team countered. Brochin's unconstitutional argument was "patently spurious." Tracing the legislative history, they showed how ATCA's jurisdiction rests on Article III's authorization of federal jurisdiction over suits "Arising Under . . . the Law of Nations," as well as under the congressional power of Article I, to "define and punish . . . offenses against the Law of Nations."

Next, Brochin played the *forum non conveniens* card. The most convenient forum to pursue justice in this suit was in Paraguay, because the continued criminal prosecution of Peña and Duarte clearly demonstrated the genuine attempt of the Paraguayan courts to adjudicate the *Caso Filártiga* trial.

Preposterous, the CCR team shot back. Presenting a letter from WOLA detailing the arrest and imprisonment in June of the Filártigas' lawyer, they explained how Mario Melgarejo had been threaten with death, forcing him to withdraw as legal counsel in the *Caso Filártiga*.

In a sweeping repudiation of the *forum non conveniens* issue, furthermore, Filártiga's lawyers elaborated upon the impunity with which torturers escape judicial sanctions. Either they receive sanctuary in their own country—such as the Chilean dictatorships's refusal to extradite to the United States the two DINA assassins who murdered Ambassador Orlando Letelier and Ronni Moffitt in Washington—or they are protected by sympathetic foreign regimes, as for example Paraguay's shielding of the notorious Nazi Dr. Mengele.

Finally, in a new twist, Brochin tried the desperate stab of introducing one of the traditional stop signs in international law, which diplomatically says, "Mind your own business." Under the Act of State Doctrine, all acts by a sovereign state or its authorized agents, carried out within its territory and within the scope of its authority, are not subject to legal proceedings in another country.

Outrageous, CCR replied. "The brutal torture-murder alleged cannot be said to be within the legitimate authority of either the defendant Peña or the dictator-president general Stroessner himself."

To drum up maximum exposure, Rhonda alerted the press a few days before the actual Appellate Court hearing. And, shot-gunning a memo to Filártigas' supporters, she urged them to come to the hearing. Reminding them of the importance "for the Court to see that there are a lot of people interested in this case," to send the message that "this is our business, too."

9

On the morning of October 16, the three-judge Circuit Court panel accorded Murry Brochin a sympathetic hearing as he presented the defense's case. Even his rather imperious closing statement elicited no critical questioning from the judges. Insisting that using ATCA to try international human rights violations in a civil trial was "too blunt an instrument" for achieving foreign policy goals, Brochin warned that only a narrow interpretation of ATCA would "prevent the Courts from becoming a forum for propaganda trials."

As recorded in the official court transcripts, the reception Peter Weiss received was less cordial. Following a brief introductory overview of the Filártigas' case, Peter began to address the constitutional jurisdictional issue. In enacting the 1789 Alien Tort Claims Act, "Congress knew exactly what it wanted, it wanted deference to the law of nations, so that the nation which they were forging would take its place in the community [of nations]."

Judge Irving Kaufman interrupted with a theoretical question concerning the executive branch's authority in dealing with international law and foreign policy. "Can our State Department take cognizance in this case," he asked, "or is the sole remedy in a court of law?"

Taken aback, Peter thought to himself that is a strange question. Because when I went to law school, I learned that judges, and not the executive branch, were supposed to decide the law. "Certainly there have been instances when the State Department has intervened on behalf of one [human rights'] victim or another with foreign countries," Peter replied, "but obviously the State Department cannot act as a court of justice in these cases."

"That's not responding to my question," Kaufman said. "My question is, has anybody requested the State Department to intervene or file a brief amicus in this case?"

"Oh yes," Peter replied, "any number of people have asked the State Department to intervene in this case."

"And their position has been what?"

"Prior to bringing the suit the State Department has not intervened very actively," Peter acknowledged. "However, the U.S. ambassador to Paraguay has not only protested to the government there. He is on record as saying that the suit is properly brought and will aid the cause of human rights in Paraguay."

"Is there any reason why counsel has not solicited the State Department's position on this litigation?" Kaufman pressed. "Because in past instances we've received a letter from a secretary of state making their position."

"I think it is rather uncommon for the State Department to intervene in cases of this type," Peter answered, "unless asked to do so by the court. But we have had informal contacts with people in the State Department who have expressed great interest."

"What did they tell you?" Kaufman persisted. "They wouldn't intervene?"

"They didn't tell us one way or the other."

"Is it fair or unfair," Kaufman went on, "to characterize the position of the State Department as hands-off in this case?"

The judge's questioning sent a shiver of alarm through Mike. Who the hell trusts the government? he thought. It's not like the bureaucrats at State are the kind of people that CCR pals around with.

"Well, at the moment that's certainly so," Peter said. "I think there's a great deal of sympathetic interest on the part of many levels of the State Department in this case, and they're watching it with great interest. And why they haven't directly—"

"—Doesn't that remind you of a court opinion that begins by complimenting counsel's skill," Kaufman interrupted, "and ends with a decision against him?"

"I really don't think the State Department has made a decision."

"The question is whether the courts should intervene," Kaufman replied. "Or keep hands off in this particular instance because we may interfere with remedies being implemented by other branches of government."

"Your Honor, with the utmost respect, I beg to disagree very strongly with the proposition that the State Department, or any other branch of the executive, has any power in an individual case of human rights."

"I didn't say that, I didn't say that," Kaufman protested.

Cutting off his colleague's incivility, Chief Judge Feinberg stepped in and steered the proceeding back to the central issue of jurisdiction.

"It may be improper," Feinberg said. "To refer this kind of individual case to the executive branch would be a violation of the constitutional separation of powers. Even so, the State Department may have objections to recognizing that the matter of jurisdiction clearly lies in the judiciary."

"In the opinion of plaintiffs," Feinberg asked, "could the court request an opinion from the State Department?"

"Sure," Peter said.

10

That same afternoon, the clerk of courts notified CCR that the Circuit Court would request an amicus brief from the State Department.

"What a disaster," Mike told Rhonda. "State's filled with career bureaucrats who've been around forever, watching presidents come and go. They look at the big picture, what's the downside, what's this going to mean for long-term foreign policy. And like Peter told Kaufman, the opinion at State is divided."

"It doesn't look good to me either," she agreed. "Wouldn't it be much easier for State just to see these cases go away?"

"I am not so sure," Peter answered. "After all, this is the Carter State Department we are dealing with. And, regardless of the administration's compromises, human rights are a serious component of its foreign policy."

What Peter had failed to mention to the court, was that for months CCR had been carrying on an informal dialogue with Charles Runyon, one of the most respected human rights lawyers at State. And while such contacts with outsiders were frowned upon, as Runyon, who was approaching retirement, later told me he felt strongly about *Filártiga v. Peña* and simply did not give a good damn.

Early on, the CCR team understood that the court's acceptance of jurisdiction in a case with such far reaching implications, would be as much a political decision as a legal issue. In fact, beginning in July, Rhonda had made several trips to Washington to confer with Runyon, and build bridges with the handful of other lawyers at the Departments of State and Justice, who upon their own initiative already had begun working on a joint amicus brief.

The Circuit Court's formal request to State's legal adviser, Robert E. Owens, for a memorandum "setting forth its position concerning the proper interpretation of 28 USC 1350 in light of the facts of this case," ended CCR's access. When Rhonda called to schedule a conference before State sent in its amicus brief, Owens' office informed her of its recent change of policy: It no longer allowed informal hearings concerning the preparation of its opinions for the courts.

Cut off from direct communication with Runyon and their other contacts, CCR tried to influence the amicus brief by sending letters to "interested parties" suggesting they contact State to urge them to support the Filártigas' position. Further, on November 19, CCR wrote Owens soliciting the government's views concerning the issues presented in *Filártiga v. Peña*.

After waiting a month without a response, the center requested that upon receiving State's legal opinion, the court give them a copy to provide an adequate opportunity to respond.

Bogged down in the Iranian hostage crisis, more months passed before State completed its amicus. However, the legal, and extralegal, action in Paraguay, had been running on the fast track.

11

Left without counsel since Melgarejo had been forced out, in August Nidia went to the churches' human rights lawyer, Heriberto Alegre, to seek his representation in the *Caso Filártiga*.

"I wanted the case with a passion," Alegre later told me. "Any criminal lawyer would want such a famous case." But first, he secured the moral and financial support of the Paraguayan Ecumenical Council of Churches. Upon receiving from the Filártigas an initial monthly installment of 50,000 guaraníes, worth about $300, matched by an equal amount from the church council, Alegre took the *Caso Filártiga*.

Alegre entertained no illusions of winning the case and bringing the guilty to justice. Rather, with the myriad of problems assailing Stroessner, he hoped that the popular clamor in Paraguay and the intense international pressure would provide the leverage for the dictator to let some of the truth come to light, particularly clarifying the mysteries surrounding Joelito's murder.

But the regime continued with its legal harassment. The Paraguayan court banned Alegre and the Filártigas from attending the depositions of Juana's sons, Nery and Jorge Villalba. The court denied Alegre's motion for a reconstruction of the crime—including a reexamination of the whip and knife wounds, bone fractures, and the other mutilations Joelito had suffered—the court also rejected his petition to depose the coroner and judge at the scene that night, ruling that their original reports were sufficient.

Supported by widespread press coverage, and privately coached by Horacio Galeano Perrone, in September Joel sent the Paraguayan Supreme Court two open telegrams protesting the lower court's decisions. Partially backing down, the lower court then notified the Filártigas that they would be allowed to attend the September 17 deposition of Duarte's mother, Sara Arredondo, as well as Juana Villalba's deposition.

Just a week before Juana's court appearance Peña's lawyer, Gorostiaga, submitted a never-before-revealed letter from Charo to her mother, dated April 16, 1976, two weeks after Joelito's death. She admits to having an affair with him, and offers other details supporting the regime's "crime-of-passion" story. *Patria* published her confession. However, convinced that Charo had been coerced into writing the letter, the Filártigas denounced it as a gambit to bolster the defense's case. Worse yet, the public's lampooning of Charo's letter left Stroessner's face dripping with egg.

So it came as no great surprise when a few days after Juana's October 1 deposition—repeating the party line and condemning the Filártigas for their attempt to besmirch President Stroessner's government—the court received yet another previously unknown communication from Charo. In an elaborately detailed affidavit, supposedly certified by a notary on April 14, 1976, again Charo backed up the "crime-of-passion" defense. Although hailed by *Patria* as "the final proof," few took the regime's fabrication seriously. On top of the suspicious timing, throughout the flawlessly prepared affidavit, far beyond Charo's writing skills, she consistently referred to herself in the third person.

12

With Gorostiaga's legal stratagem in disarray, in November 1979, Filártiga accepted the Gaffneys' invitation to make another trip to the States. Joel's tour, financed by their Esperanza Fund and his growing coterie of supporters, was timed to add further international pressure on the dictatorship.

Filártiga's seven university exhibits and lectures—including Harvard, Harvard Medical School, Columbia, and Yale—were received with what by then had become customary enthusiasm. Along with raising funding for the clinic, during his major presentations, as well as at numerous less-formal appearances, Joel condemned Paraguay's latest wave of repression that had gripped the country since June. From students to members of Congress, he pleaded with everyone to join the WOLA-led campaign protesting Stroessner's imprisonment of political prisoners.

Among the new adherents to the Filártigas' cause, fresh out of medical school, was the Spanish-speaking Dr. David Smotkin, who decided to accompany Joel back to Paraguay. Actually, beginning with Peña's bust in April, Smotkin had come to know Dolly, and through the Esperanza Fund provided small sums to help defray her commuting expenses. And beginning in July, when Dolly moved from Washington to New York and entered the International Rescue Committee's program to study English, they offered her a modest stipend to help with the salary she earned at her afternoon clerical job.

"Peter says Dolly has been invaluable," Joel told me when we got together in Washington. "Coming by the center, always ready to help out."

"She certainly is carrying the load when you're not here. And things are a lot better with the CCR people. Still it's tough, making the move to New York. But she knows the importance of the appeal, keeping Stroessner walking a very careful line."

"Dolly's political asylum too," he said. "That also holds Stroessner back. Here she is out of his reach. So whatever happens to us there, he can do nothing to shut her up."

"And David Smotkin's presence will offer some further protection," I suggested.

In June, drawing on the popular upsurge brought by his defiance of the regime, Joel had established a "medical cooperative" in Asunción. After purchasing a large building in a modest barrio in the capital, and enlisting the collaboration of a dozen colleagues, Filártiga opened the Policlínica La Esperanza. Working on a rotating basis—Joel spent Sundays at the new clinic during his weekends in Asunción—the team began providing low-cost, high-quality medical care for the poor.

"Yes, David will serve as a deterrent to the dictatorship," Joel agreed. "But even more, the Asunción clinic is still in need of basic equipment—to say nothing of the chronic lack of medical supplies. I think that Ybycuí may not be the best place for Dr. Smotkin's introduction to third world medicine. Perhaps Asunción would be more beneficial for everyone." Indeed, David spent most of his three months in Paraguay at the Asunción clinic, his dedication greatly contributing to the growth of the new Policlínica La Esperanza.

Even before Drs. Filártiga and Smotkin left the States, they received good news from Paraguay. On December 23, 1979, the day before their arrival in Asunción, Stroessner released most of the political prisoners. Among those who gained their liberty in time to spend the holidays with their families, after seven months in an Investigaciones cell, was Domingo Laino.

13

As we all waited for the Appellate Court decision, Stroessner attempted to grease the skids of U.S. justice. Overturning the lower court, in May 1980, the Paraguayan Supreme Court granted Heriberto Alegre's appeal for a full reconstruction of the case—a complete reevaluation of the evidence and introduction of new facts: the exhumation and reexamination of Joelito's body; new depositions questioning the original statements given by the coroner, judge, and police officials following Joelito's murder—the whole works.

Again, at first glance, it might seem that at last the regime would give the Filártigas a fair shake. And yet once more, a closer look revealed that the "concessions" meant nothing. Employing Stroessner's standard stalling ploy, the Paraguayan Supreme Court failed to mandate a date to implement its decisions.

14

That same month, on May 29, the Appellate Court received the long-awaited "Memorandum for the United States as Amicus Curiae in *Filártiga v. Peña*." Excluded from the government's work for the last six months, CCR was stunned by the document that the Departments of State and Justice jointly submitted to the court.

"This is absolutely amazing," Rhonda exclaimed to Peter as they studied the twenty-six-page amicus. "It could hardly be better if we'd written it ourselves."

The government brief began by refuting the traditional narrow interpretation of the Alien Tort Claims Act. "Since the law of nations had developed in large measure by reference to evolving customary practice the framers of the first Judiciary Act surely anticipated that international law would not be static after 1789." Consequently, it reasoned, "The law of nations in Section 1350 refers to the law of nations as that body of law may evolve."

Tracing the evolution of international human rights, the amicus quoted key provisions from the 1945 UN Charter to its 1948 Universal Declaration of Human Rights, and through the 1951 OAS Charter before getting into its meticulous review of the 1975 UN Declaration on Torture. Drawing upon more than another two dozen treaties, charters, conventions, and agreements, it determined that "the constitutions or other important laws of over 75 states," had incorporated the principles elaborated in the Universal Declaration of Human Rights, establishing "that human rights obligations are now part of customary international law."

Moving on, the U.S. amicus rejected Peña's Act of State Doctrine defense. "While some nations still practice torture, no state asserts a right to torture its nationals. Rather, nations accused of torture unanimously deny the accusation and make no attempt to justify its use."

Moreover, the amicus brief cut the legs out from under another argument that could be used in an appeal later on. Traditionally, the Right of Action doctrine holds that only nations, and not individuals, have the right to bring a legal action in matters concerning international law. The amicus, however, declared that should a federal court determine that a plaintiff "has suffered a denial of rights guaranteed him as an individual by customary international law . . . there is little danger that judicial enforcement will impair our foreign policy efforts. To the contrary, a refusal to recognize a private cause of action [jurisdiction] . . . might seriously damage the credibility of our nation's commitment to the protection of human rights."

In its conclusion, quoting part of the Alien Tort Claims Act, the amicus from State and Justice to the Circuit Court left no room for misunderstanding: "The only question presented is whether official torture is a 'tort . . . committed in violation of the law of nations. . . .' Because the district court erred in concluding that it is not, its judgment should be reversed and the case remanded for further proceedings."

15

A month after receiving the government's brief, on June 30, 1980, the Circuit Court issued its ruling. As chief justice of the Appellate Panel, Feinberg reasonably would have been expected to write the opinion. Instead, Judge Kaufman managed to gain the opportunity to put his name on this landmark decision. Indeed, the U.S. amicus seems to have had a formidable influence on Kaufman. In a 180-degree turnabout, the opinion he wrote surpassed even the government's strong support of the Filártigas' case.

Only on two occasions had the federal courts granted jurisdiction in a suit based upon the Alien Tort Claims Act—the 1795 *Bolchos v. Darrell* and a 1961 child custody case. In the 190 years since its enactment, all other cases brought under 28 USC 1350 had been dismissed for lack of jurisdiction—the opinion listed ten suits that had been denied, including four in its own Second Circuit.

However, employing the same treaties and arguments presented in the CCR motions and amicus briefs detailing the evolution of human rights in international law, the Circuit Court now refuted the traditional narrow interpretations of ATCA. In fact, citing the government's criteria to establish what is "customary international law—the usages of nations, judicial opinion and the works of jurists—we conclude that official torture is prohibited by the law of nations."

Remanding the case to Judge Nickerson at the district court for trial, the Circuit Court declared that under "this rarely-invoked provision [28 USC 1350], we hold that deliberate torture perpetrated under color of official authority violates universally accepted norms of the international law of human rights, regardless of the nationality of the parties. Thus, whenever an alleged torturer is found and served with process by an alien within our borders, 1350 provides jurisdiction."

Moreover, the Appellate Court addressed several legal issues not taken up by Judge Nickerson, for his decision dealt solely with the question of jurisdiction. Shooting down Brochin's contention that even if torture did violate modern international law, ATCA was unconstitutional, the court found: "The claim is without merit . . . [because] The constitutional basis for the Alien Tort Statute is the Law of Nations, which has always been part of the federal common law."

Likewise, while the Act of State defense had not been advanced in the district court proceeding, and therefore was not part of the appeal, Kaufman parroted the government's amicus. "We note in passing, however," he wrote, "that we doubt whether action by a state official in violation of the Constitution and laws of Paraguay . . . could properly be characterized as an act of state."

And, noting that on remand Nickerson would likely be required to adjudicate the *forum non conveniens* issue, Kaufman seems to have overlooked the previous decisions denying jurisdiction in ATCA cases. Instead he praised "the wisdom of the First Congress in vesting jurisdiction of such claims in the federal district courts through the Alien Tort Statute."

In an eloquent declaration, cribbed from the briefs, Kaufman concluded: "From the ashes of the Second World War . . . humanitarian and practical considerations have combined to lead the nations of the world to recognize that respect for fundamental human rights is in their individual and collective interests. . . . Indeed, for purposes of civil liability, the torturer has become—like the pirate and slave trader before him—*hostis humani generis*, an enemy of all mankind. Our holding today . . . is a small but important step in the fulfillment of the ageless dream to free all people from brutal violence."

16

Caught up in the jubilation when they learned of the Circuit Court's decision, in a rare discourse the normally restrained Peter Weiss became downright expansive.

"Just at the level of simple personal gratification," Peter told the team at CCR that afternoon, "all those who laughed when we sat down at the piano, and most people did laugh at us, were wrong.

"This is more than a victory for the Filártigas," Peter said looking at Dolly. "More than a victory for the center, or any of us individually. It is a victory for human rights, a victory for the law, in a world in which most governments act in a lawless way."

Even so, while recognizing the court's decision as a groundbreaking victory, everyone knew that *Filártiga v. Peña* had still not triumphed; the legal battle was far from over. From the start, the government of Paraguay had hired the best legal talent to contest the suit. First, during the proceedings to win Peña's deportation, all the way up to the U.S. Supreme Court. And then through every step of the long and expensive fight to the Circuit Court's ruling accepting jurisdiction in the case, and sending it back to Nickerson's district court. Among CCR and the legal cadre backing the Filártigas, no one doubted that Stroessner would pursue litigating against this attack besmirching the Fatherland's honor.

"In itself, the Circuit Court's recognition that ATCA gives federal jurisdiction over torturers is a legal milestone," Peter elaborated. "But not until we win the case will *Filártiga v. Peña* take its rightful place alongside the other historic decisions in U.S. jurisprudence."

And with that, they all went out for a celebratory dinner, drinks, and dancing.

17

Fearing the consequences of a successful Filártiga suit in the United States, Stroessner attempted to settle the matter through Paraguayan-style diplomacy. "Among the senior government officials there was anger," Ambassador Robert White told me. "I mean true anger. Because in this case there was a plausible explanation, so why are you guys going after us? The fact that they were torturing and killing people all the time wasn't germane to their arguments. To them, it was like Al Capone getting convicted for income tax evasion.

"They really panicked," he laughed. "About once a month Stroessner's chief of staff, Conrado Papalardo, would invite me to lunch. We were relaxing in the back seat of his car after a great meal at the best French restaurant in Asunción, when he says, 'Robert, you just have to do everything possible to get the decision reversed.'

"'Conrado,' I told him, 'there's absolutely nothing I can do. The U.S. courts are independent.'

"'But you must,' he insisted, really upset by now. 'If the judgment is upheld, then no Paraguayan government figure will feel free to travel to Miami. Any one of us could be arrested for just even being in any state in the United States.'

"They were so smart," Bob mused, "and at the same time so dumb."

18

The press coverage of the Circuit Court's landmark ruling reinforced Stroessner's alarm. The following day, July 1, the *New York Times* quoted Peter's prediction that the decision would have the practical effect of eliminating the United States as "a safe haven for human rights violators from other countries."

Throughout these years, for the *Caso Filártiga*, the timing could hardly have been better. Reflecting the esteem accorded international human rights, in 1975 the imprisoned Soviet dissident Andrei Sakharov received the Nobel Peace Prize. Then, of course, in 1977 Amnesty International was awarded the same honor. And in 1980 the Nobel committee bestowed the prize upon Adolfo Pérez Esquivel, the persecuted Argentine human rights activist.

It was within this context that, during the following weeks, NGO press releases and articles provoked the first serious reaction from the opponents of the Circuit Court's ruling. The proponents of narrowly interpreting ATCA attacked the decision as intervening in the sovereignty of other nations. Entering the fray with its August 20 editorial—"Foreign Torture, American Justice"—the *New York Times* hailed the changing attitude of U.S. courts. "To critics of judicial imperialism," it declared, the Circuit Court ruling "may seem a presumptuous assertion of judicial power." Then, after presenting a review of *Filártiga v. Peña*, the editorial concluded, "but if American courts rejected such suits, they would only encourage malefactors, hoping to avoid accountability, to come here. It is to the oppressed that America should wish to give refuge."

19

But our legal process, as Peter had warned, allowed for a lot more maneuvering. The government of Paraguay could appeal the decision of the Appellate Court's three-judge panel to the full Circuit Court, and then on to the Supreme Court. Because of the extraordinarily strong opinion, however, that seemed doubtful. Rather, CCR thought it more likely that Stroessner's strategy would be to first fight it out back at the District Court. For, even if he lost there, he still then could appeal the lower court's ruling.

Even though the Appellate Court had settled the constitutionality of ATCA's juris-diction in *Filártiga v. Peña*, Nickerson's ruling left open several matters for the defense to argue. Were Peña's alleged crimes exempt under the Act of State doctrine—and if not, should he be judged using U.S. or Paraguayan law? Will the statute of limitations on torts bar prosecution? And then, of course, there still remained the big *forum non conveniens* question, whether the U.S. courts were a "convenient forum" to try Peña.

"The way I see it," Peter said, "the whole thing comes down to what happened that night. The factual issue is whether it was a crime of passion, as the regime claims, or an act of torture by Peña."

"And there's this blank spot in the evidence," Rhonda added. "We can show Joelito was dragged off to Peña's house. And his threats to Dolly that 'this can happen to you.' From which we can infer knowledge, even responsibility.

"But in court, we're going to have to prove not only that Peña tortured Joelito, but also that it was officially endorsed. That he was acting as an agent of the regime. Unlike slavery, private torture isn't a violation of international law."

"Yes, it is going to be a tremendous uphill fight," Peter acknowledged, "with con-tested facts of great complexity."

"And what about the witnesses?" Rhonda asked. "If we can't get them here for the trial, then the defense has a strong argument that our courts do not constitute a proper, convenient, forum. This isn't a criminal case where we can extradite Peña. For that matter, he doesn't even have to be present in court for a civil case. His lawyers can represent him at the proceedings."

"True enough," Peter said, "but we have the Filártigas' depositions detailing the government's persecution. Newspaper reports verifying the truth of their statements, everything from the imprisonment of Dolly and Nidia to the arrest and disbarment of Horacio Galeano Perrone. Along with the series of Amnesty and other NGO reports, there are the International League for Human Rights on-site reports condemning the regime's policy of gross human rights violations.

"And we have the record of the *Caso Filártiga* trial proceeding to present to the court," Peter went on. "Dr. Godoy's independent autopsy, the fact that Joelito died under professional torture, and all the other evidence contradicting the government's crime-of-passion tale. These documents are an official chronicle of how the regime has purposefully denied the Filártigas even the semblance of justice."

"Hell, a trial up here against one in Paraguay," Mike scowled. "That's like compar-ing apples and mangos."

"And this is a civil, not a criminal case," Peter said. "We are not required to prove guilt beyond a reasonable doubt. The standard in civil suits is that the preponderance of evidence supports our claim. So, yes, I think we can show that Peña, with the com-plicity of the government of Paraguay, denied Joelito his fundamental human rights by torturing him to death."

20

Two weeks after the U.S. Circuit Court's ruling in mid-July, the Paraguayan courts reversed the promised reconstruction of events; and in early August they rescinded yet another concession, prohibiting the introduction of new evidence in the *Caso Filártiga*.

With the case yet again mired down, Filártiga left the mess to his attorney and came to the States. Since the Appellate Court's historic decision, Filártiga's celebrity status had soared. Along with his usual exhibitions and lectures, now he gladly took the opportunity to reciprocate for CCR's support, which increasingly featured him at its fund-raising events.

On November 9, 1980, after spending three months touring the States, Filártiga was preparing to go home. Richard Claude, Joel, and I passed a few hours the afternoon before his flight the next day kicking around the new twists. Taking us all by surprise, Stroessner had decided not to contest the suit in the district court. Indeed, informed by Gorostiaga that Peña was unable to pay for further services, Murry Brochin had asked the court to withdraw from the case. On November 7 Judge Nickerson granted his request.

But of most immediate concern, with Stroessner retrenched into a hard line in the *Caso Filártiga* trial, once again, international pressure became our only effective weapon to restrain the regime. Suddenly Claude shook the room with an infuriated "I'll be damned." His indignation increased as he read us excerpts from that Sunday's *New York Times Magazine* article, "A Legal Remedy for International Torture?" by the Honorable Irving R. Kaufman.

Assuming the posture of a jurist-statesman, in his sweeping seven-page missive, Judge Kaufman pontificated on the course of jurisprudence in advancing international human rights through the history of western civilization. In protecting its own citizens, he explained, the English and American Bill of Rights eliminated the stamp of approval torture had enjoyed in ancient times.

Still, Kaufman observed, there prevailed "a deeply rooted, hands-off attitude" to confront human rights violations in other lands. Then, the Nazi horrors of World War II shocked the world into beginning the arduous task of incorporating human rights into international law. Yet, "despite the emergence of an international consensus condemning torture, the abominable practice remains with us."

But now, he went on to counsel, "What is important, however, is that the world-wide momentum on behalf of human rights be carried forward." Indeed, since for the first time the U.S. courts accepted jurisdiction in *Filártiga v. Peña*, Kaufman concluded that "where torture is concerned, on the state or international level, the Federal courts have no choice."

"That hypocritical weasel," Richard exclaimed. "Kaufman even gets in that he wrote the Circuit Court opinion. This is not the first time he publicly has taken credit for important decisions, as if he was behind it all the way, did it from the beginning. It's as if he's trying to make up for collaborating with the FBI in the Rosenberg trial."

"Yes. It was in that context that I first heard Kaufman's name," Joel said. "And lately I have learned much more about your government's domesticated judge. But of importance just now is the impact of this powerful article on international opinion, the added international pressure it will place on Stroessner.

"That is not to say I do not understand your anger at Kaufman's hypocrisy," Filártiga assured Claude. "It is hardly uncommon among those who in their hearts know what is right, but have pursued a career of opportunism. As they approach the end of life, often they seek redemption. Kaufman's eloquent defense of human rights is an attempt to save his soul."

"The repentance of a lickspittle," Richard grumbled.

21

Back home, Filártiga found his legal situation worse than ever. By November 1980, the Paraguayan Supreme Court had ruled against all his lawyer's appeals. Further, while sustaining the defense's motions by Gorostiaga—now supported by the state attorney, the prosecutor supposedly helping the Filártigas—the decisions came with an official warning that further action by Heriberto Alegre would be considered in contempt of court.

Concerned about the safety of his family, and convinced that there was no hope of justice in Paraguay, in early February 1981 Alegre resigned, yet again leaving the Filártigas without legal representation. Meanwhile, with the open collaboration of the courts, Gorostiaga, and the sell-out state attorney, the sham *Caso Filártiga* trial continued on its programmed course.

Undeterred by his failure with Ambassador White to quash the U.S. suit, and expecting that Joel by then had been beaten down, Stroessner proposed an extrajudicial solution of the troublesome matter. In early March, less than a month after Alegre's withdrawal, one of the dictator's top troubleshooters, Martínez Meza, arrived at the Sanatorio La Esperanza in Ybycuí.

"Dr. Filártiga," he began, once alone in the office. "I have come with an offer of comfort for you and your family. The government is under a lot of pressure and desires to find a solution for your situation. There were six people who killed Joelito, and we are prepared to deliver their corpses to you. All of them. We only ask that you drop the suit in the United States, and remain silent."

The more he talked, the more Filártiga wanted to know. Excitedly, he peppered Martínez Meza with questions. "Who are these people? How could I be sure they are the ones?"

"Because I was there. I saw."

"Where was Joelito killed? Investigaciones? The Sajonia police station?"

"I can't tell you that."

"Why were you there?"

"That also I am not at liberty to say. I swear that I did not personally harm your son, but I was one of the first to touch his corpse."

"I want the names. Who else besides Peña? Chief Domingo Galeano? The other police on duty that night in Sajonia? Crispulo Salcedo? Celcilio Torales? Díaz?"

"I can't tell you that either. But what I can assure you is that this world can be a beautiful place for you and your family. You only must stop everything here and in the United States. And the bodies of the men who killed Joelito will be brought to you. All of them. Here to Ybycuí. The death of your son will have been avenged. You can feel at peace."

For hours, Joel futilely pressed to learn something, anything, more about Joelito's murder. At last his rage passed.

"It is justice, not more deaths, that I want. And what you ask is impossible. No longer am I in control of what happens with the case in New York. It is out of my hands. Like feathers scattered to the wind cannot be gathered up one by one."

The wounded healers, this couple represents Joel and Nidia Filártiga
trying to comfort each other.

TWELVE

THREE MONTHS LATER, the Filártigas won their suit in the U.S. district court. Shortly after the Circuit Court's June 1980 decision, when it became clear that Stroessner would no longer fight the *Filártiga v. Peña* suit, the Center for Constitutional Rights filed a motion for default judgment with Judge Nickerson. For nearly a year, the government of Paraguay had refused any further participation in the proceeding, not even bothering to reply to the court's communications. On June 23, 1981, Nickerson granted the center's motion for a default judgment against Peña.

Nickerson's ruling left CCR both surprised and relieved. The default judgment of Peña's guilt meant the center would not have to fight a long, expensive, and always uncertain jury trial, especially with all the thorny legal hurdles that *Filártiga v. Peña* presented. "Frankly," as Peter Weiss confirmed, "nobody likes to litigate if they do not have to. So yes, we were pleased."

1

And then, Judge Nickerson did a most surprising thing. Instead of presiding over the damage hearing, he sent the case to Magistrate John L. Caden to determine the financial award due the Filártigas.

"What is he thinking about?" Rhonda Copelon asked Peter incredulously. "This is the biggest decision out of the Circuit for years, forever concerning international law. The most important case he's going to have. And usually judges want to be part of something like that, put their stamp on it.

"When we first went back to Nickerson, he was happy to see us," Rhonda said. "And he knows we hardly have any records, hard documents. It's all about the Filártigas' pain and suffering, and you can't just put dollars on that, like it's some malpractice damage hearing, settled on the medical bills.

"And now Nickerson is farming out the evidentiary hearing to a magistrate? Who's just a court-appointed lawyer whose function is to hear evidence, clear up the facts of a case. Instead of doing it himself? Weird."

"It is strange," Peter agreed. "Almost as if he is somehow distracted. Treating the damage award like it is perfunctory."

"And it's not perfunctory," Rhonda retorted. "It's our chance to make a statement. We want a full court hearing, not something sloughed off to some magistrate that'll get less attention from the press.

"It's an important piece of the educational process," she insisted. "It's the most profound human aspect of the case, the first time that Dr. Filártiga and Dolly are really going to tell their story."

"I don't understand it either," Peter said. "But it's up to us to see that the Filártigas get their chance to speak. And be heard."

2

Reacting to the *Filártiga v. Peña* victory in the U.S. courts, Stroessner retaliated through the *Caso Filártiga* trial in Paraguay. Perhaps encouraged by the Reagan administration's foreign policy deemphasizing human rights, ten days after Nickerson's default judgment—on July 3, 1981—the Paraguayan state attorney informed the court that the evidence failed to support the Filártigas' claim that Joelito's death involved more than one person.

Hugo Duarte alone was responsible for killing Joelito, Stroessner's obedient prosecutor declared. Upon finding his wife committing adultery, Duarte suffered "an explosion of nerves that night, making him lose control over himself." Therefore, since his action was justified under Penal Code 7, all charges should be dismissed and Duarte set free.

Even without the Filártigas' own legal representation to contest this farce, it took several months for Paraguay's ponderous judiciary to issue its final decision. On September 10, the court dismissed all charges against the coconspirators Américo Peña, Juana Villalba, and her two sons Nery and Jorge. Further, accepting the cuckold husband defense, Duarte was absolved of all responsibility for killing Joelito and released from the National Penitentiary. And finally, the ruling ordered Dr. Filártiga to pay all court costs.

And as if all this were not enough, the regime leapfrogged the legal proceedings in the States. The next day, September 11, Gorostiaga filed a civil suit on behalf of Hugo Duarte who, although spending five years in prison, had never been convicted of any crime. It took but one week for Stroessner's court to award 5 million guaraníes, worth about $31,000, in damages for the slander and defamation of character that Duarte had suffered because of the *Caso Filártiga* criminal trial.

While a body blow to the Filártigas' struggle, Stroessner's legal persecution did not quite mark an end of the *Caso Filártiga* legal battle. Given the dictatorship's traditional legalism, Paraguay's judicial process allowed the Filártigas the right to appeal. But to carry on the legal fight, they needed independent representation of their own. During the following months, however, the Filártigas could find no lawyer willing to take the case.

And then more pressing matters demanded Joel's attention.

3

In mid-January 1982, Joel arrived in New York to prepare for Magistrate Caden's damage hearing. Already, the CCR team had mounted a campaign soliciting additional amicus briefs, affidavits, and letters, and they had lined up several expert witnesses to testify at the evidentiary proceedings.

By then Dolly had been adopted into the center's family, even taking a part-time secretarial job in Peter's office to work more closely with the team. CCR's public relations officer, the Spanish-speaking David Lerner, made a special effort to watch over her, and in many ways filled in as Dolly's friend and confidant for Mike Maggio, whose legal practice required him to spend most of his time in Washington.

While preparing Dolly for her testimony, Rhonda was impressed by her near total recall. During the sessions, though, Rhonda also saw Dolly's great emotional distress, how incredibly painful it was for her to relive the events in Paraguay. They worried if she could hold up telling her story in court.

If Dolly was volatile, Joel was like a stone. He just could not talk about what happened, replying to Rhonda's questions about his feelings with the most laconic, even one-word, answers. "It's as if I'm not even in the room," she told Peter. "He isn't preparing for court. Rather it's all between him and Stroessner. He won't open up, let it out, admit that Stroessner has gotten to him."

A few days before the hearing, Rhonda took Joel and Dolly to talk with Jacobo Timerman, the former Argentine newspaper publisher. After being arrested and tortured for his crusading campaign against the dictatorship's human rights violations, Timerman had spent years in prison until international pressure forced his release.

For hours in the New York hotel room, Jacobo and Dolly carried on a dynamic, enlightening exchange. "A lot of people who have been tortured can't live together any more after that, with their families," Jacobo said. "Everything has been destroyed, the relations with my sons, with my wife; there is something, always something, between us."

"Yes," Dolly replied excitedly, "it's just like that." And she went on to tell him similar experience of her own.

In contrast, Joel remained all but frozen as he sat in a corner chair. Maintaining his stoicism, when Timerman would try to bring him into the conversation, Filártiga answered only with curt, almost hostile, replies.

More concerned than ever about Joel's testimony, to demonstrate the depth of his pain, the center put together a presentation of Filártiga's art and poetry as exhibits to present to the court.

4

Peter was in Washington on another CCR case involving the burning to death of a young man, the same age as Joelito, by the Chilean dictatorship. So Rhonda and Mike handled the evidentiary hearing at the Magistrate's Courtroom in Brooklyn on the morning of February 12, 1982. David Lerner had done his job. Among the audience were a number of reporters. Not long after the proceeding began, it struck Rhonda that the Honorable John Caden's attitude did not make sense.

She had thought there would be some spark of excitement at having such an important case. But nothing. Nothing. Caden was totally phlegmatic; as Rhonda put it, "a very cold fish."

Not even the affidavits from psychologists specializing in torture victims, detailing the post-traumatic stress disorder that explained the Filártiga family's continual emotional suffering, seemed to have any effect on Caden. Unmoved, the magistrate treated it all matter-of-factly, like an everyday car accident case.

Dolly held up for a half hour. Prompted by Rhonda, she told of the horror of finding Joelito and being forced to carry his body home, of the death threats, of her and Nidia's arrest; and of how the family could not emotionally comfort each other because they were all going through the same thing. But it was while explaining how she could not believe Joelito was really dead, how for the next year she kept waiting for him, hearing his voice in the house, that Dolly broke down.

Rhonda asked for a short break before continuing. But Caden wanted to move on, sending Dolly to his chambers to relax for a while.

5

As the official transcripts reveal, Joel set the tone of his testimony with Mike's opening question. Asked to identify himself, he answered, "I am a medical doctor, artist, and poet. I am a permanent opponent to the dictatorial regime."

Filártiga went on establishing his credentials by describing his treatment of torture victims and relating in detail the times he had been tortured and forced to watch others being tortured. Asked what thoughts most lingered about his experience, he described his feelings when arrested and brought to Investigaciones headquarters in downtown Asunción.

"It is a sensation of being tremendously isolated, a sensation of sudden fear, the feeling of being a prisoner. And thinking of all the people walking by the police building. There were seventy or eighty of us in there, and that night ten were tortured. And the same the next night, another ten. And the people passing by did not know what was going on in that place, unaware of the criminality of the regime."

"You mentioned that you had intimate discussions with Joelito about the dangers of opposing the dictatorship," Mike prompted Joel.

"I told him that I was living in a state of permanent depression and of permanent fear for myself and for the family. And that if you are taken by the police don't lie. Don't say anything because you do not know anything. But don't lie. Because one lie brings another, and they will know it is not true and keep going."

Maggio then led Filártiga through a lengthy explanation of what happened upon learning of Joelito's death; racing to Asunción to find his son's mutilated body being washed by relatives; Nidia's collapse; and taking photos of Joelito's wounds, which he recognized as professional torture. "The first thing I thought was I know what happened, but how could I make the world know what happened?"

"Did you institute legal proceedings in Paraguay to try to obtain justice?"

"The death of my son was suffering. But trying to obtain justice in Paraguay is another suffering in itself. It would be something like reading *The Trial* by Franz Kafka. That is Paraguayan justice. It is something without end. It is a machine that grinds down people psychologically."

Filártiga then went on to describe the endless legal obstacles and drawn-out proceedings; the disappearance of Charo, the key witness; the harassment of his lawyers; and the recent court decisions absolving Duarte and the others, as well as the civil judgment against him.

Switching gears, Mike held up one of the exhibits—a drawing by Joel depicting a man and a woman in a clutching embrace, crying, with screws drilled into their hearts—and asked, who are these people?

"They represent my wife and myself. Giving to each other as much consolation as we are able. Fighting the pain of our isolation, of our powerlessness."

As Joel spoke, Rhonda, Michael, and Dolly glanced back and forth at each other in awe. Everyone had been worried about how Joel would come across. From the beginning of his testimony, he had opened up his most intimate feelings; saying things he had never said before, in words no one had ever heard from him. At long last, this is his day in court, Rhonda realized, to tell his story to an impartial tribunal, and he is doing it with an eloquence that no one had anticipated.

"What has been the effect on you and the relationship with your family?"

"Life has changed completely for me. And I have terrible guilt feelings about my responsibility for the death of my son. Frequently my wife has become hostile to me, seeing me as perhaps a monster who is perhaps guilty for the death of our son. Many times she has threatened to leave me, to come here and live with my daughter Dolly, who also unconsciously blames me for Joelito's death.

"I have tried to rebuild my life. Right after Joelito's murder, I felt a little suicidal—and homicidal. Regardless of my being a medical doctor, I felt within me a desire to kill. It took two years fighting with myself to recover from these disorders, to accept that it was not the right way to seek justice. And now here I am, in this room, trying to continue the struggle."

6

Rhonda asked to recall Dolly, but Caden called the next witness, Jacobo Timerman. The former newspaper editor and political prisoner had caused an international sensation with his bestseller *Prisoner Without a Name, Cell Without a Number*—a brutally honest account of his imprisonment and its impact on his life that had been published in thirteen languages. Currently spending a semester at Princeton University's Institute for Advanced Studies, Timerman was still a man shaken to the core of his being. To concretely establish his credentials, Rhonda wanted Jacobo to relate to the court the torture he had suffered during the years he spent in Argentine prisons.

"Why don't we start with your experience—"

"I think we can only have so much of that in one day," Caden interrupted. "I prefer not to have the witness tell us about his personal experiences."

Working around the magistrate's preference, Rhonda brought Jacobo back to his ordeal. "Once you have been tortured," he said, "torture is with you forever. And there is nothing you can do about it. It is pain and humiliation. But more than that, the moment you are tortured, and the days after torture, and the years after torture, they have changed your human condition. It is a biological change. Your feelings are different. Your relation with the rest of humanity is different.

"And now, I still, after two years, having written a book and having the support of my family and my sons, friends, human rights institutions, and many people all over the world, I still cannot accept that it happened. I couldn't be an editor. I haven't the strength to be an editor. I couldn't go back to the man I used to be."

"From your experience," Rhonda asked, "what can you say about the impact of torture on society as a whole?"

"The incorporation of torture into a society or civilization means that there is somebody, many people, who believe they have in their hands an instrument to discover everything they want, to obtain anything they want to obtain.

"They act like God because they have the power not only to kill you. That is nothing, because to kill is a power that is in the hands of every human being. They have a bigger power to torture and to discover, find out, and change everything they want to do. And this is the danger.

"The moment torture is incorporated to a society as routine, a fixed feature of life, a permanent instrument—the moment you accept that, you haven't changed society, you have changed civilization."

7

After lunch, the court swore in the last witness, former ambassador Robert White. During the final year of Carter's presidency, Bob had left Paraguay to become ambassador to El Salvador. However, due to fundamental policy differences in that trouble spot, in early 1981 the Reagan administration forced his resignation from the Foreign Service. As the controversy exploded in the media, Bob employed his position as senior associate at the Carnegie Endowment for International Peace to speak out against Washington's hard line in Central America. Indeed, in the United States, White's celebrity—or notoriety, depending on one's politics—approached that of Timerman.

"Could General Stroessner's regime survive if it did not employ torture?" Rhonda asked him.

"No. That's what keeps the government in place. Torture is basic to the overall repression. It's at the heart of the system that enables the Stroessner dictatorship to maintain itself in power.

"Really, it's something routine. I mean perfectly normal people, who appear normal, get up and go to work. And their work is torture. And then they come home after work and do whatever normal people do."

"Beyond the direct victims, what is the effect of torture?"

"Well, there is almost no one in Paraguay who hasn't been touched by torture, in the sense that either they or someone in their family has been tortured. This is true in the upper class. And if it's true there, where people have connections and so forth, you can imagine what it's like in the countryside, where people are poor and illiterate.

"These people don't torture for the fun of it. It goes in waves, depending upon the pressures on the government. Mostly, they torture when it is necessary. And if you torture for a certain period, you cow the people. Then you no longer . . . it is institution-alized in Paraguay."

Rhonda steered Bob's testimony around to the *Caso Filártiga* in Paraguay, and the central question facing Caden. The amount of the Filártigas' award, and therefore in good part the strength of the message *Filártiga v. Peña* would send to other international human rights violators, depended upon the Magistrate's Choice of Law decision.

Paraguayan law permits damages to compensate for expenses incurred by the victims. And though there are provisions for pain and suffering, these so-called "moral damages" can never be punitive. U.S. law, however, allows not only for compensatory damages but also punitive damages. So the Filártigas could be awarded the suit's $10 million claim only if Caden chose to apply U.S., and not Paraguayan, law in determining the settlement.

"Did you become engaged with Dr. Filártiga while you were ambassador in Paraguay?"

"We became very interested in the Filártiga case from the first month I was there," White made clear. "Not only because of our human rights mandate under the Carter administration. But also because we were deluged with letters from the United States after every trip that Dr. Filártiga made here. We would get letters from university professors, human rights organizations, and just ordinary citizens, senators, congressmen, and others, in effect saying, please do everything you can to protect Dr. Filártiga."

"Is there an independent judiciary under Stroessner?" she asked.

"No. Total power belongs to the president. In issues in which the government is interested, there is total arbitrariness. The only law is the law that the president decides upon. There, in effect, is no law."

"What role do you think that civil remedies for victims of torture, as we here in this court, might play in the overall effort to stop torture?"

"Well, the only thing that Paraguay responds to is international pressure. Traditionally, the Stroessner regime has survived pressures by not responding to them, by postponing action, by waiting things out. But international pressure is the only way."

Ambassador White then went on to relate the pathetic attempt by Stroessner's chief of staff to get him to reverse the Circuit Court's *Filártiga v. Peña* decision; the panic among government officials that they could be arrested simply by being in the States.

"Based upon your knowledge of the system," Rhonda concluded, "in your opinion can the Filártigas get justice in Paraguay?"

"No. It is impossible."

8

"Dolly," Rhonda began when she resumed her questioning, "I want to turn your attention back to the period after your brother was killed. I want you to tell the court about the dreams that you began having during that period."

"Why don't we go on to something else?" Magistrate Caden suggested.

Again, skirting the court's discomfort with "pain and suffering" testimony, Rhonda led Dolly through the trauma of seeking political asylum, and her continuing fears of reprisals against her family in Paraguay.

"Do you still want to be a doctor?"

"No. My life has changed a lot. Seeing my father and the work he does, I think I may not be prepared to handle more pain."

Noting her need for continuing therapy, Rhonda asked how she felt in social situations, with other people?

Much as Timerman had discussed with the Filártigas during their visit—how he would hide in his room for days at a time, avoiding social interaction—Dolly said, "I feel different to others . . . times when all I want is to be alone."

"How about normal activities like reading? Can you read? Can you do things like that?"

"I cannot concentrate."

"How often do you think of your brother?"

"Always."

"Do you feel you'll ever be free of that?"

"I think that only if I could be brainwashed."

9

Realizing that again Dolly had reached the verge of tears, and gauging Caden's demeanor, Rhonda figured she had pushed it enough. Because she had been unable to take Dolly through reliving the most painful and devastating period following Joelito's death, Rhonda requested that Dolly be permitted to finish her testimony by way of an affidavit.

Caden readily agreed. In her May 17 affidavit, Dolly recounted her recurring dream, denying Joelito's death that night when she was brought to her brother's body. "I dream that Joelito is rising from the blood-soaked mattress upon which I found him with all his wounds and that he is telling me that nothing happened. I wake up screaming." In a classic symptom of survivor's guilt, Dolly told how she then would spend the next hours asking herself why, instead of Joelito, they had not taken her.

Wrapping up the damage hearing, Caden suggested that CCR also send him other relevant materials, "especially with regard to the applicable law. Because it seems to me one of the more difficult problems this case poses is not so much the testimony of the witnesses and what occurred, but assuming for a moment the law that applies in this case is the law of Paraguay. That seems to me to pose some interesting legal problems."

Rhonda assured the court that they would include an affidavit from a Paraguayan legal expert, to help in the Choice of Law question. However, because CCR thought the suit should be determined under international law, she said, "that's what we will address in our memorandum."

"That's the $64 question," Caden replied.

"That's right," Rhonda agreed.

"Okay. This hearing is closed," the magistrate declared. And then, indicating Joel's drawings, Caden added, "Please take all of these exhibits back."

10

Regardless of Caden's acerbic attitude, for Dolly and Joel, testifying at the hearing offered them the moment of most profound fulfillment: not only in the *Filártiga v. Peña* suit, but in all the years of the *Caso Filártiga* struggle. Rhonda—struck by the depth of the Filártigas' moving testimony—witnessed Dolly and Joel's sense of vindication with tremendous satisfaction.

"After six years of fighting Stroessner's crushing legal apparatus, at last the Filártigas had their day in court, an honest court of law," she told me later. "Every once in a while there is something mystical about lawsuits. And I felt it happen most dramatically for Dr. Filártiga. His testimony, letting down his guard, was an emotional catharsis. By opening the floodgates and revealing his most intimate feelings, he came to terms with a critical piece of the struggle—his intense personal anguish of despair and impotence."

After the hearing that Friday night, they all went out for a drink. Joel, Mike, Rhonda, and several other CCR staff members tried to cheer up the still-shaken Dolly, who felt she had failed the team by breaking down. Everyone assured her that she could not have come across more effectively; the torment she expressed powerfully showed the trauma caused by the persecution of her and the family. Soon, Dolly's self-criticism abated, allowing her also to feel the emotional purge of testifying.

It was Joel's irrepressible elation, however, that dominated the gathering. "Never had I seen Filártiga so gay, so happy," Rhonda exclaimed. "And he was so proud. It was like a ton of bricks came off his shoulders. If you ask me how old he was, it was maybe five or six when the hearing was over. It was an amazing, wonderful thing."

Rhonda's insight into the "mystical" force of some lawsuits would soon gain concrete confirmation. In the coming decades, thousands of human rights victims testified before truth commissions in Argentina, El Salvador, South Africa, and more than a dozen other nations. No longer crushed by the despair of governments that suffocated all hope of justice, for the first time people had the opportunity to air their suffering before an authentically impartial tribunal. Like the partial closure the Filártigas felt after Caden's hearing, by openly bringing their stories before the world in a public forum, the truth tribunal victims attained an even greater comfort—for the moral vindication they gained went a long way in lifting the overwhelming burden of helplessness they carried.

As a grateful Dr. Filártiga put it after his testimony: "Finally, somebody listened."

11

Recounting the highlights of Timerman and White's testimonies, the next day the *New York Times* gave a strong account of how the witnesses "graphically told a hushed Brooklyn Court yesterday how Paraguayan authorities use torture tactics to crush dissent."

Virtually every article probed into the $10 million damage claim. The Filártigas held no illusions of collecting the award, David Lerner told the *Times*; for them, money had never been a major consideration in the suit. Rather, as Mike Maggio explained to the *Daily News*, they sought such a large amount "as a public renunciation of torture."

Joel had intended a six-week visit, but the news from Paraguay persuaded him to prolong his stay. Since intimidating Alegre into dropping the *Caso Filártiga*, nothing could be done to hinder Stroessner's courts from absolving Duarte and the coconspirators and from imposing the $31,000 award against the Filártigas. For the past year, it seemed to the dictatorship that all was under control.

Then, in late February 1982, Nidia convinced their neighbor, the eccentric attorney Julio Regis Cabrera, to take the case. With little hope, he filed the automatic appeal of Duarte's and the coconspirators' criminal acquittal. And, appealing the civil judgment, he pointed out that Filártiga never leveled any accusations against Duarte and did not even believe his confession that he killed Joelito; therefore, Cabrera argued, the *Caso Filártiga* could not be considered "malicious," as required under Paraguayan law to prove "slander and defamation."

The whole Filártiga mess burst back onto the front page. Fed by the international wire services' accounts of the Caden hearing, the Asunción press prominently reported the accusations of the witnesses "defaming the Fatherland," only to be followed by widespread coverage of Cabrera's appeals opposing the *Caso Filártiga* decisions.

Infuriated, the dictatorship attacked Dr. Filártiga's life's work. During several burglaries at the clinic, the vandals stole stores of medications and destroyed medical equipment, leaving the Sanatorio la Esperanza unable to function. As rumors spread that the government planned to seize the clinic to pay the damage award to Duarte, Nidia took to hiding the remaining medicines and equipment at the homes of friends.

But most frightening of all, as Nidia warned Joel on the phone, Stroessner intended to drive Dr. Filártiga into permanent exile. Informed by an opposition congressman as well as several sympathetic government officials that Joel would be arrested the moment he set foot in Paraguay, Nidia pleaded with her husband not to come back.

Hoping that in time things would calm down, Joel postponed his return.

12

As the reports of Stroessner's threats increased, the NGOs and local support networks mobilized. Arranging further appearances for Joel, their requests that messages be sent to high-ranking officials at State—especially Secretary of State Alexander Haig—along with the Paraguayan ambassador in Washington and directly to Stroessner in Paraguay, met with an overwhelming response.

On top of letters from members of Congress, countless more arrived from individuals, from the ACLU to the Maryknoll Justice and Peace Office, from Amnesty-USA to Americas Watch, from WOLA to COHA, and many, many others.

Ever more frequently accompanied by Dolly, Joel carried on a demanding schedule at East Coast universities and other institutions, such as the Albert Einstein Medical College in the Bronx and Brooklyn's Saint James Cathedral. Moreover, CCR sent out direct mail solicitations, along with sponsoring fundraising receptions with patrons in Manhattan and the Hamptons.

"Filártiga is a wonderful presence and performer," David Lerner explained, "totally inspiring. Speaking like a poet, he often brought people to tears. They wanted to help, do something, like give money, write letters, collect medicines, go down there."

While Joel appreciated the measure of protection such an international campaign provided, he well knew that it offered no guarantee against Stroessner. Still, the idea of remaining here in safety was not an option. Following his exhibition and lectures at Yale Law School, the *Hartford Courant* asked him why, in the face of such persecution, he was so determined to go back.

"Dignity," Joel answered with disarming simplicity, "I am not a delinquent. The government of Paraguay is."

13

Frequently, Dolly and Joel gave joint appearances. And invariably, it was Dr. Filártiga who commanded the limelight. Even though the follow-up press coverage usually included a quote or two from Dolly, always the articles centered upon Joel. As the focus of the campaign moved to Washington, however, Dolly emerged from the shadow of her charismatic father.

Perhaps realizing that upon his return the weight of carrying on the campaign would fall upon his daughter, Filártiga took the second seat while Dolly gave the major presentation at the Antioch Law School reception on March 23.

"It is Dolly's turn to relate her brother's torture and murder," the *Washington Post* journalist Carla Hall began her feature article. "She stands in the center of the room and recites the details: the 1976 abduction of Joelito in Stroessner's police state, being brought to the police inspector's house where she found his mutilated corpse, ordered to 'Take your brother's body away, because if you don't we'll throw it in the street.'

"She interlocks her fingers in front of her, wringing her hands in confusion. Around her, plates of cheese and crackers set out on tables for the reception wilt in the stuffy room. Dolly Filártiga smiles wanly. She doesn't want to go on and starts to cry again. The audience applauds her fervently. Her father, physician Joel Filártiga, stands calmly next to her as they are given a plaque from the law school honoring them for their human rights work."

The *Post's* article—"In Paraguay, a Death in the Family: Dolly Filártiga's Crusade for Human Rights"—goes on to illuminate why "the brunt of the speaking, the explaining, the criticizing of the Paraguayan government for what they feel it has done to them and others' lives falls on the shoulders of the father and his oldest daughter.

"'We don't want them to have to do it,' says Dolly Filártiga of her younger sisters, aged eighteen and twenty-one, both married. 'We don't want them to go through it all. They are so little. We want them to have a different life.'"

The account of the landmark *Filártiga v. Peña* suit, "an action that has made legal history," led into the damage award. From the beginning, Dolly explained, the family held no expectations of collecting any monetary compensation.

"At this point it is publicity that they seek for their cause," the *Post* article made clear, "publicity that Joel Filártiga can wear as a protective mantle against further reprisals."

14

The day after their Antioch reception, WOLA arranged for Dolly and Joel to speak with a group of congressional aides. By 1982, of course, human rights had lost ground in U.S. foreign policy. In fact, returning to anticommunist realpolitik, the previous year the Reagan administration had channeled over $6 million in U.S. economic aid to Stroessner.

Even so, the high-profile *Caso Filártiga* was something of an exception, a matter to be handled with extreme caution. On April 2, WOLA's efforts produced a strong letter of support signed by twenty-four members of Congress. Even though "President Reagan has determined that Paraguay is no longer a gross violator of human rights," the legislators warned Stroessner, "should Dr. Filártiga or his family be harmed or jailed upon his return to Paraguay, it would bring into question that determination by the Reagan Administration."

By then, the campaign had wound up to high gear. Letters flooded the U.S. and Paraguayan governments. And on top of everything else, Amnesty's London Secretariat did its customarily spectacular job on the wider international level. Even before Joel returned, and for weeks after, letters of solidarity poured in from Holland, Sweden, Turkey, New Zealand—indeed, from all corners of the world—expressing to Stroessner their concern for Filártiga's safety.

Among the contingent of well-wishers who had come to see Joel off at JFK Airport on April 8 were several reporters. The *Daily News* article—"A Healer in a Wounded Land"—told how everyone was "struck by the courage of this man who was returning to his country in spite of threats he would be arrested, knowing that he stands a good chance of being submitted—as he has been in the past—to questioning by the torture squads of General Alfredo Stroessner."

For, as Filártiga remarked as he boarded the flight home, "If I don't return, then it is a victory for terror."

15

Evidently, the intense international pressure had an effect on Stroessner. Met at the airport by his family and the U.S. consul who escorted them home, without further harassment Dr. Filártiga resumed his work at the Ybycuí and Asunción clinics.

Most noticeably absent at Joel's departure from New York was Dolly. For years she had been adopted as a member of the CCR family. From the legal secretaries to Peter and Rhonda—for whom she had a touch of hero worship—everyone at the center had taken her in. Dolly found companionship and encouragement at CCR, mixing with the staff during coffee breaks, joining them for an evening of dancing and a few drinks.

But, beginning with her testimony at the Caden hearing in February 1982, things began to change. And with her presentations at Antioch and before the congressional aides in Washington, Dolly gained strength and confidence, and the conviction to become more deeply involved.

"I've remained covered up for a long time," Dolly had told her friend David Lerner, CCR's publicity officer, when they had returned to New York. "Since I came here in 1978. Maybe because I really wanted to just forget, or insecurity and not knowing what to do. I don't care. I could have done much more. And now I see that I can, that I must do more. Especially, now that Papi will soon return to Paraguay."

"What do you have in mind?" David asked.

"Something more useful than being a part-time clerk for Peter, or working in a clothing store just to survive. I want to become more active, maybe give talks on my own."

Within the week, Dolly was in southern California on her inaugural solo speaking tour.

16

On Monday April 5, Dolly gave her first address to the UCLA School of Law; her two talks the next day at the Loyola Law School and Amnesty's journalists chapter sharpened her presentation; and by Wednesday, when she delivered her speech at Southwestern Law School, she had it down, coming across as an accomplished and persuasive advocate. No longer did Dolly display any awkwardness as she spoke, or when handing out the prepared telegram and letter-writing campaign information. Readily, Dolly pushed through her rounds of fundraisers, private receptions, and press interviews.

The April 28 *Los Angeles Times* above-the-fold piece, "A 6-Year Quest for Justice: Paraguayan Dolly Filártiga Pursues a Killer"—reprinted nationwide through the *Washington Post / Los Angeles Times* wire service—was a major media coup. This extraordinary feature article went on for 3,600 words relating the Filártigas' struggle.

Unabashedly plugging the international campaign for Dr. Filártiga's safety, the article told its readers of Dolly's request that "politically worded" letters be sent "to General Stroessner, the U.S. Embassy in Asunción, your congressional representatives and the State Department demanding the cutoff of U.S. economic and military aid to Paraguay."

Probing Dolly's feelings toward Peña, who by then had returned from Brazil and was working as a bodyguard for a highly placed government official, the reporter asked her about Joelito's murderer: "'I hate Peña,' her reply came without hesitation. Yet she does not want to see him die—'I don't think that giving back to him what he did to my brother is a good thing.'" Instead, "In his comfortable middle age, she would like to 'make him work for the peasants' of Paraguay."

In the coming years, along with her frequent fundraising and speaking engagements, Dolly kept CCR abreast of events in Paraguay. As Rhonda later explained to me: "Dolly had an important part to play, and she played it well. She knew what was happening every step of the way. From this time, Dolly remained engaged, a tremendous force in the process."

Throughout it all, the center remained her anchor, a true second home. "I think without that," Dolly later reflected, "I would have been unable to live."

17

By the end of 1982, CCR had submitted to Magistrate Caden all the supporting documentation. As expected, the affidavit by the Paraguayan civil law expert, Alejando Miguel Garro, confirmed that though the Filártigas were eligible for compensatory damages, under Paraguayan law they could only recover "moral damages;" such as for physical pain, mental suffering, and the loss of companionship. In cases involving particularly heinous crimes causing the plaintiffs exceptional pain and suffering, however, the monetary award could be increased—but never as a means to punish the defendant; that is, Paraguayan law did not permit punitive damages.

CCR's brief included a compensatory damage claim of $439,734 for the costs of Joelito's funeral, loss of income, and the Filártigas' past and future medical and legal expenses. The $10 million punitive damage award sought in *Filártiga v. Peña*, however, all depended on the court's Choice of Law. And that meant CCR not only had to persuade Caden that Joelito's death was an act of government sanctioned torture, but also that there could be no fair redress for the Filártigas under Paraguayan law.

As a key part of its argument, among other NGO documents, the center included the 1980 International League for Human Rights' report *Mbareté: The Higher Law of Paraguay*. In his accompanying affidavit, the Reverend William Wipfler, one of the two experts who conducted the on-site investigation, explained that the Guaraní word *mbareté* meant "superior power over others," the unwritten code assigning rank and influence within the hierarchy of power; superior to any and all norms postulated by the judiciary, it was the highest law in Paraguay. Presenting the sham *Caso Filártiga* trial as a prime example of institutionalized torture in Paraguay, Wipfler concluded that, when *mbareté* clashes with the legal system, it is the courts that must, and do, give way.

The CCR brief followed up by stating that Stroessner's judiciary precluded any chance of justice; particularly in the *Caso Filártiga* because Peña "has escaped all sanction in Paraguay, being immunized by the system of *mbareté* from criminal as well as civil liability." Furthermore, it emphasized that while the Paraguayan Constitution and Penal Codes explicitly ban torture, the prohibition of punitive damages "does not satisfy the unusually strong interest of the international community in explicitly penalizing the torturer given his status as *hostis humani generis*."

As part of U.S. common law under the Constitution, their brief reminded the magistrate, ATCA provided jurisdiction in *Filártiga v. Peña*. Even so, the primary interest of the United States was not in applying its own law in the suit. For the demands of the community of nations—universally concurring that torture is absolutely forbidden and that its practice violates international law—cannot be met by the mere application of the law of one or another nation-state having an interest in the matter.

Rather, the paramount consideration of the United States was to ensure that international wrongs were properly redressed in our courts, in accordance with the principles of international law. For precisely this reason, CCR's brief requested that Caden employ U.S. law and impose punitive damages; for, guided by the intentions of the community of nations to express their outrage and deter future offenses, his decision would reinforce the principles of international law.

18

"It's almost incomprehensible," Rhonda told Dolly and Peter, "but Caden completely rejected our argument and based his ruling entirely on Paraguayan law, and in the tightest possible way." That morning, May 13, 1983, the court had sent the center a copy of the Magistrate's *Report and Recommendations* prepared for Judge Nickerson. Caden not only denied any punitive damages, but had cut the compensatory damages to $375,000.

"The way it breaks down," Rhonda read from the report, "is he granted $150,000 each to Joel and Dolly for their emotional pain and suffering, loss of companionship, and disruption of family life. Then he added $50,000 for Joel's funeral-related and medical expenses, and loss of income. And $25,000 for Dolly's future medical and psychiatric treatment. That's it."

"But what of Joelito's suffering," Dolly asked, "when they tortured him?"

"Here Caden cites Gorostiaga's 1979 affidavit to the Circuit Court," Rhonda said, "'that Paraguayan law permits no recovery for the decedent's own pain and suffering.'"

"What about all the money the criminal trial has cost Papi?" Dolly persisted. "And the civil award for Duarte?"

"Caden says all that is irrelevant," Rhonda answered. "He dismissed these claims because, like Nidia's suffering and medical expenses, they were not part of our original complaint to Nickerson."

"He not only ruled against our claim for legal fees," Peter noted, "on the grounds that CCR was representing the case pro bono. Caden even rejected the Filártigas' request for compensation to cover their costs of pursuing the case in the States—airfare and telephone calls to and from Paraguay, their housing, and other expenditures."

"But they found Peña in Brooklyn," Rhonda protested. "Joel and Nidia had to come, they were essential to the trial proceedings!"

"Of course," Peter agreed. "Even so, he found 'no merit whatsoever in their claim.'"

Getting deeper into the magistrate's report, Peter soon uncovered the reasoning behind the "hands-off" decision. "Look here. The old curmudgeon is still caught up in the traditional narrow interpretation of the Alien Tort Claims Act. He is worried about the Parade of Horribles. Comes right out and says the application of Paraguayan law 'would prevent U.S. citizens from being tried abroad.'" Reading on a bit, Peter found Caden's other major objection in employing U.S. law in our courts to settle *Filártiga v. Peña*. "And here is the 'floodgate' canard. 'Furthermore,' Caden says that should punitive damages be granted, 'such an award would be contrary to our own policy against forum shopping.'"

"That's preposterous, completely unfounded by the facts," Rhonda retorted. "Dolly came to escape harassment, possible imprisonment, and torture, not to file a suit—never mind shopping around for a sympathetic court to hear it. And Peña certainly didn't come here to be sued. And besides, the Circuit Court's decision said that torts are transitory, that a defendant such as Peña can be sued wherever he may be served."

"But the Appellate Court's ruling did allow some wiggle room," Peter reflected, "leaving it up to Nickerson to decide if 'fairness' might require application of Paraguayan law. And that is what Caden latched on to. He claims that the injury occurred in Paraguay, both the defendant and plaintiffs were Paraguayans, and the only U.S. connection being that Peña was sued here."

Peter and Rhonda tried to comfort Dolly, pointing out that even without punitive damages, by Paraguayan standards, the award represented an enormous settlement. In reality, though, they were outraged and began preparing their arguments against Caden's recommendations to present to Judge Nickerson.

19

"Ay Papi, it makes me nauseous," Nidia sobbed when Joel told her of Caden's $375,000 award. "It will burn my hands. Even if they left Joelito mutilated, in a wheelchair, at least I would have my son."

The idea that money, any amount of money, could somehow make up for the loss of Joelito caused the fury of her mother's anguish to lash out.

"Richard failed me," Nidia cried.

"You must not judge Richard," Joel replied. "He did everything he could."

"No, he betrayed me," she raged, "because he had in his hands the man who destroyed my son's life. He could have liquidated Peña. Nobody would have known who did it. Nobody would find out. And now Peña is back again. What happened to Richard, that he didn't cause any damage to him? Explain it to me, because I can't understand it."

In the privacy of their bedroom, the couple lay down together. And as they shared a bottle of beer, Joel told Nidia that he would try to explain what happened, that one day she would see how it was.

"At first, I wanted to kill Peña. When we first found him, before Peña was arrested, we discussed what to do. Dolly, Richard, and I thought about it a lot. Very seriously. And we decided it was better this way.

"Last year," Joel said, "I went to the Georgetown University Library with Professor Claude. This was after we won the appeal, just before I came back in April. He put 'Filártiga and human rights' into the computer, and the screen filled with a long list of articles about the case. And not just from newspapers. Publicity is important to keep the case before the public, to raise consciousness and support."

Nidia glared at him.

"Yes *querida*, you are right," Joel soothed her. "Money can never be a compensation for Joelito. But seeing all those scholarly articles in professional journals. How our case condemned torturers like Peña as international criminals. I knew for sure we had made the right decision. It is greater than we hoped, when we did not kill Peña. And this is just the beginning. We are changing international law. It will help keep other young people from dying like Joelito."

"No. Richard failed me," Nidia said. "It is a mistake to let Peña live, because he will still have his moments of happiness."

"He won't be happy," Joel replied. "His stained hand, the one stained with Joelito's blood, will always be too heavy. And the people will see him walking on the street and they hate him."

"How can you say it is better that Peña can walk around and my only son is dead? He is still eating, he is growing fat, he is a pig! Nothing can cause sorrow to him. He is a murderer who killed my innocent boy."

20

Two months later, on July 12, 1983, the center submitted to Judge Nickerson their "Objections to Magistrate Caden's Recommendations." Caden's theory of mutual exclusivity—that since torture violates Paraguayan law, it cannot simultaneously violate the law of nations—CCR argued was a misreading of the Circuit Court's decision.

For, even if Paraguayan law be applied in *Filártiga v. Peña*, under the Alien Tort Claims Act an alleged tort still is actionable if it violates the law of nations. Indeed, precisely because Paraguay does not provide for punitive damages, the matter of dual applicability becomes of cardinal importance. Pointing out that the Filártigas had shown they are entitled to punitive damages under international law, the center's brief insisted: "It is a generally accepted rule that where two theories of damages lie, claimant is entitled to the greater of the two."

A month later, throughout the long, mid-August hearing before Judge Nickerson, the CCR lawyers reviewed the mass of evidence that over the years had come to make up the *Filártiga v. Peña* case file. And while Peter engaged Nickerson in a discourse concerning the more technical legal points, the seasoned litigator Rhonda abandoned her hard-driving courtroom persona.

"Given that there exists no hope for justice in the Paraguayan courts," she argued passionately, at times close to tears, "U.S. policy should maximize the international enforcement of human rights, not relegate plaintiffs to fora in which an attempt to vindicate their human rights only ends up with further deprivation of those rights."

21

With remarkable speed, it took only three months for the ponderous Paraguayan judicial machine to issue a ruling denying Julio Regis Cabrera's criminal appeal in the *Caso Filártiga*. In June 1983 the government had notified the OAS of the Supreme Court's decision upholding the exoneration of Duarte, Peña, and the other coconspirators.

For six years Stroessner had played his stalling game—agreeing to the OAS request to conduct an on-site investigation, while rendering his promise useless by refusing to set a specific date. Nevertheless, on September 26, the Inter-American Commission on Human Rights neatly closed its Filártiga investigation, reporting that its "findings had failed to demonstrate that the Government of Paraguay had violated human rights guaranteed by the American Declaration of Human Rights."

And then, on November 23, the Paraguayan Court of Appeals upheld the lower court's civil suit award. Moreover, the ruling embargoed the Sanatorio la Esperanza in Ybycuí as surety until Filártiga paid off Duarte.

At this time, however, Joel was back in the States for another tour. Traveling with Dolly from October to December, the Filártigas covered the now-not-unfamiliar rounds: Along with appearances to raise funds and medicines, press coverage expanded beyond their university exhibitions and presentations to the wire services, whose stories were picked up around the country in countless small-town newspapers. Apparently, their activities generated enough international pressure to permit Dr. Filártiga's safe return to Paraguay for the holidays.

22

A few weeks later, on January 10, 1984, Judge Nickerson issued his eighteen-page *Filártiga v. Peña* decision. "Spread upon the records of this court," he declared, "is the evidence of wounds and of fractures, of burning and beating and of electric shock, of stabbing and whipping and of mutilation, and finally, perhaps mercifully, of death; in short, of the ultimate in human cruelty and brutality."

The judge's ruling began by acknowledging the appropriateness of first looking to Paraguayan law, given the human rights guarantees contained in Paraguay's Constitution and Penal Codes. However, it was precisely these prohibitions against torture that invalidated Peña's Act of State defense, for his actions could not have been lawful under Paraguayan law. Indeed, drawing upon the *Mbareté: The Higher Law of Paraguay* report, Nickerson issued his most scathing condemnation of Stroessner's judiciary. "Despite Paraguay's official ban on torture," he declared, "the 'law' of that country is what it does in the fact . . . and torture persists throughout the country."

Nickerson went on to overrule two related recommendations proposed by Magistrate Caden. Explaining why the U.S. courts constitute the proper forum, he wrote, "*Forum non conveniens* depends on whether the courts of Paraguay are not only more convenient than this court, but as available and prepared to do justice." Further, he put aside the magistrate's concern of forum shopping. Recognizing that the Filártigas stood no chance of redress in Paraguay, and had sued Peña where they found him, Nickerson accepted their additional claim of $10,364 for compensatory expenses incurred in pursuing the suit in the United States.

He then moved on to punitive damages. Because "Paraguay will not undertake to prosecute Peña for his acts," Nickerson reasoned, "the objective of the international law making torture punishable as a crime can only be vindicated by imposing punitive damages . . . [that] are designed not merely to teach a defendant not to repeat his conduct but to deter others from following his example."

Employing the logic and language of the Circuit Court ruling, he stated that "for the purposes of civil liability, the torturer has become—like the pirate and slave trader before him—*hostis humani generis*, an enemy of all mankind." The human rights principles of international law, however, would remain incomplete until a remedy for a specific case was accorded in our courts. Further, he declared, to adhere "to the universal abhorrence of torture held by the community of humankind . . . any remedy [U.S. courts] fashion must recognize that this case concerns an act so monstrous as to make its perpetrator an outlaw around the globe. . . . Thereby the judgment may perhaps have some deterrent effect."

In keeping with the custom of referring to similar cases as a guide in determining damage awards, Nickerson noted the 1980 *Letelier v. Republic of Chile* case. Unlike *Filártiga v. Peña*, since that case did not involve a dispute between two aliens, it had not been brought under the Alien Tort Claims Act. Instead, employing a different U.S. law, it charged a nation-state with violating international law in the 1976 Washington assassination of Ambassador Letelier and Ronni Moffitt. Even so, the $2 million settlement influenced his decision.

"This court concludes," Nickerson ruled, "that an award of punitive damages of no less than $5,000,000 to each plaintiff is appropriate to reflect adherence to the world community's proscription of torture and to attempt to deter its practice."

23

"It would seem," Rhonda said, "I might have been a bit premature in worrying that Nickerson didn't appreciate the importance of *Filártiga v. Peña* when he sent the case to Caden. Even when he seemed so sympathetic and taking us very seriously at last year's August hearing, I was still leery about the outcome."

The whole CCR team—Dolly, David Lerner, Peter, the other lawyers and interns, along with all of the staff—became caught up in Rhonda's exuberance. "And now, this wonderful, groundbreaking decision," she exclaimed. "I had no idea that he was going to order the entire $10 million punitive damages. Never mind kicking up the compensatory damages by another ten grand."

The following day, with *Newsday's* "Judge Sets $10.4M for '76 Murder," Nickerson's landmark ruling began hitting the press. The *New York Times* held back its report for its widely circulated Sunday edition. "This court must make clear the depth of the international revulsion against torture," the *Times* piece of January 15 quoted Nickerson, "and measure the award in accordance with the enormity of the offense."

One week later, while applauding the momentous award, *Newsweek* magazine opined that the milestone decision had "more importantly served notice that . . . [United States] courts are open to judge actions in any corner of the world." And, in what proved to be an understated prophesy, "Justice: A Verdict on Torture" concluded: "The case is of more than academic interest because it may foreshadow similar suits against other torturers and death-squad members who may want to seek refuge in the United States."

24

In what had become almost a way of life, that autumn of 1984 Filártiga was in the middle of another intensive U.S. speaking tour. Although we had stayed in contact with letters and telephone conversations, more than two years had passed since Joel and I had had the chance to meet in person.

With the outbreak of turmoil in Central America in the 1980s, and the *Caso Filártiga* in the capable hands of CCR and others, I had taken a job as an analyst at a Mexico City–based think tank. And while like Joel, I made frequent trips to the States, our visits never seemed to overlap.

In October, however, we finally got together. I was in New York testifying at the War Crimes Tribunal on U.S. Policy in Central America, when Joel, Dolly, and Rhonda returned from a presentation at Northwestern University School of Law in Chicago.

We were both running on outrageous schedules. While I had to be in El Salvador as an election observer that weekend, Filártiga's back-to-back engagements were even more demanding. Right after a two-day trip to Puerto Rico, Joel would leave for Europe, with stops in London for talks and interviews, to confer with Amnesty International and hold preliminary discussions with a producer who wanted to make a feature film about the Filártigas' saga; and then on to Geneva for meetings with the World Council of Churches to arrange donations of medical supplies. Even so, we cut out a few days to spend together at Dolly's Manhattan apartment.

"In Ybycuí, the Sanatorio La Esperanza continues to function," Joel told me. "But Stroessner's harassment has placed the Asunción Policlínica La Esperanza in jeopardy. Every other month we lose another physician. Even many of the specialists now find pretexts not to accept the patients we send them.

"Last Christmas I returned home to find the Paraguayan Appellate Court had upheld the defamation ruling for Duarte. But in January, CCR and Amnesty mounted a big protest campaign against this latest persecution by Stroessner's courts."

"Has Duarte collected the award?"

"Not yet. But we have reached the last appeal," Joel sighed. "It is hopeless. You remember Senator Luis María Argaña, Stroessner's fanatic defender at the 1978 OAS conference? The one who ridiculed the *Caso Filártiga* as a 'Romeo and Juliet tragic comedy'? Well, Argaña is now president of Paraguay's Supreme Court of Justice."

The proceedings dragged out for a further six months, until April 30, 1985, when Argaña's Supreme Court issued the final order. By then, however, Paraguay's rampant inflation had devalued the original 5 million guaraní award from $31,000 to about $5,000.

"And Hugo Duarte, since his release?"

"Well rewarded for keeping his mouth shut," Joel replied. "Stroessner repaid him with a position of corruption. Today, Duarte is taking his share of the smuggling traffic as a customs inspector."

"Peña?"

"For a couple of years after he came back from Brazil," Joel explained, "Stroessner's son, Gustavo, hired him as his personal bodyguard. But then he deteriorated and was fired. Drunken bar room fights, even with high-ranking police officials. His violence became so uncontrollable that even Juana left him. Peña now is fighting her for custody of their son. Living with his sister."

Filártiga had some good news, too. After eight years, Horacio Galeano Perrone had gotten his law license back, and he was well on his way to rebuilding a lucrative legal practice.

Inevitably, our conversation drifted to the Filártigas' fantasies, should they somehow ever collect the $10 million court award. Dolly wanted to set up schools for the peasants of Ybycuí; Joel dreamed of building a medical complex to serve the entire Ybycuí Valley.

"Of course, we will never receive a dollar," Joel said. "Quite the contrary. Stroessner's courts will make me pay Duarte. So far, international pressure has staved off the worst of the dictatorship's punishment for bringing the suit here. But, that, too, cannot always be counted upon. There are more reprisals to come."

"I know you're not saying that it wasn't worth it."

"Of course not," he replied dismissively. "In a life of permanent opposition, the effort becomes the goal. The means are the ends. They become the same thing—the reason for living.

"Peter Weiss told me once that because of *Filártiga v. Peña*, international human rights are no longer just an airy principle to be thrown about at diplomatic conferences or in presidential statements. Peña has been publicly tried and sentenced in court. He is an international criminal—like all the other torturers who defile humanity. For the first time, international human rights is backed with the force of law. How can a price be placed on such a triumph?"

Filártiga paced around Dolly's small apartment.

"No, Richard," Joel said, "we have broken the silence of people to speak out—the taboo of shame and fear that the dictatorship has always counted on to cover up its crimes.

"Joelito was only one who died of torture that day. One among hundreds every day, all around the world. But they go unnoticed, forgotten, without any testimony. It is as if their suffering and deaths never happened.

"Our struggle has opened a channel of hope. For them, for all the more to come. It is Joelito who has won. Because death only counts if it leaves a legacy."

Like the archer's arrow, the impact of the *Caso Filártiga* is shot into the future.

EPILOGUE

As he was rushing home from his 1984 European trip to be with his family for the holidays, Dr. Filártiga was arrested by the Paraguayan political police on December 24 at Aeropuerto Presidente Stroessner. After subjecting him to a humiliating strip search by a female officer, the police grilled him for hours. But Joel's family, which had witnessed his detention as they waited for him at the airport, immediately contacted the Center for Constitutional Rights and Amnesty. Together they launched an Urgent Action Campaign, and the international pressure forced his release on Christmas Day, albeit to house arrest. At Investigaciones headquarters the following day, they returned Filártiga's confiscated medicines and books with an apology.

By 1986 Joel had paid off Hugo Duarte and saved the Sanatorio la Esperanza in Ybycuí. The continuing harassment, however, forced him to close the Asunción Policlínica La Esperanza in 1987.

On February 3, 1989, a military coup ousted "Latin America's most durable dictator" after thirty-three years in power. By then, Luis Maria Argaña had become minister of foreign affairs, and even as General Alfredo Stroessner left for exile in Brazil—where at age ninety-one, he awaits his comeback—Argaña's fortunes prospered. Since then, Paraguayan governments have consisted of shifting coalitions from among Stroess, Colorado Party, and Argaña's star continued to rise, taking him to the vice presi of Paraguay. However, on the afternoon of March 23, 1999, three men in camo gear opened fire with automatic weapons on his vehicle, cutting short his career

A number of others involved in the *Caso Filártiga* also pursued ambition the "gangster state" politics that still blights Paraguay. Judge Diógenes Martín minister of the interior—Paraguay's top cop—but Colorado Party infightin resignation in 1996. While the involvement of his faction in the assassinatio has held back Martínez, he still exercises his public service as a senator.

Horacio Galeano Perrone held several cabinet positions in the goverg for eral Andrés Rodriguez, who overthrew Stroessner. But suspicion for the at his nation also fell on Horacio and his brother, sending them both into A several years. Currently, all is well with Galeano Perrone, and he is ntinues to legal practice.

Domingo Laino, after failing in his 1993 and 1999 presidentia Villalba got harass the successive Colorado governments as a key opposition sena

Time has been less kind to Américo Peña. For a while, he aPeña relapsed to back together, when they both were "born again" Christians. Bu his old ways, and their relationship fell apart. Juana left him again, and since her death in 2002, Peña has continued his downward slide into alcoholism and depression.

Sometime during the 1980s, Charo returned from her forced residence in Argentina. She got back together with Hugo Duarte, who is running an Asunción pharmacy, and they have had two more children.

1

During the 1980s and 1990s, the Filártigas kept up the international struggle. Their public appearances ranged from cocktail party fundraisers—such as the Manhattan benefit for Andrei Sakharov—to university auditorium lectures. They appeared onstage with Yoko Ono, Muhammad Ali, Paul Simon, and other celebrities at the 1986 Amnesty International "Conspiracy of Hope" concert, which was broadcast live around the world from the New York Giants' Meadowlands stadium. And in 1991, HBO put out *One Man's War*, in which Anthony Hopkins plays Dr. Filártiga.

Today, Peter Weiss continues his trademark legal practice and is a vice president of the Center for Constitutional Rights. Rhonda Copelon teaches at the City University of New York School of Law and is the director of the university's International Women's Human Rights Law Clinic. David Lerner is the president of Riptide Communications, a New York public relations firm focusing on social justice and human rights groups, and he still works closely with CCR.

Michael Maggio is a senior partner in a Washington law firm specializing in immigration law. Robert White is the president of the Center for International Policy in Washington, which promotes a U.S. foreign policy based upon demilitarization and human rights.

Larry Birns is still plugging away as the director of the Council on Hemispheric Affairs, and I continue my affiliation as a senior fellow.

Shortly before Judge Kaufman's death in 1992, admirers established Harvard University's Irving R. Kaufman Public Interest Fellowships program, which ironically awards fellowships to promote careers in public interest law, such as human rights.

Of the others, Colonel Robert LaSala is a stockbroker in South Florida. After leaving Paraguay in 1980, Father John Vesey spent twelve years in Guatemala and now is in Brooklyn working as a diocesan priest in a Hispanic parish. Walter Gaffney is development director at a health care facility for the elderly, and Jeannette Rodgers ing in a public school, both still in New Haven, Connecticut. In 1985 Father M. Nouwen left academia to live at the L'Arche Daybreak community near here he continued writing and working with the handicapped until his death thirt

An lives in the States, with her husband and their daughter Paloma, now in Paragu age. "I no longer hate," she says "it takes away from my life." ves in Caraguátatuba, Brazil, while Katia is with the rest of the family

2

Ever the irrepressible critic, Dr. Joel Filártiga is regularly featured in Paraguay's print and electronic media, speaking out against government corruption, human rights abuses, and deplorable public health conditions. And even though Joel and Nidia Filártiga have not received any of the $10.4 million U.S. court award, they have been able to establish the Joelito Filártiga Grammar School in Ybycuí. Moreover, at his own expense, Joel also publishes books and pamphlets. Some he distributes for free, such as his 2003 booklet *What They Give Us to Eat*—written in a simple style for a widespread popular readership—which denounces the health hazards of the fare served up by the fast-food chains that now proliferate in Asunción.

Today, Joel and Nidia's major concern at the Sanatorio La Esperanza is the effect among their patients of agribusiness's unrestricted use of insecticides. Joel is convinced that these agritoxins are responsible for the epidemic of spontaneous abortions, the increase in ovarian and testicular cancers, and the dramatic rise in infantile mortality among their patients. In April 2002, flouting government warnings, he signed twelve certificates of death "caused by prolonged exposure to agricultural pesticides."

Filártiga's stubborn outspokenness does not go unnoticed.

Several weeks later, on the morning of April 30, 2002, home invaders terrorized the Filártigas' Asunción household. In a commando-type raid, six armed men in ski masks burst in and rounded up everyone. For three hours, at gunpoint, the invaders forced Joel and rest of the family—including two grandchildren—to lie face down on the floor as they stuffed documents detailing government corruption in dumping waste toxins, as well Filártiga's notebook and personal computers, into canvas duffel bags. Filártiga refused to give them the combination of his safe, which contained other documents, cash, and family valuables. Finally, the intruders called collaborators on their cell phones and had dollies and other equipment brought in to carry off the ancient 400-pound safe.

In March 2004, as president of the Organization for the Defense of Campesino and Indigenous Human Rights, Filártiga publicly denounced the killing of two campesino activists that he ascribed to agribusiness interests. So reliable were the death threats that followed that even Joel felt it necessary to go into hiding for several months until, yet again, international pressure forced the soybean growers to back off—for now.

3

"In April 1983, after the traditional seven-year waiting period," Filártiga reminded me during a 2003 visit with the family, "we had to move Joelito to Nidia's family pantheon because so many people came to pray to Beato Joelito. Humble people desperate for a miracle. And students, before a big exam. Because he too was a student and is special to them. And today, it is still the same."

Several years ago, someone smashed out the windows and broke open the doors of Joelito's pantheon. And though the individual vandals were never caught, Dr. Filártiga was able to win a civil suit against Hugo Duarte for damages.

At the Cementerio del Sur, evidence of Beato Joelito surrounded us. Bundles of dried flowers littered the ground; and dozens of burnt-out votive candles, several with flames still flickering, lined the windowsills and doorways of the crypt. Inside, through the glass windows of the casket, the young Joelito could be seen. It is a vivid memorial to the Pascua Dolorosa, as that Easter of 1976 is still called during the yearly commemorations held by the survivors of the massacres of campesinos, the killings of the OPM members, and Joelito's murder.

And as something of a counterpoint, in 1996 Soledad, the former comandante of the OPM guerrillas, paid a surprise visit to the Sanatorio La Esperanza, to introduce her daughter to the Filártigas. Nidia González and Mbyja, now a mother herself, live in São Paulo, Brazil.

4

Joelito's death still reverberates locally and globally, personally and publicly. And no one has felt that more than the Filártiga family members, who through their loss and grief pursue their work, love, and struggle.

Until the *Filártiga v. Peña* torture case, victims were caught up in a stacked-deck game, with no place to turn. Like a catch-22, human rights violations were considered exclusively an internal matter of the very countries that had perpetrated them in the first place. The *Caso Filártiga* reshuffled the deck.

During these years, scores of *Filártiga* progeny cases have been brought against individual human rights abusers, as well as class-action suits against corporations for violating environmental and labor rights. This second wave of class-action cases that began in the mid-1990s also took governments to task for the historical wrongs they had committed. Five years of litigating *Filártiga* Alien Tort Claims Act (ATCA) suits in U.S. federal courts resulted in the 2001 Swiss Bank $1.25 billion settlement to claimants whose assets had been held by the banking establishment of Switzerland since World War II.

Similarly, *Filártiga* progeny suits finally delivered a measure of justice in the big "Nazi industrialist cases" against German corporations for profiting from slave labor. Since the end of the war, Holocaust victims had lost every one of their criminal suits for indemnification. Again, forced to settle by *Filártiga* ATCA cases in U.S. courts, in 2002 a conglomeration of corporations and the German government began distributing more than $5 billion in reparations to the former slave laborers. Like O. J. Simpson escaping criminal charges only to face a large civil action, because of the *Filártiga* principle, the corporations had to pay up.

The *Filártiga* interpretation of ATCA has spawned a global movement to file civil cases on behalf of human rights victims in order to punish violators, deter others, and compensate survivors. Into the fray have come not only the Center for Constitutional Rights but also many others such as Human Rights Watch, Earth Rights International, the International Labor Rights Fund, and the Sierra Club. In 1998, supported by Amnesty International, the United States–based Center for Justice and Accountability was established for the exclusive purpose of locating torture victims and bringing *Filártiga*-style ATCA suits against their persecutors.

Further, the worldwide awareness that the *Filártiga* progeny cases have helped to create has given rise to facilities to help human rights victims. Today, more than 100 programs in about seventy countries offer treatment for victims suffering from post-traumatic stress syndrome.

The underlying principle of the Filártigas' struggle is that human rights is about human beings—and Joelito's death gives a human face to international human rights. Over and over during the past twenty-eight years, I have seen the *Caso Filártiga* story evoke authentic expressions of interest, revulsion, outrage, and sympathy. Through this process of basic human identification, people make the startling breakthrough of internalizing the concept of international human rights—in much the same way that they have come to regard civil rights—as an everyday, working part of their values and beliefs.

From what was once scoffed at by many as a quixotic quest, the Filártigas' struggle has come to be seen as one of those extraordinarily rare occurrences in history—an act of individual courage that truly makes a difference.

GLOSSARY AND ABBREVIATIONS

ACLU: American Civil Liberties Union.

AI: Amnesty International, a London-based human rights NGO that won the 1977 Nobel Peace Prize.

AI/USA: Amnesty International, United States of America section.

amicus curiae: A "friend of the court" brief, containing the written opinions of specialists and other interested parties who, though not principals in the suit themselves, offer the court their expert advice.

APO: Army Post Office. International postal service operated by the U.S. Army and used by other official U.S. institutions abroad to send mail to and from the United States.

ASU: Anti-Smuggling Unit of the U.S. Immigration and Naturalization Service.

ATCA: Alien Tort Claims Act. Also referred to as the Alien Tort Statute (ATS).

barrio: Neighborhood.

beato: A blessed soul, but not quite a saint, favored by God.

campesino: Peasant farmer.

CAT: Campaign Against Torture of Amnesty International.

CCR: Center for Constitutional Rights. New York-based legal-advocacy NGO.

COHA: Council on Hemispheric Affairs. Washington-based Latin American information-dissemination NGO.

forum non conveniens: An inappropriate court, or nonconvenient forum, in which to try a case.

IACHR: Inter-American Commission for Human Rights of the Organization of American States.

ILHR: International League for Human Rights. New York–based human rights NGO.

INS: U.S. Immigration and Naturalization Service.

Investigaciones: Paraguay's political police during the dictatorship of General Alfredo Stroessner.

jefe: Boss or superior.

LADOC: Latin American Documentation Center. Lima-based research NGO that publishes weekly reports on hemispheric news.

mbareté: Superior power over others. The basis of Paraguayan governance, replacing the rule of law as the governing principle during Stroessner's dictatorship.

NGO: Nongovernmental organization. A nonprofit advocacy organization unaffiliated with government.

OAS: Organization of American States.

OPM: Oganización Político Militar, or Political Military Organization. Paraguayan insurgents opposing the regime of General Alfredo Stroessner during the mid-1970s.

OSI: Office of Special Investigations. A part of the U.S. Department of Justice established in 1980 to investigate Nazi war criminals living in the United States.

pyragüé: Paraguayan police informer.

Semana Santa: The traditional Holy Week, filled with religious observances, leading up to Easter Sunday.

solicitada: Paid newspaper announcement.

TRO: Temporary restraining order.

UCLA: University of California, Los Angeles.

UN: United Nations.

USCC: United States Catholic Conference. Washington-based institution representing the Catholic bishops' interests, and including an active human rights office. In 2001, it merged with the National Conference of Catholic Bishops to form the U.S. Conference of Catholic Bishops.

WOLA: Washington Office on Latin America. Washington-based NGO promoting Latin American issues in the U.S. Congress.

INDEX